SECOND EDITION

CULTURAL AWARENESS IN THE HUMAN SERVICES

A Multi-Ethnic Approach

James W. Green
University of Washington

Allyn and Bacon
Boston • London • Toronto • Sydney • Tokyo • Singapore

Be not forgetful to entertain strangers;
For thereby some have entertained angels unawares.

—*Hebrews 13:2*

Vice President & Publisher, Social Sciences: Susan Badger
Executive Editor: Karen Hanson
Managing Editor: Judy S. Fifer
Editorial Assistant: Sarah L. Dunbar
Production Editor: Catherine Hetmansky
Editorial-Production Service: Ruttle, Shaw & Wetherill, Inc.
Cover Administrator: Suzanne Harbison
Composition Buyer: Linda Cox
Manufacturing Buyer: Louise Richardson
Executive Marketing Manager: Joyce Nilsen

Library of Congress Cataloging-in-Publication Data

Green, James W.
    Cultural awareness in the human services: a multi-ethnic approach
  / James W. Green.—2nd ed.
        p.   cm.
    Includes bibliographical references and index.
    ISBN 0-13-202631-7
    1. Social work with minorities. 2. Multiculturalism. I. Title.
HV3176.G73   1995
362.84—dc20   94-19617
                                                              CIP

Printed in the United States of America
10 9 8 7 6 5 4 3 2   99 98 97 96 95

CONTENTS

FOREWORD

Cultural awareness was a new, even a controversial, idea when the first edition of this book appeared in 1982. It is now becoming well established in university training and workshops. New research clearly acknowledges the importance of cultural factors in providing effective service delivery.

This second edition includes new material on ethnicity and social services as that topic has emerged in the literature of human services, psychology, sociology, and anthropology over the last decade. In addition, the innovative help-seeking behavior model developed in the first edition has been refined and expanded with more social service applications.

The new chapters on ethnic communities include more material on minority groups, placing greater emphasis on their internal diversity and providing more explicit guidelines for learning about them. Exercises and conceptualization draw heavily on the experiences of minority professionals who know their communities well and have published materials about them.

For teachers and students, the section on exercises and activities has been considerably strengthened and can be easily adapted to a variety of social services courses. The applicability of cultural knowledge and skills to areas as varied as aging, drugs, family conflict, and illness is made explicit.

Finally, Green has developed these topics and learning techniques in classes, workshops, and conferences throughout the country and with social and health service providers of many backgrounds and interests. The emphasis on a client-oriented interviewing style, close attention to client language, and the role of community norms in shaping individual responses to human problems has been well received by professionals in many areas.

The chapters all build on a tradition of providing human services that are both humane and culturally responsive. This second edition is a welcome contribution to the growing literature on ethnicity and culturally sensitive social work practice.

Michael J. Austin, PhD, ACSW
School of Social Welfare
University of California, Berkeley

PREFACE

My formal training is in anthropology. You may think that anthropologists dress up in khaki shorts, a pith helmet, and walking shoes and go off to exotic countries where they "study" the locals. I did some of that, except I wore blue jeans and a T-shirt in the West Indies, a shalwar kameez in Pakistan, and ordinary street clothes as I rode around in cars with Child Protective Service workers in Washington State. But what I learned from the CPS workers was just as interesting as anything I saw in the Caribbean or South Asia. I noticed, for instance, that the workers had a terribly frustrating job. They were not always well trained for handling some very difficult clients, and sometimes they did not get the full backing of their supervisors or agencies. Yet many of them were incredibly dedicated to children and families, and they worked as hard as they could until burnout caught up with them. Many of the best among them are still at it and it is amazing to me what strong people they are.

Something else I noticed: Many of the workers were white, and many of their clients were not. As an anthropologist with a professional interest in ethnicity, I watched very carefully when workers and clients of differing racial or ethnic backgrounds discussed what was in the "best interests" of a child. When I began that investigation, I assumed that all CPS workers would be very skilled in multiracial situations and that the difficult decisions they had to make would reveal great insight into the dynamics of cultural variation among the families they served. I also assumed that the formal training offered in schools of social work would prepare these practitioners to be sensitive to every nuance of language, family norms, and personal expectations among clients. In a few instances, my assumptions were correct. But in many others, they were not. The reasons for that had more to do with staff training than with attitudes, with opportunities for learning than with resistance to working with diversity.

That was fifteen years ago. Since then, I have been extensively involved in training workshops and in discussions with a variety of health and human service professionals, all of whom feel that more needs to be done to prepare workers to function effectively with minority clients.

The question is always how. Should there be specialized classes within the social work curriculum, or should ethnic and minority content be diffused throughout courses on other topics such as family counseling or prison reform? Should students pick one ethnic group of interest and go off to the library to learn all they can? Are in-service workshops helpful? What of minority professionals? Is it enough to invite a guest speaker to a staff meeting to discuss "problem" clients or situations? Or should minority concerns be left to minority professionals and minority-operated agencies who, it would seem, know their client populations best?

There really are no simple or obvious answers to these questions. But they are issues that I think social service professionals ought to know more about, and they reflect my biases as a cultural anthropologist with a strong interest in using ethnographic information to help solve real human problems. I see a number of areas in which I hope this book will be helpful.

1. I think social workers need a better understanding of how people in ethnic and minority communities think about their needs and how they act to meet them. That means workers should know something about many ethnic groups and something about variations within the specific communities they serve.

2. I have watched social workers conduct interviews and I have come to appreciate how they could use standard ethnographic interviewing skills to learn important cultural information about their clients and their clients' concerns. They will need that information to plan and carry out culturally acceptable forms of intervention.

3. I think social workers need a model of the cultural context of human problems to help them see that needs are more than just personal or even family concerns. A cultural model would help them conceptualize human service issues so that everyone could understand why clients accept or reject assistance.

4. Human service professionals need to rethink their personal as well as professional relationships to minority clients and communities. Cultural difference is not something "out there" that "they" have but "we" don't. Diversity is about all of us and we need to be able to see how a *comparative* understanding of difference puts both the worker and the client under scrutiny.

5. I think social work as a field of practice needs a model of multiculturalism that is generalizable, not just to black-white relationships or to Indian-white relationships, but to Asian-black or Indian-Latino relationships as well. Not all social workers are white, after all, and not all clients come from minority traditions. It would simply be stereotyping to assume that this book is aimed at white workers, although they will probably be the majority of its readers. Rather, it is intended for everyone because we all come into contact with people who are culturally and racially unlike ourselves.

I have tried to address all of these issues in this book. I have proposed an explicitly comparative way of thinking about ethnicity, one that focuses on worker-client relationships, not inventories of ethnic traits. That understanding leads to an open-ended ethnographic interviewing style, one easily learned and one I have used in training social workers for many years. In addition, I have described a model for thinking about people's concerns as they see them within the context of their own community. This model can help all of us break out of reductionist ways of thinking about the needs of others.

If you used the first edition of this book, you will discover that this one is different in several important ways. In this edition, there are no coauthors. The first time around, a group of us decided that a book on ethnicity, culture, and human services was a good idea. We wanted it for our teaching and there wasn't anything else available so we wrote a book we could all use. That was in 1980. Since then, some of my former colleagues have gone off to other things, some entirely outside academia or social services. The new chapters are my own work and do not rely on what my former coauthors wrote. I have turned to scholars and practitioners who are well known and widely published in their fields, and from their research I have made an interpretation of how their work might contribute to an ethnographic, multicultural model for social services.

Second, this edition contains a larger section on exercises and training activities and most of them I have tried myself. Others have been used and recommended by people whose judgment I trust. There is an extended chapter on training; I hope you will find it an interesting and useful addition to the text.

I want to add that although most of the people who will read this book are probably social service students and professionals, I believe others who do "people work" might benefit as well. I have in mind nurses, rehabilitation specialists, counselors of all kinds, development personnel and foreign service volunteers, even teachers or members of the clergy. In addition let us not forget program planners and administrators. I have conducted workshops for many of these professionals and their response has been gratifying. The point of view of cultural anthropology now seems more important in these fields than it was when the first edition appeared and that has been especially pleasing.

Acknowledgments

No one ever writes a book without help. I wrote this book with the help of a slow word processor, fast acting coffee, and the incredibly fine library system at the University of Washington. I also received help from people who used the first edition of this book in their classes. I studied carefully all the advice they sent me, and for each of their recommendations I have made a change.

As social workers, you should appreciate that family life takes a beating when someone works on a book. There is all that anxiety, fussing about, and weekends at the office. It's an interesting task but not always great fun. My wife Carol tolerated it because she is a busy professional herself. My son Matthew was bemused by it. But my daughter Allison encouraged me. As a professional editor she is one of the very best and she helped make my clumsy sentences and hideous spelling readable. Thanks, Allison, you were great!

Others offered help as well. James Leigh, a social work professional of enormous teaching skill, is both friend and colleague. He and I discussed many of the ideas presented here. He originally coined the phrase "ethnic competence" during one of our conversations. Martha Richards made it possible for me to try out many of my ideas and exercises with trainees of the Washington State Department of Social and Health Services, and for that long-running opportunity I thank her. Michael Austin, now of the University of California at Berkeley, encouraged the original cultural awareness project and I want him to know how much I still value his loyalty at that earlier, and difficult, time.

The chapters on the ethnic communities discussed here were all read and critiqued by people who know those communities well. Their advice was important. Again, my thanks to Jim Leigh, and also to M. Jocelyn Armstrong (University of Illinois at Urbana-Champaign), Marlene Comenout (Yakama Nation), Karen Eckert, (Bureau of Indian Affairs), Joseph Gallegos (University of Portland), Albert W. Black, Jr. (University of Washington), Michiko Epstein (University of Washington Medical Center), and Keith Basso (University of New Mexico). Thanks also to the reviewers who provided feedback for this revision: Aida Bruns (Bridgewater State College), John D. Bower (Bethel College), Peter B. Vaughan (University of Pennsylvania), and Deborah H. Siegel (Rhode Island College).

The Humanities and Arts Computing Center at the University of Washington transferred written text to disk, greatly speeding the editing. The National Association of Social Workers granted permission to quote portions of their Code of Ethics. Mark Madsen very capably prepared the charts. Of course, all these words on all these pages are mine so if there are faults or omissions, write to me, not to them.

I would like to know if something in this book worked for you, as an instructor, a student, or a practitioner. Which of the exercises did you like, or not like, and how did you modify them? What ideas in the text were helpful to you, and are there any changes you would recommend? Write me and I'll write back. I'm at the Department of Anthropology DH-05, University of Washington, Seattle, WA 98195. Even better, use email to contact me at *jwgreen@u.washington.edu* for a quicker reply. I'd like to hear from you.

And finally, my regards to Gary T. Henderson for all the mirth his presence once inspired.

JWG

PART I

CULTURAL DIVERSITY AND SOCIAL SERVICES

Part I addresses four basic issues: (1) how we understand, and misunderstand, race and ethnicity; (2) what culture has to do with how people resolve problems and meet their needs; (3) how cross-cultural interviewing is done and why it is a critical social services skill; and (4) what is meant by "ethnic competence" in professional practice. The chapters present an ethnographic approach to social services, emphasizing how we can better understand cultural differences generally and how we can use that understanding with specific clients from diverse communities. Familiar social service issues—individualizing the client, demonstrating empathy, identifying the ecological context of problem resolution, and effective communication—are examined from a cross-cultural perspective.

1

RACE, ETHNICITY, AND SOCIAL SERVICES

Novelist James Baldwin once said of his homeland, "This is the only nation under heaven that contains the universe—east and west, north and south, black and white" (1985:124). But, he said, the history of this American universe is murderous and distorted. European explorers and colonizers unilaterally claimed land, resources, and souls that were not theirs to own. Africans involuntarily labored on sugar plantations in the world's first and longest-running experiment in international industrial production. Native peoples gamely resisted invasions by foreigners and their diseases, but finally yielded half the world. Greed, heroics, compassion, and death were present in abundance, and in all colors. Reflecting on the "American universe" from his self-imposed European exile, Baldwin both raged and hoped, angry over his country's legacy of racial hate. Yet he indulged a faith that America really was a last, best chance for everyone.

Five hundred years after Columbus, it is easy to romanticize and sanitize the history that Baldwin deplored, and difficult to imagine its ruthlessness and the precariousness of life for so many for so long. We forget that explorers and colonizers built their enterprises, from the Atlantic seaboard through the South and into the West Indies, Mexico, and Brazil, on a volatile mix of ethnicity, class, and race. Racism was essential to the economic viability of their sugar and cotton plantations and to justifications for territorial domination and state building. Their old plantations are now tourist destinations and much of the hemisphere has been converted to suburbia, but racism endures. It is the "Evidence of Things Unseen," Baldwin's title for his essay on his homeland. It still confounds the very best efforts of those who would make right some very old wrongs. Race, class, and ethnicity, and their complex manipulation for the preservation of advantage, remain the troublesome demons of the American experience. The conflicts that inspired the American Civil War were only partly settled and their final resolution has been deferred by each succeeding generation.

The congruence of race and racism with advantage and disadvantage—in housing, education, health, justice, and mortality itself—is a continuing, dominant theme in American life (Omni and Winant 1986). Yet in popular ideology and by administrative decree, Americans prefer to think of themselves as "color-blind," living in a nation that is moving toward an integrated, pleasantly pluralistic, and less troubled future. The tension of this contradiction, between a past that, as Baldwin reminds us, is not yet undone and a future that may be an illusion, is perhaps the most distinctive feature of the American cultural landscape.

How should those who define their profession as service to others, particularly others in need, respond to this contradiction? Should public policy and professional practice assume the long-term existence of racial diversity, acknowledge that multiculturalism sometimes leads to conflicts of interest, and then deliver services that strengthen ethnic and racial pluralism? Or is it more reasonable to expect that through sufficient goodwill and well-financed human services, we can eventually create a less contentious and truly open society, one grounded in a set of core values we can all share?

It is useful to remember that cultural and racial variation are among the most enduring characteristics of our species. Diversity is certainly a fact of our past, about three to four million years of it, and we can be reasonably assured of it in the future. The recent interest in finding one's ethnic "roots" in faraway places suggests that even in a society in which the imagery of the "melting pot" is widely held as a proper model of ethnic interaction, people still feel a need to define their distinctiveness. Cultural differences reflect not only a history but also fundamental variations in what people hold to be worthwhile. As long as variations persist, they will invite comparison and questioning of the practices and preferences of others. It may be disconcerting to have to acknowledge that members of historically stigmatized racial and ethnic groups often things their way, not just because they have been excluded from mainstream institutions by prejudice and discrimination, but because they find the values and institutions of the larger society inferior to their own.

The preference for cultural homogeneity, whether expressed as ethnocentrism, racism, or some other principle of exclusion, runs deep in any society. In a multiethnic society such as our own, it is a source of conflict between groups and individuals. That is particularly troublesome in social services, where social workers often deal with individual problems of the most intimate kind, brought to them by people they do not always understand. As professionals with authority and power, they can have enormous influence on people's choices and values. But that creates a dilemma. In providing services to ethnically distinctive clients, should a worker's suggestions for problem resolution be based on a belief in the essential similarity of all people's needs and desires? Or should social workers attempt to solve problems in terms of the distinctive values and community practices of their clients, however "unusual" they may seem?

The argument made here, and made very explicitly, is that social services can and should be provided to people in ways that are culturally acceptable to them and that enhance their sense of ethnic group participation and power. When Barbara Solomon referred to this as "empowerment" in 1976, the term caught on as a general point of view within human services. Although for some empowerment has become more a buzzword than a practice, her idea was that workers, service agencies, policies, and educational and training programs must work to meet client needs in ways that are congruent with each individual's cultural background and community setting. More than that, empowerment to her meant that people and communities should be encouraged to define their own best interests, promote their self-sufficiency, and be free to live out their historical values. But how can that be done when the institutions that are to provide empowering services are essentially monocultural, and their dominant perspective is that of one group—college educated, English-speaking whites mostly of middle-class origins and with professional class aspirations?

The problem is *not* that it is inherently bad, or good either, that most social workers (and nurses and teachers) are white, or that most speak only English, or that most are middle class. That is simply what they are. The problem lies in the inevitable limitations of those who are monocultural and monolingual in a society that clearly is not. Despite much discussion about "pluralism," most Americans do not think about what that term implies and, comfortably monocultural, they do not believe it has much to do with them. Social service and health professionals, however, cannot afford that level of comfort, and there are important reasons for them to consider the implications of pluralism for their work. The challenge of cultural diversity is the future of us all. Responding to it is a professional obligation since ethnic and minority group clients are as entitled to sensitive and competent services as anyone else. Because of the current prominence of consumer movements and political demands for improved services, minority persons can be expected to become more critical and outspoken about how they are treated in the future. The growing number of programs and agencies oriented to the problems of specific ethnic groups, with services managed and staffed by members of those groups, also suggests the inadequacy of existing programs.

Like minority clients, minority professionals look forward to an end of tokenism, both in services and in professional employment and advancement. They expect and sometimes insist that programs and policies change to accommodate their concerns and those of the people they represent. Majority group workers, especially those who cannot perceive the coming changes and who may not be prepared for them when they arrive, may find themselves more a part of the problem than contributors to solutions. That would be an awkward position for individuals and for a profession explicitly committed to the welfare of others.

There is an additional reason why social workers should give careful attention to the quality of their cross-cultural work—their own unfortunate history of insensitivity to ethnic and minority groups. That is an odd thing to say about people whose profession is caring about others. As a teacher and trainer who has worked with a variety of service professionals, I have known white counselors, nurses, social workers, teachers, occupational therapists, agency administrators, and others who are exquisitely sensitive to the formalities and nuances of face-to-face encounters with minority persons. But I have also come to see that their dexterity in "handling" racial otherness is not always a sign of cultural sensitivity; sometimes it is a response to a professional imperative to appear competent, officially color-blind, and never, ever, confused with Archie Bunker. The language and style of how one "cares" can mask great ignorance or even hostility which, even when Archie doesn't see it, Edith Bunker in her unadorned innocence usually does.

Examples are not difficult to find. Applied anthropologist Barbara Joans (1992) reports on the case of a group of Bannock-Shoshoni Indian women residing at the Fort Hall reservation in southeastern Idaho. Their supplementary security income (SSI) was cut off by a local service agency on the grounds that they had not reported all their income. In this economically poor region of their state, some of the women who owned small plots of land had rented them out to local farmers, making a profit of about a thousand dollars. The agency wanted the money back, money the women no longer had and could not return. To help resolve the dispute, Joans was asked by a legal aid service to determine how well the women understood English and if they had understood what was expected of them by the agency. Her evidence would be used in court proceedings.

Through carefully planned interviews, Joans discovered that all the women were familiar with everyday English as they used and heard it on the reservation, in local shops and businesses, and in conversations with whites. But only one woman understood simple jokes, puns, double-entendres, and other subtle nuances of usage, all evidence of her ability to understand fine gradations of meaning. Further, most of the women were not able to use or understand English in other than casual conversations; they had difficulty with the English of whites who represented social service, law enforcement, and other mainstream institutions. Their misunderstandings were compounded by their lack of familiarity with the rules and procedures of off-reservation bureaucracies.

Through participant observation, Joans found some of the reasons for the women's difficulties in understanding whites who spoke with them in an official capacity. For example, SSI people who came to the reservation often met with groups to discuss the aid program in general terms. They did not usually meet with individuals who had specific concerns about the use of funds. In describing SSI, they used the language of their own culture, the professional and bureaucratic culture in which they were immersed all day, and spoke of "regs" and other features of agency policy and practice. Much of this information was poorly understood by the Indian women, partly because it relied on vocabulary they did not know but, more importantly, because the vocabulary assumed knowledge of a system entirely outside their experience. In the critical area of SSI compliance, the differing usages and understanding of English were sufficient that the judge ruled in favor of the Native-American women. Joans's research demonstrated the importance of "linguistic patterns as criteria for cultural understanding" (Joans 1992:148) even when the nominal language of communication, English, was the same for everyone.

A somewhat older but still relevant example is presented by Jones (1976), who describes a survey conducted among a group of social service workers in Alaska who had daily contact with urban Eskimo individuals and families and who insisted on their genuine insight and understanding of their clients' "needs." The survey findings reflected a variety of worker attitudes toward Eskimo clients. One worker observed that "Natives have been improperly socialized. They haven't even been socialized to drink properly" (Jones 1976:335). That Eskimo drinking patterns might be situationally and culturally specific apparently did not occur to this worker nor enter into his calculations of what kind of intervention might be most helpful. Another worker spoke of "Natives [who] have no long range goals. They don't understand anything about planning for the future." This worker's statement seemed, to him, a sociological truism, despite the fact that the Eskimo have survived for thousands of years in one of the world's harshest environments. And although the Eskimo have long been known to anthropologists as a people with an incredibly subtle and refined sense of humor and decorum, a demeanor which assures emotional survival in tiny living spaces during the Arctic winter (Briggs 1986), one worker told an interviewer that the "Natives have no psychological awareness; they don't know how to verbalize and express their emotions." He added that in his work with Eskimo clients, "it doesn't matter what they say because our central task is to teach them to verbalize and express emotions: nothing can deter us from that" (Jones 1976:335).

It would be too generous to refer to these comments as instances of simple misunderstanding or ignorance. They were hostile, judgmental, and blatant expressions of racism. The fact that they were decorated with psychological phraseology, presented authoritatively as official "expertise," does not make them less vicious or hurtful. Nor is the problem ameliorated by the fact that "good intentions" and a "desire to help" motivated the people who offered these remarks. (Their use of the term "Natives" is itself highly revealing, although by now most workers have probably moved away from such obviously demeaning speech habits.) Did these workers really "care" about the people they served? In some ways they probably did. But their comments reflect an unfortunate ethnocentrism and condescension. If their remarks now seem unworthy and unrepresentative of the service professions generally, they did not seem so to the people who made them.

A final reason for examining cross-cultural encounters in social work has to do with how the profession has conceptualized its involvement with ethnic communities generally. Despite years of work with minority clients, practitioners have only recently considered their relations with minority communities systematically (Rodwell and Blankebaker 1992; Christodoulou 1991). Descriptions of social work among minority clients, which are now more common in social work journals, emphasize a client's individual characteristics, or problems in communicating with service workers. Much less attention has been given to understanding the cultural background from which these clients speak, or of finding ways to translate cultural understanding into improved social, health, and counseling practices. Even those who prefer "ecological" approaches have generally limited themselves to immediate family relations or personal networks, with little reference to the larger cultural settings in which family life and social networks are embedded. And only recently have texts in the field made other than passing reference to ethnicity as a factor in human services, community organization, or policy and planning. The National Association of Social Workers has on occasion addressed the issue (White 1984; Jacobs and Bowles 1988). But with the exception of a few texts and readers such as Lum (1992), Sue and Sue (1990), Devore and Schlesinger (1987), Ho (1987), Dana (1981), and McGoldrick (1982), ethnicity in the social work literature and teaching is hardly prominent. It is more often treated as an adjunct to other substantive concerns such as mental health or child welfare.

There are many reasons for this, but several are worth mentioning because they remain problems in developing an informed and truly holistic approach to multicultural social services (Pedersen 1985). First, there are disciplinary barriers. Sociologists, psychologists, anthropologists, and social workers rarely show much interest in one another's research. They are even more reluctant to teach in one another's programs. Turf issues are as common in academe as elsewhere. That may never change, but a few brave individuals will always be needed to work at overcoming this insularity.

Second, demonstration projects and intervention research are usually limited to abnormal behavior, viewed in clinical settings. This kind of research looks at individual pathology, not the communities where pathology is generated. There is rarely any attempt to discover a "cultural baseline" against which behavior, intervention, and outcomes can be compared or evaluated. In addition, many social service researchers have an overriding concern with variables that can be isolated and described quantitatively. Their faith in the predictive control they expect their research to produce divorces them from the human context and the lived realities of personal problems. Meaning-centered or ethnographic research is often thought of as yielding data that is "soft" (unquantifiable) and therefore less desirable. Consequently, the issues that might be most interesting to a teacher, social worker, or a nurse are avoided.

Finally, the current popularity of the family systems approach tends to exclude cultural features that may be important in understanding the sources of some problems. Menicucci and Wermuth (1989), for example, contrast individual, family, and cultural approaches to drug treatment. They note that in cases of clients with long histories of abuse, individual and family systems treatment modes are less useful than treatment that takes account of cultural variables such as life cycle, gender, and social variations within target communities. In their view, overlooking cultural data makes impossible a truly holistic framework for problem assessment and treatment. Where clients come from ethnic and minority communities unfamiliar to the worker, the risks of misunderstanding and treatment failure are simply compounded.

Regular contact between social workers and ethnically distinctive clients, ignorance of cultural differences that may be present, and the absence of a cross-cultural theoretical framework within social work—all seem to suggest a need to look more carefully at client diversity in human services. What, really, are "problems" for some people? What different patterns of problem resolution are common in various ethnic and racial settings? Other than social workers and those in institutional positions of authority, who do troubled individuals turn to in their own communities? And with what impact? What exactly is an intervention "outcome" and who decides if it is a useful one? These are just a few of the issues that a comprehensive program in multicultural services must resolve. They call for a research and practice agenda that would help improve both our understanding of ethnic communities and the quality of services that are provided.

At a minimum, a model for culturally responsive social and health services would require us to do the following:

1. Define a model of cross-cultural social work and caring services. The model must be systematic, and it must take account of cultural complexity in a genuinely pluralistic society. But it must also point to ethnographic features of clients that are explicitly salient to presenting problems and to the services offered. Generalized models of ethnic difference, with generalized principles of cultural awareness, may have been acceptable in the 1970s and the 1980s, but they will not do now. Something more analytical and more client-specific is needed.

2. Describe how the model is applicable to any cross-racial or cross-ethnic relationship. The model must be useful regardless of the participant's cultural identity. It cannot assume that the service professional is always a member of the dominant group, or that the recipient of services is always a minority person. Nor can the model assume extensive background knowledge among workers about the communities they seek to serve. Indeed, it ought to assume they have relatively little cultural information about their clients beyond what they know through casual contact, brief impressions, and perhaps unexamined assumptions.

3. Specify how the model would be useful in a wide range of service activities, whether oriented toward children, the aged, the physically challenged, or the abused. The service provider's professional specialty, or the provider's ethnicity, should be irrelevant to the model's utility. We simply require that it be applicable whenever contrastive cultural experiences and perspectives are part of a service relationship. The model should be useful in a variety of service relationships, whether they involve social workers, nurses, teachers, career counselors, ministers, doctors, administrators, volunteers, or others.

4. Generate explicit training procedures for improving the skills of service providers. Training must have a knowledge as well as a skills component. It must result in improved services as measured by professional and also community criteria. The model should suggest ways of adapting agency procedures, policies, and evaluation criteria to the ethnographic issues that workers meet in their clients and their client's communities. Without administrative follow-up and support, cultural sensitivity skills training will have minimum impact and might well be construed as little more than a faddish interest or, worse, the current face of tokenism.

In addition, the model ought to suggest hypotheses for applied research on the service needs of minority groups, the impact of policies on both clients and workers, and culturally appropriate criteria for program, agency, and staff evaluation. With such a model service workers would themselves be empowered, to critique what they offer and to know when and why they have been genuinely helpful.

One further point about the model is worth noting. I have made frequent reference to ethnic and minority groups, and will continue to do so throughout the book. Those are the groups I am most interested in here. But at various points, I will discuss other communities of interest as well, communities not explicitly racial or ethnic. For example, I will refer to a school for the deaf, the experiences of elderly street women, a psychiatric clinic, and a drug house. My reason for doing this is consistent with my overall approach: I am interested in how the concept of culture can be used to better understand a variety of communities and differing ways of life. My belief is that a cultural or ethnographic dimension will be helpful to professionals serving many people, especially those who identify with ethnic traditions, but also those in other kinds of communities as well. It remains true that the most obvious cross-cultural boundaries in American society are those that differentiate ethnic, racial, and minority groups. But we often differentiate people on the basis of power, age, gender, accent, religion, and education as well. The ethnographic approach directs our attention to the significant *cultural* features of any defined and distinctive community. In that sense, the skills of ethnic competence are widely applicable in human services generally. They should not be artificially confined to professional work with ethnic or minority peoples alone.

RACE AND CULTURE

There is, unfortunately, a multitude of ambiguous ideas about race, culture, and ethnicity that too often confuse rather than clarify what we need to know about these controversial and even painful subjects. All the more reason to be as clear as possible as we begin. My feeling is that conceptual accuracy is important, not just for academic neatness, but because the ideas we use when we think about "others" and "otherness" have explicit consequences for our behavior and for the quality of our services. Social workers often emphasize, and rightly so, the value of knowing "where the client is coming from." But it is equally important that professionals know where they themselves are "coming from." Their biases and assumptions should be explicit, at least to themselves. Assumptions, even assumptions that attain the status of scientifically validated theories, are usually culture-bound and expressive of some set of values and interests. What passes for objective, "factual" theory, especially in a complex and emotionally laden area like race, may be something else. "Theoretical assumptions, like all basic cultural assumptions, tend to be so deeply held, so much a part of one's personal commitment, that not only are they resistant to refutation by the 'facts,' but instead tend to transform the nature and significance of those 'facts' themselves" (Thompson 1989:4). I emphasize this point because I see many students, and many workers, who are so motivated to get on with the job of providing service that they think time taken for study and reflection is an unnecessary diversion. I don't think it is. Intellectual clarity is too important to be treated as a luxury, especially when the issues are as volatile and difficult as those of race and ethnicity.

We can begin with the idea of "race" by stating unambiguously that it has no standing of any kind as a scientific concept. A "race" is neither a culture nor a brute fact of nature, two erroneous beliefs that Margaret Mead and other anthropologists of her generation fully discredited more than half a century ago. Yet the shadow of these ideas still flits through everyday speech. Many of our current folk beliefs about race come from eighteenth- and nineteenth-century ideologies, some of which had their origins in religious thinking. Others derive from political ideas once associated with empire and conquest and used to justify European expansion and the doctrine of Manifest Destiny in the settling of North America. People of various "races" were described then as "primitives," "heathens," or subhuman creatures, all of whom would benefit from exposure to a conquering, missionizing civilization. Their cultural and racial diversity was expected to melt and finally disappear, although what they were to "melt to" was always rather vague. Modern racial supremacists and hate groups, with their calls for separate homelands, still rely on religiously and politically motivated racial stereotypes that originated in the divisive history that James Baldwin lamented in his essays on America.

In the natural world there are no clear, discrete things called "races." That term has no taxonomic validity and there is no way that a "race" can be objectively defined or consistently measured. Physical anthropologists and biologists rarely use the term except to warn the rest of us away from it. They speak instead of populations (more correctly, "gene pools") that slowly change due to the long-term effects of natural selection, genetic drift, mutation, and reproductive behavior. Whatever the seeming diversity of races in the modern world, *all* contemporary human beings trace their origin to ancestral populations that lived in east Africa about 200,000 years ago (Klein 1989). The slow movement of those early people out of their African homeland and into the rest of the world, during a period of tens of thousands of years, is an incredibly complex story. But its essence is that they migrated, diversified, evolved, and became us. The current distribution of "racial" groups, such as the peoples of southern Africa, southeast Asia, or northern Europe, is far more recent than 200,000 years. All populations, be they plants or animals, change over time and it is a certainty that our species' physical variation was different 10,000 years ago and will be different 10,000 years from now. Race simply is not the immutable, heaven-ordained order of things the hate groups would have the rest of us believe.

It is important to mention this mutable dimension of our biological heritage because Americans tend to think of race or "a race" as something inevitable, as an unchanging part of the "natural" world, even as something ordained by God. Objections to interracial marriage, dating, eating together, and riding in the same part of the bus have always been based on the seeming "naturalness" of racial divisions. Yet no one is a member of a "race" simply because he or she has a given amount of skin pigmentation or a particular type of nose, eyes, or hair. These physiological features, when we make an issue of them, are really representations of something else, namely our creativity and perverseness in devising social categories, sticking individuals into them, and making moral evaluations.

As an interesting illustration of this, Lieberson (1985:128) has shown the tenaciousness and seeming "naturalness" of racial categorization in everyday habits of speech and thought. Consider the following two sentences:

1. Americans are still prejudiced against blacks.
2. Americans still earn less money than do whites.

Williams (1989:430), who quotes this example, comments that the first sentence is perfectly clear in a quick, casual reading. But the second is not. That is because the conventional use of the word "Americans" assumes a white point of view. "Americans" is a linguistic "cover term" or gloss for whites, and that makes the first sentence "correct" both grammatically and socially. The second sentence initially confounds, however, because "Americans" now stands as a linguistic gloss for blacks. To grasp its meaning, we must consciously extricate the statement from conventional usage and make its unfamiliar categorical logic explicit. It defies both a quick gloss and the routines of thought implicit in our taken-for-granted world of everyday discourse. In this example, Lieberson exploits our linguistic habits to expose the social (and arbitrary) way language implicitly defines experience for us. It is a useful illustration of how the partitioning of the world into races is a social convention that we reproduce every time we speak, thus convincing ourselves that our favorite dissections of reality are indeed "true" in some fundamental, normative, and moral way.

But is the persistence of racial beliefs simply a matter of inappropriate language? Probably not. Many social scientists argue that racial logic expresses a concern, both linguistic and psychological, with orderliness (Douglas 1966) and a need to preserve and enforce order. In the instance of race, orderliness is constructed around notions of descent, exclusiveness, privilege, and most especially notions of moral purity. "Blood" is one of the most common and potent metaphors for that purity. As a consequence of historical assimilation and federal regulation, American Indians commonly speak of themselves as having varying percentages of "blood," and sometimes that percentage is the basis for who can and cannot claim tribal membership and benefits. African Americans have sometimes referred to one another as "bloods" and the chapter on African-American culture discusses the ethnomedical significance of "blood" in some black communities. In the nineteenth and early twentieth centuries, whites often described and evaluated one another in terms of their "breeding," an idea not unconnected with notions of bloodlines. References to one's "breeding" would be quaint and a little humorous now because it is language we usually use to describe the pedigrees of dogs, cats, and horses. Whites, therefore, usually describe their ethnicity as proportions of nationality, such as one-quarter Irish and one-eighth German, but the implication of "blood" purity and descent is still there.

Speculation about descent, one's blood, and degrees of mixed nationality from European ancestors is more than a parlor game. Serious attention to the purity of metaphoric bloodlines always comes to the fore in discussions of "mixed" marriages. The specter of racially or ethnically "mixed" marriages is, for some people, only slightly more troublesome than "mixes" that cross disapproved religious, language, educational, or class lines. Nor is this concern with preserving purity a problem only for whites. Virtually all ethnic groups in America have strong feelings, if not explicit objections, to "marrying out" for fear that the group's integrity will be compromised or contaminated. Some of my Asian-American students have described the less than charitable feelings their parents would have were they to marry someone white. Some Jewish students have expressed a strong preference for marrying within their faith, not only to keep their parents and grandparents happy, but also to minimize conflicts over the religious training and identity of their children. And authorities (of sorts) no less than talk show hosts Oprah Winfrey and Phil Donahue regularly capitalize on our fascination with unlikely mixtures of intimate preferences. All cross-racial contacts, whether they involve marriage, sex, or advice on how to manage a personal problem, invoke deeply held beliefs about the purity and separateness of social types. We can appreciate, then, that race is far more than a matter of biology. To reduce it to that is a sentimental and dangerous delusion. Race is always a point of view, not a natural fact. Racial thinking is the modern mythology of purity.

There is an implication in this idea about purity and race that is worth a pause. In the American world view, if we allow that there might be such a singular thing, two explanations of our difficulties with race are common. First, it is sometimes held that racism continues because of our failure to communicate with one another. If we would just listen more carefully, just try to connect, we would see that our problems are not really so large. In communicating and sharing our needs and feelings with one another, we would find the common ground of our experiences and our humanity. Second, and related to this, is the view that racial misunderstanding comes from our ignorance about each other. Learning more, through open and caring communication, would eliminate much of what separates us. (The logic of these points, and compelling critiques of them, will be found in Wellman 1993; Varenne 1977; and Bellah et al. 1985.) In my classrooms, I hear these explanations for racism regularly. Yet it must be apparent that if racial thinking and behavior are a consequence of our need for social orderliness, and the protection of our place and privileges within a system so ordered, then any frank exchange of views is as likely to polarize differences as to resolve them. Readers who think I exaggerate should review their initial reaction to Lieberson's two sentences quoted above and then think again about the power of racial metaphors to shape the way we mentally construct the world.

The idea of "race" is not helpful in advancing our understanding of difference, but it remains a prevalent notion, which is why we need to deal with it. By contrast, a "culture" is something else. Cultural differences are both real and meaningful, especially when people struggle to protect their group identity and personal dignity. Unfortunately, however, the term "culture" lacks a clear, specific meaning; there are literally hundreds of definitions of culture in the professional literature of sociology and especially anthropology (Kroeber and Kluckhohn 1952). Some of these definitions are cognitive: they stress what people know and how they interpret the world. Culture is thought of as a shared "cognitive map" and the study of culture in this sense is the study of a people's categories of meaning (Spradley 1972, 1979). Other definitions emphasize behavior and customs and their transmission from generation to generation. Here, culture is more like a list of traits handed down over time. Other ideas of culture emphasize how people use their material and ecological resources (Harris 1968). Culture may also be thought of as "discourse," the exchanges (verbal and otherwise) that occur when people communicate. In this perspective culture is something people mutually create as they go about their lives.

Many social work texts and authors, however, continue to rely on a very general (and older) model of culture taken from Kluckhohn and Strodtbeck (1961), one that stresses values and especially value differences. In this approach, people are said to be culturally similar if they share similar beliefs and preferences. While there is some commonsense truth to this view, there is also a problem. A values theory of culture suggests that the differences between group A and group B can be described simply as an inventory of values propositions and, further, that any individual's identity is essentially the match between that person and a given list of values. Obviously, not only is this a rather wooden view of what a culture is but it comes dangerously close to the kinds of stereotyping that we would prefer to avoid. In addition, the values approach leaves out important dimensions of culture, especially those associated with power and powerlessness, situational expression of ethnic loyalties, and how these play out in interaction between persons of differing and perhaps hostile communities.

Like the terms "life" in biology or "gravity" in physics, the word "culture" has to be given some fairly precise meaning before it can be useful as an analytical tool. An obvious place to start is with differences or contrasts; someone else's culture is most evident when I contrast what I see in that person with what I know about myself. The presence of an "other" makes me self-conscious (perhaps even reflective) of my own cultural distinctiveness. The experience of contrast, the presence of an apparent cultural boundary, is certainly stimulating, perhaps even discomforting. When I confront someone I perceive as different from myself, that person's "culture" might be any number of things—what I believe his or her values or family life to be, what I think about the religious beliefs I presume that person holds, my previous experiences of people "like that" when they are in contact with people "like me." The historical or objective truth of what the other is, and of what I am, is less important than perceptions. In an encounter on a bus, in a classroom, or at the beginning of a counseling session, there is a moment in which we each decide what is important to us about the other and how much of ourselves should or should not be revealed. (The word "decide" barely describes the subtlety of what goes on in cross-cultural awareness, for it suggests conscious decision making. Verbs like "scan" or "react" might be more appropriate.) Not all of my background and experiences, or those of the other, are initially important. What counts is how we narrow and focus the relationship, through verbal and bodily clues both subtle and explicit. In our mutual presentations of self, what passes as "culture" and as ethnic identity is usually brief and very specific, little more than a glimpse of all that we are as individuals. Culture, in this sense, is not something the other "has," such as a specific value or a physical appearance; it is rather the "perspective" that guides our behavior, however brief the encounter. Culture and ethnicity are not essential or innate properties of persons; they are the meanings that two people act on in a specific relationship. This emphasis on relational rather than essentialist aspects of culture may, in fact, be the only useful way to think about cultural differences in a complex, heterogeneous society such as our own (Hannerz 1986).

This idea of culture, as a perspective that emerges when people engage one another across boundaries they recognize as significant, is an established one in studies of ethnicity (Barth 1969). It has the advantage of being more precise than generalized statements about values and it suggests where one must look to discover cultural differences. It also assumes that some of the things that characterize the individual's background and experience are, at least at the moment of communication, more important than others. This is particularly critical where, in assessment, "individualizing the client" is one of the central tasks of social work intervention.

Before more fully exploring this notion of culture and its implications for professional practice, I want to briefly say something about minority status and social class. I prefer to think of the term "minority" as referring to something different from ethnicity or culture. Minority status persons need not be perceived as ethnically distinct, although they often are. (Indeed, there is considerable debate among African-American scholars as to whether the black community's unique characteristics derive from cultural features of African origin or from caste and class relationships and a history of economic exploitation. Important voices in this debate are Ogbu [1974, 1978, 1987] and Wilson [1987]. See also Gregory [1992].) Nor must persons of minority status be in a numerical minority, as the women's movement has made clear. Minority standing refers to power, not numbers; it concerns the degree to which individuals identified with a specific group are denied access to privileges and opportunities available to others. One could speak of minorities as "communities of interest" (Weaver 1977), those who share a similar set of values, lifestyles, and expectations but whose most common and definitive trait is that they are exposed to a similar set of limiting political and economic circumstances. In this sense, the term "minority" refers to social and economic disability, not to cultural differences as such.

That viewpoint is well established in social services. In a special issue of *Social Work* devoted to oppression of people of color, the editors explicitly link minority status to oppression: "the term *minority* has been expanded to include many other offended groups: immigrants, all those with Spanish surnames, women, the physically handicapped. . . . The list continues to grow as new groups are identified or claim minority status" (Hopps 1982:3). The phrase "people of color," as used in the special issue, suggests a dimension of power and relative disadvantage. The usage, however, also reveals one of its conceptual limitations. "People of color" do not constitute a culture; the term is just too broad for that. Since I am concerned in this book with the meaning of cultural differences for individuals, families, and service providers, a phrase like "people of color" has only limited utility. A "new" group, suddenly aware of a collective self-interest, may not be an ethnic or culturally distinctive community at all and it is useful to keep that difference in mind.

Finally, what of "social class"? That term introduces what we normally think of as the objective measures of education, income, religious affiliation, housing standards, and the like. However useful social class may be for categorizing large groups of people, especially for policy purposes, it really has little to do with the central elements of culture as I am presenting it here—boundary maintenance, meaning construction, and meaning enforcement. Even if the social class affiliation of a client (and a worker) are accurately fixed early in a professional consultation, that information would provide only minimal grounds for exploring the relationship. Most human service workers would want to know much more.

ETHNICITY

The essence of ethnicity is contrast, the recognition of difference. That seems obvious. But when we try to determine what differences mean, the idea of ethnicity becomes complex and frequently troublesome. Ethnicity in a multiracial and multicultural society is often problematic, both in practice and in moral terms. In a piercing critique of contemporary race relations in America, essayist Shelby Steele (1988) put the issue bluntly: "I'm Black, you're white, who's innocent?" Moving beyond innocence, he suggested, means understanding what ethnicity is and isn't, recognizing how it works both for people and against them, and appreciating why ethnicity remains important even when racial barriers to minority disadvantage are overcome through education or earning power.

A number of theories of ethnicity have been proposed, and while I do not intend to review them all here, it is worthwhile to note the major ones because ethnicity is neither a simple idea nor an obvious social fact. Alba (1990) has categorized theories of ethnic identity into four types: ethnicity as class; as a political movement; as revival; and as a token identity (Figure 1.1). I want to review what these different ideas are about, partly because it is useful to look at the range of meanings commonly associated with ethnicity but also because I think some approaches are more useful for social service professionals than others.

Alba notes that ethnicity is sometimes associated with social class, particularly when it is used to suggest working class or lower-class lifestyles. This is an often romanticized view of ethnic distinctiveness, one associated with urban groups socially isolated in ghettos and in "little Italies" or "Chinatowns" where there is presumed to be a strong congruence between family life, social networks,

Type	Feature	Example
Ethnicity as class	Distinctive lifestyle	Urban and rural ghettos
Ethnicity as politics	Group mobilization	Ethnic power movements
Ethnicity as revival	Return to traditions	Public and family celebrations
Ethnicity as symbolic token	Minimal commitment	Remembered family traditions

FIGURE 1.1   Four common perspectives on ethnicity.

Based on Alba 1990.

world view, and language. There is also a sense that economic disadvantages are buffered by family loyalties that are warm and protecting. This conception of ethnicity is commonly linked with a political and policy agenda of assimilation. It assumes that ethnic identity will be strongest among those least assimilated to the national mainstream and that assimilation is both a possible and desirable strategy for helping those who are economically disadvantaged. In this perspective, ethnicity is essentially a relic and a social problem, one to be overcome and left behind.

A second view is of ethnicity as a political process. Individuals whose origins (and perhaps their symbolic loyalties) are in other countries, cultures, or continents have suffered and endured the disadvantages and stigmata typically applied to those who are "different" in the American context. Recognizing this commonality in their suffering, ethnicity becomes for them the basis of a call to corrective political and economic action. Redressing historical wrongs becomes the agenda of ethnic group politics. Examples of this might be the various "power" movements of the 1960s and 1970s as well as the efforts of people like Cesar Chávez to organize agricultural workers or the Reverend Jesse L. Jackson to build a "rainbow coalition." In this view, ethnic groups are really political interest groups, struggling for their share of entitlements in a ruthlessly competitive political market. To hostile outsiders, the claims of ethnicity made by community advocates are seen as little more than a cloak for political opportunism. To sympathetic insiders, the cultural symbols of ethnicity are the flags of a moral crusade against an oppressive social and economic system.

A third perspective is that of ethnicity as revival, as something "celebrated" in self-conscious returns to ethnic foods and clothing, traditional religious practices, ethnic festivals, adoption of ethnic personal names, and renewed interest in non-Western (or at least non-American) languages and folklore. Alba suggests that these deliberate efforts to return to one's roots occur when a people feel they have achieved some of what they want and, having proven their worthiness as Americans, are in a position to comfortably and safely resurrect "lost" or denied traditions. In contradistinction to the class-based theory of ethnicity, here ethnicity and its revival is not the product of those mired in ghettos but of those successfully reaching for the American Dream. The leaders, and followers, are on their way into the middle class, not stuck at the bottom. One thinks, for example, of St. Patrick's Day parades among the Irish in New York, or of summer music and food fairs built around themes of Norwegian, Greek, or Cajun identity. Some would argue that this expressive ethnicity is a healthy social indicator, not a social problem, for it "proves" the essential openness of our tolerant and liberal democracy. Others, a bit more cynical, would point to these displays as contrivances and self-congratulation, not any real commitment to living out the alternative ethnic realities they celebrate.

The fourth view, perhaps only a watered-down version of ethnicity as revival, is ethnicity as a symbolic token. It is something taken on by individuals whose real interest is maintaining a nostalgic connection to an imagined old country. This theory is often applied to whites, or "ethnic whites" (some East Europeans or Scandinavians, for example) for whom ethnicity is an avocation at best. Most of the time, in most of their concerns, these people mix more or less freely with everyone else in their jobs, in recreation, and in political and religious organizations. In fact, they often pride themselves on their loyalty and patriotism. But they choose to "feel ethnic" to distinguish themselves from others on special occasions, in ways that are essentially ornamental rather than political or economic.

For example, most of my white students define themselves ethnically as fractional quantities of European nation states and languages. Being one-quarter this and one-sixth that, their sense of ethnicity extends little further than a grandmother's Swedish Christmas cookies recipe or bratwurst and beer on a Polish uncle's birthday. (I find it interesting that their *functional* ethnicity—white, mainline Protestant, English speaking, middle class, educated, upwardly mobile, suburban—is apparently invisible to them.) Some students get very creative in locating their European fractions, with a kind of pride of place going to obscure groups (Frisian speakers, Basques, French Huguenots). This perspective is far removed from ethnicity as a political process or as a sense of participation in a distinctive community. It certainly has limited use for social service providers.

These four perspectives suggest the diversity of ways Americans deal with what, for them, is a difficult and contentious topic. But ultimately beliefs about ethnicity are about perceiving difference, accounting for it, and knowing how to respond to it. Ethnicity starts with a recognition of "the other" and imposes a set of learned meanings on what "otherness" represents. Wallman (1979:3) remarks that, "Because it takes two, ethnicity can only happen at the boundary of 'us,' in contact or confrontation or by contrast with 'them.' As the sense of 'us' changes, so the boundary between 'us' and 'them' shifts." She adds that "the difference between two aggregates of people will be *objective* to the extent that an outsider can list items that mark it, but it is inevitably *subjective* to the extent that none of these markers has a necessary or precise significance outside the perception of the actors" (1979:5). Ethnicity has less to do with distinct and enduring groups than it does with the perceptions of boundaries, with how contrasts are manipulated, managed, denied, asserted, and proclaimed. With ethnicity, we are dealing, first, with meanings that define separateness and, second, with the enforcement of meanings and separateness through power.

This insistence that ethnicity really is about boundaries, control, and meaning construction is not my attempt to spin an interesting but obscure theoretical point. It addresses directly an issue that social service and health workers need to think more about: how their own activities, behavior, and assumptions affect cross-ethnic encounters. I will say more about this in the chapter on cross-cultural social work. For now, we simply need to be clear that ethnic identity is not the natural order of things it often appears to be. It is shifting, transactional, sometimes uncertain, and almost always implies an agenda of enforcement. And enforcement is a difficult thing for many well-meaning Americans to think about. Ethnicity as a phenomenon is specific to situations and its particular meaningfulness at any given moment can be elusive and unresolved. Where the bigot sees certainty in the human condition, the rest of us see a conceptual and behavioral minefield.

This cultural sense of ethnicity, as the construction of meaning in the presence of an ethnically distinctive other, has been reduced by Nash (1989) to three major components: kinship, commensality, and the shared ideology he calls a common cult.

> *The most common ethnic boundary markers, in the ethnographic record, and the most pervasive, in any system of ethnic differentiation, are* kinship, *that is the presumed biological and descent unity of the group implying a stuff or substance continuity each group member has and outsiders do not;* commensality, *the propriety of eating together indicating a kind of equality, peership, and the promise of further kinship links stemming from the intimate acts of dining together, only one step removed from the intimacy of bedding together; and a* common cult, *implicating a value system beyond time and empirical circumstance, sacred symbols and attachments . . . (1989:10–11).*

Nash distinguishes these three core elements of ethnicity from "surface features" or "surface pointers," characteristics that allow easy recognition of ethnicity at a distance (Figure 1.2 on page 20). Surface features include clothing preferences, speech patterns, behavioral styles, physical characteristics, housing locations and types, living arrangements and decor, food items, and family and community rituals and celebrations. These secondary features are important because they mark and express difference, allowing insiders and outsiders to spot relevant boundaries. They serve as identifiers, ornaments, badges, and the fodder for ethnic jokes and small talk. They are the superficialities Americans commonly think of when they comment on ethnicity—African-American rap, East-Indian

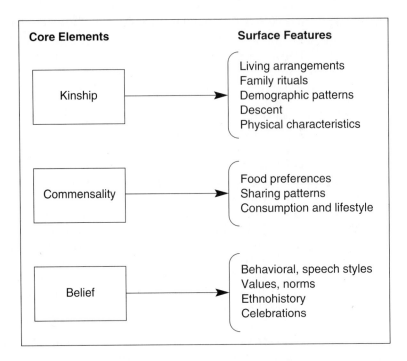

FIGURE 1.2   The core elements and surface features of ethnicity.

curries, Native-American powwows. Preoccupation with these surface features, in adulation, romanticization, or belittlement, is the "innocence" of those whites who do not recognize a racial blunder when they see it. Surface features help establish the visibility and legitimacy of ethnic affiliation. But they are not themselves what is ethnic about ethnicity.

The core elements—Nash's kinship, commensality, and a common "cult" or belief—are the real psychic and social foundations of ethnicity, boundary maintenance, and codes of enforcement. They organize the surface features into distinctive, recognizable combinations. For example, kinship is more than relations traced genealogically; it refers to all those to whom one is linked physically and metaphorically ("my people," "our kind," "by blood"). Kinship carries with it the notion of "primordial sentiments" that are widely shared, or at least believed to be widely shared. It is not accidental that African Americans sometimes refer to one another as "brothers" and "sisters," or that some Native Americans speak of themselves as "skins" or "bloods." These terms are markers for sentiments of shared moral substance; the idiom of kinship is open, flexible, even opportunistic, and hardly limited to traceable genealogical ties to specific ancestors. Kinship as affiliation can be invoked (or ignored) according to occasion and circumstance, something that bilingual or bicultural individuals often do out of necessity or convenience.

White Americans often view the matter differently for, as I have noted, many of them have difficulty in thinking of themselves as "ethnic." Typically they resort to national labels when asked to describe themselves culturally, and their idiom of ethnic affiliation is more geographical. As the dominant group, whites hear the claims of shared substance (in food, marriage, language, and experiences of prejudice) made by Latinos, Asian Americans, and others whose ethnicity they can easily see, but they do not find anything like that in themselves. That is because for them ethnicity is perceived only in the surface features mentioned above. From the point of view of whites, that is a convenient perspective to have, especially in a political sense. It locates ethnicity exclusively in others and excuses them from having to consider their own participation in the management and enforcement of separateness.

Commensality, like kinship, is an idiom for marking affiliation. Eating together suggests sharing and reciprocity with those most like oneself. Food preferences and dietary prohibitions are powerful identifiers of who is and is not a member of the community. Family meals and sometimes religious gatherings are occasions for celebrating ethnic distinctiveness. But more than that, food and taste preferences are our first experience of our culture of birth. Those preferences may be deeply embedded, even at the biological level, and highly resistant to change in later life. Even the idea of what makes a meal is culturally encoded. Douglas (1975) has argued that more than simple nutriment, food is a symbol system of great complexity that operates at two levels. First, to qualify as a meal, foodstuffs must meet established criteria of taste and color combinations, correct sequences of presentation, carefully controlled and matched temperature ranges, and functional and decorative display. Second, a meal is an event during which specific and carefully observed values govern the style of eating, the rituals of etiquette, knowledge of the history and importance of selected foodstuffs, and preferences for who eats and sits with whom. Even in a mass production culture of "fast" and "convenience" foods, a hamburger in a cardboard box is no less freighted with a complex of values than is a Thanksgiving turkey served with yams and cranberries.

In particular, foodstuffs stand for relations with others; they are a highly visible part of the boundary between "us" and "them." Douglas (1971:66) puts it nicely: "Drinks are for strangers, acquaintances, workmen and family. Meals are for family, close friends, honored guests. The grand operator of the system is the line between intimacy and distance." This sense of intimacy surrounding food is so strong that it may even extend to the dead. Kalcik (1984:49–50) notes that some Mexicans set up small altars or *ofrendas* to the dead which are covered with the favored foods of the deceased. On the anniversary of a death, many Vietnamese cook foods preferred by the departed, and both Mexicans and Italians eat special sweets and breads on days commemorating deaths. Taken out of context (as in the proliferation of ethnic restaurants catering to mainstream tastes), these specific food items are clearly "surface features." But to cultural insiders, they are emblematic of more fundamental values, especially those associated with enduring forms of reciprocity. Far from being colorful and tasty exemplars of diversity, ethnic foods are defining devices for social relationships and boundaries.

Nash's idea of common cult refers to the body of beliefs and ritual activities that celebrate and legitimate the community's collective, historical experiences. Sacred or secular, such beliefs and practices assure the individual that his or her personal triumphs and failings are linked to the triumphs and failings of the entire community, as the success of Alex Haley's *Roots* (1976) so well demonstrated. Ethnic history and autobiography are intertwined and given a cosmological dimension. Although we commonly think of these dimensions of ethnicity in religious or quasi-religious terms—a "chosen people," an "African diaspora," "manifest destiny"—their importance for social services lies at more mundane, less grandiose levels. Understanding the common cult dimension of ethnicity could help a social worker better understand a number of situations. For example, when young Indian and Eskimo men venture out of their northern villages to work for whites, how does the competitive, task-oriented environment of their employers clash with an Indian sense of time and pacing and, just as important, with what consequences for Indian mental health (Christie and Halpern 1990)? Why are "nerves" and the suffering of a "nervous attack" the idioms of physical and mental distress among poor, rural Southern women working at dead-end factory jobs (Van Schaik 1989)? How do immigrant Asian children acquire literacy in American classrooms when oral rather than written styles of learning are favored in their homes (Cheng 1987; Glasgow 1991)? These are all issues that could come to a social worker's attention and none could be resolved simply with a knowledge of surface features. They are examples of Nash's common cult in action: core beliefs about how the world is organized and how one copes with it when things seem to fall apart.

Beliefs, myths, folktales, and stories ought to be of interest to social workers for another reason. Kracke (1994) argues that mythological materials may function as templates that help resolve emotional conflicts and crises. Symbolic systems are not only condensations of major values or ideologies. They are often linked to emotional fantasies that may be distinctive to a cultural community and, as such, act as a repository of possible solutions. Based on his own cross-cultural psychoanalytic work, Kracke states that "I came to regard ritual forms as providing, for the practitioner, a symbolic medium for articulation of affective conflicts: a kind of ritual language in terms of which the person can formulate emotional conflict and reach some resolution" (1994:208). Obviously, that kind of capability in professional work requires intense, long-term study even in one's own culture, more so in that of someone else. But it also suggests another of the possibilities for social service associated with cross-cultural understanding.

Ethnicity, Nash suggests, is a complex "recursive metaphor." It is a kind of mental template through which all experiences are shaped, interpreted, and given, quite literally, their "common sense." This metaphorical quality makes ethnicity powerful, empowering, and enduring. Ultimately, ethnicity is "the place where one is fully human" (Nash 1989:128). It underlies and underlines Jesse Jackson's cry, "I am somebody." The growth of state structures, multinational corporations, and overwhelming bureaucracies—all built on rationalistic principles of affiliation and cooperation—increases rather than decreases the importance of ethnicity as an alternative to collectivist forms of social regulation. Viewed this way, we can see that ethnicity is not an archaic sentiment surviving among the misfits or malcontents of the modern world; it is a powerful strategy for resisting and even reshaping what modernization offers.

CONCEPTS OF ETHNICITY: CATEGORICAL AND TRANSACTIONAL

Theories of ethnicity are not academic contrivances. They are systematic efforts to understand people's perceptions of reality and their characterizations of others as human beings. No service profession, especially one that deals with suffering, can afford not to articulate these matters clearly. To further refine these ideas as they apply to social services, I want to consider a distinction made by Bennett (1975) between what he calls categorical and transactional explanations of cultural difference. This distinction is crucial in thinking about cross-cultural social work.

Categorical explanations for cultural difference dominate American popular thought. Categorical accounts of ethnicity begin with assemblages of ethnic "traits," lists of things believed to be descriptive of persons in group X or Y. This approach involves a mental operation of sorting and matching specific traits so that one can locate individuals on a predetermined scale of what people X or Y are believed to be like. It presumes that an individual who "fits" one criteria probably fits many of the others that define the group as well. In categorical thought one would presume, for example, that the well-known social worker Jimm Good Tracks, who has written about these issues, must be Native American simply because Indians have names like that. (In fact, some do but many others do not.) Good Tracks is immediately categorized and, depending on how cavalier we want to be about it, we can also assume we know other things about him based on whatever previous experiences (including watching Hollywood westerns) we have had with other Native Americans.

In this approach, individuals are slotted into a predetermined trait list of surface features that do not explain so much as they impose. The categorizer's intellectual task is to assess the degree to which Good Tracks or any other Native American conforms to a standardized, stereotypical expectation. But if, for example, it should turn out that a client is Native American and also has an advanced degree in mathematics, sent her two children to Stanford, and works as a software engineer for NASA, the question the categorical thinker would ask is: with all that education and work experience, how Native American is she? Categorical thought comes with a set of assumptions about assimilation and the degree of match between the individual and the constellation of traits that are believed a priori to typify all Native Americans. The presence of a software-designing American Indian client does not challenge the validity of the categorical approach; rather, the categorizer redefines her to fit preconceived ideas of what constitutes true Indian-ness. This kind of pigeonholing seems obviously misguided, especially in this example, but it is surprising how often it occurs, even in social service settings.

Since categorical thinking about race and ethnicity is the norm in American culture, all of us, whatever our background, indulge the habit at one time or another. Even those who try to be sensitive in these matters find it difficult; the subtlety and pervasiveness of categorical thinking is profound. Further, where it is relatively easy to identify and correct categorization of surface features of ethnicity, it is more difficult when we are working with the core areas of ethnicity which can be less obvious.

Consider an example that involves one of the core areas of kinship, reciprocity (a derivative feature of the more generalized commensality). During a year of participant observation and interviewing on issues of race in an integrated dormitory at Rutgers University, Moffatt (1986, 1989) documented racial attitudes among white and African-American students. He found that whites categorized blacks according to a white model of friendship. White students emphasized their fundamental individualism, especially what they saw as their "free," voluntary choice of who would be a friend. Whites assumed that friendship pairing was a purely subjective matter, one in which no constraints other than personal preference operated. Only in matters of *style,* which to whites meant food and music, did white students concede any significant differences between themselves and blacks. When some African-American students seemed to resist white efforts at making friends, whites concluded that there was an "attitude" problem, "attitudes" being something over which individuals ought to have some degree of control. The white model of friendship was voluntaristic, individualist, and ahistorical and was one source of friction between the two groups of students.

African-American students, of course, had their own model for friendship pairing, one guided more by ideas about kinship—something hardly voluntary—than white notions of individualism and unfettered free choice. In the black model, friendship was thought of as something that evolves slowly and not entered into easily. It was intended to be genuinely long term and frequently involved a series of small exchanges such as money and personal items that gradually moved the relationship to the point where someone could be described as a "friend." These reciprocities were at least as important to African-American students as the psychological compatibility which the white students emphasized. Many of the black students resented what they saw as the easy and seemingly shallower attachments the whites favored and which whites insisted ought to be the pattern for blacks as well. For blacks, the easygoing nature of white friendship seemed casual to the point of being superficial and hence not trustworthy.

This example illustrates several features of categorical thinking that usually lead to fundamental misunderstandings about what people are doing and intending. First, the members of the dominant group in the dorm presumed that everyone shared (or ought to share) their beliefs and practices surrounding a very basic and seemingly simple notion: what it means to be a friend. But that kind of homogeneity did not exist. Second, the white students did not recognize or allow cultural (as opposed to psychological) variations on the theme of friendship. As far as the black students were concerned, there was no "attitude" problem at all and certainly no "problem" that needed fixing. Third, the example illustrates how easily "problems" that arise in cross-cultural relationships are located in the ethnographic "other," never in oneself. Categorical thinking is comparative but only in the most simplistic and ethnocentric sense: it presumes a central point of reference that is a standard, myself, and measures all others against that standard.

Categorical approaches to ethnicity have dominated belief and practice in American popular culture for generations and their omnipresence is hard to avoid. Both the older "melting pot" ideology and more recent notions of cultural pluralism assume that ethnicity is a cultural fossil, a remnant of the historical past and our unhappy experiences with slavery, immigrant enclaves, and reservations. In the melting pot model, historically received ethnic traits are expected to recede as each ethnic community adopts features of the dominant culture and gradually submerges its own distinctiveness through education, social mobility, and perhaps (although this is rarely mentioned) intermarriage. Eventually, it is assumed, a new and singular national social identity, one without the divisiveness associated with race or class, will emerge. That this has not happened, and probably will not, seems evident, as Glazer and Moynihan (1963) pointed out many years ago.

(It should be noted that the "tossed salad" model of ethnicity, considered progressive by some, is not an improvement. While it postulates a happier future where everyone "celebrates" his or her ethnicity without hindrance, it still pigeonholes—separating the lettuce from the celery from the olives—as though ethnic identities are fixed, permanent assemblages of traits. It does not understand ethnicity as a matter of perspectives, shifting and changing with time. Why this insistence on the immutability of ethnicity is so persistent in American thought is beyond the scope of this book but those who want to pursue it should start with Mary Douglas's thoughtful essay on the social meanings of pollution in human relations [1968].)

Although the melting pot model no longer has credence in social science, it continues to function as our unofficial, popular ideology on racial and cultural matters (Wellman 1993). Thus, ethnic groups or individuals are described as more or less "assimilated," a reference to the extent to which they are presumed to have given up their ethnic uniqueness in favor of the generalized cultural characteristics thought to be typical and desirable by the larger society. This kind of explanation often includes an implicit scale of degrees of acculturation. Individuals who retain their native language, food preferences, or occupations fall at the "traditional" end of the scale; those who appear to have given up entirely their ethnic lifestyle are "integrated" into the larger community.

The melting pot approach is severely limited, however, for many reasons. For example, there is no historical evidence that the variety of groups that make up American society are merging into a homogeneous whole. Acculturation for Native Americans has really been a euphemism for cultural genocide. (If the word "genocide" seems too strong, review the statistics of Native-American mortality over the past two or three centuries, and the impact of federal land and education policies on Indian peoples.) Similarly, the effort to preserve linguistic distinctiveness has become a contentious issue for both Anglos and Spanish speakers, especially in the South and Southwest, where the electorate in a number of states has approved ballot initiatives declaring English the official language. That issue is more than the right of Latino children to be taught in Spanish language classrooms. What is involved is preservation of one of the most powerful cultural identifiers any group can have, its language (Gibson and Arvizu 1977). Finally, studies of Southeast-Asian students in American schools reveal that those who are most acculturated to the norms of American life have poorer academic scores than those who are less acculturated (Nathan, Choy, and Whitmore 1992). Such findings contradict established beliefs about the value of the melting pot model and suggest instead that many people might be better off maintaining their distance from mainstream culture.

Cultural pluralism, a more recent innovation in popular thinking about ethnicity, is also based on the categorical approach and, as such, shares its limitations. Cultural pluralism stresses the distinctiveness of ethnic groups and the need for them to live in a kind of separate-but-equal harmony, the "tossed salad" theory again. Unlike the melting pot view, however, the pluralist approach appreciates cultural differences and their preservation—up to a point. It argues that ethnic groups provide the individual with a primary basis for loyalty and affiliation; that ethnic differences are good in themselves; and that ethnic variation contributes strength, not weakness, to the larger community. While these claims have a powerful appeal, particularly to those of a liberal or humanistic persuasion, they are not without problems. Pluralism can and has been used as a kind of "enlightened" cultural relativism to rationalize the exclusion of some groups from full social and political participation. An example is the once fashionable "culture of poverty" theory, widely used to explain why the problems of poor people are distinctive to them and why they are the victims of their own bad choices. The current expression of this idea is in the benign pluralism that arose in the 1980s. In that period, when greed and self-aggrandizement almost became patriotic acts, troubled communities were left to "do their own thing," "walk their own walk," and otherwise deal with their problems as best they could. A conservative version of pluralism as national policy called for nonintervention in human issues as though that were a benevolent respect for cultural differences. Of course, it was not.

The categorical approach, whether of melting pot or pluralistic forms, always requires that the observer view the ethnicity of others as a combination of traits that they (rather than us) exhibit: their "color," their musical styles, their foods, and sometimes their poverty. If the fashion of the times romanticizes these things as "their" way, this provides justification for doing little or nothing to change debilitating circumstances. Carrying this view to its most extreme, one could argue that slave plantations, Indian reservations, and World War II detention camps were examples of pluralism. Of course, no one thinks of them that way because they were imposed through force by one group on another. But rural slums in the South, Indian reservations in the West, and crowded Chinatowns with sweatshop labor conditions have at times been viewed by the uninformed as quaint, romantic, and authentic. Pluralism, by itself, is not a theory that can help us understand ethnic and minority concerns because it diverts attention from the fact that many people live as they do because the larger society permits them few alternatives.

There is one additional criticism to make of categorical ways of viewing the ethnographic other. Categorization, like prejudice, would probably matter less if everyone were equally powerful. But everyone is not. In categorical thinking, one *imposes* on another, largely because it is possible to do so. Most minority Americans are acutely sensitive to racial slights from whites, far more than whites generally realize. Verbal gaffes are not mere breaches of etiquette or expressions of insensitivity. Rather, they reveal an arrogance of power, a presumptiveness that one has a right to label others, and to get away with it.

In sum, the problem with categorical ways of thinking about ethnicity and cultural difference is that it is ultimately political: the dominant group dictates the categories that help it manage and control uncertain and potentially contentious relationships. The implicit assumption is that cross-cultural relationships are essentially competitive and hostile, competitive for the scarce resources of position, power, rank, authority, goods, time, services, and moral worthiness. Cultural difference is a challenge, even a threat, one that invokes self-protection and personal distancing. In service relationships, that is hardly an effective way of learning about others or of responding to their needs.

Bennett's transactional approach to ethnicity suggests something entirely different. The surface cultural traits that are central to pluralist and melting pot thinking are moved into the background. Instead, the boundaries that groups define around themselves, using cultural traits as markers for exclusion and inclusion as situations require, become critical. It is the idea of boundedness and its invocation when necessary, not categorical bundles of specific traits, that defines an ethnic sensibility. Frederik Barth, whose work *Ethnic Groups and Boundaries* (1969) is most closely associated with this theory, writes that "The critical focus of investigation from this point of view becomes the ethnic *boundary* that defines the group, not the cultural stuff it encloses. . . . [A] dichotomization of others as strangers, as members of another ethnic group, implies a recognition of limitations on shared understandings, differences in criteria for judgment of value and performance, and a restriction of interaction to sectors of assumed common understanding and mutual interest" (1969:15). The key idea here is Barth's emphasis on socially distributed knowledge and implicit understandings, and the "restriction of interaction" that results from that. It is what individuals do with what they know, and the conditions under which they do it, that marks them off as members of a distinctive community and defines all others as strangers. Boundaries in this sense are loose, situational, sometimes permeable, always subject to manipulation. Ethnicity is an emergent feature of relationships, not an abstract identity worn publicly like a badge. Barth refers to this process as

Categorical	Transactional
• Emphasizes cultural "content" within groups.	• Emphasizes boundaries between groups.
• Assumes high level of cultural uniformity within groups.	• Expects differential expression of surface features within groups.
• Seeks conceptual simplification in response to cultural "otherness."	• Seeks conceptual complexity within a comparative perspective.
• Assimilation or acculturation are policy and intervention goals.	• Resolution within indigenous frameworks as intervention goal.
• Associated with melting pot and pluralistic ideologies.	• Anticipates resistance to political and cultural dominance.

FIGURE 1.3   Categorical and transactional perspectives on diversity.

"boundary maintenance," the things people do to make claims about who they are, under conditions that are usually specific. Figure 1.3 summarizes the differences between categorical and transactional views of diversity.

A humorous example from the growing social science literature on the transactional aspects of ethnicity comes from Basso's (1979) work among the Western Apache of Arizona. He shows that an Apache folk model of whites is important in their everyday joking behavior. Despite stereotypes of Native Americans as quiet and dour, Apache speakers interlace their conversations with spontaneous skits that mock what they see as the communicative incompetence of whites. These jokes, usually a series of one-liners, exaggerate white speech and body gestures. An enthusiastic, loud, hand-waving exclamation, "Come right in my friend! Don't stay outside in the rain. Better you come in right now" (1979:46), brings a round of appreciative laughing from other Apaches. Why should that be so funny? It's funny because it offends (as humor often does) an Apache sense of propriety on at least four counts: (1) it is an abrupt and extroverted display of uncontrolled body motion and enthusiasm, behavior more appropriate to children than properly socialized Apache adults; (2) it makes an assertive, public demand on others that violates their right to make their own choices, again, behavior that is more childlike than adult; (3) it presumes friendship where none exists and is therefore preposterous; and (4) it repeats the same message three different times, as though the speaker believed the hearer too stupid to do the obvious and come in out of the rain. What for whites would be taken as a polite, solicitous expression of concern for someone standing in the cold is, on the other side of the cultural boundary, a joke about bumbling and haplessness.

Are Basso's Apaches being ethnocentric in their own way, simply making fun of whites whose culture *they* do not understand or appreciate? Of course they are. That is just the point. Boundaries set up contrasts, and contrasts become occasions for commenting about difference, for asserting who and what one is, and for proclaiming values that are held to be eternal truths, at least among one's own people and for the present moment.

Looking at this brief example of ethnic humor as a transaction, a number of implications for our understanding of ethnicity follow. First, relations across ethnic boundaries tend to be rigid and stereotypical. They are, in fact, highly ritualized. This assures that actors in cross-ethnic encounters can more or less predict one another's behavior and carry on their business without having to learn much of one another's culture. Obviously, the more rigid the boundaries between groups, the more stereotyped the encounters will be. Caste-like relations between blacks and whites have contributed enormously to stereotyped and protective maneuvering on both sides of the racial line. Effective cross-cultural communication requires working with and eventually beyond the etiquette associated with these boundaries.

Second, the example implies (and Basso's readable ethnography amply demonstrates) that ethnic group formation is an ongoing process, one with political and economic consequences. Despite melting pot ideology, in which differences are submerged through contact, the transactional model suggests that where people can find advantage in distinguishing themselves from others, they will do so. This tendency need not be viewed as a cynical or devious characteristic of the human mind; rather, it is simply evidence that loyalty to groups and participation in particular styles of living are among the most important values we have as human beings. The specific nature of these values may be less significant than the fact that they continuously evolve and that we utilize them to justify differential behavior toward individuals we presume to be different or even inferior. Far from melting away under pressure of acculturation, therefore, ethnic distinctions are continuously defined, redefined, and reinforced as a result of multiethnic, multiracial contact. This reasoning suggests, for example, why people periodically change their ethnic group names. Changing perceptions of boundaries prompt individuals to redefine themselves and their relationship to the dominant society.

Finally, the example suggests that group members creatively manage their ethnicity. Individuals do what we might call "identity work" by self-conscious manipulating of group boundaries (in the Apache case, with jokes). The degree to which a person is "assimilated," therefore, is situational rather than absolute and can be modified to suit different kinds of cross-cultural encounters. This observation has profound implications for how individuals manifest ethnicity in different relationships. The culturally responsive practitioner will want to be aware that clients can be more or less "acculturated" as the situation demands. Individualizing the client requires understanding how people manage and manipulate the symbols of their ethnicity as a resource for building satisfying lives.

The idea of "identity work" suggests another aspect of this essentially fluid view of ethnicity. I recall the comment of an African-American colleague originally from the West Indies. In his home country, where nearly everyone is black, ethnicity is hardly an issue, at least in everyday, routine transactions. Since coming to the United States, however, he has never been allowed to forget who and what he is. He is regularly asked, even by strangers, questions such as what he thinks of Clarence Thomas on the Supreme Court, or if he likes the Ray Charles cola commercials, or if he saw a spectacular play in a televised sporting event. He feels he is asked these things because he is black and therefore must have an opinion on the Supreme Court, Ray Charles's music, and sports. (No one ever asks him about his Ph.D. in political science.) He is reminded, daily, of who and what he is (or ought to be) and he finds it exhausting and irritating. In describing his frustration, he remarked how he always felt that around whites he was expected to be "on" as an "ethnic," and that it was a great relief to go home after work and be "off" for the rest of the evening. In a predominantly white society, identity work for many minority individuals is the constant and often tiring management of an "on" and "off" self. It is something whites experience only if they are in situations where they, not the other, are the minority.

I want to end this section with an observation about the longer-term implications of ethnicity and why I think "identity work," such as that mentioned by my West Indian coworker, will be as important in our future as it has been in the past. I have already mentioned that there is nothing permanent about the racial or ethnic identities we all claim for ourselves. The so-called races that exist today did not exist 10,000 years ago. Some, in fact, did not exist in North and South America even a few hundred years ago, prior to colonization by Europeans, West Africans, and East Asians. Some races that now exist may be less evident in a few thousand years. Certainly current boundaries will be blurred just as new ones will be emerging. Migration, human contact, sex, and evolution guarantee it.

So what does such a large, historical generalization mean for us now? Consider this: America's complexion is literally darkening, and if current demographic trends continue, that darkening will be more evident to everybody by the early years of the next century. Gibbs and Huang (1989) refer to it as the "browning of America." As the baby boomers begin to retire and vacate the workplace over the next 20 to 40 years, the American economy will face severe labor shortages at virtually every skill level. Immigrants from all over the globe will converge on Baldwin's first universal nation, as they always have, but in much greater numbers than before. Those immigrants will meet and mix with the indigenous African, Latino, Asian, and Anglo population as they always have, but with greater frequency.

At some time near the middle of the next century, people who are now cultural and racial minorities will be close to numerical and political parity with whites. At that time, they may well demand economic and social parity as well and, for the price of civil peace, they will probably get it. Half a lifetime from now, all the meeting and mixing will be evident in the faces of everyone and the phrase "people of color" may mean something else, or it may mean nothing at all. From an anthropological point of view, that process seems perfectly natural, much more natural in fact than our historic insistence on racial separation.

Similarly, we may come to see that while cultural diversity has always been with us, the contents of ethnic categories are of more recent vintage. Perhaps they are even fictions, inventions of convenience (Anderson 1983). Most claims of ethnic identity, purity, and pride rest on assumptions about an original homeland and the special status of a favored people endowed by their gods and culture heroes with unique moral substance. When we speak of our ethnic origins, that assumption is there, however uncertain or vague we might be about it. Yet the mixing of peoples and cultures over thousands of years belies any such constancy, making it impossible for any of us to trace reliably our ultimate origins. Claims about traditions—racial, ethnic, religious, or nationalistic—are always created anew to meet current needs and circumstances. They may be the most creative and complex form of mythmaking of which we as a species are capable (Williams 1989). If that is so, we should recognize our myths for the double-edged sword they are: assertions of pride and distinctiveness, but also justifications for privilege and advantage. They may serve us well, or not at all, and how we use them is our own choice, not one dictated to us by history.

SOCIAL WORK—ETHNIC GROUP RELATIONSHIPS

If ethnicity resides in the boundaries between distinctive cultural communities, then the persons who mediate boundaries are critical actors in the communication of information and regulation of resources affecting minorities. The social science literature has numerous terms for such persons: mediators, facilitators, ombudsmen, cultural brokers, go-betweens, and the like. In their work with minority clients, social workers are often mediators who help clients get things they cannot get alone. But mediation can be expressed in a variety of ways and each way presupposes an implicit if not explicit value orientation and matching intervention style.

At least four modes of intervention with minority groups can be defined. Following Cowger (1977), I will identify these as (1) group advocate, (2) counselor, (3) regulator, and (4) broker (Figure 1.4 on page 32). Of course, these categories can and do overlap, but they suggest ways of understanding the immense variety of social work–ethnic group encounters. I will use this simple but useful division of professional-client relationships to consider some of the implications of ethnicity for professional services.

One approach to intervention is advocacy, sometimes described as a radical response (Statham 1978). The forms of advocacy vary widely, from efforts to fundamentally reorganize community services in New York's Harlem (Day 1987) to making mental health services more available to people in Appalachia (Keefe

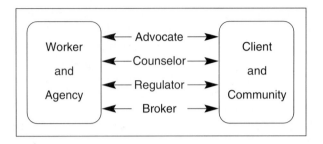

FIGURE   1.4   Worker-client relationships.

Based on Cowger 1977.

1988). Advocacy assumes that conflict is inherent in minority and dominant group relationships and that the dominant social institutions must be challenged and changed. The advocate views the client's needs and problems as a result of unfair and unjust practices and an inequitable distribution of resources. Advocacy has an explicit value orientation. Taylor (1987) notes that the National Association of Social Workers Code of Ethics calls for "marshaling of community resources to promote the well being of all" and "action for improving social conditions" (1987:4). Advocacy is in fact interference and partisanship which, of necessity, challenges institutional procedures and habits that interfere with the legitimate expectations of those seeking help.

The important issue raised by the advocacy approach is the culpability of dominant institutions, including the institutions that provide social services and social service education, in the problems minority clients experience. Advocates point out that problems are often perpetuated and aggravated by accepted practices: drug misuse by intensive commercial promotion of medications; slums by the investment practice of banks and landlords; job discrimination by the rhetorical insistence on maintenance of hiring and promotion standards. Social work has also been criticized for ignoring the political, social, and economic forces that contribute, in both direct and indirect ways, to the concerns that clients bring to workers.

One of the classic (and controversial) statements of advocacy is that of Cloward and Piven (1975). They charge that schools of social work train students to acquiesce to the organizational demands of social service and government bureaucracies. These demands, they maintain, perpetuate the agency and its agendas at the expense of the legitimate needs of clients. Established service organizations tend to blame the victim for psychological deficiencies, instead of working to change the oppressive social and economic circumstances that are part of the victim's problems. They cite health care: "Social workers are used by hospitals and their medical rulers to appease anxious or dissatisfied patients, to cool out the mark. What we ought to do instead is to challenge the doctors and hospital authorities, and encourage patients to do the same" (1975: xxxiv).

One of the more interesting recent attempts to provide a theoretical basis for advocacy in social services is that of Rose and Black (1985). Explicitly empowerment oriented, they criticize what they call the "decontextualization" of patients and clients—treating individuals as nonhistorical, nonsocial units to be therapeutically acted upon, their background experiences and associations subjectively replaced with a controlling language of procedures and formulas. They find decontextualization evident, for example, in implicit, often unspoken professional criteria of what makes a "good" client:

> *After a time, the externally imposed new social order [of the clinic or hospital] becomes incorporated subjectively—the problem definition coercively held out is tacitly accepted. But in the process, the patient undergoes an experience of anomie—of an abrupt withdrawal of norms and forms. . . . The experience of such extraction of one's known universe of meaning is profound (1985:30).*

Unlike many of the overtly political models of advocacy of the 1960s and 1970s, Rose and Black's program is intended for work with individuals, not just groups. For them, empowerment is the conversion of dependent help-seekers into self-consciously autonomous persons. Their challenging model calls upon the worker to learn the subjective meanings of the client's everyday world (they use the social science term *Verstehen*, implicit knowledge) and the cultural themes of that world (1985:60–69). The social worker learns of cultural issues prior to making technical assessments and evaluations. This strategy, which makes cultural meaning a central concern, goes well beyond the political mobilization of groups which is the traditional sense of advocacy. Rose and Black show how their approach applies to case management, legal advocacy, and mental health day-care programs.

While there are many instances of advocacy based on prior cultural knowledge, one older but still excellent example is provided by Jacobs (1974a, 1974b, 1979) in her work with a Midwestern African-American community where she helped establish a neighborhood health center. In that community, infant mortality rates among African-American children were considerably higher than those for nearby white children, a problem that has become worse rather than better in recent years. The established health organizations attributed this difference to underutilization of existing health services by black families and an apparent unwillingness by expectant mothers to comply with their physician's advice. Jacobs's research and advocacy team discovered different reasons. These included explicit acts of racial stereotyping of black patients by white physicians, collusion among white-dominated health organizations to exclude black physicians, and adoption by health providers of a white model of health services, which at that time was crisis oriented rather than preventive. As she documented these issues, Jacobs also examined the health care preferences and behavior of community residents. Working with black patients, clients, and a variety of black professionals, she helped design health care practices that were more closely aligned with community expectations. The work was time-consuming and difficult, but it resulted in a high level of trust between Jacobs and community members and in a demonstrably more useful health care program. It also showed the utility of an explicitly cultural orientation in taking on a significant community concern. Long-term problems in the transactions between the white health care establishment and black patients had contributed to a serious health problem. Jacobs's work as an advocate unraveled the threads of that problem, thus enabling the community to better plan its own initiatives.

Schensul and Schensul (1978) have suggested that advocacy involves a number of skills and techniques, including research capabilities, knowledge of community institutions, in-depth awareness of community values and of community relations with the larger society, and an ability to promote linkages between minority and dominant institutions. The key issue, however, and the one that Jacobs addressed early in her work, is that of identifying the person or persons to whom the advocate is accountable. Once Jacobs established that the patient's needs had priority, and that research, planning, and service delivery had to meet those needs, it became apparent that the participation of community residents was critical. This ability to identify and utilize community-centered information characterizes the culturally responsive service provider who acts as an advocate.

In the second intervention mode, that of counseling, practitioners intervene by focusing on the client's specific problems, particularly on client feelings, ideas, and behavior, and on ways to develop positive responses to specific issues. This is the usual clinical style, with the practitioner functioning as a counselor, and it is the one many social work texts and training manuals address. Professional practice is viewed as neutral in terms of larger social implications. The target of change is the individual, not power structures or class relationships, and change is achieved one-on-one or in small groups. The practitioner's first responsibility is to the client, not to the client's community as such. This approach, as Cowger points out, was codified in an earlier version of the National Association of Social Workers' statement of ethics: "I regard as my primary obligation the welfare of the individual or group served, which includes action for improving social conditions" (1977:27). To change social conditions is usually interpreted as subordinate to changing clients. While the clinical model has the advantage of recognizing that individuals do have concerns that must be addressed through supportive personal services, it often slights the institutionally generated sources of individual difficulty.

A persistent problem in counseling has been the sometimes awkward match between the individual counselor with his or her clinical approach and the cultural diversity of clients. Social work researchers have generally looked no further than the degree of comfort felt by clients and clinicians in same-ethnic and mixed-ethnicity combinations and, in practice, most social workers have relied either on personal experience or empathy to carry them through cross-cultural encounters. This is surprising, because cross-cultural counseling is an area of vigorous interest in such fields as education and psychology and it has a number of applications, particularly in government and business programs involving contact with people in other countries. Anthropologists, although they have not often specifically focused on the interests of social workers, have done extensive work in interethnic communication (Ross 1978) and in communication issues in medical settings (Kleinman 1980, 1988b), schools (Spindler 1982, 1987; Spindler and Spindler 1994), and specialized areas such as aging (Sokolovsky 1990b), child abuse (Korbin 1981), abortion (Ginsburg 1989), and American marriage and divorce patterns (Johnson 1989). Some have even proposed that ethnographic interviewing has therapeutic functions for minority clients (Davidson 1994; García-Castañon 1994).

But the availability of information, whatever its source, is probably not the real issue. In what has become one of the standard works in cross-cultural counseling, Sue and Sue (1990) list what they see as the impediments to effective communication between mainstream, white counselors and minority clients. These impediments include a number of culture-bound values, including extreme individualism in the conceptualization of client concerns; an insistence on verbal and emotional expressiveness as a therapeutic technique; demands for self-disclosure; simplistic, linear cause-and-effect models; reliance on mind/body distinctions in arriving at clinical judgments; and missed body and linguistic cues. Language is of particular concern not only because some clients have difficulties with English but also because social service providers tend to rely on technical vocabulary that mystifies clients. Using euphemisms and jargon, the language of "empathy," "caring," "engagement," "openness," "holism," and even empowerment can inappropriately substitute for learning the meaning of personal issues within the context of another culture.

Vontress (1976) has described examples of some of the problems of using well-known counseling techniques in cross-cultural encounters. Self-disclosure, for instance, is particularly difficult in relations between white counselors and African-American clients, as it presumes a degree of trust that blacks generally have no reason to extend toward whites. Short-term, task-oriented styles of social work may conflict with an emphasis on personalism in social relations, a preference common among blacks and whites, especially in rural areas of the South, and among many Mexican Americans and Puerto Ricans. While brief, task-centered contacts with a large number of clients may be desirable to agency administrators who must watch budgets and schedules, they may be ineffectual with clients who feel that time spent "just talking" is an important way of entering and maintaining a trusting relationship.

Obviously, examples like this could be listed and described endlessly. But that would not lead to a satisfactory way of thinking about cultural differences; it would simply encourage a categorical approach to ethnicity by producing lists of traits and procedures to be memorized for use whenever a client of X or Y ethnicity appears at a social worker's desk. As an alternative, Mayes (1978) has identified some of the characteristics he feels make for effective intercultural relationships, including critical insight into the limitations of one's own experiences with minorities, cognitive and attitudinal openness to signs of difference in others, a sense of adventurousness in exploring with others what their cultural distinctiveness may mean, flexibility in adapting to the interests of others, and a very large measure of informed skepticism toward all diagnostic and assessment procedures when these are applied to persons who are not mainstream whites.

He concludes that the effective cross-cultural communicator is one who adopts a value stance in which he or she can "understand, believe, and convey that there are no 'culturally deprived' or 'culture free' individuals and that all cultures have their own integrity, validity, and coherence" (1978:39).

As principles and goals for cross-cultural counseling, these are worthy ones. But there remains the task of defining what they mean in day-to-day encounters with specific individuals. Cultures differ in the way decision making is structured, in the life events that are emphasized, in how the developmental cycle of household and family units are ordered, and in how individuals and households react to crises and to external interference (Sundberg 1976). That kind of information, of critical importance in making an intelligent response to the needs of others, has yet to be gathered and presented in a framework suitable for training social workers. Clearly, it will have to come from a variety of sources, including academic research and publications, intensive participant observation, and detailed consultation with ethnic and minority social workers. Then cross-cultural counseling will have acquired the theoretical and empirical basis it must have in order to contribute to resolving the problems brought to social workers by their ethnic and minority clients.

In a third intervention mode, the practitioner is seen as an extension of the larger society, in effect a kind of regulator who is concerned with helping clients modify their behavior or attitudes. Resocialization of clients, especially involuntary ones, is a standard strategy in this approach. There is an important social control function that clearly reflects society's mandate that some kinds of problems be corrected or controlled. In the area of child abuse, for instance, the idea of serving the "best interests of the child" may be viewed as one of changing family discipline practices. The social worker may indeed act as a counselor to an abusing parent, but the aim of intervention is to modify family patterns. How these patterns are modified, in what direction, and under what authority are critical issues that often reflect the mandate placed on the social worker-as-regulator. Ethnic community leaders often cite this control-oriented function as evidence that the profession is more committed to protecting the status quo than assuring just and fair treatment for those who need it most. Whatever the merits of these complaints, these critics raise an important issue that goes beyond mere rhetoric. How should deviance, discontent, maladaptation, and nonconformity be defined and judged, and who is to do the judging?

One of the most dramatic illustrations of the regulatory functions of social service providers can be found in the history of control over Native-American children, first through government boarding schools (Blanchard 1983), then in attempts to deal with suicide, alcoholism, and delinquency (Wise and Miller 1983; Robbins 1984), and finally in the slow development of Indian-oriented and Indian-operated service programs (Shore and Manson 1983; Grafton 1982). Indian children were often removed from their homes, not because of abuse or neglect, but because of perceived deficits in the home and community environment. Tribal authorities and agencies were not always consulted nor did parents understand the nature of the legal proceedings against them (Blanchard and Unger 1977). In the boarding school system, parents and tribal authorities did not always know where children had been sent. These injustices are far less frequent now, in part because of the militancy of tribal leaders and Indian social workers but also because of the growing sensitivity of social workers generally to the values and strengths of Indian communities (Edwards and Edwards 1984). But this example raises larger issues about the regulatory role. In managing the expression of apparent deviance, who decides what is and is not acceptable, and by what standards? To whom ought social service providers be accountable for their decisions? This is both a cultural and a political issue, and the culturally sensitive worker will need to be able to defend counseling, referral, and placement choices in ways that make sense not only to individual clients but to their families and communities as well.

In the fourth intervention mode, the practitioner functions as an intermediary or broker. This approach stresses the practitioner's dual responsibility to the individual and society. Many social workers probably function as brokers as part of their professional activity, particularly when they work to mediate the needs of clients and the limitations of the service system. It is frustrating and often thankless work and, for some social workers, a primary cause of burnout.

There is more than one way to be a broker or mediator. McLeod (1981) summarizes these ways in an interesting discussion of mediation as a professional skill. She notes that the most superficial kind of mediator is the "trader," whether a trader in goods, ideas, or services. The trader is primarily interested in his or her own enterprise, the personal benefits that might accrue, and the success of the larger agenda of the "home culture," whether that is the "culture" of the trader's company, profession, or local office. A detailed knowledge of client needs and interests is secondary since clients are viewed essentially as consumers (however unwilling, at times) for whatever the trader is offering. In this relationship, one client is much like any other and moving them through the system, "processing" cases, is the trader's goal.

By contrast, the "diplomat" requires a deeper knowledge of the client's culture because he or she will be called upon to deal with unhappy "incidents" in which some member of the client community feels aggrieved. A bit more sophisticated than the trader, the diplomat is still an extension of the home territory's agendas; the services offered justify the sponsoring organization's staff and budget and the diplomat functions to advance the home culture's goals however they may be defined.

The "missionary" is a third kind of mediator, but one whose first loyalties are not to the home office or the client but to the mission itself. To be successful, the missionary must know more of the client culture than either the trader or the diplomat, but that knowledge is intended to serve first the needs of the mission. Clients, of course, are the presumed beneficiaries, but it is the mission that is at issue. Missionaries are usually individuals with zeal, something that may not typify the trader or the diplomat who have more circumscribed interests. Fueled by enthusiasm for their cause—cracking down on crack, extracting support from errant fathers, gaining convictions against abusive spouses—the missionary is really a crusader, concerned more with a principle than the idiosyncrasies of individual cases.

The fourth kind of broker McLeod calls the "teacher." She states, "I use the word *teacher* to refer to the true mediator, because his success can be measured in terms of what is learned by those with whom he has contact" (1981:40). Teachers undoubtedly have vested interests, just like other kinds of mediators, but they succeed when they can persuade members of differing cultural communities to better understand, respect, and perhaps care about one another. Both sides receive benefits. Not all teachers (in the occupational sense) are mediators, but all good mediators are teachers because their professional work leads to new levels of understanding by everyone.

What special skills do mediators as teachers have? First, not surprisingly, they have knowledge, lots of it, about the communities they serve. Their knowledge is neither superficial nor encyclopedic; it is specific and deep. Second, they have communication skills. That does not mean they know two or three languages but that they understand the importance of vernacular in discussing and clarifying personal and family problems. They know how to use language in specific ways that are helpful in their work, a skill I address in a later chapter. Third, teachers have technical skills, acquired through formal training and refined through apprenticeship. Fourth, they have social skills that enable them to perform effectively in confusing, ambiguous, or even hostile environments. They can articulate some of the "rules of the game" of another community and recognize when rules are being violated, although they may not always know why. For effective mediators, their knowledge of another culture is a kind of master skill that allows them to know that culture much as community members do (Taft 1981). The mediator who recognizes and understands the culture-specific emotional responses of the served community has achieved the highest level of skill. At this point, he or she is truly bicultural.

Is this kind of capability too much to ask, something beyond which social workers need aspire? The answer is an unequivocal no. Many people already have these skills and presently work in human service occupations. They are social work's minority professionals, individuals who occupy a middle ground between their communities of origin and their acquired, professional ones. Whereas most white social workers probably do not experience a significant cognitive and emotional dissonance between what they do on the job and what they believe the larger society supports, minority workers often confront this dilemma. They have grown up in a minority community and perhaps continue to live and participate in it. As most minority communities in America now have a significant and growing middle class, they often share in that. But the universities in which they were trained are still predominantly white and, in at least some of these schools, the debate continues about the place of minority issues in the curriculum, what emphasis they should have, and whether or not courses designed around minority content ought to be required for everyone. Where minorities were once referred to as having a "dual perspective" (Norton et al. 1978), it may now be fairly stated that they have multiple perspectives: a community of origin, their middle class status, and a professional community. On some occasions, professional responsibilities and personal interest may collide.

I would even suggest that in some quarters a degree of ambivalence toward minority professionals remains. Their priorities, if not loyalties, are a question mark to some of their colleagues. I do not think this is due to explicit racism, although that may sometimes be the case, but to the fact that minority professionals do indeed have multiple perspectives. They are in a good position to make comparative, even critical judgments about policy and practice. Being multicultural, the authoritative basis of their insight is hard to ignore. And as professionals, they know the customs, etiquette, and preferences of the professional subculture and how that subculture is generally expressive of the value system of the politically dominant white middle class. Their "quiet presence," as I once heard a sympathetic but troubled trainee describe it, was a daily reminder that his agency's goals and activities were not always accommodating to those who had different ideas about what could or should be done.

SOCIAL WORK AS AN ETHNIC COMMUNITY

Are the differences between minority and dominant group social workers really that great, or are they minor matters of etiquette, communication styles, and personal preferences? One way to think about that is to turn the ethnographic approach onto the service professions directly, treating the subculture of social workers as an ethnic community like any other with its own arcane rituals, in-group jargon, overt and covert values, and boundary protecting mechanisms. Using Nash's model, we could say that social workers as an "ethnic group" share kinship (common socialization through degree-granting and training programs), commensality (shared physical working spaces, bureaucratic routines, time put in on tasks, and private understandings about work and the agency), and cult (motivations for entering social work as a career, the values that prompt one's labors, and a share in the legacy of the profession and one's agency). We could also say that some members of the social work tribe are, in their own ways, ethnocentric, just like the members of ethnic communities everywhere.

To understand this tribe, we can compare its distinctive features—communication styles, rituals, or implicit working assumptions, for example—with those of other ethnic communities. Native-American social worker Jimm Good Tracks has commented that "all the methods usually associated with the term 'social work intervention' diminish in effectiveness" when applied to Indian clients (Good Tracks 1973:30). The more traditional the client's orientation, he says, the less likely the positive effect of normative social work practice. This is because in many Native-American communities "no interference or meddling of any kind is allowed or tolerated, even when it is to keep the other person from doing something foolish or dangerous" (Good Tracks 1973:30).

Similarly, Wax and Thomas (1961) contrast the ways in which Indians and whites sometimes deal with personal problems. For example, when confronted with a crisis, whites often feel the need to act decisively, to "do something" before the situation gets "out of hand." Activism, courageous decision making, and the appearance of being "in charge" are important values for whites, whether they can do all those things well or not. But many Indians respond to problems with quietness, caution, careful observation, and, if necessary, withdrawal. What looks to whites as escapist is, from an Indian perspective, properly careful scrutiny and the avoidance of unnecessary pain. Personal integrity is also protected this way. Rejecting the urge of whites to be heroic and to reach beyond their grasp (failure for whites, if in a noble cause, is still ennobling), many Indians prefer to avoid the foolishness of attempting too much. They also value noninvolvement, holding that if something obviously needs to be done, at some point an individual qualified and capable will do it; there is no need for well-meaning bystanders to presume it is their responsibility to act just because they happen to be present. Further, Indians avoid direct requests to others. Direct talk, seen by whites as "honest" and "frank," is seen by many Indians as rude, behavior more typical of improperly raised children rather than of adults sensitive to what is going on around them.

Indian communities, especially traditional ones, have low levels of the kind of demonstrative action that whites accept as normal. Voluntary cooperation, at a time convenient for all concerned, is the way things get done. This is reflective of a fundamental and profoundly democratic orientation, one in which "assertiveness," "being number one," and "standing tall"—popular clichés in the white world—are seen as incredible boorishness if not folly. However well intended, intrusive behavior by whites in Indian matters is quietly noted and sometimes resented, a resentment manifest in silence or withdrawal.

From the point of view of the social work tribe, probably no Indian values are more puzzling and confounding than those associated with time and timing. "White time" is clock time, time organized to serve industrial and corporate purposes. The "fifty minute hour" and task-centered services are examples of extreme clock and calendar awareness. By contrast, Indian time is social time, adjusted to meet personal, family, and sometimes ritual needs. Philips (1974) has described how an Indian sense of time is shaped by a distinctive notion of the progression of events, be they public ceremonies, private conversations, or informal gatherings of friends. To whites, most activities have an implicit order: an identifiable beginning, a middle, and an end. At each stage, the participants know where they are in the sequence and modulate their speech and mannerisms accordingly. But for many Indians, events are defined more in terms of the availability of people; the presence of certain persons is necessary before anything can begin. Thus many Indian activities are open-ended, seemingly indeterminate, and appear to whites to have confused and ambiguous boundaries. To Indians, there is no confusion at all. As Philips notes, an event cannot happen until the right people are available and, given the value of noninterference, it would not be appropriate to coerce anyone to be at a specific place at a given time. This emphasis on people rather than the abstractions represented by a clock face is an organizational strategy that "maximize[s] the possibility that everyone who wants to participate is given the chance when he or she chooses to and in the way he or she chooses to" (Philips 1974:107). Indian time, therefore, is not an inability to get someplace exactly when one must be there; it is not an "inability" at all. It is a distinctive cultural style, subtle and complex, that is preeminently person-centered.

Are these generalizations true of all Native-American communities? Certainly not. To believe so would be to stereotype anew. Not all Indians fit this very brief summation of generalized Indian values any more than all social workers would fit a comparably brief overview of what they are like. Rather, the value of the information is in alerting the social worker to issues that may affect a relationship with Indian clients. These generalizations about white time and Indian time cannot be taken as Grand Truth but as a hypothesis, one that might have to be explored in working with specific Indian clients.

We could also compare social work as a distinctive culture with other service or bureaucratic entities in the dominant society. For example, there is a small, emerging field that studies the culture of corporations. It goes behind organizational charts, job descriptions, and management policies and looks at the implicit rules and practices of corporate life. Some of this research has been done by anthropologists, although much of it is the work of people in business studies and corporate psychology. The topics range widely: the hidden values in corporate logos; the management of stress by salespeople; company picnics and other organizational festivals; corporate folklore and myth making among top management; the manipulation of customer relations; the funeral director as ritual choreographer; and the "glass ceiling" and its effects on the promotion of women and minorities. (See Jones, Moore, and Snyder [1988] for an interesting introduction to this field.) These matters are not only interesting but useful for understanding the hidden dynamics of behavior in what seem to be highly structured, preeminently rational human associations.

For example, Deal and Kennedy (1982) describe what they call "corporate tribes," each of which has a distinctive way of doing their work. They offer amusing accounts of corporate dress, housing, sports, language, greeting rituals, and officially disapproved relations between coworkers. Deal and Kennedy do not describe social services organizations directly, but a close approximation are those they typify as "process cultures," low-risk, slow-feedback organizations (insurance companies, universities, utilities, much of government) in which "no one transaction will make or break the company—or anyone in it" (1982:119). Lacking good feedback on outcomes (sometimes even lacking clear definitions of outcomes), members of these corporate tribes are obsessed with procedures, memos, paper trails, low profiles, "cover your backside" tasks, and hunkering down when evil administrative winds blow. They are marked by an inordinate concern with titles and rank, most dramatically evidenced by office walls papered with framed certificates awarded for attendance at workshops and conferences. Their favorite rituals center on procedures: long meetings on how to organize and reorganize, and endless discussions of the micropolitics of departments, personnel, and policies. There is a studied wariness of institutional brush fires and fear of where they may erupt next. The ability to survive procedural challenges and internal power shifts makes one a hero in a process culture tribe. Heroes are also the mythological progenitors of agency policies and practices, all carefully explained to new hires but quickly forgotten when one reigning hero is displaced by another.

The literature on the corporate culture of social work is not great, and what little exists is scattered in many sources, but I want to cite briefly two examples that help us go beyond the generalizing (and sometimes amusing) descriptions of "tribal" corporations. They illustrate how the culture of a service organization can collide with the will and expectations of its clients, creating conflicts for reasons that neither client nor worker quite clearly see.

In describing what she calls "splintered visions," Wharton (1989) analyzes competing views of family violence held by staff and clients in a shelter for battered women. Her case study shows how conflicts can arise when the corporate culture of the staff is not shared by those served. Wharton states that the shelter "was founded by a grass roots feminist group, who adopted the self-help model that battered women realize their own capabilities" (1989:54). But that approach did not lead to actions desired by the residents. The staff encouraged women to separate, permanently if possible, from their offending partners; they referred to the women's abusive husbands as "assailants"; and they defined the dominant emotion of the women in the shelter as "anger," anger that must be turned into "positive energy" to put the residents "in touch" and in charge of their own feelings.

Yet the women who came to the shelter as short-term residents were not interested in permanent separation from an abusive spouse. Their goal was to wait out a husband's anger until it was safe to return home where, they hoped, things might get better. (That may or may not have been a realistic goal, but Wharton's concern was a separate issue, the imposition of staff ideology on residents.) Many of the women resented hearing their husbands or boyfriends referred to as "the assailant" since they knew their situations were more complex than that. The word "assailant" suggested to them a legal category, not a description of a lengthy and complicated relationship. Some of the client-residents became anxious about a "bunker mentality" that permeated the shelter, an us/them dichotomy that dominated staff conversations and counseling. In addition, through interviews and participant observation, Wharton came to understand that anger was not the predominant emotion of these women. They were depressed, tired, frightened, and confused but they did not define those feelings as "anger." Nor did they perceive that dwelling on "anger" and its "venting" would help them deal with hostile and even dangerous men once they returned to their homes. The client's view of the shelter was as a "people-processing" place, one where women in need could come for a short respite. But the staff saw the mission of the shelter as "people changing" according to a predetermined model of residents' "needs." When disputes among the women occasionally broke out— usually over feeding schedules, child discipline, and privacy—staff blamed clients for not really wanting to change their lives. Clients blamed staff for demanding that they accept goals they did not really want.

If ideology, and conflicts about it, is one of the things that defines an organization's culture, so too is behavior, especially behavior that is a response to internal cleavages of power. Wiener and Kayser-Jones (1989) describe what they call "defensive work" in a nursing home: protective strategies intended to shield the institution and staff from outsiders, especially state inspectors and patient's families. For example, the authors found that informally agreed-upon rules had evolved for filling out forms so that the real causes of death or illness were given different names and descriptions. One staff member told the researchers that this was known as "buff[ing] the chart" so that state inspectors would not find fault with the nursing home's procedures. The fact that the nursing home was generally well run did not matter; the nit-picking of state inspectors, with potentially damaging legal results, was perceived to require defensive work simply so the home could carry out its legitimate functions with minimal intrusion. Defensive strategies proliferated, and staff time gradually became more taken up with extensive documentation, even though the documents were unreliable. Defensive work became embedded in all staff activities, creating a massive, complex, and implicit structure of agency-specific understandings that would be as daunting to the state inspectors as it was to newly hired staff. Not only did the preoccupation with defensive work make life in the facility inordinately difficult for everyone, it also drained off the enthusiasm of those who were genuinely concerned for elderly patients. The agency's culture, with its thematic core of defensive work, made realization of that worthy intent unnecessarily difficult.

The nursing home and the women's shelter are examples of just two corporate service cultures. Obviously, corporate cultures can evolve in other ways, some more "user-friendly" for clients and staff than others. But the cultures of many service bureaucracies are similar in one respect: they tend to be grounded in an ideology of "professionalism." Older organizational research describes professionalism as a commitment to rationality, universalism, disinterestedness, and functional specificity (Becker and Carper 1956; Cogan 1953; Goode 1957). That is, professional organizations and activities have a culture that emphasizes reason over tradition as the basis for action, the uniform delivery of quality services regardless of the client's idiosyncrasies, and the provision of services without intrusion into inappropriate aspects of the individual's life. Obviously, any cultural critique of an organization and how it does its business will quickly puncture these bland dicta, revealing a much more complex world than administrative flowcharts and mission statements would suggest.

Any agency, from a state bureaucracy for adult and family services to a neighborhood office of part-time staffers offering walk-in counseling to teenagers, has a complex culture. That culture is based on shared understandings that are contingent on the organization's history, the staff's experiences, and the policies and philosophy of the funding source. Every client confronts this complex mix, usually without any awareness of its controlling effect on the quality of services.

The issue for culturally alert human service professionals is to begin thinking beyond the limitations and restrictions of embedded routines, to see their office and their agency as a corporate tribe, with all its attendant strengths and limitations. They also need to consider how clients perceive and respond to agency culture and what that suggests about utilization rates and compliance with professional recommendations. Both at the personal and organizational level, workers need to think about what tribal boundaries mean and how brokering those boundaries, using the skills of "ethnic competence," can lead to greater client as well as worker satisfaction.

A HUMAN SERVICES MODEL OF ETHNIC COMPETENCE

This chapter began by introducing some of the critical concepts for an ethnographically sensitive approach to human services. I discussed a number of issues related to race, culture, and ethnicity because clarity about the meaning of these things is important, both conceptually and in human services practice. Especially practice. My view is that a commonsense approach to race and ethnicity will not carry the worker very far, no matter how well intended and how receptive to others he or she might be. The distinction between categorical and transactional views of ethnicity is vital. It should be obvious that my concern here is not simply intellectual neatness; rather, it is that ideas have consequences for others, and the transactional and categorical ways of looking at human differences express very different ideas about the world and how one operates in it. I have tried to clarify this by discussing some of the possible relationships between social workers and ethnic communities. I then pushed the culture idea a little farther than usual by suggesting that the human services profession is a kind of culture itself, one with its own ways of doing what it does.

These topics, important as they are, are really only matters of clarification. In preparing for practice, we need a model that will help us organize our thinking, perceptions, responses, and professional behavior in cross-cultural encounters of many kinds. Sue and Sue remark that "becoming culturally skilled is an *active process*," one "that it is *ongoing*, and it is a process that *never reaches an end point*" (1990:166). How, then, can we understand what this process involves and what must be done to become proficient in it?

Given the complexity of the topic and the obvious need for specialized skills, it is surprising that more models for cross-cultural human services work have not been proposed (Ponterotto and Sabnani 1989; Ponterotto and Casas 1991). Sue and Sue (1990) represent a standard in their field of psychology and counseling. Pedersen (1985) and Lefley and Pedersen (1986) are important sources for useful ideas and techniques from a variety of disciplines. A brief but useful overview has been authored by d'Ardenne and Mahtani (1989), and in the last few years, nursing has shown significant interest in cross-cultural health relationships (Boyle and Andrews 1989). The surge of nursing research and training is due, in large part, to the pioneering efforts of nurse-administrator-teacher-anthropologist

Madeleine Leininger and her lifelong work on transcultural nursing care (1978). But what of social services?

There have been important advances in this area as well. The obvious need for new training formats and curriculum has been addressed by Chunn, Dunston, and Ross-Sheriff (1983). They point out that the state of the art in curriculum for professional social service education is very uneven, that subdisciplines within the field are at various stages of maturity, and that some minority groups have received much more attention in teaching and research programs than others. That is a function of history, politics, and funding, not the real needs of real communities.

The knowledge base in social services has been improved by the collections prepared by Dana (1981), McGoldrick, Pearce, and Giordano (1982), and Mindel, Habenstein, and Wright (1988). The McGoldrick book is useful because it moves beyond the standard categorization of American ethnic groups and includes chapters on many cultural communities not normally addressed, such as West Indians, Iranians, and Portuguese. In addition, it covers special issues such as the refugee experience of Vietnamese. The Mindel collection is valuable for its exploration of diversity within large ethnogeographical blocks: Spanish speakers, Asians, and European minorities. It also describes minorities that have separated themselves (or had separation imposed on them) for religious reasons, with chapters on Amish, Jewish-American, Arab-American, and Mormon families. Obviously, there is a richness of sources from which to extract ethnographic and overview information on a range of American ethnic communities.

Two analyses of American ethnicity and social services stand out from these collections. In a useful and penetrating study, Lum (1986; 1992) has proposed a "process-stage approach" in which he tracks the experiences, values, expectations, and activities of clients and social service workers through various stages. These stages include initial contact between social worker and client, problem identification, assessment, intervention, and termination. One of the strengths of Lum's approach is in taking categories that are familiar to social workers and filling in their ethnic and minority content. He tracks the experiences of a single family, the Hernandezes, through the entire social services system, adding tips and recommendations along the way so that social workers can more effectively help families of this type. Information on other ethnic communities is also included, making the book a readable, valuable guide for any social worker interested in minority services.

By contrast, Ho (1987) has developed an ecological approach to family systems therapy for minority communities. He notes that "at this time, there is no single integrated theory on which therapists practicing family therapy can rely. The problem is accentuated when therapists deal with ethnic minority families" (1987:12). Beginning with general propositions, he discusses family therapy as it could be applied in a variety of ethnic contexts. One strength of Ho, and of Lum as well, is their reliance on good ethnographic material, extended case studies, and detailed discussion of intervention activities.

Devore and Schlesinger (1987) go further, however, to propose a comparative model, what they call the "ethclass," as a device for comprehending the experiences of minority persons generally. The overlap between social class and ethnic group membership constitutes the "ethclass," a social formation that is often fragmented along class as well as ethnic lines. These fractures create communities with divided loyalties that makes it hard for outsiders to understand them. Their book offers a useful analysis of the variety of social work theories and models and how they relate to the service needs of minority persons. The authors look at psychosocial, problem-solving, task-centered, systems, and ecological theories of social service. They also consider cultural awareness models developed in the early 1980s and rightly observe that these models did not clearly define procedures for acquiring cultural awareness as they needed to. They then discuss how ethnic-sensitive practice can be planned and delivered for minority families in a variety of situations, including aid to families with dependent children and families facing health care crises. The Devore and Schlesinger discussion is sensitive and sensible, and it carries the work of designing ethnically appropriate models a long way.

The ethnic competence model proposed here is intended to add an additional and, I believe, essential dimension not fully developed in other approaches: the *comparative* basis for learning and for action in cross-cultural relationships. The comparative emphasis derives from ethnography, the descriptive study of cultures, and cultural anthropology, the comparative study of variation both within and between differing cultures. Figure 1.5 shows the major elements of the ethnic competence model, each of which is developed more fully in subsequent chapters. As an introduction, however, I want to offer a brief overview of the model and its components.

One of the most important elements of the ethnic competence model is the knowledge base for effective cross-cultural social work. But what kinds of knowledge? What is important, and how can the worker find it? No one can possibly know everything about all the clients he or she sees, especially when in a single day clients may come from many traditions and backgrounds. Overviews of the history of specific groups, or brief summations of their preferences in, say, child rearing might be useful and interesting, but they are at best a beginning point and may not be helpful for working with a particular client trying to manage a difficult child. Some other kinds of learning must prepare the social worker.

In this model, the knowledge base for cross-cultural human services work begins with identifying what is salient in the client's culture for the problems that routinely come before the worker. Once that is clarified—and salience is never as obvious as it seems it ought to be—the model provides a framework for filling in knowledge gaps with culturally appropriate and useful information. This is not particularly difficult, but it does require a systematic approach and a particular kind of perspective about working with and learning from others who may be culturally different from oneself.

A second element of the ethnic competence model is that of honestly addressing the personal meaning of racial and cultural differences for one's professional

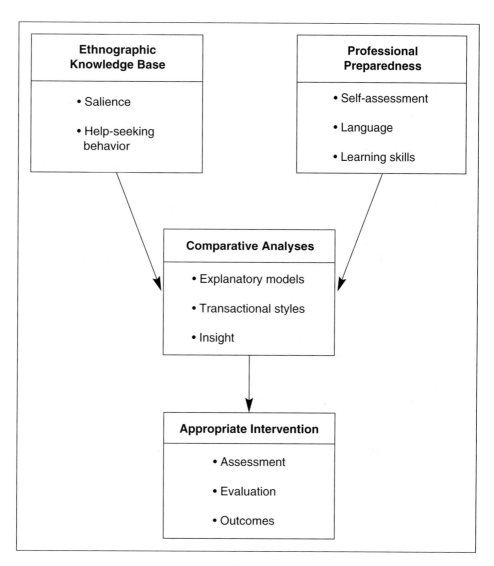

FIGURE 1.5   The ethnic competence model.

work. Articles in social service journals, statements of professional ethics, and the goals of workshops and training programs often sound as if all human service workers everywhere are fully aware of their biases and prejudices, have them under full control, and suffer no fear or anxiety of any kind when they are with minority clients. But when I go to training workshops and note what is being said and not said, when I discuss the problems of service delivery for minority clients with supervisors, when I listen to workers in minority directed and staffed agencies, I am forced to reconsider what I thought the professional position papers were telling me. Although I certainly do not believe that gross and blatant racism is a problem in social work, I am troubled by the expressions of insensitivity I sometimes hear. They are usually masked and cautiously phrased: assertions of special insight encoded in buzzwords and jargon; acceptance of superficial knowledge as adequate to one's professional tasks; and presumptions of innocence that distances the worker from culturally threatening others.

These anxieties and reactions are both reasonable and unreasonable. They are reasonable because we do live in a racially divided society, one that has never been color-blind and may never be. We have all learned the mannerisms, fears, and etiquette that get us through even the briefest of interracial contacts. But they are unreasonable because they are misperceptions, even dogmas, and offer easy truths as a substitute for the real effort one would have to make to work effectively with others. I would argue that no one can really understand the differences in others without confronting directly one's own limits and capabilities. The chapters on preparing for cross-cultural social work and on language describe ways of beginning that process.

A third element of the model proposes a form of comparative analysis for identifying in detail the salient cultural elements of a client's presenting problems. But the approach does not offer a "trait list" of the characteristics of people in cultures X, Y, or Z. Rather, it emphasizes client concerns within an explicitly comparative framework. This component of the model discusses the importance of understanding culturally different world views, of individualizing clients in reference to those differences, and exploring ways of developing analytical insight and appropriate empathy. A discussion of some of the salient human service issues and needs in a number of ethnic and minority communities follows.

Finally, the model points the social worker toward ways of thinking about appropriate forms of intervention. This is really the "frontline" work for future cross-cultural human services. Early reports from the 1990 census suggest a rate of growth among ethnic and minority groups that will put them on numerical par with whites in a few decades. Some of this growth will occur within indigenous minority groups; some of it will be from foreigners, especially migrants from Asia and Central America, who will come to fill the jobs the baby boomers leave behind. And some parts of the country are already seeing an influx of people from Eastern Europe and the Middle East. Their presence may grow depending on the vagaries of international politics and trade agreements. Methods for learning about all these new people and of meeting their needs appropriately may become a political demand as much as it is an ethical one.

Taken in total, the ethnic competence model I will describe in later chapters is really a system of learning. That is what it must be. There are simply no shortcuts. No one-day workshop or list of intervention tips and guidelines will give anyone the skills for working well with others, especially others whom one does not know or understand. The traditional service phraseology of rapport, empathy, empowerment, diversity, and caring is too vague. These terms often hide from the social services provider the true complexity of what he or she is attempting. If we really are committed to doing well by those who seek our help, we have few choices other than to spend the time and energy necessary to understand the context of their lives so we can more effectively respond to the needs and concerns they bring us.

2

HELP-SEEKING BEHAVIOR: THE CULTURAL CONSTRUCTION OF CARE

During a training workshop on "reaching minority clients" that I attended several years ago, an African-American social worker listened quietly to the advice offered by a panel of speakers during the morning session. They discussed ways adult and family services staff could demonstrate their interest in the well-being of minority individuals, and why it was important that both staff and administrators appreciate the cultural diversity of their "catchment area populations." They urged the workshop participants to revise their admissions and "people-processing procedures" (as they described it) to make their agency more "user-friendly" (again, their term). During the question and answer period, the social worker rose to say that she was encouraged by all she had heard but that it probably would not make much difference to her black clients since many of them had alternatives to going to a social service agency. Indeed, she said that on occasion she had referred clients to a local "root worker" where, she felt, they sometimes got better help than her own agency provided. She added that she did not list "root worker" in the client's records nor did she clear the referral with anyone. As the only African-American social worker in her agency, she felt the reasons for her clinical decisions with black clients would not be understood and would take more time to explain and justify than she cared to do.

Needless to say, there ensued a lively discussion on who and what a "root worker" is, under what conditions referrals to root workers are appropriate, and what the presence of a large number of "alternative" mental health providers in a "catchment area" means for social service providers. The discussion was animated but inconclusive. Yet the mental health worker had made her point: there are alternatives to official, publicly sponsored versions of care, alternatives that represent choice and even community preferences. Care includes proper staffing, worker empathy, adequate funding, and prompt service delivery, but it also includes a cultural dimension. Caregiving as a cultural system is tied to the experiences, perceptions, and needs of specific communities (Albert 1990).

In social and health services, we tend to think of care as a professional but also a personalized relationship, a special kind of service to others. My suggesting that care be viewed as a cultural category may seem an unusual, overly analytical way of thinking about it. But it is not. Despite what appears to be general acceptance of the notion that there are cultural differences among the people seen by social workers, and that those differences are important in service relationships, it is surprising to find so little conceptualization within social work about what that means. This theoretical deficiency is matched by a methodological one. There are few training techniques, evaluation schedules, or case studies in which the salient features of cross-cultural intervention are defined or analyzed. With the exception of the work of Devore and Schlesinger (1987), Lum (1986), and others cited in the previous chapter, much social work research on cross-cultural topics (including some by minority social workers) has offered little more than abstract directives and pleas that social workers give credence to the ethnic sensitivities of ethnic and minority clients. These pleas are usually supported by little more than anecdotal evidence or brief case studies. Perhaps part of the problem is a historical lack of useful social service models for defining what ethnic sensitivity means. But I would go even further: good models do not exist because the discipline has never considered "care" as a cultural category, or "caring behavior" as something that is culturally (not just clinically) organized. Much in social service education and research centers on clinically defined pathology and professional models for intervening; an alternative would be consideration of the normative practices of care in culturally distinctive communities and investigation of the ways social and health workers might build on them.

If we think of care as a cultural category, one that is reflective of a people's historical and contemporary experiences, we can begin to see why the culture concept can be a powerful way of redirecting our attention (Albert 1990). The culture concept tells us that care is several things. First, care is always ideological: it implies a worldview and value preferences. That is not the way many professionals think about their work, especially those who see professional care as an extension of scientific methodology or scientifically grounded psychological theories. Second, care is socially constructed. It is manufactured and maintained through symbols and rituals, and these are meaningful only within a given, ethnographically defined context. Care is always culture-specific, and therefore culture-bound. Third, care is a system of communication, a kind of discourse that includes language, procedures, and styles or mannerisms known by members of a particular community. It is part of what Geertz (1983) calls "local knowledge." Finally, the existence of differing forms of local knowledge, of alternative paradigms of care, implies conflict. What the African-American root worker knows is not in *DSM-III-R*, nor its successor *DSM-IV*, and probably never will be. *DSM-III-R* is the local knowledge of someone else's community, someone else's discourse, symbols, and ideology. Mechling (1990) describes the edges of alternative kinds

of local knowledge as " 'hot' border zones," contested sites "where people interpret and perform their own identities, all the while interpreting the others' and
adjusting their own performances according to understandings of how the other
is interpreting them" (1990:156). Care, then, is more than a clinical issue; it is a
cultural and even a political one.

If care is really all this, in addition to being a helping, empathic, and individualizing service relationship, then how can we get beyond the anecdotes and the
testimonials that make up much of what the research literature reports about
cultural differences and minority clients? And how can social workers develop a
cultural sense of care in their own work, one that will lead them beyond generalizations?

The model followed in this book is one called "help-seeking behavior." It is
an adaptation from the work of Arthur Kleinman (1973, 1974, 1977, 1978a, 1978b,
1978c, 1980, 1986, 1988a, 1988b, 1992), his associates, and others of what they have
called "health seeking behavior." In the last decade, in fields as diverse as psychiatry, nursing, student counseling, and occupational therapy, Kleinman's model
has become recognized as a powerful tool for comprehending the diversity of
peoples' responses to crises, whatever their cultural orientation (Shweder 1991).
Essentially, the help-seeking behavior model is a discovery procedure, not a
formulaic code, and its value to human service providers is as a guide to learning
what they can do to work well with culturally distinctive clients.

As a discovery procedure, the model rests on several assumptions. First,
language is of special importance since it is the symbolic device by which the flow
of experience is categorized, labeled, evaluated, and acted on. Shared cognitive
and affective events and the language through which they are communicated are
the ultimate bases of a common culture. Any approach to understanding the
distinctive cultural characteristics of others must begin with what they say, exactly as they say it. The discourse of personal crisis carries a heavy cultural as well
as emotional charge and is the means by which inner states are given shape and
conveyed to others.

Second, the model recognizes that any need or problem is both a personal and
a social event. It is personal in that it disrupts daily routines by creating discomfort and pain. It is social and cultural in that the labeling of damaging experiences
often involves confirmation by others as a preliminary step to corrective action.
The model recognizes the role of culturally significant others in diagnosis and
evaluation. Indeed, in some situations lay consultation may be more important to
a client's response than is information supplied by certified experts and professionals.

Third, the help-seeking behavior model rests on a fundamental dichotomy
between illness and disease. Disease is a diagnostic category, a conceptualization
originating in a professional subculture and expressive of the procedures and
preferences of that subculture. Illness, by contrast, is the experience of suffering.
It is how people perceive and live with their symptoms, how they imagine them
to be caused, and how they cope with them. Illness includes categorization,
explanation, and resort to culturally available hierarchies of care in the expecta-

tion of relief. It is personal, localized, shared, and validated by others. All illness experiences are culturally formed, whatever (and sometimes without regard to) the "real" causes of suffering postulated in medicalized or psychologized discourses of disease. Illness complaints are a genre of commentary or narrative, a genre that addresses fundamental questions: What is my problem? What is its cause? What course will it take? How will it disrupt my life? What do I fear about it? Who can help? What might help? What will not? Why me? Why now?

Kleinman (1986:145) suggests three possible ways of thinking about illness. First, there are overt and obvious symptoms of disability: an injury, a deformity, an accident, a personal crisis. One's community of family, friends, and coworkers has a pattern of discourse about symptoms, what they mean, and how well or how poorly individuals cope. Second, there are understandings about the larger meanings of illnesses. These understandings and the discourses that accompany them are not biomedically neutral. (They may not be biomedically well founded either.) Perhaps the most obvious example is the aquired immune deficiency syndrome—AIDS. In families in which it occurs, its meaning is certainly much more than a biological event; it has overtones of choice, lifestyle, and morality. AIDS even becomes a subject of national commentary for some media-oriented religious leaders who find in it evidence of celestial condemnation. Public dialogue on other issues such as abortion, child abuse, doctor-assisted suicides, and gang violence are also rich with rhetoric that mixes beliefs about individual behavior, public morality, and the fate of the nation. None of us ever has a crisis that is fully, ideosyncratically our own.

Third, if we think of illnesses or personal crises as disvalued experiences, the importance of their social and cultural moorings becomes apparent. Kleinman illustrates with several examples:

> *Heart disease for the failed businessman in Western society can become embedded in disintegrating marriage, alcohol abuse and related family violence, a demoralizing relationship with a boss, a midlife crisis in which change in body image and coming to terms with one's mortality assault a fragilely constructed ego. Or, for Chinese society, think of a thirty-year-old, disaffiliated worker, a former Red Guard and rusticated youth, whose bitterness, cynicism, and mourning over multiple losses in the Cultural Revolution (of education, career mobility, family harmony, and so forth) are absorbed into the symptoms of a chronic illness so that treatment of the physical complaints needs to include response to the particular psychological and social distress that are likely sources of symptom amplification and worsening disability (1986:145).*

In this model, the illness-afflicted individual is a moral agency, the immediate crisis an occasion for dramatizing fractured connections from some normative, perhaps idealized notion of functioning. All cultures provide explanations to which suffering individuals can turn for relief. They range from food as medicine among health food aficionados to personal prayer choreographed by broadcast evangelists. In a culture as diverse as America, with its engulfing media presence, there is a democratizing of information and advice, however useful or useless it might be. That is part of the broader meaning of cultural pluralism. But something different happens when the sufferer, trailing a concentrated mix of belief, imagery, and anxiety appears before an authorized, professional healer. The disvalued experience is transformed into the clinical "presenting problem." The erupting emotions in one's personal life become "symptoms" to be "managed." Clipboards, file folders, closed doors and modulated voices subdue, at least for the moment, disallowed interpretations of crisis. In the clinics and offices of institutional medicine and counseling, physically and functionally set apart from the client's daily life, the interplay of history, biography, and cultural context is usually subordinant to symptom identification, classification, and assessment.

The help-seeking behavior model is an attempt to reconcile these contrasts and bring together the domains of the personal and the institutional for a more complete, holistic appreciation of the client's experiences and what can be done about them. The model is constructed around a division between what individuals know and do in their privatized responses to problems and what professionals and experts know and recommend. It postulates a client culture and a professional culture (or more accurately, subcultures), each marked by a distinctive set of assumptions, narratives, beliefs about causation, and expectations for resolution (Figure 2.1 on page 56). Within these contrasting domains, any specific problem initiates differing kinds of questions, discourse, and behavior. Generally, the greater the cultural distance between help seeker and help provider, the greater the discrepancy in their perceptions, labeling, and responses to a given issue. These differences are significant for client compliance and the success of service outcomes. At a minimum, the culturally responsive social worker will assume as a working hypothesis that divergent interpretative and communicative domains accompany all presenting problems and that they will have consequences for the worker-client relationship.

There are a number of reasons for arguing that this dichotomy between the world of the client and that of the service professional is profoundly real. In his study of interaction between Chicano patients and medical practitioners, Hayes-Bautista (1978) distinguishes what he calls "stocks of knowledge," lay knowledge and professional knowledge, that vary not only in their ethnographic content but in the nature of their organization and application as well. For instance, he found in his research that patient and client knowledge about medical matters comes from a variety of sources, including friends, media, and folklore, and is acquired in slow, random, and unsystematic ways. Over many years, the individual's stock of knowledge becomes larger as new items of information are added. But little of it is ever discarded unless it has been tested for its appropriateness during specific illness episodes. Consequently, the knowledge stock grows, containing a number of disparate, even contradictory, bits of information. Lacking depth, it is essentially "cookbook information" that is utilized in ad hoc ways to explain "how things work without making clear why they do" (Hayes-Bautista 1978:85). By contrast, the stock of knowledge of medical practitioners (and, by implication, other professionals) is marked by a high degree of formality, acquired during a

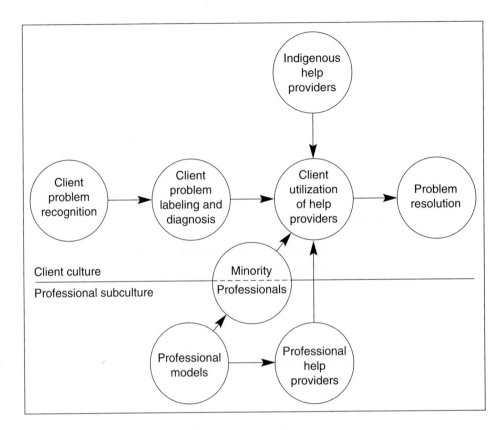

FIGURE 2.1   The help-seeking behavior model.

Based on Kleinman 1977, 1978a.

rigorous learning process and from increasingly specialized rather than comprehensive sources. Rather than retaining information for ad hoc retrieval, the professional seeks to eliminate contradictory bits of information through systematic testing. Clarity, precision, narrowness, and depth rather than comprehensiveness distinguish the practitioner's stock of knowledge from that of laypersons.

This sociology of knowledge approach is useful in suggesting that there are differences, even oppositions, between the interpretations and expectations of laypersons and the judgments and procedures of professionals. In human services work with minorities, however, the client-professional contrast may be more complicated than the Hayes-Bautista model suggests. How formal and rigorous, for example, is the social worker's stock of knowledge of specific minority communities? How much of that knowledge is really generalized or so-called common sense that is widely held in the social worker's home community? How much of it is the "local knowledge" of the agency, of the department, of one's co-workers and professional peers? How rigorously is that knowledge compared with the latest research findings reported in social service journals, applied to one's professional practice, and systematically evaluated in careful analysis of client outcomes? In human services agencies, there may be more at work than a dualistic opposition between the stocks of knowledge of clients and professionals. Instead, the clinical setting may contain at least four sets of knowledge, all competing for authority in defining the clinical encounter: what the client knows from daily experience, what the practitioner knows from formal education and training, what the practitioner knows as a private citizen, and what the agency allows given its institutional history and policy directives.

All this suggests that there are multiple, competing voices in virtually all cross-cultural helping relationships. They include the voices of the client, the social worker, the local office, its larger agency, the worker's professional subculture, the mandates under which the service organization functions, and the community with its political divisions and interests. The precise form this mix will take in the clinical experience of any particular client is always an open question, and will have consequences for service quality and outcomes.

HELP-SEEKING BEHAVIOR: A MODEL FOR CROSS-CULTURAL SERVICE RELATIONSHIPS

The help-seeking behavior model has a number of components, each of which is part of the "cultural baggage" both clients and workers bring to a service encounter. From the client's side they include (1) recognition of an experience as a "problem" of a particular kind, one that is conceptualized out of the individual's stock of knowledge and the prevailing local knowledge of the community; (2) a narrative that establishes the conceptual framework within which the problem will be controlled; (3) knowledge of helping resources in the community and the decision making involved in their utilization; and (4) criteria for determining that a satisfactory resolution has been achieved. Each of these four areas is an example of Mechling's "hot" border zones, where competing values, assumptions, and restorative procedures operate. For example, in an ethnographic discussion of chronic pain sufferers, Kleinman lists some of the issues that make their illness more than physiological:

> *What is at stake for the sick person and family? What is learned from the encounter with pain by those who undergo it and those who provide care? How is the meaning of pain created, expressed, and negotiated? How are meanings reflected or constituted in stories people tell? What is the relation between such narratives and lived experience (Kleinman 1992:15)?*

Issues like these are part of the cultural context of problem resolution and understanding them is essential in planning intervention. Kleinman is very specific that patients and clients of all kinds have a "stake" (his word) in their problem, that their concerns are not just "how do I find relief?" but also "what in my life is at risk?" The client's stake, always culturally specific, is part of what the ethnically responsive social worker will want to understand before moving on to the technical procedures of diagnosis, treatment, and evaluation.

To make more evident the cultural dimensions of this model, with its dichotomy between disease and illness, pathology and risk experience, I will illustrate each component of the help-seeking behavior model with examples from the ethnographic and human services literature. All of the examples are intended to show that informed ethnographic understanding is critical to planning and delivering culturally responsive social services.

The Individual's Definition and Understanding of an Experience as a Problem

The presenting problems of clients and patients may be general or specific: vague feelings of pain, loss of appetite or a job, a death in the family, violence. But how these objective conditions are interpreted is also a significant part of the experience. This is particularly true when issues of mental health are involved. Any culture provides a repertoire of explanations for problems, explanations related to etiology, symptom recognition, and the course of illness episodes. A culture also provides a sick role for those who suffer, expectations concerning treatment, and a definition of desirable outcomes. These explanations and expectations amount to a "cognitive map" (Wallace 1970) more or less shared by members of the culture. This map or "explanatory model" (Kleinman 1978a) is part of the conception of the problem the client brings to the service provider. Some individuals may be better able to articulate their experiences of suffering than others but all know the local, implicit knowledge of body and self that makes interpretation possible.

But are "folk models" of illness true or false, and how seriously should we take them? Should the trained expert correct an incompletely formulated explanatory model, or an illness narrative that may be medically or psychologically "faulty?" Are some clients' beliefs akin to folklore and superstition? Or are clients' perceptions of a different nature altogether, suggestive of ideas and explanations quite different from those of helping professionals but valid within a particular body of local knowledge? This question goes to the core of cultural difference. My view is that if clients routinely draw on localized knowledge to find meaning in illness or trouble, then professionals cannot afford to ignore interpretations of misfortune, however odd they may seem.

I take it for granted that until shown otherwise, ethnic or minority clients have a view of the world that is not the same as that of the help provider, a view that is a mix of idiosyncratic and community elements. There is adequate evidence for making this assumption. Indeed, the idea that variations in world view are associated with distinctive cultural communities has been a central philosophical and scientific preoccupation of the social sciences for a long time. Years ago Ruth Benedict (1934) wrote of "patterns of culture," suggesting that all cultures have their own implicit, governing values, evident in a people's myths, rituals, family patterns, and behavior. Other anthropologists have elaborated on this. Kearney (1975) has noted that the "world view" of a people, their outlook on life that makes them distinctive from all others, will always include culturally distinctive notions of self, others, relationships, even time and space. It seems self-evident, then, that to understand others one must first understand something of the distinctiveness of their vision of the world and their sense of their place in it.

These are complex ideas, but they are easy to illustrate. The examples that follow are really vignettes, chosen only to clarify specific parts of the help-seeking behavior model. They are *not* intended to be representative of whole ethnic groups and should *not* be read as "typical" or "exemplary" of behavior or belief in any particular community. That distinction must be kept very clear so that stereotyping does not occur. Rather, the vignettes show how ethnographic data can help us understand the cultural realities behind specific problems faced by some individuals in particular communities.

The ethnographic description of Native-American drinking is one illustration of how the world view of one community can differ significantly from that of another. Years ago Zola (1972) noted that the recognition of symptoms and the concept of "trouble" are not value free. Problem recognition occurs in a values context, and there may be instances where what is perceived by clients as normality, or as the working out of some inevitable sequence of events, is to outsiders an instance of pathology. The question that must be asked at this stage of the help-seeking behavior model is: "What is a problem?" What has been a problem for the white community may be something else for some American Indians.

Native-American Drinking

No people have been more stereotyped in reference to drinking behavior than American Indians. The orthodox view on alcohol and Indians is that of a whole continent of uncivilized tribes, incapable of resisting the white man's "fire water" and reduced by it, along with warfare and the reservation system, to near total loss of their lands, livelihood, and dignity. This popular image of Indians and Indian drinking has remained, despite changes in thinking about alcoholism as a disease rather than a personal moral failing. Some Native-American leaders have agreed with this view, calling drinking a "most grave problem" (Locklear 1977: 203) for all Indian peoples and, indeed, in the eyes of many Indians, it is. Yet there is considerable diversity in drinking patterns within Indian communities (Waddell and Everett 1980; Christian, Dufour, and Bertolucci 1989), enough to suggest that beliefs surrounding usage are also variable. The question posed here is the nature of that variability. If drinking is an issue among American Indians, what kind of issue is it? How is it experienced, perceived, and acted on in Indian communities, and in particular, what is its meaning within specific communities? Those things must be clarified before it can be decided that ameliorative action is necessary, especially if action is proposed by people who are not themselves Indians.

In its most naive form, speculation on Native-American drinking has assumed that all Indians are possessed of an inordinate desire for alcohol, coupled with an unfortunate genetic incapacity for dealing with it. Neither of these beliefs is true. More sophisticated approaches have associated problem drinking and alcoholism with the social disorganization created through white contact, particularly when access to economic rewards is blocked (Graves 1967) or when individuals feel that they have no sense of belonging to either traditional or white communities (Ferguson 1976). These studies suggest that the incidence of Indian drinking can best be taken as a measure of cross-cultural relations and their difficulties, not an indicator of biological deficiency. This does not explain, however, what drinking means to Native-American individuals, nor does it offer insight into the social context of drinking.

An alternative to this "social breakdown" thesis is one that views drinking behavior, first, as an extension of cultural traditions deriving from precontact as well as postcontact times and, second, as a category of learned behavior specific to differing tribal and cultural groups. This approach has been developed by MacAndrew and Edgerton (1969) in what they call the analysis of "drunken comportment." They argue that in conventional research wisdom, it is assumed that the effects of alcohol on human beings are more or less uniform. That is, whenever and wherever people drink, there is a progressive deterioration of sensory-motor functions and superego controls. Alcohol is presumed to have a "disinhibiting" effect, with results that are predictable: jocularity, lewdness, aggression, and overt expression of things normally concealed or at least suitably managed. Alcohol as a "superego solvent" reduces normally decent individuals to something less than honorable.

But if one looks at the historical and ethnographic record of drinking among American Indians, a more complex picture emerges. There is instead an infinite series of gradations in drinking practices and experiences, ranging from individuals who become boisterous and violent to those who remain sedate or only titillated when inebriated. Among some groups, such as the Menomini of Wisconsin, religious ceremonies focused on the attainment of visions and dreams, and alcohol was used, often generously, within carefully controlled ritual settings to advance that aim (MacAndrew and Edgerton 1969:118). Lemert (1954) notes that there was little aggression associated with heavy drinking among the Northwest Coast groups he observed, and Levy and Kunitz (1974), in a careful and thorough study of drinking in the Southwest, found that the Hopi who abjured public drunkenness were very heavy drinkers in the privacy of their homes. They also found that Hopi drinking contrasted markedly with that of the neighboring Navajo and Apache, both of whom practiced public drinking and the public intoxication that went with it. In Canada, Kupferer (1979) found that among the Cree of Ontario drinking contributed to a sense of community solidarity. Because the Cree valued individual autonomy and normally shunned emotional intensity in their relationships, weekly drinking was an occasion for relaxed animation and the venting of strong feelings. From these few examples, hardly a random sample but at least illustrative, one could not conclude that there is a uniform effect of alcohol on all Indian individuals nor a homogeneous response to alcohol by all Indian groups. Similarly, we could argue that these ethnographic findings are consistent with an approach to providing services that does not generalize from a few cases but rather is specific to the needs and experiences of particular communities.

To account for differences, MacAndrew and Edgerton (1969) argue that drinking behavior occurs "within limits," limits that are culturally defined and that individuals know and observe even while inebriated. Most important, they suggest that not only in Indian societies but in some others as well, alcohol use occurs during special "time out" periods, occasions when the rules of normal comportment are expected to bend. Religious ceremonies may be special "time out" periods, and the "within limits" rules that govern them are precisely defined. Occasions of public drunkenness may also be "time out" periods, moments when the standards of decorum of the household, the workplace, or the religious ceremonial are not expected to dominate. The "drunken comportment" that is displayed at these times has its own set of understandings, which, however benumbed by excess, are not normally exceeded by the drinker (Hill 1978).

How does this work in practice? Price (1975) has argued that there are both positive and negative consequences of drinking among Native Americans and that there are also external and internal sources of control. The negative consequences of alcoholism (injury through accidents) and the external controls (police, detoxification cells, government treatment programs) are well known. Less well known are the positive consequences of the activities of "time out" periods and the internal controls, community expectations, and sanctions that establish the "within limits" rules for drinking activity. I have already mentioned the spiritual significance of intoxication where vision states are valued. But there is also the fact that drinking provides an opportunity for camaraderie, especially among young men new to urban areas and who are unfamiliar with the hazards of such places. For some of these men, a period of freedom, of "time out," before taking up the responsibilities of jobs or permanent settlement in reservation communities, is important. Price notes that a 1969 study of alcoholism by the Indian Health Service found that heavy drinking was primarily a young man's pastime, that it occurred infrequently among women, and that it declined rapidly after age forty. Perhaps most important, however, the study found there are many Indians of all ages who do not drink at all (Price 1975:20).

Indian drinking, when it becomes a problem for the dominant society, is handled in two ways. One is by police and courts. Arrest and incarceration rates for Indians are generally higher than they are for whites, even when whites consume greater quantities of liquor (Price 1975:22). A second approach is Alcoholics Anonymous. But AA is a white model, both in the perception and definition of the problem (it is a "disease") and in the treatment required (abstinence and public confessions). It cannot be assumed that all Indian communities, reservation or urban ones, will find AA perceptions of drinking behavior and drinking treatment compatible. How many Indians, for instance, think of heavy or compulsive drinking as a "disease"? Or do they see it as something else? And would they see public confessions as a reasonable method of control? Is there precedent for confessional behavior, of any kind, and would Indians see that as an appropriate response to a disease? These are cultural issues that need to be considered as part of implementing a treatment program.

Drinking in many American-Indian communities is a major problem. That seems clear enough. What too often is not clear is the kind of problem it is. That will vary among Indian communities and perhaps even within them. The point here is, simply, that drinking is culturally conditioned behavior like any other; it can become "excessive" but the meaning of excess is subject to the normative expectations of drunken comportment specific to a group. When and where drinking is determined to be a problem is something dependent on the beholder's point of view. One cannot know a priori that a "drinking problem" exists, or the kind of problem it is, unless one knows as well the values of "time out" and "within limits" within a given ethnographic context.

Indian drinking, as briefly as we have considered it here, points to one of the important issues in all cross-cultural problem identification and labeling. Alasuu-tari (1992), a Finnish sociologist, recently completed a provocative study of worldwide drinking patterns and their management. He notes that the meaning of drinking is highly dependent on cultural variables, especially ideas about in-dividualization, beliefs about the body and its reactions to alcohol ingestion, and expectations of drinking outcomes and their control. He concludes that in an important sense, heavy alcohol consumption is a culture-bound syndrome, a constellation of features that vary from community to community and lack any universal etiology, and therefore any universal treatment. To successfully interdict the outcomes of drinking, if and when that is deemed necessary, requires an exquisite knowledge of the local conditions under which drinking takes place and the cultural evaluations that go with it. Not all drinking is pathological, not even all heavy drinking, although it may be, and no control program can succeed unless the local meanings of drinking behavior are fully understood and built into the management regimen.

The Client's Semantic Evaluation of a Problem

In one sense, a culture can be described as what people know—the knowledge, information, and beliefs they share with one another, Geertz' notion of local knowledge. Shared cognitive materials mark off one group as culturally distinc-tive from all others. This view of culture was expressed by Goodenough (1957:167) as follows: "A society's culture consists of whatever it is one has to know or believe in order to operate in a manner acceptable to its members, and to do so in any role that they accept for any one of themselves. . . . It is the form of things that people have in mind, their models for perceiving, relating and otherwise interpreting. . . . " Even if one is not willing to accept the argument that culture is equivalent to what people know, it remains true that much that is culturally distinctive within any society is its stock of information, including everything that is linguistically labeled and communicated in speech. Identifying linguistic labels, therefore, and exploring their meaning, is critical to under-standing how people construct their world.

The organization of information in any society is partly a matter of categorization. Thus, the semantic label "family" refers to a culturally specific category or domain. Of course there are different kinds of families, and the variations among them are important. These variations are called the "attributes" of the members of the domain. Thus, in American popular culture, we have the domain of "families," and we recognize such attributes as "nuclear," "broken," "extended," "mixed," "single parent," and the like. The attributes themselves can be more minutely divided in order to give finer shades of meaning. Thus, "single parent" families may have a male parent, a female parent, biological parent, or adoptive parent. Similarly, an attribute such as "mixed" can be further subdivided. In its most general usage, the folk attribute "mixed" refers to adults of differing "racial" background (Root 1992) but it might also refer to married adults of "mixed" religious background. In addition, there are gay and lesbian couples who already have or who adopt children, and there are other people who refuse to think of them as having a "family" at all. The complexity of the domain "family" is made more evident when we appreciate that in our culture native speakers not only use the term "family" in a descriptive but also in a metaphorical sense, applying it to entities that clearly are not families. Thus, someone could suggest that the members of a large corporation are "one big happy family," and religious figures sometimes refer to their congregations or denominations as "families."

This latter usage of the native label "family" suggests one of the critical features of folk thinking and the semantic labels attached to folk categories. Semantic labels have both a "referential meaning" and a "social meaning" (Spradley and McCurdy 1975:541). The referential meaning of "family" is its dictionary definition or, when more precision is required, the kinds of definitions found in a sociology text on family life. The social meaning, however, refers to usages that are contextual: appropriate times and places for using the term, its metaphorical associations, or the emotional weight it carries among those who hear it. Appropriateness has to do with subtle variations in meaning that are contextually dependent and that would be recognizable only by those who are members of the speech community. (Humor, for example, is probably the most contextually sensitive form of speech.) This level of understanding is called "communicative competence" (Gumperz and Hymes 1972). Speakers who have communicative competence, or what I call ethnic competence, are intimately and intuitively familiar with both the referential and the social meanings of language in a specific speech or ethnic community.

Language is the storage medium of any individual's stock of cultural knowledge, his or her "cognitive map" or "explanatory model" as Kleinman (1978a) would call it. For example, a parent comes to a worker concerned about a child's health. The parent has an implicit explanatory model of how the child became sick, the probable meaning of the symptoms, what has been observed to be effective with such symptoms before, why certain therapeutic procedures are deemed useful or not, and why some kinds of health advisors are preferable to others. All this conceptualization of the child's illness is something that the client knows, whether or not it is articulated well. It is knowledge that may or may not be held with conviction; the explanatory road map might not be very reliable. But it is the framework within which new information is stockpiled. If the worker is concerned with truly knowing where the individual is "coming from," then the semantic dimensions of the client's explanatory model are the only place to reasonably begin. To start with the client's emotions, as many social workers are prone to do, presumes that the worker *already* understands, exactly like a native, the sensibilities and meanings those emotions express. But if one is not a native in the client's culture, then such a presumption is dubious and exploration of emotions may be superficial at best.

The section below explores exactly this point—the complex features of an explanatory model of illness and health. In this instance, it is one that is at some variance with established, biomedical knowledge. Yet it is a model that is widely known (but not universally practiced, and that should be noted) by Spanish-speaking persons in the United States.

Latino Disease Categories

Among Spanish-speaking persons in this country, beliefs and knowledge about disease derive from at least four sources (Saunders 1954:141). Medieval Spanish traditions were brought to the New World by colonizers, and these influenced and were influenced by indigenous Indian beliefs. Elements of Anglo popular traditions, particularly as represented in the mass media and advertising, and "scientific" or biomedical knowledge, are also part of the body of medical concepts found in many Latino communities. But these diverse disease concepts are not equivalent to those of scientific biomedicine. They have their distinctive etiology, nosology, symptomatology, and treatment methods (Maduro 1983; Gleave and Manes 1990). An examination of several major disease categories, as they are defined by many Americans of Spanish heritage, reveals something of their cultural significance.

Latino disease categories do not rest on a dichotomy between the physical and mental sources of *enfermedad* or illness. Rather, they come from a notion of disturbed balance in one's physical and social well-being. As in the ancient Hippocratic system, the individual in a healthy state is believed to be a harmonic mixture of contrasting elements: hot and cold, wet and dry, and the various "humors" of the body. The ethnosemantic labels for three significant disruptions of this balance are *empacho, mal ojo*, and *susto*. These medical categories have been described in a number of studies carried out in South and Central America and in communities in this country (Martinez and Martin 1966; Madsen 1964; Clark 1959; Saunders 1954; O'Neill 1976). The detailed descriptions provided by Rubel (1960, 1964, 1966, 1984) and Finkler (1985) are particularly useful because of their emphasis on the social functions of these disease concepts.

Empacho is a physiological condition, affecting both children and adults, in which the manifest symptoms of stomach pains are believed to be caused by food that cannot be dislodged from the sides of the stomach. The food is said to be in the form of a ball that can be broken up and eliminated through back rubbing and the use of purgatives. A diagnosis of *empacho* is made only after other problems, such as indigestion, have been considered.

Mal ojo is the result of dangerous imbalances in social relationships, and, in its advanced form, can be fatal. Its symptoms include headaches, sleeplessness, drowsiness, restlessness, fever, and, in severe cases, vomiting. The individual's sense of equilibrium is in danger of being disturbed in any encounter with other people. Particularly if one has been the subject of covetous glances, admiring attention, or intense interest by another, *mal ojo* is likely to result. The eyes of another person can be the virulent agent for initiating this condition, although evil intent need not be present. Children are particularly susceptible to the admiring looks of adults, and women may be exposed to danger from the glances of men. This unnatural bond of power that one individual may hold over another can be broken by prayers, by gently rubbing the body with a whole egg, or by having the perpetrator touch the victim's head, thereby draining off the threatening power of the relationship. *Mal ojo* or the "evil eye" is one of the widely distributed value complexes in the world, found in cultures from India through the Middle East, North Africa, southern Europe, and South and Central America. By no means is it limited to Spanish speakers, although it is associated with Spanish cultures in this hemisphere. As a value complex it was not common in northern Europe nor among the English speakers who came to dominate much of North America.

The *susto* syndrome has a number of characteristics widely dispersed among both Spanish and Indian cultures in South and Central America. *Susto* means fright, and a victim of *susto* is one who has lost some of his or her spiritual essence as a result of an upsetting experience. The source of the fright may be trivial or truly life-threatening, but the symptoms are the same: depression, lack of interest in living, introversion, and disruption of usual eating and hygienic habits. Cure requires coaxing lost spiritual substance back into the individual's body. This is done through prayers, body massage, spitting cold water over the patient, and particularly by sweeping the body with small branches while "talking" the spirit back to where it belongs. Curing is usually undertaken by someone familiar with the condition and known to be successful in treating it. The family and patient are consulted as part of the diagnostic process to determine that *susto* is in fact present. Not all frightening experiences lead to *susto* but many can, and a link between an earlier experience and manifest symptoms must be established before treatment can begin. Clearly, a lot of individual and family counseling and intimate knowledge of the nature of this condition, are a part of the treatment.

One view of these folk illnesses, particularly the methods of diagnosis and treatment, is that they are simply historical survivals from older, now discredited, Iberian and southern European systems of medicine. They persist only in impoverished, backwater areas where people lack access to the benefits of Western medicine or are ignorant of modern medical practice. Another view, however, is that these beliefs and practices are consistent with the culture in which they occur quite apart from their historical origins. They express an underlying logic that is convincing to many people and through which they find relief for some (but perhaps not all) of their problems. Rubel (1960) has argued that the experience of stress is common to all these illnesses. In small communities, where one's position in life is a matter not only of economic success but reputation, respect, and esteem, challenges in the form of unwanted endearments or jealousy and envy are highly stressful. *Mal ojo* is resolved, balance is restored, when the unwitting perpetrator of the disease touches the victim, assuring that there is no intent of inappropriate desire to control the other. Stress is also experienced when individuals are unable to meet their role expectations. Children who feel they have disappointed their parents, particularly in a culture that emphasizes ideals of family honor and the shame that disrespectful behavior entails, may well develop the symptoms diagnosed as *empacho*.

The role stress theory of *susto* has been refined by O'Nell (1976), who suggests that it takes two forms: rationalized and precipitating fright. In the rationalized form, there is a lengthy time period between the onset of symptoms and the experience of fright. In addition, fright is usually initiated by nonhuman agents such as an attacking animal or the accidental breaking of household utensils. The patient explains the appearance of symptoms by locating a frightening experience in the past that is deemed to have been causal. This is not, however, an irrational, post hoc procedure. Rather, the patient uses this explanatory principle to define himself or herself as sick, thereby utilizing a defined sick role to withdraw from relationships that generate stress. In this way, a sense of failure in role expectations is institutionalized, and a means of treatment is made available.

Precipitating fright, by contrast, involves human causes, and in this form the appearance of symptoms is rapid. Confrontations with others, exchanges of insults, or threats of violence are all events that challenge the individual's sense of self-control and decorum. Loss of control or a sense of balance in personal relationships precipitates the fright symptoms. This is most likely to happen within the family or among kin, where the frustrations of daily life serve as tests of the individual's ability to preserve a sense of calm and composure. The appearance of symptoms is a signal to all that withdrawal and an easing of tensions is needed to restore the normal order of relationships, the balance and self-control that represent normality and good health.

Far from being an irrational manifestation of folk superstitions that have survived into the modern world, *susto* is a syndrome that is culturally specific, couched in the language of health and illness, one that many (but certainly not all) Spanish-speaking individuals use to adapt to the stresses of everyday life. For *susto* sufferers, both rationalized and precipitating frights "serve to validate the(ir) problems in culturally meaningful terms, (and) . . . facilitates the rehabilitation of the individual in social context" (O'Neill 1976:61).

How widespread are these beliefs among Spanish-speaking persons in this country? Martinez and Martin (1966) found that in a sample of urban housewives, virtually all the respondents had heard of these illnesses, and 85 percent of them knew therapeutic measures for treating the symptoms. In addition, 95 percent either had experienced a folk illness or knew someone who had. It is significant that Martinez and Martin reported their findings in the *Journal of the American Medical Association*. Physicians are not usually called on to treat *susto* or *mal ojo* because, as the housewives in the survey pointed out, doctors neither understand these diseases nor are they trained to treat them. Most physicians would probably agree! As long as that situation persists, patients will seek help from alternative health care providers who better understand the reasons for their problems.

Should the social worker assume that all Spanish-speaking patients or clients will be familiar with these disease entities and rely on them in personal evaluations of misfortune? Certainly not. Some individuals will be fully committed to these ideas, some will regard them as nonsense, and others will be ambivalent. That is why the explanatory models of illness employed by any given client are always an important topic of inquiry in an assessment. Until we know what shapes an individual's sense of order and disorder, we are not really in a position to make therapeutic recommendations.

Indigenous Strategies of Problem Intervention

There is an enormous range of help-seeking activity in all cultures. These activities are guided for the most part by lay interpretations of personal problems and by informal consultations with persons who are already within the troubled individual's network. Some types of lay intervention and help-seeking are more familiar than others: reliance on family members and friends; solicitation of advice from a minister, pharmacist, or faith healer; use of special diets or drugs; exercise or meditation; resort to religious or secular rituals to manipulate unseen forces; membership in support groups for almost every concern imaginable. There are also help-seeking activities distinctive to specific groups, such as the utilization of *curanderos* among many Spanish-speaking persons and the active use of religion in the treatment of illness in some black communities and among many whites. Even the degree to which contemporary Americans rely on television commercials and the popular media as sources of guidance for problem identification and resolution has been a topic of research interest (Bauwens 1977).

The point to be emphasized is that in virtually all communities, including highly urbanized ones that are well supplied with professional healers and therapists, there are many alternative sources of help. Over the last several decades, these alternatives have expanded both in number and in the variety of services they offer. What was once widely considered quackery is now firmly enshrined even in some segments of the middle class (Hess 1993). Indeed, so-called mainstream professionals may be the least and the last consulted for some kinds of personal or family concerns. Especially where minority communities view the social service system as a threat or as a source of social control, social workers may be the last link in the chain of help-seeking contacts.

In pluralistic societies such as our own, one of the critical problems in providing social services is the relationship of the dominant provider system to indigenous alternatives. Where service professionals are selectively recruited, trained in specialized techniques, socialized into the ideology and folklore of their profession, and certified and licensed as a condition of employment, there can be an enormous social gap between them, their clients, and community based alternatives. The lack of trust many social workers experience in minority communities can have severe consequences for the success of their best efforts. But the social worker who tries to utilize rather than replace indigenous resources may have fewer problems. If there are local individuals or organizations with histories and reputations for providing assistance, the social services worker should seek them out, determine what needs they meet, and strive to deliver services in a complementary way. As an outsider, the worker may never enjoy the prestige of such persons or groups, but he or she can work to supplement the forms of care they provide.

The African-American community is one in which these issues of legitimacy are of major importance. The social service establishment has not always served black people well and, as noted later in the chapter on African-American families and social services, black critics of the existing system have been harsh. Historically, many American service organizations evolved to meet the needs of poor European immigrants in large eastern cities in the mid and late nineteenth century. It was left to the black churches to address the concerns of their community following the Civil War. From the point of view of many established agencies at that time, blacks had always been a part of the American social landscape, they always had been poor, and their problems did not seem amenable to the psychodynamic approach that was becoming popular in much of social work at that time. But in the African-American community there were numerous, alternative ways of meeting human needs. Many of them persist in rural and urban areas today.

African-American Community Resources

For a significant portion of the black community in the United States, and also in some Southern rural areas populated largely by whites, there exists a common set of beliefs about health, illness, and general well-being derived from old European as well as African sources. The African origins of these beliefs are bodies of local knowledge common to the west coast of Africa during the time of slave trading in the seventeenth and eighteenth centuries. The European sources are just as old and were brought to North America by the earliest immigrants. There is no generalized name for this system of knowledge, although terms like "witchcraft" or "spiritualism" have been used. In its contemporary form in some areas of the African-American community, it is a consistent, self-contained set of principles for accounting for some of the problems that beset individuals. In addition, it is associated with a set of practitioners who, under certain circumstances, provide effective assistance to those who seek it.

This system of belief has been studied by a number of anthropologically oriented researchers, not only in this country but also in the West Indies and in Africa (Snow 1973, 1974, 1977, 1978, 1993; Whitten 1962; Wintrob 1973). It is very widespread and, in its geographical dispersion, surprisingly homogeneous as well. The system is based on a fundamental division of physical and mental illness into two kinds: that which is natural and that which is unnatural. It is important to understand this distinction in order to appreciate the power of those individuals who are recognized within their own communities as proficient healers.

Natural illness results from the individual's failure to properly care for the body. It may also come about as divine punishment for one's misdeeds. In either event, a lack of wellness is due to an improper relationship with natural forces. Cold air, strong drafts, misuse of alcohol, or poor diet can all be responsible for illness and can signify the individual's inattention to basic health and hygiene requirements. Similarly, illness that is a consequence of God's displeasure results from failure to respect principles of decency and morality as they have been established by Biblical and church authorities.

Unnatural illness, however, is the result of evil influence. It may range from obvious physical ailments to psychosomatic symptoms to problems commonly classified as mental health concerns. But these are all similar in that their origin is in the evil intentions and hostile actions of others. Unlike natural illness, unnatural illnesses are initiated by a human agent against a victim, and they fall outside the orderly domain of the universe established by God and in nature. Various terms for this activity are "hexing," "rootwork," "fix," "mojo," and "witchcraft," but these words change and new ones come into being as needed. It is believed that evil intentions and actions are efficacious because all events in the universe are interconnected. If one knows the interconnections and how to use them, one can have a measure of influence and control over them. It is the wrongful use of this power, not knowledge of occult things per se, that is evil. Thus, individuals who suffer with inexplicable physical or mental problems have reason to suspect that someone else is the cause of their misery. It is important, therefore, to find a specialist who can identify the source of the problem and who can deal with it effectively.

Clearly, neither mental health specialists nor biomedically oriented professionals are in a position to respond to individual complaints based on this model of illness and misfortune. But there are individuals in the African-American community who are effective as far as they and many of their clients are concerned. These healers are variously known as psychics, "root workers," counselors, "root doctors," conjurers, and sometimes witches. Snow (1973, 1978) has described in detail the skills and procedures of a woman she calls a "voodoo practitioner," and what is remarkable are the similarities of her techniques to those of mental health professionals. The woman's practice was located in her home in the downtown section of a large southwestern American city. Her clients included African Americans, whites, Indians, and Mexican Americans. Snow had difficulty locating the woman because she was known only by word of mouth. Yet her place of business was similar to that of many doctors, counselors, and other professionals. She had an office, she kept nine-to-five hours, and patients met her in a waiting room. The woman had received her training from her grandmother, an individual who also possessed special powers of healing and who was widely known among local blacks for her skills. The training consisted of learning ways to utilize her "gift" in helping others, a gift with which she was born and which could not have been obtained any other way. Portions of her therapy involved touching and massage but much of it involved talking through a problem with the patient. Using an idiom with which most black patients were intimately familiar—the personalities and events of the Bible—she was able to illuminate the source of personal difficulties and suggest practical ways of coping with them.

This practitioner acknowledged the critical distinction between natural and unnatural forms of illness, claiming no medical skills for those problems that were clearly within the domain of medical providers: "Now an unnatural sickness, well, that's a person that's sick in the mind. Mentally sick. Doctors can't find that. They Xray and they can't find it. . . . And yet they are sick, mentally sick in mind. And then, I'm a counselor, I counsel them. . . . I give 'em medicine you know, through their mind. I call that spiritual medicine" (Snow 1973:278). Judged by the enthusiasm of her patients and the size of her clientele, this woman was very successful in her community. She did not compete with established medical professionals since both she and her patients recognized that she dealt with problems such practitioners were not trained to handle. Furthermore, she had an intimate knowledge of the pressures of life in her community and of how poor people are vulnerable to forces they cannot control. Many of her patients came to her after having seen professional counselors. They were disappointed with the kind of treatment they received and concluded that professionally trained experts could not treat the kinds of things that afflicted them.

It is important to note, as Snow does, that these beliefs in unnatural illness are not simply the legacy of prescientific superstitions. It would be a serious error to interpret them that way. Rather, unnatural illnesses "are those which have to do with the individual's position as a member of society. . . . Some arise from the tensions and anxieties of everyday living. Worries about money or family problems, for example, may produce a variety of symptoms that informants call 'mental' illness. Hostility in interpersonal relationships, on the other hand, may cause the individual to become the target of witchcraft" (Snow 1973: 272–73). When social relationships are strained because of the problems of poverty, discrimination, and exclusion from full participation in the larger society, beliefs in the efficacy of evil influences are one response to the abrasiveness of everyday living (Rainwater 1970). The problems persist, and so does this culturally defined answer to them, as Snow's (1993) most recent research makes clear.

Foster and Anderson (1978) have identified a number of the characteristics of healers and curers, traits that they believe are the marks of indigenous helpers in many societies. They include selection and training, specialization, certification, projection of a professional image, expectations of payment, and, significantly, an ambivalent public image. Snow's practitioner fits all these criteria. She had a specialized store of local knowledge—the treatment of "unnatural" forms of mental and physical illness—and she was specially selected and trained for her task. That selection came about through the influence of her grandmother, but it was also a divine choice. "I was born just exactly with the gift," she said. The idea of a "gift" to be shared with others was important to her legitimacy in the community. Certification of competence came from patient testimony and did not require framed certificates issued by hallowed institutions attesting to her skills. Further, this healer conducted her practice as a business and, as she herself admitted, her public image was a mixed one. Some in the community accused her of manipulating dark and forbidden forces. Yet she responded that she was simply implementing the power, the "gift," that God had given her.

To the extent that Snow's respondent had success with her patients, it must be attributed not only to her personal skill in counseling others but also to a local awareness of the value of her services to the community. It is this latter quality of legitimacy that professionals who are cultural outsiders, and who are stationed in agencies that are themselves outposts of larger, alien bureaucracies, will always find difficult to obtain. Formal training and the completion of specialized, degree-granting programs are not effective substitutes. But professionals can acknowledge the importance of indigenous help providers and, to the extent feasible, attempt to learn something of their methods and the reasons for their success. Cultural awareness does not require imitation of the skills of knowledgeable insiders, however desirable that may sometimes be. It only requires an honest sensibility as to who and what is really helpful for persons seeking advice on matters that trouble them deeply.

Culturally Based Criteria of Problem Resolution

One of the core tasks of any care system, according to Kleinman (1978a:87), is the "management of a range of therapeutic outcomes." This is a particularly difficult issue in social services, where the specific relationship of treatment to outcomes is not always obvious. That difficulty is compounded when cultural differences contribute to failures in communication and misunderstanding of intent. In transactions with clients, particularly minority clients, social workers have traditionally responded to this problem in two ways, neither of which is useful in enlarging the worker's sense of cross-cultural effectiveness.

One response has been to focus on the idiosyncratic characteristics of each client, taken one at a time. Differences in ethnicity, race, or power between the client and the worker are underplayed or ignored altogether. The rationalization for this strategy is the often expressed desire of social workers to "individualize the client" and get straight to diagnosis and treatment. There is a great deal of support for this position in the social work literature, and, indeed, it is one of the implicit if not explicit values and ideological components of social work's professional subculture (Levy 1976). But from an ethnographic perspective, this orientation can have the effect of stripping the individual of just those things that may be supportive of a healthy sense of individual identity and capability: familiar communication styles; use of indigenous resources; accustomed family patterns; standards of reputation and respectability with family or peers; and styles of demeanor and conduct that are recognized and meaningful among those who count in one's life. To perceive the client's individuality as something beyond, behind, or irrelevant to these ethnographic features leaves only an insubstantial ephemera of what the individual must really be like. It also leaves open the possibility of easy stereotyping, justified by whatever theory of human behavior the social worker brings to the client encounter, whether Freudian, behaviorist, or eclectic. Pursued vigorously, the decision that one need only "individualize the client" in order to come to a full understanding of his or her needs is really a decision to ignore the greater part of the individual's biography.

The other response is the urge to find cultural "reasons" for client "problems" that cannot be accounted for in any other way. In this approach, what clients do or say is viewed as causally related to something in "their culture." A social worker worried about an "inability to self-disclose" among his Asian clients once commented to me that "their quiet culture" was the cause of their reticence to speak about painful family issues. Sometimes workers relying on common, every-day explanations for cultural differences make superficial, even stereotypic judgments about their clients, judgments they believe show them having "insider" information. Typically, the more difficult it is to account for the behavior in question, the more intense the search for some "likely" cultural generalization that explains everything (Neutra et al. 1977). This reliance on ethnographic trivia, things known anecdotally rather than from systematic observation and analysis, suggests the truth of the cliché that "a little knowledge is a dangerous thing." Lacking an organized, comparative framework for accommodating cultural data, anecdotal information becomes the social worker's primary, and most misleading, source of knowledge.

One way of resolving this difficulty is to gather information about how people solve problems within their own communities and what, to them, are reasonable outcomes to those efforts. If the social worker is knowledgeable about the recent history and the day-to-day experiences of the client's home community, there is little likelihood that inappropriate intervention techniques or goals will be pursued. Similarly, the worker who is alert to cultural variations within the client's community will have some sense of how different individuals respond to specific therapeutic techniques. Of course, the greater the cultural difference between the social worker and the client, the more the worker will need to learn in order to be effective. Diagnostic and intervention techniques must always be adapted to the needs of specific communities; there is no such thing as a generalized cultural awareness (Chin 1983). The recent immigration of Southeast Asians to this country, particularly the Vietnamese, provides one example of how social workers can respond to clients in ways that build on reliable cultural knowledge.

Asian Immigration

The evacuation of Vietnamese from South Vietnam in 1975 represented a major challenge to social service organizations in many parts of this country. Unfamiliar with American culture and the English language, many Vietnamese discovered too late that what they thought was to be a temporary retreat before returning to their homes was instead permanent exile and relocation in a strange country.

Many apparently came to accept the fact that their future would be an American one (Kelly 1977). But this acceptance was not easy, given the suddenness of their emigration and the difficulties of life in the refugee camps (Rahe et al. 1976). The need for social services, both advocacy and long-term counseling, was and still remains great. It is a need that is complicated by the fact that the refugees came from a culture with little tradition of publicly sponsored social service programs and with considerable stigma attached to the kinds of problems that practitioners in this country are trained to help resolve (Rutledge 1992).

The stark cultural differences separating Vietnamese and Americans suggest the importance for human service providers of acquiring both an overall background knowledge of Southeast-Asian peoples and some guidelines for using that knowledge in professional practice. Both of these objectives can be met through a careful study of the cultural history of the immigrant population and the translation of dominant cultural themes into service techniques and objectives. The results can and should be the resolution of individual and family problems in ways that are acceptable and useful to clients. I will briefly mention here some of the skills and knowledge areas that have been important in this effort in the last few years.

As is true of most areas of the world, the population of Southeast Asia is culturally diverse. Excluding tribal peoples, of which there are numerous distinctive ethnic groups, there are two major civilizations in the region (Keyes 1977). Buddhist-oriented traditions evolved as the result of extensive borrowing from India. That borrowing was followed by the cultural infiltration of people and ideas from southern China. Consequently, refugees from Burma, Thailand, Cambodia, or Laos are commonly affiliated with a Buddhist world view. The Vietnamese, by contrast, represent a distinctly Chinese tradition, one influenced more by Confucian ideals and Chinese patterns of social organization. The historic Vietnamese "push to the south" along the eastern edge of the mainland led to a lengthy period of instability and conflict, a condition that still persists. Part of that conflict came from colonizing activities by the French, whose influence is seen in the colonial and postcolonial importance of Catholicism in the country and among many Vietnamese in America today.

Aside from these major variations, however, it is important to mention several general themes that are common to the region. One is the exceptionally high value placed on family life. Asians and Pacific Islanders have been called "the most family-dependent" among America's ethnic communities (Sokolovsky 1990: 208), and the Vietnamese are an example of that. Their pattern is based on a Chinese model of the patrilineal extended family, one in which the senior male has high status as head of the family unit. In predominantly Buddhist areas, less emphasis is given to lineality in family and kinship structure, although the predominant importance of senior males is often preserved.

A second theme is the role attached to fate in everyday affairs. The Buddhist notion of karma suggests that all life involves suffering but that the individual can reduce his or her share of it, at least in any future existence, by the performance of meritorious acts now. To some degree, one can influence one's own fate through morally upright behavior and thoughts. Salvation is the ultimate reward. However, the Vietnamese view excludes this possibility and the likelihood of modifying one's fate. The world simply is, and the individual's goal must be harmony in this life, not salvation in some future one. Since there is no escape from fate, preserving a sense of harmony and balance is an important value in the present. What is especially honored is harmony in the "five fundamental relationships of society," those between ruler and ruled, father and son, husband and wife, older brother and younger brother, and friend and friend (Keyes 1977:195).

The refugees who came to America were a special, perhaps atypical, segment of Vietnamese culture. Although many came as family groups, rather than as lone individuals, most refugees were young, half of them under the age of eighteen. Almost half were Catholic, over a quarter were Buddhist, and two-thirds were from highly educated, well-to-do, urban and professional households (Montero 1979). Confronted with American cultural traditions and offered jobs that were for the most part menial and low paying, the refugees were certain to face adjustment difficulties. A number of problems have occurred repeatedly.

Many Vietnamese have experienced disturbing readjustments in family roles, a matter of particular concern to social workers. Under crowded, less affluent living conditions, inherent strains in family life have become more apparent. These include potential conflict between the wife and her mother-in-law and the resultant strain for the husband, who must balance important filial obligations with his responsibilities to his spouse. Similarly, the strict obedience expected of children in their relations with parents, relatives, all adults, and older siblings is challenged by American practices that foster a sense of independence, assertiveness, and inquisitiveness. The American preference for autonomous action conflicts with Vietnamese notions of subordination of personal interests to those of the family group. In addition, physical violence, drinking, divorce, open criticism of others, and direct, face-to-face confrontation are all highly offensive. Yet these have all been a part of the experience of many refugees and have added to their burden of economic marginality, isolation from other Vietnamese, and uncertainty about the relevance of their traditions and experience to their new lives in America (Vuong 1976).

Yet sometimes these traditions can be turned to advantage and great success. One of the most striking features of the Vietnamese adjustment to American life has been the success of children in the public schools and universities. Many have been drawn into the natural sciences and engineering, areas where the analytical skills of mathematics are more important than full native fluency in English. Others have been attracted to business programs, partly in response to enormous family pressure to achieve in education and in the commercial sector. Recent research by Caplan, Choy, and Whitmore (1992) has suggested that it is the preservation, rather than acculturative abandonment, of traditional family practices that accounts for this remarkable academic success. For instance, they found that among Vietnamese students who were high achievers, there was no perceived discontinuity between family life and what went on in the classroom. At home, older children tutored younger ones, parents insisted on a nightly study table that lasted nearly three hours, and learning was verbal and interactive in a group setting. In fact, group learning, with parents in attendance even when their English was markedly weaker than that of their children, was a normal part of family life. By contrast, the Vietnamese children most acculturated to American youth culture and to American family norms did consistently poorer in school. The researchers concluded that cultural factors, not academic ones, accounted for Vietnamese school success and that the preservation of ethnic distinctiveness and more traditional family values was important to that achievement.

The Vietnamese represent only one kind of Asian adjustment to American life, and it would be a serious error to assume that all Asians have experienced America in the same way. Yet there are some overall uniformities about which a culturally sensitive social worker would be aware. These include a concern with orderliness in relationships, especially hierarchical orderliness with deference to those older than oneself. The preservation of order includes control of emotions and emotional displays. "Talk therapy," as a standardized therapeutic style, does not always fit well with this kind of cultural and personal predisposition. Family responsibilities and family preservation, with a clear sense of internal roles and obligations, are important. Ideas about family protectiveness include conceal-ment of stigmatized conditions from outsiders, especially mental illness, drink-ing, and related behavioral issues.

Tsui and Schultz (1985, 1988) have described some of the problems that occur when outsiders (usually white) attempt therapeutic work with Asian clients. Group work in particular is a Western invention as far as many Asian clients are concerned, and the insistence that they participate often has predictable results: a surface pleasantness and willingness to be agreeable, indirection in discussion, sometimes withdrawal into silence. Some social workers may become overprotec-tive or oversolicitous with individuals they (correctly or not) identify as spokes-persons for the local group. Tsui and Schultz suggest several ways of avoiding these problems in service work with Asian clients.

First, recognize that personal and family problems are often presented as physical symptoms. That is logical in cultures where "mental" problems are heav-ily stigmatized and certainly not discussed with strangers. Clients often come to social workers, whom they see as authorities (again, the hierarchical idea), seek-ing very specific suggestions for treating symptoms. Tsui and Schultz describe a client who recounted her physical symptoms to a therapist, to which the latter replied: "Do you feel depressed? That is, feeling sad and possibly hopeless?" The client was confused by the question because to her it wrongly attributed physical illness to "underlying" mental conditions. She reversed the causal sequence when she replied, "Yes, I feel very ill, and my illness is making me sad" (1985:563). At the very beginning of the encounter, the worker and client invoked differing "causal" models, for differing cultural reasons, and the worker missed what it was that the client was trying to say.

Second, Tsui and Schultz urge therapists to consider how the therapeutic alliance is created. Many Asian clients respect the education and academic de-grees held by professionals. But responses to a question such as "Tell me more about that," or "When these things happen, how do you feel?" or "Can you tell me something about the things that happened to you when you first came to America?" tend to undermine the perceived authority and expertise of the social worker. The client wonders: Why is he or she asking these questions? Is this inappropriate prying by a stranger? Is it evasion because the counselor really doesn't know what to do? Does the therapist not care about my problem? Is dislike of Asians behind an apparent refusal to take on the issue authoritatively? These are the images some workers create when they impose, at least at the start, a distinctly American, middle-class model of therapeutic questioning. It is a model many Asians do not recognize either as an intervention technique or a useful rhetorical style. Tsui and Schultz state that such interviews may go well on the surface, with a gentle kind of agreeableness all around, but that the Asian client may not come back. To some workers this unaccountable lack of compliance evokes images—more often thought about than spoken in these politically correct times—of "inscrutability" or of "model minority" clients who can be left to fix things up for themselves. Is that response racism? Perhaps, perhaps not. But it *is* ethnocentric and, for the social services professional, it is an opportunity lost.

HELP-SEEKING WITHIN INSTITUTIONS

It is not necessary to think of help-seeking behavior only in reference to specific ethnic groups and their communities. The model is applicable to behavior within institutional contexts as well, and it suggests that help-seeking and the management of suffering go on in a variety of settings. Sometimes the forms of help-seeking are almost silent, feeble, and barely visible. Yet if we think of help-seeking as the effort to manage distress, then we are obliged to look for it even in unlikely places. It is not confined to ethnic neighborhoods or found only among alternative help providers. It can be seen in client and patient behavior in hospitals, nursing homes, youth centers, drug rehabilitation centers, halfway houses, emergency rooms, homes for the disabled, and a variety of other settings where services are routinely made available.

Just as the model asks us to look at the contrasting versions of a problem or its treatment held by clients and professionals, so too at any institutional site we can locate at least two, often competing versions of what is being done to provide care. Clients and staff each have their own, sometimes very different images of the reality of what is given and what received. This is an old idea in the study of social service institutions, going back at least to the work of Goffman (1961) who suggested that when people enter people-processing facilities they are both the "objects" of professional activity and the "products" of invested labor, intended to result in defineable "outcomes." When an object/product/outcome perspective is clearly articulated and behaviorally dominant, we have what Goffman called "total" institutions, places where governing ideologies and routines swamp subordinate, competing ones. The behavior of everyone, clients and staff alike, is driven and constrained by a single organizational model that invokes industrial, production-line imagery.

But people are not "products," nor do they respond like so many widgets to the ministrations of authorities. Any service facility is a diverse mix of motives, behavior, and objectives. Conflict and subterfuge, not compliance, may be normal (or at least frequent) behavior in those situations. In her study of an inner-city emergency psychiatric facility, Rhodes (1991) found it more useful to describe her mental health field site as a "field of power" rather than a "people-processing" unit, one where numerous competing claims, games, and defensive maneuvers transpired daily. The cultural reality of the site was not its official organization chart, the job descriptions, state mandates, or the contents of the annual report sent to higher authorities. "Rather, administrators, staff, and patients were engaged in a situation of shifting, reciprocal, and multidirectional power relations" (1991:6). In managing that power, every activity, from intake interviews to treatment plans to discharge, became an opportunity for challenging administrative controls over a situation that was almost chaotic. Rhodes observes in her ethnographic study that "this subversion was not peripheral to the 'real' work of clinical practice, something that would end were the institution to be retooled to more perfectly meet the needs of its constituents. It was part and parcel of the work itself, and to the extent that the work had meaning to the staff it was because they made something tangible out of their experience of disjunction, contradiction, and absurdity" (1991:7).

Problems of control exist in any human organization, be it a totalizing one in Goffman's sense or the organized chaos of Rhodes's study site. This is most especially true when goals or "outcomes" are vague, as they often are in social service activities. Institutional uncertainty makes it difficult to see the hidden realities of client's lives and the efforts they make to assert their own models of distress and damage control. In these situations, the help-seeking behavior model is useful as a way of thinking about what those unnoticed realities might be.

Elders, Time, and Nursing Homes
The dependent aged, those seventy-five and older, are more numerous in industrialized countries than ever before, and their social and health needs require more in the way of services and expense than in previous years (Johnson and Grant 1985). The "nursing home" as a custodial institution for the aged hardly existed prior to the passage of the Social Security Act in 1935 (Dunlop 1979), but it has so flourished in the latter half of this century that it is now an "industry," as its managers and owners like to describe it. It is also a technologically complex and much regulated one, modeled after acute care and mental hospital wards, not after anything recognizable as homelike. The institutional features of nursing "homes"—regimentation, social enclosure, exclusion, and dependence on strangers—contradict the familial model as Americans usually think of it (Johnson 1987). This is especially true where the residents are of ethnic and minority backgrounds (Green 1989). The idea that nursing homes have their own, distinc-

tively institutional culture is a novel one both in the social sciences and in human services. Yet research based on cultural models of institutional settings has begun.

In a remarkable study of daily life in a nursing home in the Northeast, Shield (1988) describes the routines of staff and elderly residents using a dependency model. There is nothing new in looking at the elderly in terms of their dependency, but Shield saw it in things much more subtle than wheelchair restraints or set meal times. For her, time itself was an issue. There were multiple models of time operating at her research site: secular calendar time, Jewish calendar time, clock time, shift change times, television program times, "meds" times, and a host of other markers that identified the passage of moments. But the ultimate passage, the time of death, was a timing issue that was kept deliberately ambiguous and almost never discussed.

Shield quotes a social worker who described for her what happened whenever a resident died:

> *I was uncomfortable each time I saw how a death was managed. All the residents are taken into the dining area and the doors are closed. Mysteriously, two men in black suits appear on the floor with a stretcher between them. They take away the body and five minutes after the residents have been taken into the dining area, they are let out again. No one ever says what just happened (1988:71).*

Death was not publicly acknowledged, partly for reasons of policy but more often because people working in the facility didn't know whether or how they should discuss it. The institutional agenda for "managing" a death was to say as little about it as possible, on the presumption that the residents would neither know nor notice that it had occurred. Following a death, staff time was spent on completing charts and files, cleaning up the former resident's room, sanitizing it, and removing personal belongings for pickup by the family. Death meant closing a case in ways not much different from checking out of a motel.

However, in the corridors, the sitting area, and the dining room an alternative, almost invisible reality developed, a sense of quiet gloom that Shield calls "future peril." The residents constructed a sense of time very different from that of the staff. To them time was an endless and unmarked flow in which they saw themselves quietly sinking toward dementia and an unnoticed death. Residents repeatedly told her that they knew almost immediately of every death that occurred and that they resented how they were unable to memorialize them. Even discussing death was not permitted; one resident was told cheerfully that "we don't talk about dying here. We talk about living." Yet aging and death were the two most obvious events in this institution, they were its reason for being, and the residents had a desperate need to articulate their relationship to that fact. The mood of "future peril" became their "cognitive map" for the reality of the nursing home.

The help-seeking model directs our attention to the buried agendas that can operate in institutional settings. Clinicians are prone to think of "problems" as things like depression or misuse of drugs, things "presented." But the help-seeking model requires that we look at context and think about "problems" in ways not always obvious. For example, time is something that people in every culture organize and respond to; it is neither a neutral nor a natural category of experience even though people take it for granted. "Time" is a cultural category and for staff in the nursing home it was measured as a succession of administrative events. Its principal unit was the work shift and all else was organized around that. But time for the residents was the time of life remaining and, when that ended, their need for a suitable demarcation. Funerals in all societies are our final rite of passage, the marker of our exit. More important, they are a public declaration that says for each individual: "I was here!" The substitution of an open-ended "future peril" suggested for the residents a fearsome reality in which they noted one another's unrelieved decline but felt blocked and powerless to respond to it. In the institutional denial of that need, the residents' reality, the validity of the moods and motivations that defined the nursing home for them, was regularly dismissed and denied.

My suggestion that time be thought of as a "problem," in exactly the clinical sense that the help-seeking model suggests, is not an academic fancy. In any culture, rites of passage, including death rites, are devices that remind individuals and groups where they are in an orderly sequence of things. Rites mark beginnings, middles, and ends. They affirm the reality of some larger context, create a sense of where the world is headed, and dramatize how one is moving with it. The absence of rituals and their marking functions leaves a void that has been described as a sense of "liminality" or marginality, a betwixt and between, a place neither here nor there (Turner 1969; Myerhoff 1982). For the residents of the home described by Shield, their uncertainty and quiet desperation did not have to be.

In *Number Our Days*, Barbara Myerhoff's (1978) classic study of a California day-care center for elderly Jews, ritualized events were everywhere. Elders enjoyed not just the traditional Jewish holidays and foods, but they invented activities and new rituals that defined who and what everyone was. For example, after attending a series of seminars and discussions, the residents created a high school graduation ceremony explicitly for the older women in the center. It was an unusual mixture of American secular and Jewish sacred elements, one that was remarkable because it occurred in an immigrant community that historically placed far more emphasis on education for men than women. It was a creative response that mixed indigenous traditions and American experience.

Myerhoff also describes a ritual event of supreme subtlety and managerial insight, one in which the director of the center arranged the giving of food to its needy members in a way that preserved a complex Jewish ideal of personal honor in relations between those who are givers and those who are receivers. Anyone who needed food could take it and do so without feeling beholden to those who offered it. No one was stripped of their identity; no total institution "processed" people in unrelieved routines. And at the center deaths were always fully marked with a grand sense of accomplishment and participation by all. "Outcomes" were clearly consistent with the struggle of the elders there to make sense of everything they had all been through—the Holocaust, migration to America, the work that led to their success as the "one-generation proletariat," and their last, best efforts to die honorably and with full, formal acknowledgment.

IMPLICATIONS OF THE MODEL FOR SOCIAL SERVICES

The help-seeking behavior model, as a culturally sensitive approach to integrating ethnicity and human services delivery, contains the following components: (1) group-specific criteria for problem identification; (2) group-specific linguistic categories of problem labeling; (3) indigenous strategies for problem referral and resolution; and (4) group-specific standards for knowing when a need has been successfully met. It should be apparent that these are all cross-cultural categories that are applicable to any group or community, including institutional ones. They only require that the social worker think about service problems in comparative terms.

Culturally sensitive practice has important implications for how social workers approach their tasks. It may mean adjustments in intervention techniques and perhaps even in professional values and agency practices. The culturally responsive worker, functioning in a service system designed to accommodate racially and ethnically diverse clients, might be described in the following way:

1. A worker capable of thinking about clients in terms of group characteristics and group strengths as well as clinical pathology and agency protocols of problem resolution. Since the concept of culture applies to groups, not to single individuals, the skill of linking cultural features to individual behavior is a critical task. Stereotyping or reliance on culturally devoid psychological explanations is antithetical to ethnically sensitive practice.

2. A worker willing to undertake an examination of group strengths as they are understood by community members themselves. This may require modification or abandonment of some established theories and interpretations of how or why clients experience the problems they do and what the social worker can do about them. It also means that clients ought to be viewed as potential teachers to the worker as well as recipients of services. Such a view of clients would result in substantial rethinking of the client role in the social service system.

3. Open utilization of indigenous sources of help. This is not only a cultural issue, it is also an explosive political one. It suggests granting credence for intervention effectiveness to lay practitioners, some of whom may lack formal training and recognized credentials or degrees. Some of these practitioners have skills that social workers need and can not learn from other sources. This is one area in which minority practitioners can make important contributions to identifying the components of culturally sensitive intervention skills.

4. Modification of the criteria of successful intervention so that they are meaningful to clients and their community. It is possible that some agencies may have to revise their thinking on such matters as agency accountability, professional service standards, or standards of service evaluation. It may also be true that there will remain conflicts between the interests of the client and the client's community and the agency.

In summary, the help-seeking behavior model is a way of thinking about social services from the perspective of the client and the client's culture. It is applicable cross-culturally, and the sensitive and alert social worker can use it at virtually any work site. What is required is a willingness to suspend temporarily all professional or agency priorities in order to look at services from the recipient's perspective. The model raises questions as to what alternative sources of help may exist and how those sources can be encouraged and complemented.

Finally, the model suggests that the road to cultural awareness requires much effort and learning on the part of the social worker. The kind of person the worker happens to be—open, caring, empathic—is not sufficient without the acquisition of cross-cultural knowledge through sustained effort. A systematic learning style and a supportive agency environment, aimed at recognizing culturally distinctive modes of behavior and responding to them appropriately, is required. The worker who can do all that will know how to individualize clients, and can legitimately be described as "ethnically competent."

3

CROSS-CULTURAL SOCIAL WORK

How far must one go to learn about the experiences of others, the differences that make a difference to them? There is a cliché that we must walk in someone else's shoes if we want to know what their world is like. Several years ago, a 26-year-old product designer in New York City did just that. Not only was Pat Moore dissatisfied with her gerontology courses at Columbia University. She resented commercial products that are difficult for the elderly to use and architectural design that assumes everyone is young, athletic, and fully able to move about. So with the help of an NBC makeup artist, she transformed herself into "Old Pat," an elderly woman of limited means who for three years ambled along the streets of New York and over a hundred other American cities.

As reported by the British newspaper *The Guardian* (August 1, 1989), Moore wore a wig and latex mask, put steelworker's wax in her ears to impair hearing, and used baby oil drops in her eyes to cloud her vision. A heavy wrap forced her to walk stooped. Balsa splints taped to the back of the knees both shortened and slowed her steps, and heavy tape on her hands, hidden under bulky gloves, simulated the restrictions of arthritis. Crayon stains were applied to her teeth, and she gargled a pasty saltwater mix, deliberately irritating her throat in order to create a raspy voice. Columbia students did not recognize her when she attended her own classes as "Old Pat."

Out on the streets, Moore experienced directly the life of an elderly woman. She was shortchanged by merchants and muscled out of her place in lines. People pointedly talked down to her, she was physically assaulted, and at one time she was left for dead by teenagers looking for drug money. At times she was so frustrated "it was all I could do to stop myself from ripping off my wig and giving them a very unladylike piece of my mind" (1989:17). But she didn't, and over time she felt herself becoming increasingly timid and submissive, doing and saying whatever was necessary to get through each demeaning situation with a little dignity. Once during the research she revealed her identity to a small group of elderly women she knew and trusted. Seeing who she really was and wanting to help in the research, they took her shopping, explaining the nuances of getting through the hazards of each day. From them she discovered why the elderly have a reputation among some researchers for concealing, even lying, about how they live. Secretiveness and reduced visibility are important strategies for survival in a world that does not care if you are old. She recalls that one of her best memories as "Old Pat" was a conversation with a six-year-old boy at a beach. He responded to her presence naturally and without affectation because, she said, "he didn't know any better."

Moore now designs commercial products that are simple, ingenious, and foolproof: easily opened laundry soap boxes; pill dispensers that keep count; sensors that make it simple to park a car in a small space. She has also created a hybrid social service institution, a day-care center for children that doubles as a senior center. Moore's experiment suggests some of the interesting research issues one confronts in learning about any culture one does not know. For example, what is the research technique we call "participant observation"? Why is direct experience useful as a precondition for cross-cultural understanding, especially the kind of understanding that is sometimes described as "empathy"? Is it necessary for those who want to be of service to all the "Old Pats" in the world to have an experience of participatory involvement? Are there other ways of expanding one's personal and professional sensibilities? What is cross-cultural learning anyway, and how can human service workers use it productively?

Cross-cultural social work is both similar to and different from other kinds of human service activity. It is similar in that it can be integrated into the vocabulary and procedures common to any health or social service facility. It is generic, not a distinctive field of practice such as substance abuse or community development. But it is different in that it requires explicit, informed utilization of ethnographic information for planning, service delivery, and evaluation. That information must be specifically and demonstrably salient to client issues within a communal context. Cross-cultural social work is much more than regular contact with clients who are culturally or racially different from oneself. Certainly, it is more than vague and simplistic notions of "tolerance" or "awareness," which sometimes come from casual association with minority staff or clients.

Effective cross-cultural social work combines deliberate preparation with an alertness to the cultural as well as clinical features of the client-worker relationship. It involves specific ways of acquiring the knowledge and skills appropriate for working with ethnically distinctive clients. It supplements traditional social service training methods, and it is eclectic, relying on a number of academic and professional fields in which cross-cultural learning and communication are critical. Finally, it is a discovery procedure, a way of accessing and learning about the world of people different from ourselves. As a professional style, it is explicitly comparative, requiring us to self-consciously contrast our own view of things with that of others, and find the patterns and values in them both. This chapter discusses these procedures and how workers can use them to improve their ability to serve others.

There are several reasons social workers would want to acquire cross-cultural knowledge and capabilities. First, many workers know little of the *cultural* characteristics of the client communities they serve. This is not surprising as it is only in the last decade or so that multicultural counseling has appeared in the curriculum of many social work training programs (Ponterotto and Sabnani 1989). Unfortunately, many course offerings in this area are little more than supplements to existing curricula, in effect ghettoizing the topic in specialized, "minority issues" courses rather than integrating it into the widest possible range of social work teaching. Much that passes for "cultural sensitivity" training, be it in university classes or on-the-job workshops, is simplistic and anecdotal. Frequently it relies on minority representatives who are asked to give what amount to testimonials. Sometimes it is polite and academic, offering "background" information that is interesting but lacking any clear relationship to specific client issues. It can be simplistic and distorting, emphasizing "norms and values," as Longres (1991:55) put it, avoiding the realities of power and systemic inequality. In addition, a lack of interest among staff and administrators and a lack of willingness to follow through on training initiatives often limit the degree to which cultural awareness penetrates the profession.

Although this situation has begun to change, and some of these changes are an improvement over past practice, still the best current efforts are minimal when compared to the needs involved. It is necessary, therefore, to think about ways of acquiring cultural information more systematically and more efficiently than has been done in the past. Anecdotes, testimonials, role plays, and short-term workshops with no follow-up are no longer adequate either for social workers or for their clients. Gallegos has put it harshly but succinctly by suggesting that "social work practitioners who lack the skills, attitudes, and knowledge to work effectively in cross-cultural settings are incompetent" (1984:1).

A second reason social workers would want to acquire cross-cultural capabilities is that problem solving with those who are culturally or racially different from oneself can be highly stressful. That will not be news to most minority social workers, who deal with people different from themselves everyday! But to many whites, especially those whose contact with minority persons is infrequent, working with minority clients may be particularly difficult. Ratliff (1988) lists some of the symptoms of "burnout" in the helping professions. Among them are stereotyping clients, judgmental attitudes toward clients who seem particularly difficult, discussion of clients in distancing, jargonistic terms, and a sense that whatever one does with a particular individual, it will never make a difference. These reactions are exacerbated when workers do not comprehend their client's moods and motivations and the cultural sources of them. There is a need for training that goes beyond altruistic desires to help, and well beyond cultural "awareness" workshops that "raise consciousness" but provide little more.

Third, among most Americans the expression of prejudicial attitudes in public and professional settings is much less acceptable than it was even a decade ago. In educated circles, at least, bigotry is boorish. But institutional forms of insensitivity and discrimination persist. As I suggested in chapter 1 on the relationship of ethnicity to social work, institutional forms of mistreatment are harder to see and more difficult to correct. That is partly due to the fact that sometimes individuals benefit, in direct and indirect ways, from the status quo. Privilege is at stake. Institutional practices that are long established also carry the authority and inertia of tradition. Tradition can be used as dogma, as a rationale for continuing program and agency practices because they have a momentum of their own. A cultural approach to social services, however, makes explicit the dichotomy between the values and procedures of those who provide services and the values and responses of those who receive them. Much of the dynamics of crosscultural social work involves the juxtaposition of these two, often contrary, traditions, that of the profession and that of the client's community. Recognizing the reality of this contrast can make it easier to identify and change institutional deficiencies.

Finally, it is important to recognize that within social work even our counseling theories presume that some cultural values are "better" than others and hence more deserving of our attention and encouragement with clients. This kind of "theoretical ethnocentrism" can be as detrimental to effective communication as outright bigotry. For example, Ponterotto and Casas (1991) note that psychodynamic approaches to therapy, with their emphasis on intrapsychic conflict rooted in early childhood events, often discount the small, day-to-day stresses of racism and prejudice. They also favor a verbally active expressive style in counseling, something that may not be appropriate or encouraged in some communities. The person-centered approach of existential and humanistic theories, commonly associated with Carl Rogers and Viktor Frankl, emphasizes self-awareness, selfesteem, and self-acceptance. Yet these values are just the opposite of those preferred in communities where the welfare of the group—family, kin, ethnic or linguistic compatriots—is more important than that of the individual. Even behavioral approaches, generally preferred by ethnic and minority therapists and their clients, still assume the central importance of middle-class, white values associated with self-directed independent action, task-centered problem solving, and a linear construction of time (Ponterotto and Casas 1991:61). The task of developing a genuinely cross-cultural, ethnically sensitive social work is just that much more difficult when the discipline's guiding paradigms assume (without making their assumptions explicit) the greater importance of one's own community's values over the standards and preferences of others.

CROSS-CULTURAL LEARNING

It is an axiom of social work that the successful worker must establish rapport and develop empathic relationships in order to further treatment objectives. Truax and Mitchell (1971), for instance, found empathy, warmth, and genuineness to be frequently reported characteristics of individuals considered effective in helping others. A number of training approaches have been devised to promote acquisition of these "helping" capabilities. The literature on skills development in social work is very large, covering many kinds of intervention activities, and cannot be completely reviewed here. But it is common in these approaches to stress the student's need for enhanced perception of verbal and nonverbal cues, attentiveness to emotional states during interaction, and sensitivity in questioning and responding. Typically, rather general kinds of desired behavior ("self-involving," "encouraging," "assertive," "engaging," and the like) are described, and then problems for practice and relationship-building are presented. The goals of this kind of training are usually (1) empathic understanding that results from putting oneself in the other's place; (2) nonpossessive respect and warm, unconditional regard for the other; and (3) genuineness in the therapeutic relationship so that what one seems to be is in fact what one is. There is no holding back of one's full attentiveness to the other.

Useful as these may be as goals, they are also limited and limiting concepts. Behind them is an assumption that a specific "helping skill," when sufficiently practiced, ought to be helpful when employed with most clients. There is also an emphasis on personal "style," on practicing the techniques with which one feels "comfortable." Practice should lead to "skills" that help one develop the trusting relationships that are the mark of the competent professional.

Egan (1986), however, has described certain problems that can arise from the simplistic application of these high-sounding communication ideals in social service encounters. He calls them "counterfeits of accurate empathy." Examples include (1) inaccurate responses to the client because the interviewer is excessively focused on technique; (2) inattentiveness because the social worker is mentally anticipating what to say next; (3) assumptions that the client will understand the worker's "validating" gestures and "affirming" subvocalization; and (4) restatement of what the client has said as a device to maintain the worker's end of the conversation. Egan believes that empathy is not really a "skill," certainly not a trained "bedside manner" that can be turned on and off at will. Rather, he sees it as something that is part of how good professionals deal with others all the time. He argues that the way to avoid counterfeit empathy is to look instead for the "core messages" that clients attempt to express, the messages that emerge from their life experiences, rather than focusing on clinical management skills and elaborate diagnostic procedures.

Egan's concern with "core messages" points to one of the essential tasks of effective cross-cultural communication. I want to suggest that interpersonal skills or techniques are not in and of themselves a sufficient basis for working with minority clients. (They may not be adequate for working with many non-minority clients either.) Although personal qualities of warmth and caring may be important as work styles, they are not an adequate basis for comprehending what troubles another person or for knowing how that individual may be helped. Rather, we need some way to identify and learn the significance of our client's "core messages," especially when we are with clients whose cultural background we know little about. Further, we need a way of learning that can be adapted to a variety of cross-cultural situations, since it is impossible for any of us to know enough to effectively serve clients from every cultural community in a large, pluralistic society.

How, then, does one learn about another culture? Children learn the patterns and pieces of a culture as they are presented to them, somewhat randomly and over a long period of time. A monocultural adult entering an unfamiliar social world is forced to learn the same way. Anyone who has served in the Peace Corps or who has had overseas experience knows that events, objects, and language may appear strange at first but that strangeness recedes into the background as places, people, and contexts become familiar and taken for granted. The adult's advantage over the child is the capacity for critical assessment of the pieces as they are presented. The disadvantage is that a lifetime of learned preferences can act as blinders to much that is going on, or may lead to erroneous interpretations of the "core messages" that others transmit to us.

The framework developed by Taft (1977) suggests several beginning steps for acquiring knowledge of other cultural systems. The first level of learning is cognitive. One must simply go to the trouble to learn some of what members of a culture know, including their beliefs about their history, their values, and what they see as their relationship to the rest of the world. At this stage of learning, it is not necessary to rely solely on library-type research and generalized, background reading. What matters is what people believe to be true about themselves and others, since that is what is most real to them. At the cognitive level, then, the task of the skilled learner-practitioner is to try to determine something of the normative beliefs and behavior of a given community as the members of that community perceive and act on them. The social worker must be concerned with a new version of "common sense," the taken-for-granted things that people in a particular community rarely question. For example, there are ways of treating children, of serving food, and of offering greetings that are "right," and ways that are "wrong." The worker will simply have to learn what they are—by combining reading, listening, watching, and consulting with knowledgeable insiders. By paying attention to the regularities of conduct and finding out what they mean in context, the worker begins to discover "core messages" and to acquire empathy as a personal and professional trait.

But knowledge of another culture is more than information. What people do and what they prefer are always associated with an expressive tone. Sometimes that tone is identifiable in such overt activities as singing, dancing, arguing, playing, and working. But affective or expressive tone can also be discovered in offhand comments, facial expressions, joking relationships, exchange of favors, and styles of demeanor. In all cultures, people play largely predetermined roles: spouse, child, friend, or co-worker. But how they play their roles, how they incorporate expressive gestures into what Goffman (1959) called the "presentation of self," is a clue to the affective tone of a community. Affect, feeling tone, and intuitive sensitivities are subtle, complex, and sometimes difficult to detect, but they suggest the gut-level realities of people's experiences and cannot be ignored. It is probably impossible to appreciate them fully in a tradition that is not one's own. To pretend that one has fully crossed into the expressive realm of another culture is not only preposterous but usually embarrassing to onlookers. But to be able to recognize the core messages of expressiveness, and to respond to them even somewhat appropriately, is a sign of growing empathy. Rapport comes from one's willingness to learn about others at that level and intensity. Rapport *cannot* come from a practiced technical style.

One implication of this approach is that the competent learner-practitioner may on some occasions attempt, but with a great deal of caution and humbleness, to simulate culturally appropriate role performances if invited by others to do so. For example, I have seen white social workers who were totally at home in a Northwest Coast Indian potlatch, an all-night ceremony of dancing, eating, speech making, and ceremonial gift giving. Some joined in the dancing because they were qualified and capable of doing so and their presence was acceptable. This is, as Taft notes, the "ultimate test of enculturation" (1977:136), when one can recognize and respond appropriately to the feelings of the members of an ethnic community. When one can act "correctly," and have the act recognized by others as culturally genuine, then one has achieved the broadened understanding that exemplifies the best in cross-cultural social work.

Perhaps that level of capability is beyond what most practitioners really need to do their jobs. Yet it would be difficult to argue that a profession committed to helping others in sensitive personal, family, and community matters could proceed in ignorance of those realities. The typical injunctions to be patient, genuine, and open fall far short of real cross-cultural comprehension.

We need to put a label on this elusive capability, for it represents the essential characteristic of the social worker who knows, appreciates, and can utilize the culture of others in assisting them with their concerns. I call it "ethnic competence," a term coined some years ago by my colleague James Leigh. *One who is "ethnically competent" can provide professional services in a way that is congruent with behavior and expectations that are normative for a given community.* Figure 3.1 summarizes the minimal components of the ethnic competence model.

It is important to understand what the definition of ethnic competence says and what it does not say. It does not say—and I want to be emphatic on this point—that the trained individual will be able to conduct himself or herself "as though" he or she were a participating member of a client community. That is clearly absurd and to make that capability a personal or professional training goal

---

- Awareness of self-limitations
- Interest in cultural differences
- Systematic learning style
- Utilization of cultural resources
- Engagement with diversity

FIGURE 3.1   Basic points of the ethnic competence model.

would be misleading and dangerous. In my own workshops, I am always amazed at how regularly someone announces, usually in a holier-than-thou sort of way, that they have worked with clients from the "X" culture "for years" and so are authoritative on how the "X" feel about things. No training program can deliver that and I distrust the claims of those who think simple longevity guarantees that level of understanding. Ethnic competence means only that the worker has a systematically learned and tested awareness of the prescribed and proscribed values and behavior of a specific community, and an ability to carry out professional activities consistent with that awareness.

ETHNIC COMPETENCE

In some ways, it is easier to define what cross-cultural sensitivity is not than to pinpoint what it is. In a well-known article, Pedersen (1976) described what he called the "culturally encapsulated counselor," an individual unable or unwilling to engage the client on any but the counselor's own terms. Such a counselor capitalizes on the status differences that separate him or her from the client and uses those differences to manage the relationship. The client's life circumstances or personal problems are evaluated according to criteria more suitable to the personal or professional milieu of the counselor than to the day-to-day realities of client experience. Encapsulation is often evident when the counselor has been socialized into a set of professional values and theoretical orientations that isolate the individual within a specific, clinically defined focus. Only minimal reference may be made to the client's larger social setting, with the possible exception of family life. But that too is seen as an isolated site, a locale of pathology, to be diagnosed and treated. From the point of view of the encapsulated counselor, each client is a unique, nonhistorical, culturally unconnected entity.

Given this narrowly conceived orientation, the professional's clinical task is to "strip away" or "get behind" cultural appearances that mask and confound the "true" or "deeper" meaning of the client's problems. Pedersen notes that a "technique-oriented job definition further contributes toward, and perpetuates, the process of encapsulation" (1976:24) by canonizing some therapeutic principles while closing off alternative perspectives. The encapsulated counselor has an a priori commitment to a set of beliefs about "processes" and techniques, themselves part of established professional and institutional loyalties. Given that most social service workers have great latitude in the micro-management of their contacts with clients and patients, it seems natural to the encapsulated counselor that dominant agency perspectives would be reproduced in worker-client relationships. In effect, what the encapsulated worker brings to an encounter is ideology as a substitute for the openness and risk taking that real empathy would require.

Perhaps this is an unfair and exaggerated characterization. It has been almost twenty years since Pedersen formulated the idea of counselor encapsulation and, in that time, some of the rough edges of race relations in America may have become a little less raw. More has been written on cross-cultural counseling and communication for social services specifically, although much of it remains narrowly descriptive (sometimes in ways that are painfully brief) or is limited to anecdotes and short descriptions of single cases. The field of cross-cultural communication is only partially helpful in moving us beyond encapsulation. (That subject area is much too large to be reviewed here, but good sources include Gudykunst and Kim (1984) and the new edition of Sue and Sue (1990). Further, the discovery procedures of ethnic competence have not been well defined for social services, although in nursing (Boyle and Andrews 1989), health services (Waxler-Morrison, Anderson and Richardson 1990), and cross-cultural psychology (Pedersen 1985; Dasen, Berry and Sartorius 1988) there is considerable research and training on the topic.

We can begin, therefore, with some general features of cross-cultural capability that Mayes (1978) suggested some years ago and that are still useful in contrasting ethnic competence with other kinds of social service training. I will list these and discuss some of their implications for the model to be developed here.

Ethnic Competence as Awareness of One's Limitations

Barbara Solomon's work on "empowerment" is well known in social services. Usually, empowerment is thought of as a quality to be encouraged in the client or as an activity that "aims(s) to reduce the powerlessness that has been created by negative valuations" (Solomon 1976:19). In a discussion of empowerment as a strategy in assessment, Kopp (1989) argues that self-observation (through things like diaries, checklists, and the like) and self-monitoring are useful to clients. They help them (1) to see themselves as active agents in the solution of a problem; (2) to understand both environmental constraints and possibilities; and (3) to "perceive the practitioner as a peer-collaborator or partner in the problem solving effort" (1989:277).

I want to suggest that the same model is applicable to the social worker. Ethnically competent practitioners are sensitive to environmental limitations but also open to new and perhaps challenging experiences. In particular, they usually appreciate that ambiguity (and its resulting anxiety) in cross-cultural relationships is normal. Both the worker and the client bring to their engagement a "presenting problem" and the worker's problem is the ambiguity and uncertainty of the encounter. To cope with that, the worker needs to see the client as a "peer-collaborator" for managing anxiety.

In learning about others, the social worker learns about self, and clients can be among the best teachers. That seems rather obvious and simple, almost a cliché. But I believe it is very difficult for some workers to grasp and accept because it goes to the heart of what Solomon was talking about—power. The worker who has academic degrees, who has attended all the right workshops and has the framed certificates to prove it, who has the job title and career aspirations, may find it quite difficult to grant a teaching role to those he or she is paid to serve. Why should that be so hard?

Think again about the "culturally encapsulated" counselor and that individual's commitment to an a priori set of beliefs. What kinds of beliefs might they be? Some years ago Stewart (1969) listed five values or assumptions he thought characterize mainstream American culture, values often translated into institutionally dominant modes of planning and delivery in mental health services. Those values are (1) active self-expression; (2) equality and informality in social relationships; (3) achievement and accomplishment; (4) control of self and one's destiny while in pursuit of a better future; and (5) individualism and autonomy experienced in democratic, nonauthoritarian relationships with others (Stewart, Danielian and Festes, 1969). A more recent commentator discussing American popular culture developed what he called a "mantra" of white, middle-American virtues: conscience; industry; success; civic-mindedness; usefulness; antisensuality; and conscience (Brookhiser 1991). And in a work of great erudition, Bellah and his associates (1985) described individualism and its two subvarieties, utilitarian individualism and expressive individualism, as master metaphors of American life.

These are all admirable values, at least to persons whose socialization has included years of public education followed by advanced training in university programs marked by liberal, humanistic learning. But they may not be the values of those who are immersed in a subculture more oriented toward day-to-day survival, or who participate in a community that has preserved old, even ancient, traditions transplanted from another continent to an American setting. For example, some clients may have a sense of impropriety in discussing intimate matters outside the family, and for them the notion of "active self-expression," especially with a stranger, may be offensive. Nor can it be assumed that the ability to articulate for others one's most private feelings is a sign of a healthy mental state. In some settings, it may not be appropriate for the individual to independently "assert" himself or herself, for doing so could be interpreted as a sign of instability or insensitivity. Similarly, we cannot take it for granted that all cultures have a notion of "personal growth" tied to expectations of individual accomplishment. Indeed, many cultures do not, and "personal growth" that distinguishes one from others might be viewed as arrogant and unseemly.

What all this suggests is the applicability of the old anthropological truism, cultural relativism. Cultures are in fact different, and most of the differences are subtle and not always visible to outsiders. People occasionally get a sense of this when they participate in "values clarification" workshops and similar kinds of exercises. Although we may not all agree that Stewart's five postulates do indeed define the core values of mainstream American culture, we can probably agree that *any* set of values, including professional ones, is culture-bound and that we are all myopic at least to the extent that we operate with one set of beliefs to the exclusion of others. That need not be a cause of despair. It only means we need to see our own actions and values in an explicitly comparative way so that our personal choices do not keep us from perceiving why others may have different ones. Relativism is a beginning, at least, to appreciating that.

Ethnic Competence as Openness to Cultural Differences

The belief that "underneath we are all the same" and that we all share a basic understanding of what is good and valuable might well be added to my list of common American values. This idea derives from the melting pot ideology, with its assumption (and hope) that the cultural differences that separate people are less important than the things that unite them, and that manifestations of differences are best underemphasized in order to assure personal tranquility and civil peace.

Even as the word "pluralism" has become fashionable, both as a description of tolerance and even an appreciation of the idiosyncrasies of others, it remains true that cultural dissimilarity is much less highly valued than cultural homogeneity. In fact, many people are threatened by the promotion of cultural differences, especially if they think that "special privileges" may go with them. This is dramatically clear when themes of ethnicity are explicitly linked with political demands for change in the distribution of status and power (as in the Black Power movement of the 1960s and 1970s) and in the realignment of economic privileges (as in Indian land and fishing claims). Cultural differences are threatening even on the symbolic level, as when seemingly "assimilated" individuals insist that their children receive instruction in languages other than English. Real acceptance of differences has rarely been promoted in the educational, religious, or political institutions of the larger society. It is not surprising, therefore, that the response of social services to ethnic and minority communities would be occasionally awkward and hesitant.

A genuine and open appreciation of ethnic differences, without condescension and without patronizing gestures, is critical for the development of an ethnically competent professional style. At a minimum, that means that the worker ought to have a sense of how the social artifact called the "counseling relationship" fits into a client's normative expectations. Do clients perceive as normal or acceptable a deeply personal conversation with a near stranger, one who has a great deal of authority and who is a representative of another, possibly threatening, ethnic group? Is the social worker expected to give something of value— advice, goods, or an eligibility rating—in return for a proper show of deference or need? What is the agenda, and how is action begun?

One early step is clarifying the expectations in the counseling relationship. This does not mean asking such obvious and abstract questions as "What does your Indianness mean to you?" It means instead some acknowledgment that the client's and the worker's ethnic and cultural identities are different and that the differences may be important to counseling and giving assistance. The skill with which this is done, of course, depends on the social worker's maturity and capability. But it is important in that it makes clear to both worker and client that the latter has more to contribute than the presentation of a problem.

Ethnic Competence as a Client-Oriented, Systematic Learning Style

All cross-cultural encounters are potential learning experiences. They may result in the discovery of new information or in a better understanding of something that was not fully appreciated before. But learning depends on the social worker's willingness to adopt something of a student role, something not easy for everyone to do.

This lesson was particularly dramatic for Evans (1988, 1991), a researcher with long social service experience. He describes his activities in a state school for the deaf where he went to study the organization of the institution and its impact on deaf students. Of course, American Sign Language was the lingua franca of the school and, as a hearing-impaired person himself, Evans knew the language needed to communicate with respondents. What surprised him, however, was the degree to which deaf students developed their own, alternative subculture, partly out of opposition to the school's managers but also as a defensive reaction to the larger society. He describes the deep sense of a "wounded self" that typified these students and how that view shaped their responses to the authoritarian culture of their school community. Evans could explore these issues because he knew sign language but also because he allowed himself to be treated in the same way as the students. He experienced directly the slights and not very subtle insults that maintained a "safe" distance between students and staff. By adopting a learner role, he experienced these things directly and came to understand the real culture of the place and why people behaved and felt as they did.

The concept of ethnic competence assumes that clients, however plagued by personal problems and uncertainties, know a great deal about what is happening to them. The social worker needs to know the same information—local, contextualized knowledge—so he or she can integrate it into whatever therapeutic model is to be followed (Gubrium 1991).

However, this approach is not often taught in professional education programs such as social work, education, health, and public policy. Perhaps that is because the kind of information needed for cross-cultural sensitivity is not easily discovered, does not fit existing models of social welfare or health care practice, or is not quantifiable. The social worker who adopts ethnic competence as a training goal, therefore, must not only deal with the natural hesitancy of minority groups to reveal community secrets to outsiders but may also have to confront the prejudices of colleagues who see time committed to that kind of inquiry as peripheral to the "real" job of helping.

Ethnic Competence as Appropriate Utilization of Cultural Resources

The ability to help others find and make use of resources is one of the critical tasks of the ethnically competent worker. It is an important part of what Solomon (1976) meant when she wrote of "empowerment." The ethnically competent helper ought to encourage clients to draw on the natural strengths inherent in their own traditions and communities, reducing where possible their dependence on services provided by outsiders or by impersonal bureaucracies (Handelman 1976). This is not a new idea, although it has become more urgent with the failure of the federal and many local governments to adequately fund critical services. Social services have never been funded at levels that fully meet community needs, but during the last ten to fifteen years federal practice, if not policy, has been to dismantle parts of this "safety net." Out of necessity, self-help has become more acceptable and perhaps that is a good thing. Minority sponsored and operated programs that assist people in the languages and styles of their own communities have become more prominent and will certainly continue to grow.

Despite this change, however, cultural resources are probably those least used by professional social workers in their encounters with clients. One reason for this is the tendency of workers to think of "resources" only as the network of community social service organizations and "referral" agencies that explicitly serve minority groups. But these are only the visible and obvious parts of the human service system, and for many clients they may be the places they go to last. Many people prefer to rely on family, friends, voluntary organizations, ministers, pharmacists, self-help books, and bartenders. Some struggle with their problems more privately, through reading, contemplation, prayer, talking to themselves, compulsive eating, or watching soap operas on television. Choices and decisions are made at many levels, and troubled individuals usually rely on the beliefs and values that are part of their personal and communal networks long before they turn for help to outsiders or professionals.

The capacity for individualizing the client within a specific cultural matrix is the genius and the challenge of effective cross-cultural social work. To reach that goal, the social worker must know all the resources available to the client, especially the less obvious ones, and how they can be used in planning and guiding intervention. The term "resources" means much more than the network of community agencies and referral services. It includes institutions, individuals, and customs for resolving problems that are indigenous to the client's own community. Indeed, these indigenous resources may be the most important, for they are less likely to fade away when public policies or governmental funding levels change. It is critical, then, that the worker know what these resources are and how they can be productively used. That kind of learning requires moving out into the community, not just as a social worker representing an agency and its interests, but as a learner seeking to understand how clients communicate on their home turf and how they participate in the familiar routines of everyday life.

Ethnic Competence as Acknowledgment of Cultural Integrity

Those raised in the Anglo-Saxon tradition tend to think of faraway cultures, such as those once studied by Margaret Mead in the Pacific Islands, as whole and intact societies, and to think of the cultures of dispossessed and displaced American

Indians and African Americans as shattered remnants of a distant and perhaps happier time. Such a view is sometimes expressed in catch phrases like "culture of poverty," "multi-problem families," "cultural deprivation," and "the Indian problem." Yet all traditions and all extant communities are by definition rich, complex, and varied. It is only the superficiality of our understanding that conceals their richness and makes it difficult to appreciate why they are important to those who live in them.

The idea that all cultures are holistic and integrated is a philosophical one, but it is also a practical, empirical matter. For instance, years ago McFee (1968) described how, in his research among a group of American Indians, some of his respondents had one verbal frame of reference when interacting with whites and another when dealing with highly traditional members of their reservation community. At times they acted and spoke as if they were Indian and at other times they acted and spoke as though they were white. The contrast seemed not to worry them much. In his striking metaphor of the "150 percent man," McFee described individuals who behaved "75 percent Indian" among other Indians, and "75 percent white" in their relations with whites. Clearly, a simplistic understanding of acculturation as a one-way journey from Indianness to whiteness masked a great deal of the complexity of Indian-white (as well as Indian-Indian) contact. Similarly, the terms so often applied to individual deviance—marginality, incomplete assimilation, cultural loss, cultural deprivation—seemed to McFee inappropriate for describing the lives of people who were "150 percent" and just that more interesting and complex because of it.

McFee's point, and it is important to our discussion, is that any culture, including one that seems traditional or homogeneous, contains a complex repertoire of responses, and this repertoire may be expanded by contact with other cultures. Thus, a once isolated culture may become an increasingly differentiated one. That is, as a culture comes into contact with others, new traits do not simply replace old ones. Rather, old traits are modified and new ones appear. People expand their cultural repertoire and creatively develop strategies of preservation and adaptation. To recognize new forms of social complexity as they emerge in the behavior of individuals or families, and to value the creativity of people's responses to social change, is to acknowledge the integrity and capability inherent in their traditions and values. This view of culture, as a source of creative complexity rather than substitutive replacement, is the philosophical essence of ethnic competence.

This stance is radically different from the policies and attitudes that have governed contacts between whites and other ethnic communities in the past. There remains a gross unwillingness, in American society at large and in some social service programs, to take seriously the notion that a multitude of life ways is truly acceptable, even more acceptable than the homogeneous norms presented to us in the mass media. Perhaps it is our unfortunate heritage of racism, of genocidal policies toward Indians, or of easily ignited fears of peril from Asia, that prevents the just resolution of these old antagonisms. In social services, however, we are in a position to move beyond these limitations; we do not have to be accused of perpetuating the inequities of either the past or present.

FIRST STEPS TOWARD ETHNIC COMPETENCE

The five characteristics of ethnic competence described above should help orient our professional work toward the needs of minority clients. By themselves, however, they are too general. The route to greater appreciation of the role of culture in human behavior requires direct observation and participation in naturalistic settings, away from the confines of offices and their imposing routines. For instance, the practitioner who has not attended a black church service or talked with a black minister probably does not understand black clients as well as he or she could. The worker serving American-Indian clients who has not spent enough time in an Indian home seeing how extended families take care of their children and their elderly, or how ritual practices help preserve traditional family ways, really does not know enough about Indian clients. These important events cannot be observed from behind an office desk, nor can they be fully understood through classroom exercises or short-term workshops. Hasty consultations with minority social workers or minority group leaders when a specific problem with a client is overwhelming is not good cross-cultural learning either.

Ethnic competence means moving beyond the job description and learning about clients through direct observation and participation in their everyday routines in naturalistic settings. Fortunately, social workers are in a good position to do that, more than most other professionals, because their work takes them into people's homes and into people's personal lives all the time.

In learning about another culture, however, no one can operate alone and without guidance. The overly eager novice often wants to slip unobserved into an unfamiliar community for "study" and "observation." (Unfortunately, this is a too familiar classroom assignment, one which is usually misguided and does little to expand anyone's cultural awareness.) These experiences, usually brief and superficial, create a false sense of knowledge and can be more accurately described as academic voyeurism than a serious effort at cross-cultural learning. It is better for the social worker to enter a community as a guest, publicly sponsored by someone who understands the learner's goals and who agrees to act as a gatekeeper and guide. Even the task of preparing to meet with a potential guide can be lengthy and tedious, requiring patient negotiating. Entering smoothly into another community also requires study, using documents and reading materials related to the local group's history and customs. Only after careful preparation and establishment of rapport with one or more guides is the learner in a position to begin anything that approximates serious participant observation.

I will describe three steps in cross-cultural learning: (1) background preparation, (2) use of cultural guides, and (3) participant observation. The steps are summarized in Figure 3.2 on page 98. Each is important and together they amount to a systematic learning style that can be easily adapted to the needs of individual learners, small groups, and even entire organizations (Green and Wilson 1983).

Who is a good cultural guide? Guides can be found anywhere, in any community, and they may or may not be community leaders. More often, they are ordinary people who can articulate well what is going on around them. Professionals who are in regular contact with clients ethnically distinct from themselves and who generally work well with them depend heavily on informed and informative insiders. Their use of cultural guides is not occasional, occurring only at times of a case management crisis. Consultation and advice-seeking are ongoing activities.

Workers who are white have a tendency to turn first (and sometimes only) to minority colleagues. That is seen as a "safe" choice. But it also has the potential for exploitation. Many minority social workers rightly view infrequent or uninformed "cultural" questions from white workers as another form of tokenism. However well intended, some whites may be surprised when minority colleagues

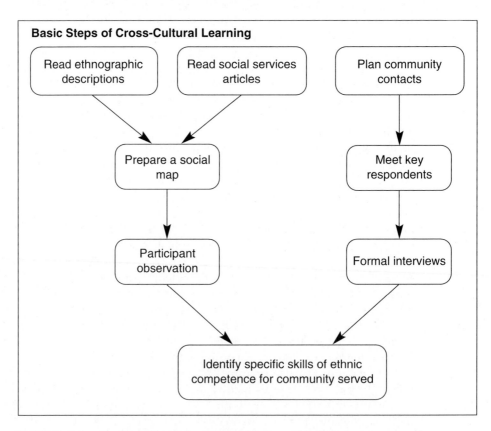

FIGURE 3.2   Cross-cultural learning involves the three processes of background preparation, use of cultural guides, and participant observation.

express irritation at requests for information on why "their people" (an objectionable phrase in itself) think and act as they do. Too often such questions are motivated by the need for a quick fix with a troublesome client, not by a desire to learn something in-depth about the cultural context of a client's needs. Cross-cultural effectiveness is possible only with a committed, long-term effort, not episodic and crisis-inspired ones. The occasional use of a minority colleague's time is not usually very effective. It certainly doesn't qualify as ethnic competence.

Entering an Unfamiliar Community

In a discussion of social research in naturalistic settings, Johnson (1975:76) notes that successful entrée into the field is not the beginning of a project so much as the result of a period of careful preparation and planning. The same can be said for the social worker's efforts to become familiar with a client community. Without careful preparation, entry into a community for the purpose of acquiring knowledge will not be as exciting and interesting as it could and should be.

Learning about unfamiliar places and people often seems to be one of the most difficult and even the most threatening aspects of acquiring ethnic competence. It appears difficult, and in some ways it is, because most of the time most of us are not required to accommodate individuals unlike ourselves except on a short-term, instrumental basis. Contact with ethnically distinctive individuals, at least for most whites, is limited to commercial transactions, routine on-the-job activities, and random encounters in public places. For most of these situations, the rules of decorum require studied indifference or cautious politeness; personal opinions about race or ethnicity, however benign or prejudiced, are not allowed to disrupt superficial agreeableness. It requires a real effort, therefore, to show more than a casual interest in others, especially when one is visiting them in their own homes and neighborhoods.

There are two helpful procedures for planning access to an unfamiliar community. The first is preparation through study of available research and documents; the second is a series of visitations for the purpose of "social mapping." These two activities should be carried out at the same time, prior to developing contacts with community members and prior to the extended interviews that will be carried out with key respondents later.

At least three sources of data are available, and all three should be utilized extensively. First, ethnographic accounts in scholarly books and articles have been written on almost every ethnic group in American society. Indeed, it is difficult to think of any group that has been overlooked by sociologists or anthropologists in their pursuit of a new, "exotic" people to study and write about. As a result of the civil rights movement and affirmative action programs at universities, many ethnic communities now produce their own researchers, and their observations can be particularly compelling. What they write should be examined closely and taken seriously. The perspectives of these writers and scholars must be a major part of any background reading program.

A second source is the literature on ethnicity and race relations that has developed within social work itself. This literature appears in the recognized, established journals and sometimes in obscure, less easily located publications. It focuses on the issues confronting minority persons in social services and on issues in developing sensitive and useful services for minority clients. Unfortunately, much of that literature is highly quantitative, or it relies on brief case reports that do not provide sufficient context. Because of these inadequacies, it must be supplemented with ethnographies or extensive case studies written by minority social workers themselves. The work of Gibbs (1988, 1989) on black youth is a particularly impressive example and her work should be mandatory reading for anyone wanting to work with this community.

A third source of information is that specific to the community or region. Because of the number of studies conducted by the government at all levels and for all kinds of reasons, it is unlikely that any city or county totally lacks descriptive information on the minority or ethnic groups resident there. The problem with this resource is difficulty of access. It is often buried in the files of government agencies, some of them social service agencies, and one would first have to learn of their existence even to ask about them. These sources, however, can be important for what they reveal about the conditions of life in many communities, and some of them are worth the trouble to find, read, and analyze.

The task of the social worker is to find and assimilate any of this information that is appropriate to his or her work and program needs. There are several reasons for doing this. No one can begin to appreciate what is going on in a community, or why, without digging into background information. A book, a scholarly article, and a government document all have something important to say that cannot be learned any other way. In addition, background research and reading provides an initial familiarity, however limited, that can help reduce the sense of anxiety and uncertainty that may accompany an initial community visit. Avoiding this necessary homework is to slight the seriousness of the job to be done.

The second procedure is to visit a community for the purpose of social mapping. Social mapping, according to Cochrane (1979), is identifying and recording the cultural resources of a community. It is making a kind of inventory at the macrosocial level. The minimal data to be included in a social map would be (1) identification and location of an ethnic group in an area; (2) description of the community's social organization; (3) description of the residents' beliefs and ideological characteristics; (4) identification of patterns of wealth, its accumulation, and its distribution; (5) description of the patterns of mobility, both geographical and social; and (6) information on access and utilization of available human services (Cochrane 1979). From a social service perspective, the development of a social map represents an effort to relate the findings of ethnographies, social service research, and other documents to the specific characteristics of the area the worker wants to understand and serve better.

The product of social mapping should be a short document containing one or more physical maps and descriptive information for each of the six items listed above, provided in sufficient detail that a stranger could read it and gain some general sense of who lives in the area, how they live, what they believe and do, and how they use social services. The document should also make clear the outstanding needs of the community, especially as they are perceived by the residents themselves. (Needless to say, that kind of information is invaluable when it comes to writing grants or justifying new services or staff positions.)

There is a good reason for taking the time to do all this background investigation. Most social service workers become aware of the characteristics and the problems of the communities they serve only after a lengthy period. The pressures of the workplace, requiring the worker to begin with clients almost immediately, delay learning about the more general attributes of the community. Information is acquired in a piecemeal way. In contrast, social mapping is highly focused and results in a tangible product; it produces a short and fast learning curve. In addition, a social map can be expanded, revised, and used by other workers in the agency. It can be used in orientations for new workers, training, and performance evaluation. It can guide improvements in the design and delivery of culturally sensitive services. Preparing such a map, especially as a personal or agency project, replicates in a small way the "community study" method that has been so productive in the development of cross-cultural understanding in the social sciences. But its basic purpose should not be forgotten: preparing social workers for a smooth entry into the community they intend to serve.

Entering a Psychiatric Client Community

There have been many studies of psychiatric hospitals and of people who are institutionalized. But with the deinstitutionalization of patients that began some years ago, and the development of halfway houses to assist them, a growing number of the chronically mentally ill have had to take care of themselves as best they could. In a major study of the culture and lifestyles of these people, Estroff (1981) spent two years doing participant observation with both clinical staff and their outpatients in a facility located in a medium-sized midwestern city. She prepared for her work by reviewing the available literature on mental illness and outpatient populations, including literature in social work, psychiatry, sociology, and medical anthropology. But to learn more about how people really lived, how they made daily decisions, and what constraints they faced on an everyday basis, she decided to live among both staff and patients as a participant observer.

Gaining access to the clinic and its staff was not difficult. Her work was in a university town and people understood that graduate students often do community research. Her entry into the client community was more difficult, partly because there were few places where they gathered as a group and partly because they were naturally suspicious of outsiders, especially "researchers" who, for all they knew, might be "spies" from the clinic.

Estroff had to construct her own social map for a diffuse community, which she considered culturally distinctive because of the particular stigmas imposed on the mentally ill. Her first task was to establish her identity and her legitimacy in living among the mentally ill when she was not so incapacitated herself. To do that she spent all the time she could in the client's natural settings: apartments, coffee shops, parks, storefronts, and alleys. "My general approach was to partici- pate *as if* I were a client in as many treatment and nontreatment aspects of clients' lives as was feasible. The purpose of these activities was twofold: to observe clients across the range of their daily lives and to participate in and experience these circumstances myself" (1981:24). She also attended staffings, participated in group work with clients, got to know community volunteers, and went to social and recreational events planned for clients. Over time, she came to feel that one of the most important elements of her subjects' lives had to be personally experi- enced: taking "meds." Under careful medical supervision, she took antipsychotic drugs for several months so she could write with more insight about the meaning of "meds" for people who were, in her words, "making it crazy."

Aside from the scholarly contribution of the research and the impact of the experience on her personal life (which was considerable), part of the value of Estroff's work was the policy and intervention recommendations she could make, based on the dual experience of researcher and knowledgeable insider. She had great sympathy for both clients and staff and generally saw staff as both commit- ted and well motivated. But they sometimes worked at cross-purposes to the values and norms of the client subculture and, lacking the kind of understanding she had acquired, they could not always appreciate why their best efforts were never enough. While it is obvious that members of the staff could not spend the time Estroff did to familiarize themselves with their own clients, it is equally obvious that they benefited from the recommendations she could make. Estroff's patience and her bravery made it possible for others to better understand the living conditions and needs of people who are poorly understood even by those who would be their benefactors.

Key Respondents as Cultural Guides

Key respondents are individuals who are knowledgeable about their community and who are able and willing to articulate that knowledge to an outsider. They can be thought of as *cultural guides,* persons who can adopt a teaching role in order to assist the worker in understanding the subtleties and complexities of a particular community. In his book on participant observation, Bogdan (1972) referred to such individuals as "gatekeepers," for they often have the power to grant access to key persons or institutions in the community. Not all key respon- dents, however, are of equal value either as guides or teachers. All that any individual knows is obviously a function of many things, including the size and composition of one's personal network, degree of participation in community organizations and activities, access to community leaders and decision makers, and ascribed characteristics such as gender and age. All these things facilitate access to some kinds of information and inhibit access to others. In judging the value of a key respondent's knowledge, therefore, the issue is not simply what information seems correct and what incorrect. The issue is assessing the significance and limits of each respondent's knowledge and knowing when it has to be supplemented or modified by information from another guide.

Simply getting information, however, is not enough. The culturally sensitive observer is often interested in things that a key respondent may take for granted, or details of daily life that some respondents may prefer to conceal. In his well-known dramaturgical model of social behavior, Goffman (1959) argued that we are all actors putting on social performances for each other. But some performances are in the "front region" of the stage, for everyone to see, and others are clearly "backstage" and partially concealed. Front region behavior is relatively open and public, and individuals conduct themselves in ways that support recognized standards of decorum. Front region behavior presumes a critical audience, present or not, to comment on the actor's behavior. In backstage regions, however, the more hidden and sometimes contradictory features of everyday life are evident, and individuals behave in ways that, while predictable or rational by certain standards of their culture, nevertheless do not coincide with publicly espoused definitions of reality.

Family life, for instance, is relatively well concealed in our own as well as many other cultures, and it could be considered a backstage region. It may be, as Leach (1968) once pointed out in an infamous remark, that the "tawdry secrets" of each and every family constitute one of the most remote and difficult-to-access backstage areas of any culture. Obviously, a key respondent, acting as a cultural guide, is not going to eagerly enter into a discussion of sensitive, often concealed matters with someone who represents an ethnic group or profession that lacks high esteem in the respondent's community. The result is that the worker seeking information is most likely to hear what the respondent believes ought to be told and little more. The solution to this difficulty is a carefully cultivated relationship of trust with a small number of individuals, relationships built over a period of time, so that the learner and each respondent come to understand and respect one another's position and purposes.

There is a tempting shortcut to working around this kind of relationship with key respondents. It is to rely on someone who identifies himself or herself as an "old hand" in the community of interest but who is a member of one's own racial or ethnic group. People like this are easy to approach, seem to be well established in their work, and appear to have all the answers and lots of "insider" information. But there are two distinct disadvantages in relying on the special cultural insights they claim to have.

First, just because someone has long association with a community does not mean they know and understand it well. Individuals can and do spend years working among persons they little comprehend, and their longevity is sometimes used as justification for flawed judgments and even obvious prejudices. From my first foreign research, I well recall white North Americans (locally called "continentals") who had lived in the Caribbean for many years and who claimed to know all about West Indian culture just because of the time they had resided there. When I started collecting my own data, however, cultivating my own guides, and spending time with West Indian families, I began to see how shallow and stereotypical the knowledge of those "old hands" really was. In workshops, I occasionally meet whites who are quite willing to "one up" others in the group with claims about their special knowledge of local Indians or Asians. Sometimes I suspect, however, they may never have extended themselves beyond a few clinical sessions with minority clients, or occasional visits to ethnic restaurants, in their pursuit of so-called "insider" information.

Second, sole reliance on a senior worker or others in an agency deprives the social worker of direct encounters outside the safe but enclosed world of bureaucracy, experiences that are essential to anyone who wants to learn about and appreciate cultural distinctiveness. Whatever knowledge the worker gets from kindly coworkers is essentially secondhand, screened through persons whose ignorance or biases may not be obvious. The kind of information they offer too often bears the mark of gossip and office folklore. It is a poor substitute for real learning about real people in situations where they, not the worker, are at home.

An additional point about key respondents is worth noting. People do not usually give their time and energy without some expectation of a return. Any relationship between the learner and a key respondent implies that a "bargain" has been struck, implicitly or explicitly. A respondent may want to aggrandize his or her own position in the community through functioning as "the expert." He or she may have a complaint concerning social services, or social workers generally, so that the appearance of the learner is an opportunity to make those opinions known. Or a respondent may expect special favors at some future time. These motives have to be kept in mind when asking anyone to commit time as a cultural guide and gatekeeper. It would be naive to act otherwise. Consequently, the learner needs to know what he or she can offer in exchange for a respondent's confidence and information.

The Joy of a Good Cultural Guide

One of the most remarkable and enduring ethnographies on the elderly is Barbara Myerhoff's *Number Our Days* (1978), a study of a Jewish senior center in California. It has become a classic in social services, anthropology, gerontology, and sociology. Myerhoff was concerned with how elderly Jews, immigrants and survivors of World War II, established and defended their Jewishness in a country where most expressions of ethnicity are suspect. The people of the center were proud, almost desperately so, of their personal and communal struggles. But as elderly parents of children who had succeeded well by the standards of the American dream, they were pained that their children had less commitment to their ethnic and religious heritage than they did.

In many ways, the senior center was a closed community. It had its formal and informal leaders, its factions, its rules of etiquette and decorum, and its prohibitions, all of which were well known to the regulars who spent their days there. Myerhoff drew the suspicion of some of the older women because she was busy being an anthropologist rather than staying home and tending to her husband and children as some of them expected. In addition, she was unfamiliar with the rural Polish and eastern European background of many of the seniors and that too put her outside their community of familiar and comfortable things. Nor did she share in many of their Old World beliefs, including the "evil eye" and the magical power of formulaic words and recitations. Being Jewish like them was not enough and did not ensure her easy entry into their small world.

To understand how these elders saw themselves—their sense of being old, Jewish, American, ethnic, and apparently forgotten by their adult children—Myerhoff worked closely with a man named Shmuel. He was well known in the center but not popular with everyone. Like many of them, he had been an internationalist, a socialist, and a Zionist, and he still was. But he also criticized freely and frequently. His targets included the policies of the Israeli government, the folk and magical beliefs of the seniors, and the compromises they made with their Jewishness as they struggled to preserve their ethnicity while affirming their Americanness. Although Shmuel sometimes referred to the others as "peasants," they respected him for his brutal honesty and his ability to articulate the subtle implications of their endless and sometimes philosophical arguments. They kept themselves warm and lively through enthusiastic talk and ingenious insight, and for that Shmuel was one of the best.

In the early weeks of her research, Myerhoff had a vague sense of the center's factional life and its leaders. The contentiousness of some in these factions astounded her. But she lacked specifics about the history and significance of their disputes. Shmuel had the answers. She also wondered why the elders were reticent to accept charitable donations when many seemed so obviously in need. Shmuel and the center manager, also a key respondent, knew why, and they demonstrated for her what correct conduct required. She was puzzled as well that the elders were so concerned that they be visible to themselves and to outsiders. She saw that visibility was a master metaphor in much of their talk. Again, Shmuel knew why that was so and he gave Myerhoff important insights that guided her work.

Could Myerhoff had written about this community with the understanding and sympathy that she did if she had not had a Shmuel to guide her? Perhaps, but he made critical observations that directed her attention to what was important to the people there. He also alerted her to missteps and misstatements and helped her understand why some things she had said meant something very different to those who heard them. Shmuel was not a formally educated man, having been a tailor most of his life, but his knowledge of the local scene was critical to her success and to the vivid picture of aging her ethnography presented. For the social worker desiring to serve Jewish elders, Myerhoff's book is obligatory reading. And Shmuel is what every social worker and social researcher would want in a cultural guide.

Participant Observation

Participant observation is a research style most commonly associated with cultural anthropology. Unfortunately, it has suggested to some investigators, particularly novices, a loose and unstructured way of acquiring information, as though one learned just by "soaking it up" through simple proximity. There is also a view among some that participant observation is a "soft," qualitative technique that results in "soft" and unreliable data.

It would be better to think of participant observation as an orientation toward research rather than a "method" as such. It is distinguished by long-term commitment to learning in detail something of the life of a community, conducted in a way that minimizes overt intrusion into the day-to-day activities of residents. Obviously, that is very different from the kinds of activity that typify most psychological and sociological research. The latter in particular, with its reliance on interview schedules, brief and highly controlled encounters, relative passivity of the interviewee, and generation of computer-friendly data, yields information that is largely divorced from social context and constrained by the preexisting categories of the interview schedule and the research team's interests. Quantitative research places the voice of the researcher in the foreground, not that of the researched. By contrast, one of the strengths of participant observation is the priority it gives to the words and behavior of people on their home territory, making it possible for the outsider to perceive subtlety and appreciate nuance.

Participant observation requires that the observer first determine, with the assistance of a cultural guide, that there are persons in the community who have specialized knowledge that is of interest for some practical reason. Then one of the specialists must be located. That is not always easy because, for a variety of reasons, people may not want contact with investigators from outside their community. That is particularly true where generations of student and academic researchers have entered and sometimes overwhelmed minority communities in their quest for data for term papers and dissertations. As most of these outsiders have been white, there is now (with good reason) a manifest resentment of further intrusion. Where social workers are concerned, there also may be ambivalence toward the profession or toward particular social service organizations. Even other social service agencies, including those organized and staffed by minority professionals, may be uneasy about the presence of outside "observers." The learner may have to depend on a cultural guide to act as a broker in finding contacts and making the necessary introductions.

It is a truism that anyone who wants to be an observer of almost any kind will have to prove that he or she is worthy of being given information. This is simply a matter of trust, and it may not come easily or painlessly. If the student-to-be can make an effective argument that, as a social service or health worker, he or she can do a better job for the people involved, it may be possible to build a working relationship with a local specialist. But that argument can also backfire, especially if the activities of the worker's own agency have not been acceptable to the host community. I vividly recall a community meeting between minority social workers and the mostly white representatives of a local university and several county and city departments, all of whom wanted to be involved with a research proposal on the minority aged. But none of the social workers wanted to be affiliated with the university or with one of the city agencies that was represented.

Throughout the meeting, I had the distinct feeling that long knives had been drawn and placed on the table. A community study of the minority aged, including participant observation, could not even begin until agreements on access and modes of cooperation could be established and, in this instance, they never were. I remember how, after the meeting, an Asian worker thanked one of the white city agency representatives for her "bravery" in coming to this failed planning session. They both knew what the difficult history of their respective organizations had been.

Once involved in a community, what should one observe? That depends on what needs to be learned. Equally important, it depends on the conceptual framework one will use in guiding observation. An explicit conceptual model is important because it identifies the issues that are important, builds on what other researchers (especially minority researchers) have previously found, and keeps the observation process "on track." In participant observation, as in any learning activity, the investigator must have some idea of what kind of information is important and what is not. It does not work to approach people with a blank or "open" mind, although inexperienced researchers and interviewers often attempt to do just that. One must have a researchable topic, some hypotheses, propositions, or testable statements. The learner needs to examine the research literature so he or she can formulate some ideas about what to look for and why it is important.

Individuals who fail to develop an informed conceptual orientation for their participant observation inevitably make two errors. First, they attempt to register and remember everything they see, thus inviting confusion, information overload, and burnout. Second, they assume a stylized (and occasionally silly) way of looking, listening, and even staring at their "subjects," using mannerisms that broadcast to everyone in the vicinity that they are being "watched" and "studied." Perpetrators of these errors invariably complain later that the situation was too complex for them to learn anything or that everything happened too fast for them to notice it all. My view is that those who indulge the conceit of the hard-boiled clinical private eye are being rude, not observant, and it is unfortunate that teachers and trainers continue to send poorly prepared student observers into minority communities (and sometimes minority agencies) to subject them to this kind of insensitivity. A theoretically explicit research plan combined with informed consent and a good cultural guide can spare both the social worker and community members these embarrassments.

Any conceptual framework must be based on previous studies in the area of the learner's interest. For example, a social worker who wants to do participant observation among traditional or alternative help providers would need to be familiar with Foster and Anderson's typology of healers (1978). They have tried to characterize what is common to all helping specialists (for example, shamen, herbalists, faith healers, or physicians) in a variety of cultures. In their formulation, all healers are recognized as specialists, people set apart in some significant way and recognized for their talents. They are also ranked; those claiming supernatural powers are generally ranked highest. They are selected and trained in some distinctive way, and that process legitimizes their claims about who they are, what they do, and where they get their authority and power. Those who seek a specialist's help are thereby assured of dealing with someone of known competence. Part of selection and training involves some form of certification, whether by a sheet of embossed paper hung on a wall or scars and regalia won by endurance in a difficult initiation ritual. All specialists have professional images and distinctive ways of working with their clients and patients. Their styles include manipulation of sacred or technologically significant objects and mannerisms that their patients expect to see during therapeutic sessions. All specialists expect some kind of payment for their services. Finally, healers and counselors often enjoy high prestige because they are believed to have powers beyond those of others and because they use those powers to enhance health and happiness.

The Foster and Anderson typology could help a social service investigator generate a list of questions to guide inquiry during participant observation. What are the distinctive signs of a specific healer's helping activity? How is he or she regarded in the community or in varying segments of it? Is there a hierarchy of specialists, and if so, where does this individual rank in that hierarchy? How were selection and training accomplished, and why do clients or patients consider them appropriate? What are the notable features of the specialist's communication style? Are there elements of it that are repeated from client to client, even expected by them as part of the curing or counseling procedure? Can these elements be described, and can their significance for helping the client be estimated?

Participant observation conducted in this way is a powerful tool for learning about the cultural features of an unfamiliar cultural scene. It is not the only research approach that can be successfully used, but it is the one most likely to elicit the kind of information that is useful to the social worker who will be confronted with culturally unfamiliar clients. When well done, the procedure alerts the worker to some of the more subtle aspects of behavior and communication and may reveal important data on client expectations that cannot be discovered in any other way. And, as should be evident, it is a technique that requires at least as much discipline as the more structured, highly quantified methods of community study favored by others.

Participant Observation among Intravenous Drug Users

Intravenous drug use is a significant risk factor in the transmission of AIDS. As police work is only partially effective in controlling illegal drugs, the problem for a group of Miami, Florida, public health workers was finding alternative ways to intervene and minimize the spread of the human immunodeficiency virus (HIV). A team headed by Page and others (1990) adopted participant observation as one of several procedures for understanding this issue more fully. Their research model called for a microdescription of the behavior associated with needles and drug paraphernalia.

Through participant observation, the researchers discovered that injection of heroin and cocaine in Miami is commonly associated with a "get-off" or "get-off house," usually a safe house or small apartment where "shooters" can go to take their drugs. "House men," just one of the many petty entrepreneurs the drug culture has created, collect fees from users both for use of the get-off house and for rental of syringes and other gear. House men assist users as needed, usually by tying an arm and locating a vein, and they generally supervise drug taking so that the neighbors or police are not alerted. Drugs are not bought or sold at these houses because penalties for selling drugs directly are more than those for possessing drug equipment (called a "gimmick"). A typical house man keeps a large number of needles in a can and distributes them to those who have paid their fee.

Over a period of time, Page and his observers discovered that in the get-offs there were strict rules for needle use and cleaning and that they were scrupulously followed. The public image of users who share needles is one of crazed and uncontrollable men, passing needles back and forth among themselves. In fact, there was an orderly and complex procedure for cleaning "gimmicks" after each use so that needles were visually clean even though they were not antiseptic. House men supplied cleaning water in small bottles, receptacles for holding "dirty" water, and even tissues for wiping out syringes. Viewed at a microbehavioral level, high AIDS risk was associated with (1) dipping needles for cleaning into the "clean" water used by others; (2) accepting drugs that someone squirted from their syringe into one's own; (3) drawing off melted drugs from a common supply used by others; and (4) contact of a dirty tissue with a needle.

The Miami group's participant observation had clear advantages to them. By observing noninstitutionalized users in a naturalistic setting, they could identify a wider range of user practices and risks than had been found in clinical studies of treatment populations. They also saw that exposure to the AIDS virus was accidental, as needles were not passed directly from one user to another. Perhaps most important, they saw that there was a clear system of rules in the get-offs and they were generally observed: the house men were key figures in assuring the orderly conduct of their business. Knowing this, health planners and social workers concerned with AIDS were in a better position to intervene by working through rather than against the subculture of the houses and their managers.

The Miami researchers note that the practices and risk behavior they identified probably vary in different parts of the country but that their participant observation would be important in researching and planning AIDS intervention with shooters in other cities: "Intercommunity variations in self-injection practices are potentially infinite, and each variant may be accompanied by different kinds of risk of HIV infection" (Page et al. 1990:69). They add that although their research was time-consuming and sometimes difficult, it was less dangerous than commonly believed and it added significantly to the knowledge base and skills of those who work to control AIDS risk. "In the fight against AIDS, it is worth the extra effort" (Page et al. 1990:69).

EMPATHY AND ETHNIC COMPETENCE

The capacity for empathy is one of the skills most social workers name as central to their profession. But is empathy really a "skill," or is it an attitude toward others that one either does or does not have? If it is a skill, how can it be learned? If it is learned, is its role in social work different when one expresses empathy with a client culturally like oneself? Social workers and social work educators often speak of "use of self" as a professional attribute. But what does that really mean when the professional knows little of the social, cultural, or psychic life of a culturally distinctive client?

These are not easy questions to answer and there is little in the way of a formula for the social worker who wishes to establish solid rapport with clients. Nor are the best of intentions good enough, for they can never substitute for good ethnographic knowledge. (As a trainer, I am always suspicious of those in my workshops who insist that an "open," "caring," or "engaged" approach will carry them through any situation.) Empathy is a complicated emotion, its behavioral expressions subtle and difficult to measure using standardized tests. It is also contextually sensitive, and its meaning for one person may not be the same for someone else. The ethnically sensitive worker will want to be alert to how his or her expressions of empathy are read by clients, especially clients unfamiliar with (or even hostile to) the habitual gestures, facial expressions, and language intonations some workers cultivate in their service relationships.

A number of researchers have looked at empathy in an effort to isolate some of its characteristics. For example, Hogan (1969) and Mehrabian and Epstein (1972) developed empathy scales that have been tested for reliability and validity and are now commonly used. Hogan found five traits often associated with empathy: perceptiveness to social cues; awareness of one's impressions on others; imaginativeness, especially as it relates to humor and to verbal play; interest in motivations, both one's own and those of others; and a high interest in verbally exploring motivations (1969:309). Empathic persons have also been shown to be nonconformists in some of their thinking and behavior, to have a strong interest in ethical behavior, and, interestingly, to be facially expressive. Empathy also involves communication. Empathic counselors are clear and unambiguous in their speech, often use words descriptive of emotional states, do not interrupt, and pace their own speech to that of their client. The psychoanalyst Kohut (1959) called empathy "vicarious introspection," a personal style that is oriented toward others but that is also analytically precise and cognitively imaginative.

But shared feelings of warmth and regard, a common view of the meaning of empathy, probably are not sufficient where the goal of the social worker is effective communication and common understanding with persons operating from different cultural starting points. Indeed, one could argue that in *any* profession that is people centered and people intensive, the capacity for "shared feeling" and "vicarious introspection" may be the minimal and weakest form of empathy. A stronger expression of empathy can be envisioned if we move away from the descriptive features of empathic persons and their capacity for introspection and focus instead on empathy as a particular kind of communication event. This is the approach adopted by Squier (1990), whose model of empathy is critical to the cross-cultural approach proposed here.

Squier argues that empathy really has two components, perspective taking and affective responsiveness. Perspective taking refers to the willingness and ability of the practitioner to elicit the client's implicit understanding of his or her needs. It also involves communicating that the client's position has been heard, that he or she may want to say more about it later, that hearing it said is important and appreciated, and that the client's views will be important in planning any services offered. Perspective taking in this sense is primarily informational. But it is also affirming or "validating" in that the social worker clearly signals that what the client has been willing to communicate has been taken seriously and the topic is still "open" so that more can be said about it later.

Affective responsiveness is the feeling tone associated with what is essentially an information exchange. Gestures, mannerisms, body movements, eye contact, and facial expressiveness must all support perspective taking. Affective tone is not in itself empathic. Rather, it is an endorsement or underlining of the importance of the information exchange. The focus of affect, at least initially, is *not* on the internal state of the client since the social worker really cannot know much about that anyway. Pretending to "feel for" or "feel with" a client is usually obvious and therefore minimally helpful. Where the worker can legitimately show great concern and interest, however, is in the client's words, thoughts, and patterns of expressiveness. These things can and should be given great seriousness in any discussion, however brief it may be. Words, not feelings, are the objects of interest. Nor is that interest an academic one. The seriousness one shows about what the client says is the core of empathy. All else is embellishment.

When empathy is understood this way (Figure 3.3 on page 112), what does it look like when it is present in a professional relationship? Squier uses a medical example to help illustrate the difference between an empathic and nonempathic response. In the first, a physician says to her patient: "It must seem almost impossible for an active person like you to come to terms with having the kind of heart condition that might limit your activities." In the second, the physician says "You are to stop all strenuous activities immediately in order to avoid any further heart attacks" (Squier 1990:332).

As examples, these two bits of discourse only begin to suggest the differences between an empathic and a technocratic care provider. Clearly, the first statement was preceded by a discussion of the patient's routine activities and what the patient hopes to return to after recovery. The empathic physician heard what the patient wanted to discuss and has acknowledged that those concerns are important. She has also conveyed that she understands that the patient's crisis is not simply a medical event but is also about a way of living. Her phrase "come to terms" indicates that she understands that "coming to terms" is the work the patient must now do. The second statement, that the patient "stop all strenuous activities immediately," is a command, not an acknowledgment of anything the patient said, and is issued from an authoritarian standpoint. It leaves nothing to discuss; it certainly does not address the readjustments that the patient must make while his health is returning.

Empathy and Ethnic Competence

- Perspective taking

     Information

     Context

     Clarification

- Affective responsiveness

     Seriousness

     Language focused

**FIGURE 3.3   Empathic communication involves
perspective taking and affective
responsiveness.**

Based on Squier 1990.

Why does the idea of empathy as a specific kind of communication event, rather than an urge to emotional engagement, make sense in a cross-cultural model of ethnic competence? Part of the answer has to do with the culture-bound nature of emotions and an appreciation of how middle-class, generally educated Americans (including those who are help providers) usually think of them. In a critique of popular American folk beliefs about what constitutes a "person" or "self," Lutz (1988) argues that Americans tend to think of emotions as "natural," as experiences that are distinct from thought or reasoning. In contrast, ideas, preferences, values, and principles of morality are believed to originate in learned experiences, taught to us by our parents, teachers, and friends as we grow up. Learning is cultural. But emotional states—fear, desire, empathy—are seen as natural, innate processes that some people have more of and some people less. She explains that:

> *emotions [in American culture] are primarily conceived of as precultural facts, as features of our biological heritage that can be identified independently of our cultural heritage. Although there is variation in the evaluation of the effect of culture and the natural substrate of our emotions on each other, the element of natural emotion counterposes itself to either the civilization of thought or the disease of alienation and forms the basis for much everyday and academic talk about emotions (Lutz 1988:70).*

When emotions are thought of as "natural" rather than cultural processes, it is a simple and obvious step to the conclusion that the same emotional experiences are widely and commonly shared by all peoples, regardless of their cultural affiliations. In this view, it is self-evident that what I feel in response to a need must be what everyone would feel. Empathy is my demonstration to you that

I literally know how you feel. However, if we put this concept of emotions within its own cultural context, we can see that it is only a variant of another American folk belief discussed above in connection with ethnicity, the belief that "under the skin" and at our inner core we are all "basically the same," desiring the same things and responding to the world in the same ways. Differences of emotional experience, like differences of ethnicity and race, are little more than ornamental covers hiding the presumed sameness of our common human nature.

Clearly, from an ethnic competence perspective, assumptions like these (and the practices that derive from them) must be approached with a most determined skepticism, especially in a field where working with the inner states of others is a significant professional activity. People of varying ethnic, racial, linguistic, or religious communities *may* share with many other Americans a bundle of similar psychic experiences and a common language for communicating those experiences. But there is no certainty that they do, and in cross-cultural relationships such similarities cannot be assumed. I would argue that where significant cultural boundaries exist, it is far more reasonable to work with the hypothesis that worker and client do *not* share an emotional universe, and that even where their language of emotional states derives from a common grammar and lexicon, that is not proof that they are expressing identical emotional states. As a rule of thumb, it makes much more sense to assume that the more remote the client's culture and experiences are from those of the social worker, the greater the possibility for distortion and failed understanding of emotional signals, whether those signals are communicated through words, body language, or facial expressions. All the more reason that empathy should be recast as attention to communication and information, not displays of emotional congruence.

The insights of Squier and Lutz undercut any claim that empathy is a matter of imaginatively putting oneself in the other's shoes. Rather, empathy is a deliberative effort to learn what one's clients or patients are trying to convey, of adopting a learner stance toward their perspective and their words. It comes not in trying to feel what the client feels but in *discovering* that there is a covert set of meanings, the "core messages," that drive the client's concerns. Language is the most important and most powerful tool the social worker has for acknowledging that. Key words, metaphors, modifiers, and other linguistic elements are direct pathways to the implicit knowledge underlying client behavior, beliefs, and expectations.

What kind of information about clients is one likely to find as part of this kind of perspective taking? Price (1987) has shown how illness stories can be a rich source of cultural knowledge, knowledge that would be critical to a social service provider seeking to develop empathy with culturally distinctive clients or patients. Illness stories contain "traces" of underlying models of illness causation, duration, and prognosis. They reveal tacit knowledge of roles, responsibilities, and sources of support. They comment implicitly on the natural, supernatural, and moral dimensions of crises. Equally important, they communicate through narration the feeling states of the speaker, often in delicate and indirect ways

(Labov and Fanshel 1977). Through the telling, the speaker tries to construct an account that others can agree is both descriptive and in some sense "true" of what one is experiencing. Empathy is the act of creatively entering into the story and becoming, with the patient or client, one of its characters.

4

LANGUAGE AND CROSS-CULTURAL SOCIAL WORK

The African-American actor Ossie Davis once complained that the English language was his enemy (1969). Bigots and discriminatory hiring practices offended him, but so did the language itself. English, he argued, perpetuated in its vocabulary all the habits of mind and verbal responses that are associated with racially founded inequities. Davis's point is obvious enough if one thinks of the slang terms used for labeling members of ethnic groups. But words do more than label. They impose an order on perception; they create categories of things and suggest something of what the categories are worth. Perhaps it was a victory of sorts when "colored" became "negro," then "Negro" was capitalized, and finally "black" replaced "Negro." Labels identify, but they may also prescribe and limit the possibilities of the persons to whom they are applied.

Words are weapons, and in Davis's view they have to be handled as such. Misuse of words can be a kind of aggression. Individuals are labeled and boxed into categories that do not apply to them. Or words are used to "mystify" others, to suggest the speaker's expertise and superior insight (Jones 1976). Language commonly becomes a weapon when people rely on clichés and buzzwords, particularly the clichés and jargon of institutions, professions, and higher education. For many in minority and ethnic groups, such use of language is threatening and offensive because it is, among other things, the language of power and coercion. The recent "English-Only Movement" is a political example of the same process, operating as it does through state legislatures and the initiative process, seeking to impose a single language throughout the country despite the significant linguistic diversity that has always characterized the American experience. Blatantly hostile to immigrant communities, such movements create special problems for those who deliver social and mental health services to non-English speakers (Comas-Diaz and Padilla 1992; Padilla et al. 1991).

But words are more than weapons. They reveal a "mental lexicon" (Aitchison 1987), the individual's storehouse of information about how the world is organized and how it operates. Words are the conveyers (and some would say the creators) of a world view for they reveal a particular and distinctive construction of reality. This is obvious enough when we think of individuals who speak languages different from our own. But it can also be true when two people use the same vocabulary and grammar. They may have different mental lexicons and distinctive if somewhat overlapping world views.

This point has been demonstrated dramatically by Gilligan (1982) and her colleagues (Gilligan and Murphy 1979; Gilligan and Belenky 1980), who looked at the speech of English-speaking men and women to see what gender differences, if any, were revealed by common speech conventions. They found that by puberty, American males and females had acquired sharply contrastive attitudes toward the world. Gilligan tested her hypothesis about gender differences by asking her subjects to discuss a number of issues bearing on personal responsibility, including responsibilities toward parents, friends, partners, and society at large. The males she interviewed commonly used a *categorical* frame of reference. That is, they described responsible conduct as a social, moral, and sometimes legal imperative, believing that "proper" behavior was best understood as rule-governed activity. They were especially concerned with restraints on action and with finding the balance between individual freedom and obligation to others. For them, responsibility was a matter of achieving that balance within a defined framework of permissible action. In their conversations with Gilligan, many men felt impelled to invoke large, abstract principles, and their primary way of thinking about personal morality was through general principles. For men, matters of fairness, justice, rights, and privileges were important, and these concepts organized even their informal, casual talk.

Women, by contrast, answered the same questions with language that was *contextual*. They described personal responsibility as the extension of self through action, as in noticing the needs of others and then doing what was necessary to meet them. Care and reciprocity, not rule formation and rule qualification, were the underlying themes in their answers. "The moral imperative that emerges repeatedly in interviews with women is an injunction to care, a responsibility to discern and alleviate the 'real and recognizable trouble' of this world. For men, the moral imperative appears rather as an injunction to respect the rights of others and thus to protect from interference the rights to life and self-fulfillment" (Gilligan 1982:100). Women also showed a tendency to think of personal responsibility in terms of relationships, in how their actions might affect others, and whether those effects were desirable in some concrete sense. In contrast to men, their thinking was "horizontal" rather than "vertical," and they cast their discussion in terms of networks and linkages rather than conceptual hierarchies.

Does this mean that women are by nature more focused on specifics, whereas men are more conceptual and abstract? Certainly not. What it suggests is that men and women in English-speaking American culture have learned to formulate their understanding of personal responsibility in ways that are both distinctive and gender-specific. To some degree, men and women live in differing cultural universes, and that is revealed in the implicit organization of their speech. Gilligan concluded that men and women spoke not only "in a different voice" but that they approached a basic American value—responsibility—in fundamentally different ways.

Gilligan's argument contains several important implications for how social workers can think about and understand cultural diversity. First, she suggests that even where men and women are homogeneous in matters of income, education, class and race, they may still live in differing conceptual and experiential subcultures. Those differences are more than minor variations in beliefs and attitudes. They have to do with how the individual confronts the world and perceives himself or herself as a participant in it. The appearance of cultural similarity or of shared language is to some degree illusory and should not be accepted at face value.

Second, Gilligan is explicit that language is a very sensitive and revealing device for identifying differences. In seeking to understand another's perspective, she looks carefully at the choices of words, phrasing, implicit and explicit themes, metaphors, and stories—exactly as they are stated by interviewees in open-ended and gently guided conversations. This linguistic data is her prime source of ethnographic information and the basis of her insight into another's world. She argues that "the way people talk about their lives is of significance, that the language they use and the connections they make reveal the world that they see and in which they act" (1982:2).

It is this idea of language as a type of behavior that I want to stress in this chapter. Social workers have not always been sensitive to their use of language with ethnic and minority clients, a criticism which is made even within the profession (Sotomayor 1977). Gelman (1980) has described the use of esoteric and jargonistic language in the helping professions as a "zero sum game." He notes that the use of such language by social service workers serves a number of functions, including the demarcation and protection of professional turf; assertion of authority over clients; and pretensions to specialized knowledge when in fact such knowledge may not exist or be fully understood. Esoteric language is one of the "rituals unique to professional culture" (Gelman 1980:50), and its misuse can have serious and unfortunate consequences for the worker-client relationship. Judith Lee (1980) has documented the hostile use of language in professional descriptions of the poor, and most social workers are aware of behind-the-scenes office discussions that include unflattering depictions of clients. Noting that "how we talk and think about a client or, perhaps more importantly, a 'class' of clients, determines how we act toward the client," Lee (1980:580) suggests that language is more than a matter of simple utterance. Speech also formulates and legitimates attitudes and behavior, almost as a causal agent.

Nor should we overlook the fact that much social and health service interviewing involves participants of differing social status and power. Feminist critics of standardized interviewing practices have drawn attention to this issue in an important and useful way. Raymond Lee notes that:

> *These [feminist] writers have argued that within the "traditional" survey inter-*
> *view interviewers have power because of an asymmetrical distribution of rights*
> *and obligations. In particular, there is a disparity of disclosure rights. The*
> *interviewer may obtain revelations from the respondent but need not reveal*
> *anything in return. Despite admonitions in the literature to establish "rapport"*
> *with the respondent, the disparity of rights between interviewer and interviewee*
> *gives that rapport a spurious and ultimately instrumental character (Lee*
> *1993:108).*

The manipulation of language, especially jargon that presumes professional expertise, is one way that power differentials are maintained. They override and discount client speech preferences and the community and beliefs which the latter imply. The problem is not that professional speech is explicitly bigoted; rather, it is that it denies an equal place to the client's voice in the interview process.

More recently, social workers, health workers, and various kinds of therapists have begun to rethink the role of language in their practice. This is an important development because Americans commonly view language as a neutral feature of everyday life. Oral and written language are popularly seen as devices for conveying information, and the information, not the way it is delivered, is all that is of interest. But language is more than referential. Sands (1988), for example, has shown how a sociolinguistic analysis of a mental health interview can lead to important insight into the client's sense of self. She found that for a depressed client, verbal repetition was a means of "cognitive rehearsal," that is, of trying out new ideas and testing old assumptions during therapy. She suggests that language analysis has an important place in the organization and evaluation of intervention. Similarly, Rumelhart (1984) has identified strategies commonly invoked by both social workers and clients in interviews to keep the discussion deliberately off target, to impose new agendas, and to manage asymmetrical power in the relationship. Her language-sensitive approach is an indication that many social workers are moving beyond language as a "tool" and thinking of it reflexively and critically. This trend is consistent with early work in counseling and therapy, perhaps best represented in social work by Labov and Fanshel (1977).

The emerging view within social and health services is that language is a cultural product, a behaviorally active agent, as well as a signifier of an individual's ethnic affiliations. Thinking self-consciously about language is one way the culturally sensitive worker can move beyond personal and professional ethnocentrism. The worker who wants to humanize the service relationship will find a focus on language helpful because it makes explicit the ways in which clients also use specialized or esoteric language to depict their particular concerns and loyalties. As does language among social workers, client language defines boundaries, conceals "insider" information from those who would attempt to penetrate group boundaries, and helps preserve a sense of specialness and dignity among those familiar with the jargon. In this sense, "language is more than a means of communicating about reality: it is a tool for constructing reality. Different languages create and express different realities" (Spradley 1979:17) and different uses of a single language create alternative realities as well.

LANGUAGE AND WORLD VIEW

Although the connection between speech and thinking is not entirely clear, one important hypothesis suggests that language influences the way people perceive the world, that it has an important role in molding the individual's perception of reality. The linguist Edward Sapir argued that language "defines experience for us by reason of its formal completeness and because of our unconscious projection of its implicit expectations into experience" (Sapir, as quoted in Mandelbaum 1949:578). He suggested that the natural world bombards our senses with stimuli and that these stimuli are sorted according to learned linguistic categories. These categories are in some sense "real" for us and are the fundamental tools of our thought. Assuming that we require language to think, and knowing that languages vary, Sapir felt that speakers of different languages will perceive and therefore construct reality in ways as distinctive as their languages. "The fact of the matter is that the 'real' world is to a large extent unconsciously built upon the language habits of the group. No two languages are sufficiently similar to be considered as representing the same social reality. The worlds in which different societies live are distinct worlds, not merely the same world with different labels attached" (Sapir, as quoted in Barnow 1963:96).

Benjamin Whorf, also a linguist, took a similar point of view and argued that the ways in which individuals organize their perceptions of the world do not constitute a uniform process that can be assumed to be the same in all groups or cultures. He argued that for any individual, the world is not objectively known, but is filtered through a cultural lens, the most important feature of which is language. He agreed with Sapir's statement that the "real world" is constructed according to the received linguistic traditions of a culture. "We see and hear and otherwise experience very largely as we do because the language habits of our community predispose certain choices of interpretation" (Whorf, as quoted in Carroll 1956:134). The work of these two linguists is well known as the Sapir-Whorf hypothesis, and it has been one of the most interesting and challenging ideas in linguistics for many years.

It is useful to see how and why Whorf came to this point of view. Before he was a linguist, he worked as a safety inspector for an insurance company. He was impressed that the name for something could influence people's behavior, even when that behavior was "objectively" inappropriate or even dangerous. He noted, for instance, that people working around gasoline storage drums and pumps were appropriately cautious in order to prevent fires. But where people worked with "empty gasoline drums," they were careless with the equipment and with their cigarettes and matches. The phrase "empty gasoline drums" suggested an absence of danger, when in fact the empty drums were at least as hazardous if not more so than the full ones, as they contained highly explosive vapors. Dangerous behavior, such as smoking, was a response to a linguistic cue, not an objective condition. In this way, language habits masked the reality of the situation and substituted a conventional and, in this example, dangerous interpretation.

Semantic labels are part of the reality-defining process. They are also indicative of sharp variations in how people classify and interpret behavior. This is well illustrated by research done some years ago on how linguistic labels were used by policymakers and researchers to categorize ghetto residents in Washington, D.C. Liebow (1967), an anthropologist, was concerned with the needs of poor people in general and of urban blacks in particular. He recognized that much of the academic research carried out among economically depressed African Americans had either implied or concluded that they were largely responsible for their own problems. While paying lip service to such factors as societal racism and unemployment among the poor and poorly educated, existing studies normally concluded that there was something pathological about urban black life itself. These studies usually identified the "female-centered family" as the scapegoat, but they often cited other things as well: "faulty childrearing practices," "illegitimacy," "absentee fathers," "inability to use money wisely," "low value placed on formal education," and a "psychological inability to make future plans and to work consistently toward the realization of those plans." This last factor has often been described as an "inability to defer gratification" and a poor sense of time management. Thus, it was assumed, poor people are poor in part because they have never learned the importance of planning and saving for the future. When they get something in the way of a financial surplus, their impulse is to spend wildly and then come up short before the next payday or the next welfare check. Indeed, this is one of the most common stereotypes about the poor and is often used to justify reductions in assistance programs.

The terms I have put in quotation marks here are semantic labels that both classify and "explain" the behavior of the people in question. But the terms are not "objective" in the sense that they represent critically examined, unbiased, and cross-culturally applicable analytical constructs. They are, rather, the linguistic habits of a particularly small segment of the larger society: largely white, highly educated researchers and policymakers, whose own value orientations derive in part from their participation in highly structured, bureaucratically organized research, teaching, and government institutions. Their language reflects some of the concerns of those institutions: pathology, legalism, analytical understanding, "intervention," and abstract generalization. The issue I raise is not whether these concerns are legitimate; for some purposes they may be. The issue is whether the labels are appropriate for understanding the people they claim to describe. How might that appropriateness be tested?

Living in close contact with those he called street corner men and their families, Liebow looked at these "problems" but from the inside, from the perspective of those involved with getting along on very little. He discovered that to phrase the issue as one of middle-class financial prudence ("deferred gratification") as opposed to lower-class psychological hedonism simply obscured the reality of the situation. From the perspective of economically poor black men and women in urban ghettos, planning and saving for the future made very little sense. They could look around at those older than themselves and see what the future would be like, and it was nothing much worth investing in. Most of those who did have jobs were in dead-end positions. No matter how hard one worked at sweeping floors or washing dishes, these things never made anyone anything other than a hardworking floor sweeper or dishwasher. Liebow's respondents perceived the future only as a continuation of the present, and the life experiences of friends and relatives were evidence for that perspective. Although the middle-class virtue of thrift may be appropriate for those who have a future to work toward, for those who do not, investing in the future makes little sense.

Viewing these issues from the point of view of participants at the bottom of the social and economic system, Liebow could not conclude that the poor have a hedonistic present-time orientation. Their "inability to defer gratification" was not an obsession with present pleasures but instead a despair for the future. Liebow's subjects could see very clearly what their future was likely to be, and they made a decision that it was not the place to risk what little they had. Thus what appears to the undiscerning outsider as a narrowly present orientation toward time is, in fact, an accurate assessment by the chronically poor of their life prospects. In this sense, the poor are as future-oriented as anyone else, perhaps even more so, and they have decided that the demands of the present must be met, because they are not likely to be different tomorrow. Phrases like "inability to defer gratification" and "present-time orientation" are, as Whorf suggested, linguistic constructions that stand for a reality that outsiders have created to suit their particular interests and needs. Whether labels like that accurately depict the real living conditions of the poor must always be taken as a hypothesis, not a fact.

LEVELS OF UNDERSTANDING

The accuracy of descriptive labels for behavior, especially when applied by members of one ethnic group to those of another, is an old problem in the social sciences. Late in the nineteenth century, anthropologists who were attempting to develop a scientific approach to the study of culture became aware of the need to overcome the ethnocentrism that was endemic to the descriptions of so-called primitive peoples made by missionaries, government agents, merchants, and travelers. Many of the pejorative terms currently used to stereotype racial and ethnic groups came from these misinformed descriptions. In challenging stereotypes, anthropologists insisted on examining and interpreting behavior in context and from the point of view of the actors, rather than from the perspective of uninformed outsiders. Thus they began to collect verbatim texts and lengthy, detailed descriptions of mundane as well as exotic customs. This approach placed a premium on gathering and interpreting information from the "native's point of view." Franz Boas, who taught the first generation of academic anthropologists (including Margaret Mead and Ruth Benedict), and who did extensive field research among the Indian inhabitants of Vancouver Island in Canada, set the tone for this approach by arguing that "if it is our serious purpose to understand the thoughts of a people, the whole analysis of experience must be based on their concepts, not ours" (Boas 1943:314, quoted in Pelto and Pelto 1978:55). That kind of work, begun in anthropology almost a century ago, is what we would now fashionably call "holistic" and "ecological."

The distinction between "their concepts, not ours" is central to any cross-cultural approach to understanding behavior, thought, and even emotion. Language is central to that task for language provides a model, if only by analogy, for the analysis of cultural features. Just as every language has its own grammatical structure, vocabulary, and distinctive vocalization, so too each culture is organized according to its own underlying logic. Based on this analogy between language and culture, an important distinction has been made in social research between "emic" and "etic" levels of analysis. Because these terms have begun to appear in a small number of social service research articles, it is important to know what they mean and their relationship to ethnic competence.

The word "etic" comes from phonetics, the study of speech sounds. Phonetics is concerned with all the possible sounds found in all languages, regardless of time or place. An international phonetic alphabet of standardized symbols is used to record those sounds and it contains, of course, many more symbols than are needed for describing any specific language. "Emic," by contrast, comes from phonemics, which is the study of the sounds that speakers of a particular language identify as "real" or "correct" to them. Phonemics concerns only the sound categories that convey meaning within a restricted community of same-language speakers.

Based on this distinction, then, anthropologists have identified two kinds of analysis. An etic analysis uses highly abstract global categories, imposed on data by a researcher in order to make some kind of large-scale comparison. It is the point of view of the outsider looking in and making analytical distinctions and judgments according to the outsider's predetermined categories. By contrast, an emic analysis is one based on localized, group-specific categories and is intended to generate an "insider's" perspective. It is the insider's world as the insiders understand it. Etic analyses are useful in making broad-scaled, cross-cultural generalizations or global statements. Emic analyses delineate the structure of a single culture in terms of the cognitive and behavioral categories that are specific to its members. Etic approaches normally obscure fine-textured detail in order to achieve generalizing power. Emic approaches forego comparative generalization in favor of a close look at a specific case.

An example can help make this important distinction clear. Suppose we are interested in doing a study of child abuse, and we want to answer two kinds of questions. First, we want to know how common the problem is in the country (or the world) as a whole, what kind of people are generally implicated in it (by class, income, occupation, gender, age, etc.), and what is being done at the national, state, and local levels to control it. Second, we want to know something about child abusers themselves, what they personally consider abusive (in contrast, for instance, to discipline, hitting, slapping, kicking, shouting, or whatever else it is they do), and what they feel triggers an episode of abusive behavior.

The questions in the first category are posed at an etic level of analysis. To answer them, we would have to agree upon a nationally (and even cross-culturally) valid definition of child abuse, something that so far has been very difficult to do (Parke and Collmer 1975; Korbin 1976). We would need to see a list of the social and personal characteristics that the research literature suggests are typical of child abusers, so that we could better predict who might or might not become an abuser. Finally, we would need good statistics from all areas of the country, or even the world, so we could be sure of the validity of our conclusions. The research might lead us to a definitive statement about the frequency of child abuse nationally or worldwide, a description of a statistically typical abuser, and policy and treatment suggestions for intervention and rehabilitation. Our understanding of abuse would be greatly enhanced by this information, because we have operated at a high level of generality and with definitions and counting procedures of interest to us as external, perhaps remote analysts of abusive behavior in the aggregate.

The second group of questions are of a different order. They concern the meaning of child maltreatment to the abusers themselves: how they think children ought to behave, what they view as permissible discipline, and how they justify harsh treatment that the law, society, or their neighbors will not permit. At an emic level, the problem for analysis is one of getting the "insider's" point of view, the reasons why maltreatment of children is acceptable or unavoidable for some adults in some circumstances. Here we are no longer working at the level of cross-cultural generalization or national statistical overviews. Rather, we want individual abusers to speak for themselves, so we can explore in depth the cognitive and affective content of their utterances. In an emic approach, it is the respondent as much as the investigator who establishes which topics are relevant for analysis of the problem. At the end of a period of detailed questioning with a small number of individuals, we may have identified many of the things that account for abusive behavior, at least among those who have participated in our study. Having viewed the world through their eyes, we may be more sympathetic to their plight. But more important, we may have gained real insight into why people mistreat children and how we can get them to change their conduct.

For purposes of cross-cultural learning, it is the emic approach that I want to emphasize. Social work does not always function at this level of understanding. Global explanations of client behavior, when they are accurate, typify a large number of people at an abstract level. Such descriptions may be useful for planning and policy purposes. But because they do not approximate client knowledge and self-awareness, they omit much that is part of the client's natural, "holistic" sense of the world. Yet it is just that information that is most needed by the worker who wants to provide culturally sensitive social and health services.

WORDS, MEANINGS, AND CLIENT PERSPECTIVES

An old idea in psychological anthropology is that the human mind organizes information by filtering it through linguistic "mazeways" and that they constitute a template that is a mental "map" of the culture in which we grow up (Wallace 1956, 1970). Thus we create order, specifically a cultural order, out of the chaos of stimuli to which we are exposed. Of course, "maps" and "mazeways" are metaphors, ways of expressing an idea for something difficult to grasp. But the principle of mapping is useful as a way of thinking about how people know what they know, and how their language reveals some of what is important to them.

In this metaphor, specific words can be thought of as points of interest on a map, the cities, roads, and topographical features that are landmarks for the user of a particular language. This point has been made by Aitchison (1987), who proposes a way of thinking about the relationship of people to their culture that, as in Gilligan's research, emphasizes words. Words are useful as indicators of how people construct meaning because we use so many of them and because they are organized in a particular way. Aitchison estimates that the average, reasonably well educated person may know as many as 250,000 words although most people underestimate their word inventory by half or more. Not only is there an abundance of thought topics contained in so many words, but the fact that we can find and organize the topics we want as quickly as we do suggests very sophisticated patterns or "mazeways" of word organization inside the brain. Aitchison's metaphor for this complex system of word storage and organization is the "mental lexicon."

In a mental lexicon, words have an "identification function." That is, they stand as a proxy for specific things, ideas, relationships, and actions. This identification function is more than a matter of dictionary-type definitions, however. Word meanings in the mind can change, quickly if necessary, and, unlike dictionaries, they are never out of date. In addition, the amount of information each of us has about a single word is far more extensive and complex than the amount of information supplied in typical dictionary entries. But the most important feature of the mental lexicon is that the meaning of words in the mind is not fixed. Their appearance on a printed page suggests that words have clarity, solidity, and permanence. But in the mind they have a different aspect, one that Aitchison calls "prototypical." That is, words only approximate the natural world we see and hear. They represent prototypical characterizations of our experiences rather than dictionary descriptions of an external reality. This makes it possible for us to use language with flexibility, economy, and especially efficiency.

It is important to have a clear sense of this seemingly obvious distinction between dictionary and social usages of language. Lakoff (1972) has said that words in natural languages (in contrast to words for technical or scientific use) have "fuzzy edges." That is, they don't have crisp, highly delimited definitions because that is not the way they are used. Their fuzzy edges are what make them prototypical. Suppose that on a hot summer day a friend says to you, "I could go for some ice cream about now," and you agree. What meaning has been communicated? Does your friend mean "a rich, sweet, creamy, frozen food made from variously flavored cream and milk products churned or stirred to a smooth consistency during the freezing process and often containing gelatin, eggs," etc.? That is what the second college edition of *Webster's New World Dictionary* says. Does that mean your friend won't settle for nonfat ice milk? How about sherbet, or frozen yogurt? Would a root beer float be out of the question? Is the part that melts and runs down the cone onto your thumb no longer "ice cream" since it is not "frozen" as the definition specifies? And what of the drips (again, no longer frozen as required by Mr. Webster) that dried, leaving a chocolate stain on your freshly laundered jeans? Is that still "ice cream"? Unless you want to get caught up in quasi-legalistic formalities with your friend, it is far better to think with words that are "fuzzy." Maybe what was being asked was if you wanted something cold, wet, and sweet, and for that a cola or even a flavored ice cube will do. One has to be a bit dense to miss the point, especially on a hot day, but we are not dense precisely because natural languages are more than compilations of dictionary renderings. They are full of nuances and implied meanings, sensitive to culture context and known, emically, by cultural insiders.

The ability to use words prototypically, as fuzzy entities in a mental lexicon, rather than as eternal verities stored up in dictionaries, is what gives spoken language its richness and flexibility. Each word doesn't have to be a perfect match to each object or action in the natural world. It is sufficient that it contain (1) identification criteria (the ice cream in our example and what a native English speaker knows "ice cream" as a physical substance happens to be) and (2) an area of reference (ice cream as cooling on hot days, something fun to eat, and associated with relaxation or even moods of nostalgia or romance).

If we make the jump from ice cream to something more serious, for example the conditions we label "depression," "abuse," "disability," or the recently fashionable "co-dependent," it becomes obvious that in ordinary talk the fuzzy edges of these words are sometimes very fuzzy indeed. Like "ice cream," they all have dictionary definitions intended to give them legal or clinical precision. But also like ice cream, they carry a richness of prototypical meanings which can make their use ambiguous in legal, clinical, or everyday conversations. Moreover, these words originated in popular speech and were imported into the thought and speech habits of professionals. That alone ought to make us even more concerned about what it is that is being communicated by clients as they describe in their own terms their emotional states, domestic crises, or accounts of recent illnesses.

This point about the slipperiness of words is of sufficient importance in the ethnic competence model that we ought to consider, if only briefly, its application to what is often taken to be explicit and scientifically useful language. The third edition of the familiar *Diagnostic and Statistical Manual of Mental Disorders* (1987), or *DSM-III-R*, defines "depression" or, more specifically, a "major depressive episode," by listing a number of diagnostic criteria. These criteria are presented as a taxonomy of episode types (pp. 222–224). The taxonomy includes such items as depressed mood, loss of interest in pleasure, weight loss or gain, sleep problems, and psychomotor agitation. Categories related to severity, duration, and seasonality are also described. However, none of these descriptive categories for a "major depressive episode" suggests anything of how patients actually experience these symptoms in their daily lives, or what they might mean to them. The manual's taxonomic approach to depression is intended for making clinical distinctions that separate depressive states from other possible disease conditions. Although such categorization is certainly not wrong as an initial strategy in diagnosis, the *DSM-III-R* representation suggests that depression is essentially a clinically isolatable entity. That means the professional's task, in this perspective, is to correctly identify clinically recognizable symptoms lurking beneath extraneous presentations such as the patient's personal idiosyncrasies and unique life experiences, thereby producing a diagnosis.

Whatever the value of these categorizations in diagnosis, they can only serve as very preliminary guides to understanding the complexities of a "major depressive episode," especially in individuals whose cultural history is different from that of the clinician or the authors of *DSM-III-R*. That is because the categorizations do not address the emic level of understanding that the social worker must access to learn, quite literally, what is on the client's mind. Our concern as cross-cultural communicators must be with meaning, and with how words represent blocks of meaningful cultural material in an emic sense. How, then, might the ethnically sensitive professional begin to assess a client or patient who has been diagnosed according to standardized criteria such as those contained in the *DSM-III-R*?

Shweder (1985) has discussed the kinds of culturally specific modifiers that must be invoked whenever psychological or psychiatric categories are used to describe or diagnose emotional functions. (Although Shweder discusses these modifiers in the context of non-Western cultures, I am suggesting that his discussion applies to cross-ethnic, cross-racial, and perhaps cross-gender and generational expressions of emotional states in our culture as well.) He describes a number of such modifiers, but for our purposes five are significant because they highlight the cultural context of psychological language, the "fuzzy edges" that are emically significant in cross-cultural relationships. His modifiers point to features often overlooked in dictionary and handbook definitions that emphasize clinical rather than cultural precision. They are summarized in Figure 4.1.

First, Shweder suggests that the culturally sensitive counselor must know something of the types of emotional states commonly reported for a given population. Even if we assume that all people have somewhat similar emotional lives and consequently suffer from a common set of emotional problems, the distribution of mental illnesses such as depression may vary by social class, ethnic group, or other social markers. Having information about that distribution is obviously useful to the counselor or social worker simply as a hedge against making gross errors of diagnosis. Data on that topic is scattered throughout the research literature of social work, psychology, and psychiatry, and the ethnically alert worker would want to make some effort to be informed simply as a matter of professional preparedness in addressing the needs of a specific population.

> • Common illness states and their descriptions
>
> • Individual interpretations
>
> • Community-wide meanings
>
> • Associated expressive styles
>
> • Illness, power, and social position

FIGURE 4.1   **Five significant cultural modifiers needed to understand psychiatric diagnostic categories.**

Based on Shweder 1991.

Second, he suggests that all emotions, illnesses, and problems have a situational or ecological aspect. The problem for the social worker is to identify those components. What specific situations in culture X are likely to invoke depression or anger or generosity? Some workers try to individualize clients by separating them from their social and cultural context. But every client is a representative of his or her own culture, and every biography is part of a group history. Individualizing the client in a culturally sensitive way means locating that individual within a specific context. Client tellings and retellings of personal concerns are usually rich with clues about what is believed about causes, circumstances, and aftereffects of illnesses or crises. These private understandings are also culturally grounded, and knowing the range and types of cultural scripts associated with particular difficulties will greatly aid the worker in deciding what can and cannot be done with a particular client bearing a specific problem.

Third, the social worker needs a sense of the culturally generated meanings attached to specific emotions or conditions. For example, in culture X is depression and discussion of it highly psychologized and individualized, as among many middle-class Americans? Or is it understood in terms that are equally metaphorical but different, perhaps through somatizing or reference to the supernatural? The meanings assigned to emotional states in many ethnic communities can go well beyond standard *DSM-III-R* categories and may involve foods conceived as medicine, mental states understood as physical sensations, and maliciousness in others attributable to hostile spirits. (It should be pointed out that highly educated middle-class whites are "ethnic" in this sense as well: hence the presence of chapels and chaplains in most hospitals and even airports.) Client accounts of their private grievances are not devoid of standardized (if fuzzy) meanings shared with ethnic compatriots, and an awareness of those meanings is essential for the ethnically responsive worker.

Fourth is the communicative aspect of emotional functioning. In some cultures, expression of emotions such as depression, anger, hate, or pride is viewed as dangerous, if not to oneself then to others. In other settings, the danger is in not expressing them but burying and avoiding them. Much of the current national interest in what is loosely called the "men's movement" focuses on acceptable ways of being masculine in a post–John Wayne era. This and other issues are the fodder of well-known television and radio talk shows in which celebrity guests help their viewers and listeners articulate their personal and emotional problems. Given this national mood of expressing what was once "hidden," it is no accident that the common metaphors of middle-class speech about communicating emotions are metaphors of physical containment ("bottled up my feelings") and explosive release ("blew my stack," "venting"), a long list of which has been compiled by Lakoff and Johnson (1980). All communities have their styles for the expression of emotion and their implicit rules on managing talk about misfortune. Indeed, in all cultures communicative competence in reference to misfortune is one of the criteria by which onlookers judge the veracity of statements about private emotional and physical states. The ethnically competent worker needs to have a sense of what that style is in his or her client's community.

Fifth, and flowing from the previous points, Shweder suggests that there lurks in all descriptions of emotional and problem states issues of power, its distribution, and its availability. How, then, does "depression" or any other debilitating condition signify relations of power and powerlessness? In what ways are personal complaints also social commentaries about other issues? These questions are not posed out of a narrowly academic research interest. Indeed, the ability of the social worker to perceive those connections and to help the client do so as well may be a significant part of intervention and empowerment. How individuals manage their own depression—through bodily denial in fasting or sleeplessness, for instance, or through indulgence or destructive behavior—is more than idiosyncratic. It is an attempt, however ill-advised, at reconstructing one's world and righting perceived wrongs. Shweder and others who favor a culturally informed approach to understanding emotional and personal problems would argue that the appreciation of power, including power differentials between those who are troubled and those who offer comfort, may be the beginning not only of humbleness about one's knowledge and skills but also of effectiveness in working with the problems of those who need our help.

LANGUAGE AND MEANING

Words are more than a quarter-million points of cognitive light in our mental lexicons. Aitchison's model also suggests that words link up to one another to make the lines, boundaries, and connections that are the second feature of our cognitive maps. Words in the mind, she says, are organized into semantic networks or fields so that they tend to cluster, again a feature very unlike a dictionary which presents each word standing alone as though it were as important and independent as every other one. These semantic networks form in several ways but we will look at only one because that is sufficient for getting a sense of the importance of word linkages for the skill of ethnographic interviewing to be discussed later.

One form of word linkage in the mind is "co-location." The idea is simple enough. Several words cluster around a single conceptual location and, sometimes, in the mind of the speaker, they seem "naturally" and automatically linked. This idea recalls psychological tests and word games where respondents are asked to give their first response to word cues. But for the social work investigator, the first response to a word cue is not what we want. Rather, we seek a full, well-elaborated response. We want to know what words the speaker uses to explicate a prototypical cluster and how other clusters are linked to it. The clustering of linked word ideas is an indicator of how the individual is conceptualizing an issue. Examples of co-location in everyday English are fairly easy to find. We commonly use expressions that reveal the power of word linkages to formulate our ideas. For example, when I "catch a cold" I attribute it to "a bug that is going around." There are two different, even contrary, notions of causation implied here but that does not trouble me. My semantic field links the verbs "catch" and "going around" to a folk medical noun, "cold," which does not rely on biomedical notions of cause and effect anyway. The point is simply that my way of thinking about "colds," and what I intend to do when I have one, is very much influenced (Sapir or Whorf might even say regulated) by the semantic network my culture has taught me and on which I rely for a self-diagnosis and treatment. How much more complicated the issue becomes when someone says, "I think I am losing my mind" or "I think people who get AIDS are being punished by God." The semantic linkage networks, and the moral urgency behind them, are truly potent in organizing perceptions and beliefs.

A second example of co-location in a semantic field is more complex and takes in much more territory than my simple example of how some American-English speakers account for their upper respiratory infections. Diabetes is a major health problem in American-Indian communities, one that has become more pronounced since Indian people have begun to substitute commodity foods (especially high-fat and sugary ones) for traditional choices. "Traditional" really has a double meaning for it covers pre-contact food sources, which for many Indian communities are still important symbolically if not economically, and government surplus foods supplied at times by Federal programs. In a study of food resources and the conceptualization of disease among the Devil's Lake Sioux in North Dakota, Lang (1990) recorded word-for-word descriptions of diabetes, a disease that is new to the Devil's Lake community. She found that "when I asked about why people thought they had diabetes, conversation invariably turned to the diabetic diet, then to traditional foods, and to reflection on their history" (1990:284).

What has history to do with diabetes? In the minds of the Dakota Sioux, a lot. They had all heard diabetes and its causes described by the mostly non-Indian staff of the local Indian Health Service clinic, and they accepted the medical explanations as probably true. But that was not their interest. In their minds, diabetes was linked with the eclipse of traditional foods and traditional medicine by commercial food and packaged pharmaceuticals. Further, diabetes was linked in their semantic networks with tuberculosis, measles, smallpox, and alcohol, all problems brought by whites. They spoke regularly (and longingly) of "old time cures" that had been forgotten and of medicine men and women in distant tribes reputed to still have healing powers. Thus diabetes, a clinically describable syndrome with a lengthy dictionary-like entry in physician's reference books, was for the Dakota Sioux an issue of the symbolic boundaries between the Dakota and white worlds.

But semantic linkage was only one part of the Dakota Sioux' alternative construction for the meaning of diabetes. Lang found that the style of talk they favored for explication of a disease model was the personal narrative. When asked to explain how they came to have diabetes, and what they thought diabetes was, her respondents went into lengthy, sometimes rambling discussions of their personal experience, told in a quiet, gentle way. Lang recognized this form of presentation as a common one for the Dakota Sioux, as well as some other Indian groups. To be able to hear and understand the semantic links that govern their ideas surrounding diabetes, she spent hours in active and patient listening. Their emic model of diabetes, once elicited, gave her insight into many other issues of health in the community; she had a "handle" on how the Dakota Sioux relate illness to their everyday experiences.

Was Lang's work (1990) of eliciting semantic data about diabetes a research extravagance, one done largely for the benefit of other research anthropologists? Hardly, and that is the point. Lang spent the time she did with Indian respondents because the local clinical staff either could not or would not. They often expressed their distress that Indian patients were "noncompliant" with dietary and medical recommendations. Lang's ethnographically sensitive approach, directed toward understanding the conceptual system that makes up the Indian view of things, led her to propose ways that clinical staff could work more effectively with their patients. She was able to do this because of her willingness to hear what the Devil's Lake Sioux had to say and why they said it the way they did.

INTERVIEWING FOR EMIC INSIGHT

The goal of the culturally responsive social service worker is to approximate what has been called "communicative competence," that is, to learn "what a speaker needs to know to communicate effectively in culturally significant settings" (Gumperz and Hymes 1972:vii). To accomplish this, the worker needs to have a strong grasp of the meanings that clients attach to behavior, events, other persons, and especially words, just as they occur in naturalistic or "culturally significant" settings. This is an obvious but often forgotten point. The practitioner whose primary concern is "getting in touch with feelings" is unfortunately limiting his or her ability to acquire and utilize cultural knowledge. "Empathy" and "openness" as primary techniques are inadequate because they presume an ability to enter into the sensibilities of another without first learning the context from which those sensibilities arise. The real skill in cross-cultural social work, as in any kind of cross-cultural learning, is to comprehend what the client knows and how that information is used in the mundane traffic of daily activities. Stylized "caring responses" are not an effective way of doing that. Rather, it is what our clients tell us about themselves, and how they do the telling, that is crucial to genuine understanding and insight.

It is surprising that in a field like social work, where interviewing is a primary work activity and where minority clients are served in numbers often higher than their representation in the total population, social work researchers have given so little attention to the dynamics of cross-cultural interviews. There are, of course, a number of studies on racial and cultural matching and the problems that may occur when the interviewer and interviewee are of a different background (Atkinson 1983; Leong 1986; Pedersen 1989). And there are many guides to interviewing as a general social service skill (Benjamin 1981; Barker 1990; Epstein 1985; Schubert 1982; and Ivey 1983 are examples). But what are the special issues for social service providers who work across cultural boundaries?

The classic statement on the social work interview is that of Alfred Kadushin (1990), whose book of that title is now in its third edition and which every practitioner should have as a desk reference. His advice is eminently sensible, presented in such an orderly way that even the casual reader will pick up useful tips on interviewing style. He describes how interviews serve a variety of purposes—exchanging information; establishing trust; and changing people and situations. They have specific phases and sequences, usually determined by the social service provider and the kind of assistance that is available. Kadushin gives special attention to what might be called the subtle intimacies of an interview—humor, knowing glances, posture, silences, mood, and personal style.

One chapter takes up cross-cultural interviewing. He presents the essential problem of communication at the very beginning:

> *The statistically typical social worker is middle class, college trained, white, young, and female. The statistically typical client is an older, lower-class female member of a minority group with less than high school education. The only significant social characteristic they hold in common is that the typical social work interviewer and the typical social work interviewee are both females (1990:303).*

So what should the statistically typical social worker make of these differences in planning and conducting an interview? Kadushin notes the error of one common worker response: that "race" or "culture" makes no difference because we are all human and pain is no less painful whether one is black or white. Although there is a fundamental generosity in such a response, there is also a fundamental problem. It discounts the value of an individual's heritage as a reservoir of experiences that help define, shape, and perhaps resolve the crisis of the moment. Official color blindness exalts what Kadushin calls the "myth of sameness" (1990:304), as if all the things a person has been over a lifetime are not relevant to what is happening now. The myth of sameness also implies that the worker has a superior insight into the nature of the presenting problem and how it can be resolved. In the color-blind response, generosity is linked with power and difference with deficits (two interesting semantic nodes!). Although the worker may in fact have considerable insight, and that is certainly what she or he is paid to provide, that insight becomes useful only when the worker can approach a problem in ways both affirming and familiar to the client. "There needs to be receptivity toward such differences and a willingness to be taught about them by the client" (Kadushin 1990:306).

What does "receptivity" in interviewing mean? Two caveats about interviewing styles in social services and related fields need to be mentioned. First, there is sometimes a tendency in interview training to promote a "stance" toward clients rather than knowledge acquisition. This idea is really an extension of the "sameness myth." Honesty, genuineness, and caring are urged as appropriate and necessary traits to help the worker break through mistrust or misunderstanding. Although laudable as personal qualities, they are not in and of themselves adequate for developing an understanding of others. Even as traits, they are highly abstract and difficult to translate into directives that can be passed on to a learner. Being open, patient, and concerned are useful in many relationships, especially those in which troubled individuals need our help, but they are not "skills" to be handily picked up in workshops or through role play.

The second limitation has to do with the skills that are needed in social work interviewing. Because one really cannot teach people to "care" about others in their professional relations, discussions of interviewing often turn from broad generalizations about rapport to specific techniques. Techniques are often described in terms of anecdotes or with reference to the results of controlled studies of interviewing, such as the effects of white interviewers on black interviewees. Generalizations about appropriate behavior are then drawn from the anecdotes and the research conclusions, as guides for students to follow. Techniques, strategies, and tactics are one response to the need to go beyond global statements about helping and caring for others (Gordon 1969). They are usually specific, and therefore they are learnable with a little practice. But the cultural appropriateness of techniques and their acceptability to ethnic group clients are highly variable. Interviewing skills that may work well with Puerto Ricans (Ghali 1977) may be quite unacceptable to Japanese Americans (Kaneshige 1973) or American Indians (Youngman and Sadongei 1974). It is difficult to speak of any specific interview techniques that can be assumed to be successful with any or all classes of minority clients.

Ethnographic interviewing from an emic perspective, however, is one way to move beyond the limits of culturally bound tactics in information gathering. It is really an interview style that doubles as a process of discovery. "Its object is to carry on a guided conversation and to elicit rich, detailed materials that can be used in qualitative analysis" (Lofland 1971:76). In particular, the interviewee's voice is given preference, and that has major implications for the helping relationship. It means that in some respects the interviewer, the worker, is also a student, and the interviewee is an instructor, guiding the student through the labyrinth of the interviewee's semantic network and culture. Attentive listening means more than just hearing the client out as part of the therapeutic process. It means that the client is in some sense an expert in defining the depth and breadth of a problem, and that the opinions of this expert must be clearly understood before analysis of the problem can begin. Simply allowing the client to ramble at length will not produce information in an efficient way, nor will it increase the social worker's understanding of the client's problems. The central idea in the ethnographic interview is that the worker channels the flow of the interview by using linguistic features of the conversation as they are provided by the client.

There is no single, standardized procedure for ethnographic interviewing. What I describe here, however, is an adaptation to social services of selected principles and methods common to cross-cultural research in the social sciences. As the preceding discussion would suggest, the model is cognitive and word oriented. It is not untested in social work, however, having been presented in a number of regional and national social work forums (including the Council on Social Work Education) and taught extensively by myself and others to social workers on the West Coast. Where I have offered the model, both in teaching and in workshop settings, I have been gratified by the positive response of both white and minority social workers. The procedures of ethnographic interviewing in social services are straightforward and, once their rationale is explained, really quite obvious. They are an attempt to move beyond exhortations to empathic understanding and make good interviewing and good listening rigorous, teachable, and learnable activities.

PLANNING THE ETHNOGRAPHIC INTERVIEW

The cross-cultural interview in social services is an adjunct to other interviewing styles. It is not intended to be a substitute for what the worker already does but rather to supplement what goes on in the normal course of interviewing, inquiry, and advising with clients and patients. The ethnographic style rests on several assumptions which I will discuss first. The basic elements of the interview are presented in Figure 4.2.

Features of Ethnographic Interviewing

- Exploratory
- Salient
- Language centered
- Efficient

FIGURE 4.2 The ethnographic interview is intended to supplement the normal social services interview.

The first and central issue, of course, is language and how it is to be understood in the interview. Kadushin (1990:3) defines the social work interview as "a conversation with a deliberate purpose, a purpose mutually accepted by the participants." There are two elements here, purpose and conversation. Clearly, purpose may be problematic, and client and social worker may have to negotiate what can be "mutually accepted" as the goals of the interview. But the meaning of a conversation is problematic as well, and it is that part of the interview I want to consider in some detail. Language communicates, but it also defines, categorizes, and establishes the meanings speakers assign to their experiences. As I have argued, language is not simply a tool for transmitting information. In the hands of a skillful interviewer, language is a window to the reality that people create and act on. To a considerable degree, then, the focus of the ethnographic interview must be on language, how the client uses it, and what it suggests about the client's state of being and thinking. Language, and especially its exploratory potential, is central to our interest.

A second concern in ethnographic interviewing is salience. In social services, we do not want or need to know everything about the cultural background of every client. What is needed is cultural data bearing on the presenting issue. If family violence is an issue, then a culture's funeral customs or food preferences are probably not salient to our interests. Family violence is a major topic in its own right, and any social worker will be fully occupied in learning about it without wandering off into other areas that are perhaps interesting but not immediately pertinent. Our concern as culturally sensitive interviewers is, at least initially, the context of the presenting problem.

There is a good reason for keeping the issue of salience prominent in any cross-cultural learning activity. In my own experience as a trainer, I sometimes see a tendency for workshop participants to go off on tangents that are interesting but not obviously relevant. Ethnicity is a field that is ripe for distractions. Some common ones include scheduling workshops around ethnic foods or visits to ethnic restaurants, or bringing in a speaker who may fairly represent the interests of a particular group but who has little knowledge of the audience's specific training needs. Generalized films, artistic performances, and tourist-like forays to minority agencies or community centers are other diversions. Some social workers have immersed themselves in the history of a particular group, a fascinating exercise in its own right but not always useful in face-to-face encounters with someone who needs help with a difficult child. On occasion, I have seen workers overwhelmed by thinking they must learn everything about another culture and, perceiving the clear impossibility of doing that, giving up in frustration. The idea of salience is to keep attention focused on what we really need to know about specific clients, the kinds of problems each one brings to us, the cultural context in which needs are embedded, and the language used to describe personal or family concerns.

A third principle concerns the veracity of what clients say. If someone seems to be stretching a point for the hearer's benefit, in the ethnographic interview that is acceptable because they are still telling us something, however encoded, about themselves, how they perceive us, and how they view the rest of the world. Yet veracity is more than simple truthfulness. We want to recognize that every client or patient has a perspective, however ill formed it might seem to be, and that we need to understand it so we can be more precise with our procedures of assessment, diagnosis, and treatment.

For example, some years ago while doing participant observation among child protective service workers, I was impressed that some workers made a special effort to understand how child abusers conceptualize their violent behavior. They wanted to find out more about what their clients believed about discipline, about child-adult relationships, and about the situations that led to violence in their home life. These workers were most explicit about their desire to get beyond "presenting problems," partly to enhance their professional effectiveness but also because they saw the effort as a means of coming to terms with a stressful and often discouraging job. Their approach was, in some ways, distinctly ethnographic because they were interested in understanding their clients at an emic as well as clinical level. Their reasoning was: Who, after all, is more of an expert on child abuse than someone who beats kids? Assuming that language is a window, and that what people say about their experiences and expectations has some kind of truth in it, working with what people say—exactly as they say it—may be the closest we can ever come to knowing why they respond to crises the way they do.

Fourth, the ethnographic interview, when combined with other kinds of social and health service interviewing, is the most efficient way to learn about cultural differences. No amount of reading in libraries, role playing in classrooms, shared experiences in staffings, or listening to experts in workshops as they go through "how to do it" lists will ever match the learning curve of a dedicated social worker who sees each client not only as an opportunity for service but also as someone who can be a teacher about some aspect of his or her life. That may seem an ambitious statement. But I believe it is true precisely because in too many workshops and years of classroom training I have been one of the so-called experts and I appreciate how my very best efforts are small compared to those of the dedicated worker who wants to add ethnographic procedures to his or her work style. The issues of language and salience combine to create a learning opportunity for the worker that is far more revealing of the realities of ethnic differences than the hours and days so often committed to training sessions on cultural awareness and racial sensitivity. I am optimistic that those practitioners who really want to use the ethnographic approach to inform and guide their efforts will experiment with the method and make it work for them.

Searching for Salience: Global Questions

Finding salience in the ethnographic interview is partly a matter of sorting among possibilities: what do I want to know that might have some significance for my work with a specific client? The technique of the guided ethnographic interview assumes that there is something problematic that is of concern to both the interviewer and the interviewee. Unlike interviews with highly structured, close-ended questions, the ethnographic interview calls for the social worker to identify in advance those aspects of the client's life that may be personally and professionally puzzling. The interviewer can list topics of general interest, write questions, and arrange them in an order that seems to make sense. The choice of opening topic is really one of personal preference. Sometimes, the specific topic is less significant than the fact that the worker is organizing his or her thoughts around some point that will be used to lead off the interview. Lofland (1971) calls this process "global sorting and ordering" and in this practice it is best to define and order problems in a way that is straightforward and obvious. "Deep" sociological or psychological probing about the "true" nature of the client's situation is not appropriate at this early stage.

For example, suppose a mental health worker is assigned to an unfamiliar area of New York City that is Puerto Rican and, further, she does not know Spanish. But as a native of the city, she heard Spanish in stores and on street corners for many years. She takes a drive through the streets with a colleague who is an "old hand" in the area. He reveals that it was predominantly Jewish until the late 1940s when Spanish-speaking people from the Caribbean—Puerto Ricans, Cubans, and others—started moving in. The housing stock is diminishing and disintegrating, the schools are underfunded and not well maintained, and those who have jobs are paid minimal wages. There is increasing crowding and the demands on public health facilities are far greater than the allocations of local government can possibly meet. Nevertheless, street life and neighborhood activities suggest a strong sense of community and a determined effort to preserve West Indian values, especially Hispanic ones, despite the evident poverty.

The new worker notices that in addition to the government-funded health centers and several hospital outpatient clinics, there are a number of private physicians, numerous pharmacies, and a pediatric clinic. There are also *botanicas* or herb shops, and many *centros*, small storefront or basement "churches" in which believers in *espiritismo* gather for services and for indigenous forms of mental health treatment, *consultas*, provided by specially trained folk healers. Although it is true that not all Puerto Ricans in New York City believe in *espiritismo*, many Puerto Ricans, other Spanish-speaking West Indians, and many Roman Catholics of other nationalities know of it, and many of them accept some of its premises and seek out its healers in times of need. Thus, formal adherence to the ideology or even great familiarity with it is not required for the many who, on occasion, make use of these practitioners. Knowledge about and utilization of *espiritismo* is far greater (if sporadic) than a simple count of *espiritismo* adherents would suggest.

This is exactly the situation studied by Harwood (1987) and others interested in indigenous healing systems, how they function as alternatives to scientific biomedicine, and why they not only persist but grow in popularity. Harwood shares a view held by many researchers with interests in Puerto Rican popular culture and its healing traditions: "(1) that spiritism resembles mainstream psychotherapies in certain specific ways and therefore undoubtedly works by the same processes and, by implication, at least as well as those therapies; and (2) that spiritist healing rites are consonant with Puerto Rican culture in important ways and for that reason are more likely to be effective than mainstream psychotherapeutic services, which in certain respects are antithetical to Puerto Rican expectations and values" (Harwood 1987:viii). The companion escorting the new worker through the neighborhood explains casually that although there is no "official" use of spiritualist healers by the agency, and certainly no funding for it, nevertheless some in the agency make informal referrals. For many clients a decision is made informally about mixing and matching service modalities. He explains that even though it is not agency practice, encouraging some clients to see spiritualists is at least suggested as a good thing in the research literature (Comas-Diaz 1987). Some workers in the agency are inclined to do that but many others are not. The new worker will need to decide what is best, one case at a time.

So what do these spiritualists do, and what makes them effective? Like all therapists, they treat people's problems, but the symptoms, diagnosis, and intervention may involve supernatural powers. Our hypothetical social worker may need to know more about that and if a visit and a formal interview could be arranged, that would be an opportunity for her to prepare a list of global questions. Starting with what is personally and professionally puzzling, she might come up with these:

1. What are the various activities of the *centros*?
2. How is a healing session conducted?
3. What other persons assist the healer, and what do they do that is important?
4. How are healers trained, and what specific skills do they say they have?
5. What distinguishes problems that are physical, supernatural, or both in their origins?
6. What are some examples of diagnoses the healer makes?
7. What are the causes of the problems healers see in their practice?

In thinking about the coming interview, the mental health worker knows she will probe in order to collect more detailed information than these questions alone would provide. They are simply a starting point. She will continuously refine the global questions, both before and during the interview, relying on the principle of salience to limit the scope of her inquiry. She will continue to ask herself: what remains that is personally and professionally puzzling? (She is, after all, planning to meet with the competition, and she needs to know what they do and why their clients like it.)

One final point needs to be made about the use of global questions in learning from clients, alternative practitioners, and even co-workers. Discourse patterns in American middle-class culture include a marked preference for "filling air time." This is not true in many communities, including many American-Indian and some ethnic European groups. For them, periods of silence are a normal part of any conversation. But most professionals in most fields are trained to be outgoing and analytical in an explicitly verbal way. As a teacher, I am well aware that I cannot hold the attention of a class if I include long, thoughtful pauses in my lectures. Similarly, interviewers who feel that they are supposed to be "in charge" often express their anxiety by keeping up a heavy flow of words. "Dead air" is seen as a failing, as though there was nothing else worthwhile to communicate. For some, it suggests a loss of control or direction. My recommendation is that when you lead off with a global question, allow the client time to answer, even if there is a period of silence, or a struggle to find the right words. Many trained workers are so anxious to help they want to jump right in and almost literally put words in the client's mouth. Yet it is the client's perspective, and especially the language, that we want to hear. Both what people say and what they don't say are valuable to us. They need to have air time too and permission to participate in the interview as they choose.

The Cultural Guide

In addition to selecting topics for the guided interview, the social worker will need to have an explanation of why the interviewee's cooperation is important. Spradley (1979:58–68) has suggested that an ethnographic interview be thought of as a friendly conversation in which the interviewer makes explicit at the beginning the purposes of the discussion but offers additional explanation only as the conversation continues. This can be an important tactic because it educates the interviewee to his or her role in the process, especially the role of "guiding" the worker through a cultural setting that is unfamiliar.

The idea of guidance is what I want to stress here. When Margaret Mead first went to a small Pacific island in the 1920s to study the experiences of adolescents in another culture, she began by listening to what young women told her both in formal interviews and in casual conversations. Although some of her research conclusions have been challenged since that time, no one has questioned the basic correctness of her approach: if you want to learn about another culture, you find individuals who can function as "tour guides" to the things that interest you. The client can be that tour guide, if he or she understands that you not only want to help meet a need but you are also interested in learning something of the individual's home community.

This is a simple point but it is one that is sometimes missed, for several reasons. First, the social worker is supposed to be the expert, and it is hard for experts to say, "I really don't know much about you and where you live." Second, clients don't usually think of themselves as being experts, especially experts in a "problem." The role of clientship, as it is established in our society, is usually thought of as a dependent, even passive one. Yet in the model I am proposing, the client's perception that there is value in one's experiences, even those that are stigmatized, is the beginning of true empowerment. The message the worker must convey is: whatever you do or have done, I want to know more about it simply because it is your experience, it is worth understanding, and you can probably teach me something new I didn't understand before. This approach is not going to work with every client. But it will work with enough that you can gain insights that might otherwise be missed.

An example will help clarify this. Some years ago, I was interviewing West Indian men who were illegal immigrants to a United States territory (the Virgin Islands) (Green 1973). Most had limited job skills, were having difficulties reestablishing their family life, and out of anger and frustration were willing to talk about their experiences as aliens in a society that did not want them. Typically, I explained that the purpose of my interview was to learn more about the needs of immigrant West Indians and that I wanted to hear about each one's particular experiences since coming to a U.S. territory. Having a list of general questions in front of me, the interviews began. The explanation of my ethnographic purposes was offered in comments interspersed throughout the conversation: "I'm new to the Virgin Islands myself, and I want to know as much as I can about what 'down islanders' do in their first week here." "Tell me how people get fake green cards since I'm not familiar with how that is done." "I've never been to [the interviewee's home island] so tell me why you think people leave there to come to St. Croix." Those kinds of questions and the small self-confessionals they contained not only established what it was I was looking for but informed the hearer that I needed guidance myself in a world filled with hazards that they knew very well. The questions elevated each interviewee to the position of "expert on survival as an illegal alien" and put me in a temporarily dependent relationship, exactly where I wanted and needed to be.

Given that my culture guides were in the island illegally, it was critical that I explain my recording procedures because there were suspicions that I might be an Immigration agent. I showed people my notes so they could see that there were no names on them. I asked them to take the pencil and write or diagram something if that seemed to help. I took no notes if they preferred that. But I always made something of a fetish about getting things exactly right, which I soon discovered was important to them. Typically, I would say things like: "I want to write all this down, word for word, so I have it just right. Is that OK with you?" "Would you say that again? I want to get your exact words here, because I'm trying to understand your anger about this." "When you talk about this with other people from your island, do they say the same things?" Such questions were intended to keep the interviewee in the "knowledgeable insider" or "tour guide" role, as one who could speak authoritatively to my interests. The technique is simple and demonstrated that I took them seriously.

There is nothing magical or difficult about this interview style. It simply keeps the learning and information collecting purposes at the center of attention. It reinforces over and over again the message that the interviewee is the expert, the cultural guide; that everything said is important and must be recorded accurately; and that as the interviewer I have a clear purpose in mind, that of getting the client's perspective, the "native point of view," as explicitly and as fully as it can be articulated. This emphasis on guiding the interview, using cues supplied mostly by the respondent, can be most helpful with individuals who ramble, who are initially distrustful, or who feel they have nothing worthy to say. Simple as it is, the procedure makes the interviewer's communication with the client much more active and productive than do the usual bland injunctions to use paraphrasing, interpretation, and "minimal encouragers" (Ivey 1971, 1983) as devices to keep things moving.

There is a subtle but important shift that takes place in an interview that moves the client into the culture guide position. As the interviewer, you want the client to know that you regard him or her as a kind of spokesperson for others in the same situation. (That is the salience issue again.) To do that, questions can be phrased so that the answers reflect a sense of speaking about the experiences of others as well as oneself. In my West Indian work, for example, I would ask: "Tell me about the different ways you have heard some people get jobs without a green card." A less helpful way of asking that question would have been, "How did you get your job without a green card?"

Consider these two forms of that question. The first says to the interviewee: I don't know or care if you are in a U.S. territory illegally but I'm very interested in what you have heard from people who are; you probably could tell me some great stories about that. The latter question suggests that as the interviewer I am interested only in what happened to my listener, not the experiences of the many others he may know about. I learned that most men would eventually tell me about their personal heroics in avoiding Immigration officers but that it was easier for them to do that after they first described what they knew happened to others. Too frequent use of the word "you" forced the person being interviewed into a narrow vision of what they were guiding me through. Personal details will inevitably appear but it is the vantage point of "expert" that the interviewer wants to keep encouraging as the stories unfold.

Culture guide questions are an example of the efficiency I mentioned above. It is one thing to delve into the private life of one person. It is something larger when we ask them to take a longer look at why they have come to us and tell us about others with concerns like their own. Culture guide questions signal an adjustment in the power relationship between social worker and client. The worker is making it clear that the client's knowledge is worth something and that part of constructive intervention is allowing the client to feel that power, to know that there are important reciprocities in the culturally sensitive interview.

Cover Terms

Neither worker nor client can specify in advance everything that will emerge in an interview, particularly in its early, exploratory stages. It would be presumptuous to assume that one could know at the start which topics are important and which are not, although many interviews are conducted exactly that way. As the interview develops, however, certain phrases and words begin to stand out, either because they are unfamiliar to the cultural outsider or because they appear to have special meaning to the interviewee. Often these are words in the vernacular of the speaker, although they need not be. These special terms, words that the respondent uses casually and with familiarity, are called "cover terms." Cover terms literally "cover" a number of ideas, objects, concepts, or relationships that are part of the client's experience. They are linked features of the individual's mental lexicon. For example, if I were interviewing a former drug user who said something like: "I quit because I just got tired of being fried all the time," the word "fried" should be immediately recognized as a cover term. It refers to a special category of experience that is familiar to those in this subculture, and it has cultural significance and psychological reality to the speaker. In my example of West Indian labor migrants, a man might have said: "You can't get into this country legally without a green card, it's your ticket to security." The expression "green card" is part of the specialized knowledge both of labor immigrants and the law enforcement officials who have the power to deport them. It is, therefore, a cover term. I occasionally hear Japanese students speak of "the Issei" and American-Indian students refer to "bloods" and "skins." Local politicians are fond of speechifying about "welfare mothers" and an acquaintance once told me how he was "born again." All of these expressions are cover terms. Cover terms can appear in nearly every sentence uttered by a respondent, and it is critical that they be recorded exactly as the interviewer hears them. They are the basic ethnographic materials around which much of the rest of the interview will be built.

Cover terms are our windows onto the mental and experiential world of others. The collection and annotation of cover terms are central tasks in seeking to understand others from a cultural, holistic perspective. Their importance became apparent to me when, some years ago at a cultural awareness training session for nurses in the Southwest, I casually suggested that they might want to learn a few of the Spanish terms for diseases they commonly saw in their Hispanic patients. I added they might even want to make up a short list and circulate it among staff on the wards, or have a Latina nurse explain to them what the disease names meant and how, in some patients, folk illness categories were as real as the biomedical ones the doctors and nurses used all the time. This simple suggestion was met by surprise ("we never thought of that before") and outright hostility ("ours is an *English*-speaking hospital and it will stay that way"). Yet without a knowledge of how their Spanish-speaking patients conceptualize illness, it would be difficult to know how they understand the medical advice they are given or how they intend to act on it.

Why are cover terms such powerful devices for eliciting information about cultural matters? In the interview, they focus attention on what the client knows, on blocks of information that can be shared with someone else. The discussion, without a lot of "you" words, emphasizes subject matter and information—client expert knowledge—rather than immediate needs or personal failings. The client in particular has less reason to feel defensive if the topic for discussion is "Why I think men want to hit someone when they are mad" rather than "Why I hit my wife whenever I'm angry." The latter issue will certainly emerge over the course of the interview but it will do so within a context in which social worker and client cooperatively reconstruct the complex of values, behavior, and expectations that surround domestic violence. Men who hit their wives are "experts" on just that kind of behavior, and if we want to ameliorate the problem we need to understand wife battering in exactly the same way they do.

Another strength of the cover term approach is the way it structures the narrative flow of the interview. The social worker's power and control is in choosing to follow the cover terms that seem interesting and worth pursuing. This is especially useful, for example, in working with older adults who sometimes ramble or are repetitive. To recall a client's previous cover term or cover phrase can keep an interview on track by redirecting attention to an earlier point. The client's control is in offering words that are points for further exploration. Using this approach, even sensitive or volatile subjects can be cautiously but systematically addressed, and neither the worker's ego nor that of the client's need be threatened because what we are talking about is our words.

In this kind of interviewing, my preference has always been to accept any statement an interviewee makes as a potential cover term or cover phrase because, if the individual offers it, it is fair game for discussion. The veracity of the client has to be the starting point and, even when I have believed I was being given a "tall tale," I have accepted it as data. A falsehood cannot be forever maintained, especially over a series of intensive interviews. Further, embellishments are important as information because they tell us what the client wants us to believe about himself or herself. In addition, some people clearly want to test the listener, to see what will be accepted. Testing is not uncommon in initial cross-cultural interviews and a willingness to accept information at face value, combined with a vigorous strategy of pursuing its implications, usually conveys the idea that we are serious about what people have to say and that we intend to stay serious, right through to the end of the conversation.

The philosophical basis for this very practical approach to speech was put nicely by Levine: "Interpersonal communication is the medium through which we discover how individuals experience their lives and how cultural beliefs shape their experience" (1982:293). To enter into other's lives, to establish empathy and build rapport, we have to enter into their conversations but in a special way, one that uses words to probe for implicit meanings and unexpected connections.

Descriptors

Words and phrases are useful because they open windows onto the experiences and thoughts of others. Alone, however, they are simply collections, additions to our own lexical inventory. The value of cover terms is that they open topics for exploration that lead to eventual intervention and treatment of the problem. By exploring the meaning of cover terms, we develop ethnographic *descriptors*. For example, suppose that the social worker and client have been discussing family issues and that the word "family" has come up several times in the conversation. What, exactly, is being discussed? Most practitioners are aware that many people live in extended families, that the nuclear, monogamous family is the mythical ideal of the white middle class, and that single-parent and even same-sex-parent families are becoming more common. Similarly, we are all aware that "family issues" and the call for a return to "traditional family values" are potent political symbols, especially in controversies that surround abortion and welfare. So what is involved when a client refers to "family" and "family life" in a particular community?

It is simply not adequate to hear a client say that her family is an "extended" one and leave it at that. The ethnically sensitive worker needs to know what "extended" means and if the client can clarify its functioning among those she thinks of as ethnic compatriots. The "extended family" is probably something quite different among immigrant Vietnamese from what it is among the Amish, Louisiana Cajuns, or barrio residents of East Los Angeles. To accept that a client's family is "extended" without pursuing the meaning of that cover term is to accept a vagueness that is not acceptable in cross-cultural interviewing. One would want to know, for example, what portion of the client's community has extended families; what its norms are and what happens when people depart from those norms; expectations of adult men and women in extended households; how money is managed and arguments are settled; what children see, hear, and do that is different from the experience of those who do not live in extended families; how elders are regarded and what expectations and practice typify their treatment. This kind of list could go on at some length but the point is clear: we need the kind of descriptive information that only careful probing of a cover term will reveal.

Collecting that information takes effort and time. So where is the efficiency in it for the busy social worker? The value of the effort is in building a knowledge base, one small and manageable bit at a time, gathered with the cooperation of a number of clients, until a general picture of life in a given community and its many variations emerges. But the effort has to be systematic. Given the chance, every client can tell us something that is new. Descriptors should be written down in a log book and periodically reviewed to see what new areas can be explored with future clients.

The collection of cover terms and descriptors over a number of interview sessions can illuminate numerous areas in the life of a community, many of them normally hidden from outsiders. The worker who is familiar with the terminology, the rituals, and daily rounds in the lives of substance abusers, illegal labor migrants, runaways, or prisoners will not only be familiar with the rationales for behavior from their point of view but will recognize familiar sequences as they unfold in interviews with new clients. Perhaps one of the most startling and exciting things that can occur, as one's sensibility to the nuances of another culture is growing, is sudden recognition of previously hidden connections, even in the most mundane and casual activities. That is when the pieces begin to fit together, we see the sense of it all, and we "get it" just the way the client does. That knowledge marks the beginning of real communicative competence and it is one of the most satisfying growth experiences the cross-cultural social worker can know.

Summary and Analysis

Raw data that have been collected from respondents over a series of interviews are just that, raw data, until some effort is made to summarize them and analyze their significance for a specific service activity. That is where we return to the issue of salience. The first step is to go through the list of cover terms and write them out as fully as possible. Group together all the descriptors associated with each term in order to fully identify its ethnographic content. At this point, most investigators will discover gaps in their information. It is wise, therefore, to begin this summary process after the first few interviews and to continue the practice with following interviews. Because data can accumulate rapidly over even a short period of time, it can soon get out of control. Systematically recording and organizing the content of cover terms is the only way to prevent information overload.

The second step is to link cover terms and their content to sequences of behavior, the "scripts" that people follow as they work through their concerns. Sequences or scripts can be described at multiple levels, from the most minute to the most elaborate. The choice of level ought to be determined in part by the practitioner's service interests. As I asked questions about the process of acquiring a green card, I identified sequences of behavior that were probably typical of many immigrants. I developed follow-up questions based on these sequences: how does a respondent find a place to live; how does he approach potential employers; what must he do to avoid detection by the immigration authorities; what does he do with the money he earns? A simple way to develop sequences is to graph them as a flowchart, using blocks and arrows to indicate the various stages of an activity and the alternative ways of accomplishing specific ends. The advantage to developing this kind of cultural road map is that the practitioner can use it to check, verify, and seek new information. As you match sequences to carefully described cover terms, an element of the client's culture begins to emerge in rough outline. That element approximates a portion of the client's psychological reality.

But sequences and their supporting cover terms have to be handled carefully, for they can all too easily lend themselves to stereotyping. Whatever interviewees may have said, each of them has a particularistic and therefore a partial view of his or her own culture. The careful social worker will want to distinguish between expectations or ideal forms of behavior and actual behavior. All people have a repertoire of idealized perceptions about how the world is supposed to work and what their place in it ought to be. But most people also recognize that there are discrepancies between the real and the ideal, even though they may not make this explicit during a conversation. It is therefore crucial to identify variations in sequences, those that are acceptable and not acceptable, according to the client's emic perspective. These variations can be explored in subsequent interviews and also described as they occur in everyday behavior.

Finally, analyze the lists of cover terms, descriptors, and sequence graphs for their implications for service delivery. This means returning to the help seeking behavior model and determining how the cover terms and descriptors illuminate client efforts to meet needs and resolve problems. For instance, many of the cover terms will probably label problem states, and the descriptors should clarify what these conditions mean to the client. You should outline how clients use helpers, whether indigenous agents or service professionals. Sequence graphs should identify alternative pathways of help-seeking and specify the reasons clients use them.

These simple steps can be followed by anyone; they do not require highly technical training. What they do require, however, is a willingness to spend the time needed to collect the information and to analyze it carefully for its relevance to your work style. Figure 4.3 summarizes the central features of the ethnographic approach to interviewing.

The result of all this effort ought to be some kind of personal guidebook or notebook, a place where you continually add to the data collected about your clients. When done systematically, this process can lead to a surprisingly sophisticated ethnographic document, one to which you can refer and which can be used in training new workers. The collection and organization of this data should have at least as high a priority as the all-too-numerous bureaucratic forms that social workers are already expected to complete. Carefully prepared information

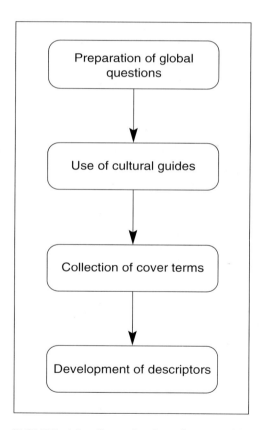

**FIGURE 4.3 Steps in the ethnographic
approach to interviewing.**

on client values, behavior, and preferences is essential for effective service delivery. Anything less means that social workers function in ignorance of what is really happening in the lives of the people they want to help. That should be professionally unacceptable. The accumulation and cultivation of ethnographic data and the shaping of such data to more accurately define the needs of clients constitutes one of the basic tasks of cross-cultural social work.

Learning the skill of ethnographic interviewing is also a way of moving beyond simplistic "cultural awareness" training formulas. In his discussion of ethnographic interviewing, Spradley speaks of "cultural scenes" (1979:21) as complex, richly organized sequences of activity where the participants understand most of what is going on but outsiders may be quite confused or uncertain. A laundry list knowledge of cultural differences (such as, "Asians respect age and defer to elders") may provide the outsider with a very minimal idea of what is taking place. But lacking any larger framework, unconnected to descriptors and a sense of scripting, the outsider really has no basis for understanding or for interventive action at all. The social worker who relies only on impressionistic observations, or on a hastily acquired potpourri of quaint "facts" about ethnic clients, will always be confused. The intent of ethnographic interviewing is not simply to acquire information but to recognize ideas, beliefs, and patterns of behavior in the contexts where they are meaningful—all as an aid to informed understanding of people's problems and appreciation of what one will have to do to effectively help resolve them.

WORKING WITH A TRANSLATOR

Obviously, not all social work can be done in English. Nor is there any reason that it should be. Even individuals who have considerable facility in English as a second language often feel that the nuances of meaning that are important to them can be conveyed best in their first or "home" language. The ethnographic interviewing style I have been describing is particularly useful in this context. Any worker who is professionally active in, for example, a Spanish-speaking community, should probably consider learning enough Spanish to understand at least some of what is being said. But what of workers whose contact with Spanish speakers is only occasional, or the worker who regularly sees a few Chinese-American clients but who perceives that learning Chinese is too much to ask? A logical solution is to collect cover terms and descriptors while working with a translator.

All languages contain an extensive vocabulary that is descriptive of physical and mental discomfort. But the goal cannot be compiling terms as though one were constructing a dictionary. What gives these terms particular power is (1) the context in which they are used and (2) their connotations within a vocabulary of suffering. That is where descriptors can be particularly useful. Descriptors are more than dictionary definitions; they are a kind of running commentary on the language of illness or pain. That commentary has to be collected over time,

- Train the translator.
- Speak to the client, not the translator.
- Discuss the meaning of cover terms.
- Repeat and summarize frequently.
- Keep the agenda short.
- Allow extra time.
- Write a summary after the interview.

FIGURE 4.4   Guidelines for working with a translator.

Based on Glasser 1983.

through the contributions of numerous social workers and clients, and it has to be written down and passed on to other workers as part of their preparation for working with clients. This process is very different from trying to learn a bit of Spanish or Japanese by signing up for classes at a local university. Cross-cultural language sensitivity for the worker is not a matter of grammar or even one of correct pronunciation. It is very much a matter of understanding contexts, especially those in which clients invoke the vocabulary of their distress.

When clients speak little or no English, a translator is essential. Glasser (1983), an anthropologist as well as social worker, has published guidelines for using interpreters. Her suggestions have the additional credibility that in her ethnographic and service work in soup kitchens in the Northeast (Glasser 1988), she learned Spanish in order to better understand the people she met. An overview of recommendations for working with a translator is shown in Figure 4.4.

Glasser notes that the social worker needs to understand the differences in power and affiliations (e.g., kin, class, or factions) that may characterize the translator and client. These issues can be especially important if the translator is someone who is simply available and is not trained or practiced in translation work. Novice translators can be expected to shield from the interviewer's "prying" unpleasant matters in their own and the client's community. Some translators may give the worker information that is so condensed (or even sanitized) that it cannot possibly convey all that the client intended.

Various suggestions for effective use of translators include facing toward and speaking to your client directly rather than speaking to the translator; keeping the translator fully involved throughout the interview; asking the client for corrections to your understanding of what was said; staying with an issue until you understand it fully; emphasizing repetition; and avoiding use of family members of clients (especially children) as interpreters (Putsch 1985). Monolingualism is a handicap in any cross-cultural, cross-language encounter and, as the service professional, it is your responsibility, not that of the client, to take the lead in overcoming it.

Good translators are usually people who are practiced in the skill, who know well what the interviewer wants and why, and who appreciate the pressures on both the client and the social worker during an interview session. They are like good umpires or referees in a sporting event: they strive to be completely fair, to maintain the activity's smooth progress, to convey information promptly and accurately, and to remain unobtrusive. A good translator can signal to the worker the client's expectations and uncertainties. She or he can also convey to the client the worker's sense of confidentiality, desire to help, and trustworthiness. Workers with whom I have discussed this and who have had this kind of interview experience are usually very enthusiastic about "their" translator and the interesting nature of this kind of communication. That satisfaction usually overrides the inevitable frustrations of the slow pace of translated interviews and the natural difficulties of communicating complex ideas across language boundaries.

IS ETHNOGRAPHIC INTERVIEWING THERAPEUTIC?

Throughout this discussion, I have described the ethnographic interview as a learning device, something to benefit the service provider. But is there a sense in which ethnographic interviewing may have benefits for clients, benefits that could even be labeled therapeutic? I do not want to make any special claims for ethnographic interviewing because there is little research or discussion of its therapeutic potential. But I think the possibility is worth considering. I mention it, too, because if such benefits exist, I suspect it will be social workers, not social scientists, who will discover them.

An example is suggestive of these possibilities. Ortiz (1985) describes how, during her work among Cuban refugee women in Los Angeles, she followed standard anthropological interviewing procedures to collect life history narratives. She met regularly with a number of respondents to tape record interviews that she later transcribed for analysis. What was striking to her, however, were the effects of the interviews on these women. First, telling others in a systematic way what they had learned and felt over a lifetime gave a sense of validity to their experiences. Several older women expressed a profound satisfaction in having told a life story that only they could tell and that others around them found interesting and important.

Second, there was a cathartic effect. Ortiz notes that these women "had never had an opportunity to tell their entire stories to anyone, to have their pain acknowledged by an outsider, and to see their lives as a process over time" (1985:108). This was important because outsiders (including other Latinos as well as Anglos) were prone to see refugee Cubans as people who had left their country for selfish reasons. The opportunity to explore the trauma of that experience, in a systematic and unobtrusive way, "was almost uniformly acknowledged as a welcome relief" (1985:109). Third, the interviews led to increased understanding among the women themselves and others around them. That was important because these women lived in large, multigeneration, extended families that were often squeezed into crowded apartments. Despite the intensity of their contact, family members often avoided or discounted communication of personal feelings or needs because it was potentially disruptive to family life overall.

How can we generalize from an example like this, to make it useful to social workers serving other clients in other communities? In a discussion of the universal features of therapeutic processes, Csordas and Kleinman (1990) suggest three healing aspects of communication, which I suggest are potential aspects of skillful cross-cultural interviewing as well. The first of these is transactional. The individual comes to perceive similarities between privatized experiences and those of some larger entity such as one's community, nation, race, or a religious figure or theme. The discovery and verbal articulation of that correspondence is a transactional event in which selfhood is linked, however briefly or imperfectly, to something larger, transcending, even universal. This connection between self and something universalizing may be somewhat indeterminant, but it is certainly not mystical or unusual. Dow (1986) describes in detail how those who seek healing for a variety of mental and physical conditions often come to terms with their illness by realizing that what has happened is part of some larger and more significant perspective. In encouraging the client or patient to explore the meaning implicit in experiences of pain, the culturally sensitive social worker is encouraging this kind of therapeutic transaction. Clearly, however, interviewing at this level is far removed from (and occurs much later than) the use of ethnographic techniques to simply gather background information.

The second aspect is social support. There is an extensive literature on the relationship of religious participation to the general health of individuals (Levin and Vanderpool 1987, for example). People who actively practice their religion tend to be healthier than those who practice none. But we do not need to confine ourselves to religion. Alcoholics Anonymous and similar organizations explicitly ask participants to forsake former ways, account for and confess behavior, and be absorbed by the group. Healing in these settings is thought to derive, in part, from the intense involvement of the participants. Although in social services such intensity in relationships between workers and clients can lead to problems in the termination phase of treatment, nevertheless the supportive aspect of the ethnographic approach is clear. Elevating the client to the honored position of "culture guide" creates an expectation that the client and worker have formed a small community of inquiry (as well as treatment) and that the client is valued, not just as the bearer of a problem, but also as someone who can contribute to the worker's professional capabilities. The positive mood that such a stance generates should not be underestimated.

Third, all storytelling, whether about oneself or what one knows about the neighbors, has a performative aspect. An interview is more than talk and information; it is a little play in which as dramatists we present ourselves to others in the way we would like them to see us, thereby making claims about the kind of person we are (Goffman 1959). These claims may be deeply held and thoroughly believed, or they may not. But in telling about ourselves, we all have the opportunity to elaborate and think about what we would like to be. Every culture comes with its own repertoire of expressive forms, in both spoken and body language. Our individualized use of these forms, bending them to suit the image we have of ourselves, is the aesthetic dimension of our selfhood. It is our style. Although we all respond to cultural imperatives, doing what we were taught to do, we are not automatons who respond unthinkingly. We are creative participants who find our unique ways for carrying out the role of bus driver, probation officer, or even town drunk. We are unique because we take what we have inherited from a history and a community and turn it to our private uses. In a sense, we are all good and earnest actors, drawing on the scripted idioms of our culture to create a satisfying persona for ourselves.

Is ethnographic interviewing therapeutic? Perhaps it can be if it is appropriately used by a skilled practitioner. It can help clients put their personal concerns in a larger, even ennobling perspective. It can help establish a relationship of trust between worker and client, a relationship that also links differing cultural communities. It allows people to describe, even invent, their persona, an essential life development task from the point of view of psychoanalyst Erik Erikson. The basic purpose of ethnographic interviewing is information gathering but that does not mean it cannot have other consequences for both worker and client.

COMMUNICATION BLUNDERS

Despite everyone's best efforts, communication blunders inevitably occur in cross-cultural work. They are a source of embarrassment and, sometimes, great pain. Why do they happen and what, if anything, ought we do about them? Can they be avoided and is there some way we can learn from them so that we do not repeat them? When problems occur, I ask students in my workshops not to look at themselves first (conscientious people are sometimes prone to self-blame) but to think about the situation instead.

For most people, interviews are not ordinary or even pleasant activities. An interview is usually the imposition of one speaker's linguistic agenda on another—the problem of power again. Kadushin recognizes this limitation when he notes that all interviews are structured by a purpose; that one partner must take responsibility to keep the conversation moving toward the achievement of that purpose; and that the relationship of the participants is asymmetrical and often nonreciprocal (1990:5). When this becomes a problem, at least in relationships intended to be helping ones, it is the more powerful speaker who imposes a linguistic style on the less powerful, especially in a manner implying that the imposition is natural or normal. This kind of verbal control makes it impossible for the more powerful speaker to hear what the less powerful speaker wants to convey. (How many times, for instance, do we all miss what someone is saying because we are mentally rehearsing what we intend to say in reply?) Mystification, domination, and distortion through the weaponry of words are the antitheses of empowerment and ethnographic approaches.

From analyzing interviews in a variety of fields, Briggs (1986a) has identified several areas where communication fails and where the likelihood of blunders is high. His own work, it should be added, is grounded in years of research and interviewing among Spanish-speaking families in New Mexico, families tracing their ancestry in the American Southwest as far back as the seventeenth century. Briggs's analysis is detailed and complex but several of the subtle and sensitive issues he discusses are what he calls "channel," "key," and "genre."

A *channel* is an idiom of communication. Generally, the most important channel in an interview is speech, but it is not the only one. Information is revealed through the most casual of gestures or body positions. The feet, hands, and head do not go into a holding pattern while the mouth speaks. They work in conjunction with the rest of the body to convey additional information about what is going on. The same can be said of posture, eye movements, and the use of artifacts such as desks or official-looking writing pads. Dress is always important, from the worker dressed for success to the client dressed to impress. Objects radiate messages which are always important to affirming self-identity and the properness of place. Most professionals do their work in offices and office codes, implicit and explicit, usually have little to do with the everyday world of clients and patients. All objects, from doctor's white smocks to the layout of conference rooms, have social histories and those histories are rarely neutral. Objects, codes, professional standards, and styles all reflect decisions about correctness and propriety, decisions made for reasons that seemed useful at one time. Whether or not they are valid for us now, they still operate as channels for saying something about who we are and what our place (and the places of others) ought to be.

Key and genre refer to performative aspects of speech events. In a language-dependent field such as social services, word choices, intonations, and speed of delivery all convey messages about what we think is important during a conversation. *Key* is the feeling tone of speech, all the expressive devices people use to say such things as "I am comfortable (or uncomfortable) as I tell you about this." *Genre* includes language forms that are creatively interjected into conversation. They may be jokes, little laughs, asides, clichés, allusions, verbal fillers, turn taking, topic shifting, rhetorical questions, and all the other linguistic devices that decorate and add interest to speech. Everyone uses them all the time, sometimes to the annoyance of others. They represent the empty spaces between grammar and elocution, tiny arenas where we are all invited to be inventive, clever, or just trite in our presentation of self. The importance of key and genre in cross-cultural interviewing is that they are very sensitive to context. They derive from an enormous reservoir of unwritten history and shared contemporary experience. Each speaker intuitively understands that and replicates a communal experience in his or her speech. To ignore that reservoir, to take a stereotypical Sgt. Friday "just the facts, mam" approach to an interview, is to cut off much that is challenging and also fun and rewarding in acquiring cross-cultural communicative skills.

What might a social worker do about channel, key, and genre in developing a personal interviewing style? The ethnographic interview is a procedure that sensitizes us to speech, the primary channel in most of our work with others. It challenges the traditional relationship of dominance and subordination in interviews, and creates a more balanced distribution of power because of its emphasis on the client as a cultural guide and teacher. Key in social services has usually been thought of as "active listening." But in the ethnographic approach, the emphasis is shifted away from listening for "deep" psychological insight in favor of listening for cultural information. We want to know more about context so we can get a holistic view of the client and his or her concerns. The worker's response, what is meant by key, is that of a respectful learner.

Genre, however, is more difficult. It includes idiosyncrasies, mannerisms, and speech habits that vary from person to person. Sometimes they are helpful ("I understand") and sometimes they are only fillers that can become wearying to the hearer ("Ya know" and "I mean" are probably the most common). Genre also includes styles of interaction that are sometimes taught to social work students. These include admonitions to rephrase or repeat what clients say, or to use minimal encouragers (things like "yes, tell me more" and "uh-huh") to keep a conversation going. More important to cross-cultural interviewing, however, is recognizing that genre is an area in which it is dangerously easy to commit a verbal faux pas. Unintended slips of the tongue, unfortunate phrases with double meanings, and assumptions about others that the others do not share, can get people into difficulty quickly. Individuals from ethnic and minority communities are far more sensitive to these matters than most whites realize. This is where minority professionals can be especially helpful. They are aware of the subtleties and the bombshells that hide in what seems to be neutral language. They should always be consulted about what is good and what is poor language etiquette with the clients from their communities.

I do not want to leave this topic, however, with grave warnings about verbally inflicted self-destruction, for that would be much too pessimistic. There is a happier side to all of this. Briggs suggests that there is an element of art in how people use language. We can think of all experience, including our own, as constructive and reconstructive, a notion compatible with Erik Erikson's ideas about life tasks and adult development. That is, we invent and reinvent ourselves as we go from place to place, contact to contact, and crisis to crisis. Reinvention is necessary because each new event is both like and unlike every other event we have encountered. We draw on personal memory but also on cultural forms, including our received language and a repertoire of standardized gestures. It may be that the highest achievement in cross-cultural communication is sharing in the creative, aesthetic dimension of other people's experiences. Such a level of engagement is probably beyond what most social service practitioners need or even desire. But its possibility suggests the very humane and humanistic dimensions of cultural sensitivity. It also helps us understand, and perhaps excuse ourselves a little more easily, when our best efforts are less successful than we want them to be.

CONSTRAINTS ON CROSS-CULTURAL COMMUNICATION

In the model of ethnic group relations discussed in the first chapter, I suggested that all communities seek to protect their distinctiveness by regulating the character and quality of intergroup contacts. I also suggested that the subculture of social work professionals is in some ways like an ethnic group, with its own values, knowledge, and patterns of organization. In the area of communication with ethnic or minority cultural "outsiders," that distinctiveness is forcefully, and sometimes painfully, evident.

Consider briefly the social setting in which many social work interviews take place. Interviews are usually held in offices, away from the more naturalistic settings where most clients are comfortable. They are highly structured events, both in terms of time (with specific, marked beginnings and ends) and the relative status (usually unequal) of the participants. Emphasis is placed on the immediate problem that has brought the participants together, and there is little time for informalities other than handshakes or cursory comments about the weather. The interview is expected to have an "outcome"—a verbal agreement, a signed document, a prod to some kind of action. This outcome is expected to be additive to the ongoing interviewer-interviewee relationship and the "work" the client is doing. Finally, the relationship is expected to terminate at some future point so that the social worker can go on to other, similarly structured encounters with other clients. In short, this style of interviewing suggests a certain type of culture: bureaucratic and corporate.

There would be nothing wrong with this as the prevailing style of worker-client communication if social workers, as members of bureaucratic organizations, only interviewed other office workers. But precisely because minority groups have been largely excluded from participation in the institutions of power, their communicative styles are adapted to cultural settings other than bureaucratic ones. Those settings are the home or the neighborhood tavern, the storefront church, or the nearby park. The people in these places have multiple interests in one another, not a single "problem" to discuss, and they are often of the same or similar status. A high value may be placed on the freedom to come and go, on entering and leaving conversations with no reference to clock time at all. In addition, personal contacts in these settings are considered interesting and valuable in their own right and do not require an "outcome" or a progression through stages toward an eventual termination. The imposition of an agency-oriented, "professional" communication style on a minority client could well be regarded, from the "native's point of view," as a highly aggressive and ethnocentric cross-cultural event.

Is there a solution to the dilemma of having to employ a bureaucratically styled form of communication when its appropriateness and utility are uncertain? One part of the answer is recognizing the limitations of all interviewing. The guided, intensive interview, with its emphasis on the client's ethnographic perspective, goes a long way toward overcoming rigidness and superficiality. But it is still a highly structured linguistic event that is intended in many ways to serve the information-gathering and people-processing interests of the bureaucratic culture. The challenge to the ethnically sensitive practitioner is to expand personal and professional capabilities beyond the superficiality of most crosscultural service contacts. That takes effort, the effort of preparing global questions, of listening carefully for cover terms, and of systematically recording and reviewing new information. It takes the effort of playing with the model, trying out ways of adapting it to one's tasks, agency, and clients. It takes the kind of critical self-awareness that most good social workers have and redirecting it toward learning a new set of relationship-building skills. It requires a genuinely experimental attitude toward one's work and toward clients, an attitude that not all agencies are willing to support.

The other part of the solution is refusing to be content with building one's knowledge base through interviews alone. Consider the background of many minority group professionals. Whatever specific helping skills they may have learned in their formal education, they have been added to prior personal experience. As I have already noted, minority professionals often make commitments of time and energy to a home community far beyond that of their white colleagues. They do this because they are a resource to those communities. But they also do it because they know that they must be kept informed of the needs of those they serve. As professionals, they do not lose their home-grown communicative competence. White professionals, and minority professionals working in ethnic communities that are unfamiliar to them, can follow this example. They can inform themselves by seeking contacts and relationships outside their bureaucratically defined responsibilities. In that way, the limitations of interviewing can be partially overcome.

PART II

ETHNIC COMPETENCE IN MULTICULTURAL CONTEXTS

Part II describes an approach to cross-cultural problem resolution and applies it to specific communities. Individual chapters discuss the special needs and concerns of African-American, Native-American, Asian- and Pacific-American, and Spanish-speaking peoples. Information is provided on the historical and contemporary diversity of these communities and how that diversity influences the way individuals view and use social services. Ethnic competence is shown to be a practical and necessary feature of service delivery to ethnic clients and their families. Consistent with the ethnographic approach, these chapters suggest an explicitly comparative way for practitioners to analyze their relationships with culturally unfamiliar clients and communities.

5

CROSS-CULTURAL PROBLEM RESOLUTION

What specifically are the cultural differences that make a difference? How can we recognize them when we see them and what, if anything, should we do about them? Are there professional guidelines for this sort of human services work? Or do we just rely on intuition and good intentions?

And what if commonsense understanding does not get us very far? Can't we call in an expert (that usually means a minority professional) for some quick advice on what to do? Wouldn't he or she help us solve our difficulties with some of our clients?

Alicia Lieberman (1990), an expert on the mental health of very young children and a researcher on the child-rearing styles of Latina women in California, was asked to discuss cultural issues with a group of service professionals who worked with women with blind infants. These social workers complained that their Latina clients were emotionally suffocating the children by trying to do too much for them. For example, they carried them about instead of letting them learn to crawl. They bottlefed them well into the years when "other" (meaning Anglo) women encouraged their children to eat on their own. The workers felt that all children need to learn self-reliance early, especially blind children, and they wanted Lieberman to give them some cultural "tips" on how to persuade their clients of the importance of autonomy for healthy children.

According to Lieberman, she refused to acquiesce in this request, and subsequent discussion in her training session became tense. She writes that "it dawned on me that we were actually unconsciously reenacting the struggle between workers and the resistant Latina mothers in their work together. I was identifying with the mothers, refusing to yield to the intervenors' demands to let go of the child and to foster the child's autonomy. The intervenors understandably perceived me as one more Latina mother who was opposing their efforts" (1990:110).

Was Lieberman being unreasonable in defending these apparently controlling mothers? Was the workers' request for her professional guidance culturally sensitive? Was the intended use of "cultural information" by the workers legitimate? What were the divergent, underlying cultural assumptions about child rearing and family life in the opposing positions of Lieberman and her trainee audience? How might those assumptions have been identified and resolved, or could they be resolved at all?

Some of the important ethnographic issues in this example include:

1. Latina child-rearing preferences that the workers apparently did not understand or recognize.

2. Anglo child-rearing preferences that Hispanic clients rejected, perceiving them as unreasonable.

3. The Latina mothers' ambivalence when encouraged by cultural outsiders to raise children in ways other than those they understood and commonly saw in their own community.

4. The Anglo workers' apparent lack of awareness of how their cultural (i.e., professional) assumptions were driving their intervention decisions, and their inability or unwillingness to articulate those assumptions.

5. The cross-cultural trainer's unwillingness to offer an insider's "tip list" that might enlarge the worker's impact on clients from an unfamiliar community.

6. The workers' and trainer's inability to generalize from specific clients to larger issues of cross-cultural social work. For example, they might have also asked: how are the child-rearing practices of other Spanish-speaking mothers with blind children, such as mothers from Panama, Colombia, or Puerto Rico, similar or different from those of the current clients, and what are the intervention implications of that diversity?

In terms of ethnically competent practice, these issues point to at least three major problem areas: (1) the adequacy of the social workers' ethnographic knowledge of child rearing among their clients; (2) how the workers determined that a "problem" existed and whether their determination was, by some clearly articulated standard, a valid one; and (3) the workers' ability to know if they had made an appropriate "fit" between their diagnosis, assessment, and treatment plans and the perceived needs and expectations of their Spanish-speaking clients.

As I have discussed in previous chapters, in an explicitly cultural approach to problem resolution, the alert and responsive social worker has several tasks. They are not difficult but they do require a way of thinking about clients and about problem solving that is only now beginning to emerge in social services training. First is the importance of a *knowledge base* adequate to day-to-day work with clients. Second is the need to identify the cultural *salience* of specific client issues and make their behavioral dimensions explicit. Third, in developing treatment plans it is critical to think of how the client functions not only in a psychological sense but in a social *context* as well. Fourth is recognition of the meaning of *power* in service encounters, especially as it relates to treatment outcomes and

- Build a knowledge base.
- Determine cultural salience of presenting problems.
- Individualize clients within context of community variations.
- Recognize power differentials between client and professional.
- Think comparatively.

FIGURE 5.1   **Five steps leading to ethnic competence in a specifically cultural approach to problem resolution.**

evaluations of "what worked" and what did not. Fifth, good cross-cultural work depends on the ability to think *comparatively,* to see individual cases as both unique and as exemplars of community-wide processes and needs. Figure 5.1 identifies each of these features. None is more important than any other, and all must be considered significant in developing a holistic approach to working with clients and patients.

PHASE I: BUILDING THE CRITICAL KNOWLEDGE BASE

It is probably the general failure of American education to deal honestly and directly with the fact of cultural pluralism that leaves most of us uninformed about what cultural diversity really means for us, or how we can proceed to understand it in a useful way. Some social workers have felt they had to immerse themselves in the history, sociology, literature, music, and even the cuisine (*especially* the cuisine) of their client communities to gain enough knowledge to function effectively as service providers. Although I don't discourage that kind of academic industry for those who have the time and energy, I think that for busy professionals there is a more appropriate and more efficient way to go about it. But it requires a comparable level of commitment and rigor. To begin, we need to rethink for a moment the earlier discussion of ethnicity.

You will recall that near the end of chapter 1, I suggested that social and health service organizations are cultural entities themselves. They develop their own set of rules, values, and expectations that govern the activities of their members. Sometimes the agency's culture comes into direct conflict with the preferences and demands of clients, which can lead to misunderstanding. Further, I suggested that none of us is culturally or racially color blind, nor could we ever be, because we live in a society that rarely permits that kind of luxurious innocence. We all acknowledge differences, sometimes by choosing to ignore them and sometimes by attempting to learn something from them. The knowledge base the culturally adept social worker will want to build makes use of the latter option. In that approach, the worker asks: what can I learn from this relationship, with this client, that will tell me more about this person's community generally, and why they come to me with this specific issue?

The most efficient way for the social services worker to answer that question is by (1) identifying general areas of the client's experience that bear on the presenting problem and (2) explicitly contrasting that information with the worker's own life experience, defining in a comparative way what the differences appear to mean for the service relationship. That procedure—not masses of book learning or the endless round of workshops and conferences—is the most effective and also the most efficient way for the worker to build a usable knowledge base about the clients he or she serves.

The general areas of client experience I have in mind are just that—general— but initially approached from the client's rather than the social worker's point of view. This is the *emic* perspective mentioned in chapter 4. If the presenting problem is something involving the client's family life, we have to ask what "family" means in that person's household and also their community. If the client does not speak English we need to find out the various words for "family" in the client's home language and understand their connotations from an emic perspective. If the issue is physical care, we need a lot of information about what people like our client believe about how the body works, their understanding of the impact of various kinds of foods and medications on it, and perhaps even their ideas about the supernatural and its links to health. These are general areas of knowledge, things people usually take for granted and which is the "common sense" of their community. The worker's knowledge of these general areas needs to be made explicit, in flowcharts, charts, or diagrams that illustrate social processes. In the chapters on specific ethnic groups that follow, I illustrate one of many possible formats that might be used to do this.

The second step, that of comparative understanding, is just as important. The trait list approach to ethnicity suggests we can understand others by itemizing, by distancing them through what an expert tells us "they" are like and what "they" do or want. That kind of thinking was behind the request for cultural "tips" sought by the social workers frustrated by the Latina mothers. In the cultural approach, our own direct participation in discovery is more important. I really cannot know much about someone else until I have discovered something of what they hold to be true for themselves and, thinking reflexively, I then compare it with my own life and experiences. Comparativism, at a very personal level, is what this kind of learning is about. Ethnographically, my concern is not with what makes someone else "different." It is what the differences between us mean.

At this stage the subject of interest cannot be the "other" as a therapeutic object. Rather, it must be the meaning of difference as we jointly understand it. We are both part of the relationship, and we are both "objects" for the learning that must take place. To achieve comparative understanding, my taken-for-granted view of things has be made explicit and contrasted with that of others. Reflexivity, not clinical objectifying, is the learning procedure. Contrasts, not differences, are what must be identified.

PHASE II: CULTURAL SALIENCE IN PROBLEM SOLVING

If comparative sensitivity marks the beginning of knowledge about differences generally, the idea of salience focuses that sensitivity on a specific service issue. The word "salience" suggests something that is noticeable, prominent, or distinctive. My suggestion is that what may be salient for clients, their ways of comprehending and working with a problem, the "commonness" of their common sense, may not always be obvious to a counselor. In reference to psychotherapy, for example, it has been suggested that minority patients have to be approached as "knowers," that is, "individuals who shape their worlds and destinies through conceptual frameworks which they develop about the world and their lives" (Tyler, Sussewell, and Williams-McCoy 1985:311). As "knowers," their experience is rich in matters that I know little or nothing of, but about which I need greater familiarity so I can better meet their needs. How can that be done?

The help-seeking behavior model is our guide for this kind of inquiry. Recall that the model was made up of a number of components: the experience of a problem; naming of the problem through labeling; selection of healers, followed by treatment and some level of compliance with their suggestions; and determination that an acceptable outcome has been achieved. The steps of the model suggest a map for tracking and identifying the salient features of client problem identification and problem resolution. For example, once a problem is experienced, what are the rationales for assigning it a particular label? Given a decision about labeling, how does that influence choices about self-treatment or referral? How wide is the range of options for consultation, and why are some chosen in preference to others?

The range of possible decisions and behavior is enormous, and some choices are more salient to a given client than others. The matter of labeling is a good example. Dufort (1992) describes the management of physical disabilities among Papago Indian children and their families in Arizona. She was interested in how client–health worker communication styles, and Papago medical knowledge, influenced the quality of care available to those with severe disabilities. The Papago were not ignorant of contemporary treatment methods, and they wanted all the help they could get. But the way nurses, doctors, and social workers defined care made it difficult for Papago patients to work closely with these professionals. Indian families often concluded that decision making had been taken away from them, substituted by lists of "shoulds" on how treatment routines were to be followed. In addition, although the Papago accepted biomedical accounts of a specific disability as the proximate cause of the condition, they added another layer of explanation of their own. That layer included moral and personal factors that were important in their etiological accounts. Dufort was able to document these factors because of the way she listened to her respondents: Papago ex-plained illness through long, personalized narratives that put the experience of illness in a dense context of meaning. They disliked the brief "patient histories" taken by the nurses and social workers, to them just bureaucratic conveniences reflecting a narrow, instrumental view of illness favored in the clinical subculture. Before they would respond to clinical suggestions favorably, they wanted their own accounts to be given a place alongside those of the biomedical specialists.

There is a second aspect of cultural salience suggested here, one more ephem-eral and difficult to access than the knowledge base described in Phase I above. That is the meaning emotions and emotional experiences have within a particular ethnographic context. Most social workers understandably take pride in their "people work" skills and their ability to respond positively and helpfully to the pain, anger, or suffering their clients endure. I suggest, however, that those emo-tional states are not "pure" in the sense of being "natural" responses that any reasonable person might have in a crisis. Like knowledge, emotions too have their cultural dimension, and the sensitive worker will recognize that and want to understand them that way.

But how can emotions be thought of in cultural terms since it seems they are preeminently psychological manifestations? And what might that mean for some-one who wants to intervene in a culturally responsive way? The argument is a complex but interesting one (see Lutz 1988:53–80) and it is best understood by considering how, in American culture, many of us routinely think of emotional states.

In the folk psychology of American middle-class culture, emotions are usu-ally conceptualized in what could be called "essentialist" terms. That is, they are "things," "energies," or "forces" of which we each have some given quantity. Conceived this way, as a kind of internal stuff that sometimes seeps out even against our will, we "work with," "control," "manage," "hide," "cope with," "release," or otherwise regulate them as best we can. On permitted occasions, however, we are allowed to "vent" them. Emotions are perceived as a physics of sensibility. They are also thought of by most Americans as universal—everyone "has" them, although some people seem to "have" more of them than others, and sometimes they are even "lost" (as in "I lost my cool") so that people feel com-pelled to reclaim and "own" them. (The latter is an interesting metaphor in itself—the middle-class depiction of emotions as comparable to commodities or property, objects that can be "spent" or "wasted" on something unworthy, or rediscovered and "owned" because they have been stolen by someone else. Thus, some people speak of "owning" their experiences.) Emotions are also thought of as "natural," being intimately associated with the body and often described in medicalized terms. Thus people experience the "pain" of grief, or they have "butterflies in the stomach" when they are under stress. Emotions as essentialist, as characterological properties of the individual, are even genderized, women presumed to have a wider range of them but those of men under more explicit, rational control.

All the words I have put in quotes, along with many others like them, are commonly used in American middle-class culture to describe emotions. The language also suggests a particular cultural bias: emotions as universal, as naturally occurring "inner stuff," stuff that has dimension, that is privately claimed, that is gendered, and that may be dangerous. If you doubt me, just keep a mental list of the linguistic descriptors you hear in a five minute conversation as someone tells you how they felt about something. The folk psychology of middle-class Americans is a psychology of quantities and uneasily managed forces, moving precariously about within an imperfect, poorly constructed container. This essentialist folk theory forces us to think of emotions as things that are "deep," "buried," "hidden," or lurking underneath the surface, always interiorized and, like goods and commodities, privately possessed and rarely shared.

This is not, however, the only way to think about emotional experience and, for cross-cultural social work, it may not be the best way either. I say that deliberately and advisedly for I am always amazed at the presumptiveness of some participants in my workshops who genuinely believe that they can penetrate and comprehend the psyche of another, especially another who is culturally a world away from their own. Sometimes the language of "growth," "change," or even "empowerment" is used to convey that presumptiveness. But such careless use of language should remind us how difficult understanding others really can be.

Some brief examples will help illustrate this point. In her field research with a group of Eskimo, Jean Briggs (1986b) discovered that any display of strong affect, or even discussion of feelings, was incomprehensible and unacceptable to her hosts. Hostility was never acknowledged and the discourse of anger was phrased in terms of protectiveness and great concern, as in a gentle advisory that "You can't come fishing with me because you'll hurt yourself on the sharp rocks" (Briggs 1986b:39). Kleinman (1982) describes Chinese experiences of depression, usually somatized and expressed as vague physical complaints. Discussing Indonesians, Geertz (1975:49) says they seek an "inner world of stilled emotions" that, following a geographical metaphor, is like a flattened plane rather than variable and contoured hills and valleys. Csikszentmihalyi (1975, 1982) has identified a "new" emotion, one that is related to total mental concentration and that temporarily dissolves the boundaries between self and activity. What he calls "optimal experience" (Csikszentmihalyi and Csikszentmihalyi 1988) may be something all people can cultivate but few bother to label or describe. Cultures that value optimal experience will develop a vocabulary and explanatory apparatus to account for it; others will ignore it or treat it as an individual peculiarity. In either case, the point is that emotions, like language, are constructed by and responsive to situations. Emotions are cultural, temporal, geographical, and contingent, never something inevitable, universal, or natural.

One could usefully think about emotion, then, as a sociocultural as well as a psychodynamic event, specifically as a kind of "discourse" that is both pragmatic and communicative. It is pragmatic because it is a commentary about the relationships that prevail (or ought to) in certain circumstances. Emotional discourse can be seen as a form of behavior that makes an assertion about the state of the world and one's place in it. In that sense, it is a profound inner or psychological event and an ideological statement as well. Emotional discourse is also communicative. It challenges an audience to affirm or deny the appropriateness of the sufferer's current state of being. Emotional behavior may be verbal or nonverbal, but it always represents commentary within a community of those who understand the messages. It can only be prudent, then, for the cultural outsider to try to understand what that commentary is about. Attempting to mimic the inner state of another through a display of cultivated empathy, without knowing the pragmatic basis or the communicative codes of that experience, is not helpful and probably not possible.

Thinking about emotions this way, as having salience not because they are internal states but because they refer to something meaningful communicated among individuals, makes them very much a cultural as well as a psychological matter. Ethnic competence requires us to learn to recognize (perhaps even to understand) the coded meanings that inhere in emotional expressions that typify a distinctive community.

PHASE III: INDIVIDUALIZING THE CLIENT WITHIN CONTEXT

All that I have said so far about the ethnography of problem resolution should make clear that the individual exists within a cultural matrix, and the idea of the individual solely and purely as a unique entity makes no sense at all. The insistence, which I sometimes hear from social workers, that individualizing the client means stripping away all social or cultural "incidentals" in order to focus on the person as person is exactly comparable to a view in biomedicine that healing only involves repair of the patient's hydraulic, molecular, or biomechanical systems. It would be like filling a cavity in a tooth but ignoring the patient's eating and brushing habits. That model may work in some areas of medicine but in human services individuals must be seen as more than damaged psychological mechanisms. Their complexity, and the complexity of their needs, derives precisely from the fact that both clients and professional helpers swim in their own cultural pond, and neither has much experience outside of it. Effectiveness in helping others must take experiential differences fully into account. How, then, can we begin individualizing others within a cultural context, one that for them is familiar but to us is a mystery?

Sanday (1976) has argued that within a culturally plural society such as our own, individuals can be viewed as belonging to one of four major categories: mainstream, bicultural, culturally different, and culturally marginal. Mainstreamers have assimilated the standardized, most widely accepted values of the dominant society, and they attempt in their behavior to emulate those values. If the individual is white with adequate economic resources and is given frequent opportunity, the assimilation and behavioral manifestation of those values are largely unthinking and automatic. Members of racial and minority groups may think and act like mainstreamers—they often become mainstreamers—but they do so in spite of the fact that their participation in the lives and institutions of mainstreamers involves constant testing and challenge of their right to be there.

Bicultural individuals, on the other hand, may participate in mainstream culture, but they are also involved with the values and interests of identifiably distinctive cultural groups. Many minority persons in American society, and certainly many minority professionals in social work, would be considered bicultural in this sense. They have a dual commitment—a loyalty to their communities of origin and a stake in the political and economic institutions of the dominant society. They move as the situation dictates between two (or more) cultural worlds.

Sanday's third category is the culturally different. These people have been exposed to the dominant or mainstream culture, but their primary affiliations and locus of activity are with a distinctive cultural entity. They may avoid contact with mainstreamers but still make minimal use of mainstream institutions, such as employment agencies and social security, and they are exposed to the mass media and mass merchandising. Culturally different individuals are often isolated in geographical enclaves, such as "Chinatowns" or "little Italys," from which they seldom emerge. Indeed, they may not use English at home, although they may know it and use it in public. The fourth category, culturally marginal persons, covers those who have little or no attachment to any identifiable cultural entity. They may come from any ethnic or racial group, but for a variety of reasons—physical or developmental needs, geographical isolation, disabling life circumstances, or sheer choice—they are truly alienated and follow a way that is distinctly their own. Some "street people" illustrate this category.

The value of this typology, and it must be regarded as a tentative one at best, is that it prepares the social worker for making an *initial* judgment about a client's cultural placement. It is not enough to know that we are confronted with a person of a particular ethnicity; we must also know where in the typology of intracultural variation that client fits. By utilizing Sanday's four categories to, in effect, "size up" the client, we begin to make cultural distinctions. But it is very important to note that locating the individual in terms of this typology is not a very sophisticated analysis nor is it an end in itself. To stop there would be simply to pigeonhole people. Rather than pigeonholing, the typology should be viewed as an initial classificatory device that suggests the kinds of options (and limitations) available in a multicultural society, a point about which Sanday is explicit.

It should be clear by now that the task of individualizing the client is a difficult one, requiring the culturally sensitive social worker to acquire as much ethnographic knowledge as possible. This point has been forcefully made from within the field of social work by Burgest (1983, 1989) who argues that individualizing the client *must* take account of each person's race and ethnicity but also their understanding of what, precisely, that means in their experience. To assume that an individual who identifies herself as Chicana necessarily believes in the health and illness system associated with *mal ojo* is to use cultural data to stereotype anew. But to know that *mal ojo* is a possible variable in the individual's experience, the significance of which must be determined on a case-by-case basis is to use cultural information in a way that helps clarify the context of behavior and its meaning for the client. It is that use of ethnographic information, in a transactional rather than categorical sense, that the social workers attempting to manage child rearing among their Latina clients did not understand. Cultural knowledge allows us to make tentative guesses and reasonable hypotheses about a client's relationship to the culture of origin and to the dominant culture. That information is only an aid to guiding inquiry, not a final summation.

How Can We "Individualize" Clients?

Making an initial assessment of how an individual "fits" into a community is a necessary but crude first step. But by itself, it barely qualifies as cultural awareness. There are important ways a social worker can and should proceed beyond that point. In a useful pair of articles, Sue (1988) and Sue and Zane (1987) discuss the applications of cultural awareness strategies in psychotherapy. Their view is that a little knowledge is most certainly a dangerous thing because often it is applied inappropriately and with negative effects on minority clients. The temptation to stereotype by using newly discovered, "insider" information is apparently too strong for some to resist. Their argument is that knowledge, to be useful in client encounters, must be "transformed into concrete operations and strategies" (Sue and Zane 1987:39). To achieve that transformation, they distinguish "distal" or distant and "proximate" or near knowledge. Distal knowledge is generalized cultural information about some group. It may have little, some, or a lot to do with the client currently sitting before the social worker. The worker who relies on distal information alone cannot know enough to evaluate the cultural similarities or dissimilarities that a particular client shares with other members of the group in question. Some kind of proximate knowledge is needed to culturally locate the individual within a given community. Sue and Zane argue that two interpersonal processes are especially important in building that awareness: credibility and giving. Credibility refers to the client's perception of the therapist as effective and trustworthy. Giving is the client's sense of having received a "gift" of some kind from the therapeutic encounter.

Each of these processes presents special problems in cross-cultural social work. Credibility is dependent, in part, on the social worker's generalized, distal knowledge about the client's community and the general expectations, preferences, and practices that exist there. The worker without such information risks loss of credibility in three ways: (1) through an inability to accurately formulate the client's concerns, as in the case of the Latina mothers discussed above; (2) by making inappropriate suggestions for problem resolution, such as self-disclosure in communities where that is not accepted; and (3) by suggesting treatment goals that may make sense in terms of textbook paradigms but which the client finds unfamiliar or even threatening. Errors in any of these areas put the worker's credibility at risk. One common client response to the credibility gap is a "failure" (as it is commonly described) to keep the next appointment.

The idea of a "gift" is equally critical. Gift giving in therapy, according to Sue and Zane, is the benefit the client feels he or she has received. Where minority clients are concerned, they recommend that benefits be forthcoming even in the first meeting. Clients are unlikely to make a commitment to a counseling relationship that seems of little use. For example, a "gift" might be reassurance that others have had a similar problem but that they found a way to resolve it. A gift could be clarification of what is involved in a current difficulty, or the opportunity to speak out without fear of judgment. But there is a caution here: gift giving should *not* be thought of as bait or bribery. Rather, it is an assurance that the therapist wants to help, will take the time to do so, and, most importantly, has credible skills that the client can depend on. Without the skills, and a demonstration that they are applicable to the client's specific situation, it is unlikely that a relationship of long-term trust can be built.

Neither credibility nor the capacity to offer appropriate gifts can be established quickly. Nor can they be expected from infrequent contacts. Both are part of a long learning curve, one that is intuitive as well as rational. Both depend on reliable ethnographic knowledge but also a strong sense of the limits of that knowledge. Sue and Zane note that the results of therapy are "the *cumulative* product of many discreet dynamics between client and therapist" (1987:44). During this cumulative experience, there are numerous points at which the client can give up, often with good reason. Credibility is always at risk and can only be earned, certainly not bought, through therapeutic gifts that show knowledge and a sensitivity to context in the client's lived reality. It is important to think of cultural awareness just this way, as much more subtle and more demanding of our best efforts than it may first have seemed.

Individualizing Others within Context

Looking at ethnographic understanding in "distal" and "proximate" terms assumes a social worker's perspective. But what does "individualizing" mean from a client's point of view? What is the client issue when we talk about individualizing others? That, too, must be part of the story.

Think back to the help-seeking behavior model. Clients don't normally use models like that because they don't have to; they have ideas of their own. But the help seeking model aids us in understanding something that our client, seeking to resolve a difficulty, is doing. That individual is communicating that he or she has something at stake. There is something to be preserved, defended, or "owned" that is important. The idea that clients have a stake in something adds a useful dimension to Sue and Zane's discussion of credibility. Individualizing the client must include the social worker's sense that people have an interest in things that transcend the immediate, presenting problem, even if they do not articulate it for us. They are concerned with coherence and predictability in how and where they live; with a felt quality of immediacy and comfort in their surroundings;

with a sense of competence that comes from handling reasonably well the minor irritations of everyday life; with the satisfaction of having survived past calamities, large and small, and knowing that they could probably do so again. These are elusive but powerful undercurrents in all our lives, states of being that are at risk when we are sick or troubled. More than that, they are conditions for living that are exquisitely sensitive to larger, cultural agendas. Our place "in the flow" of a family or community is always threatened by a crisis and our inability to respond to it capably.

In addition to that, however, every presenting problem has its larger dimensions. Consider, for example, Kleinman's discussion of illness narratives (1988a), where he states that AIDS is a direct threat, not only to the afflicted, their friends, and families, but also to the sexual and family values revered by the American middle class. For some people, AIDS even has a potent cosmological dimension, seen by them as a scourge sent by a punitive deity unhappy with sexual misbehavior. Similarly, other illnesses have their value dimensions. Cancer and heart disease clearly challenge fundamental notions of what one's body is doing, but they also indict our tolerance of air pollution, fatty diets, work pace, pressures to consume, and unreasonable career expectations. Anorexia and bulimia are now widely seen as evidences of female denigration and subordination, not simply personal failings or a result of dysfunctional family life. Menopausal crises and premenstrual tensions afflict many American women but are unrecognized as symptoms in some non-Western cultures, suggesting something of our society's emphasis on youth and pleasure. "Nerves" among Appalachian women, *susto* among Mexican Americans in the Southwest, and vodun among Haitian immigrants in New York City are similarly personal and familial issues that invoke powerful notions of orderly and disorderly relationships, matters in which individuals have an abiding concern. The point is that symptoms have meanings that transcend psychodynamic or biomedical diagnosis and they invoke issues much larger than personal complaint. The social worker who can recognize and validate the cultural and ideological framework of symptoms can help others better understand what it is they are experiencing and why they are troubled by it.

The key to learning at this level is in contrasting one's own lived realities with those of patients and clients. Classifying presenting problems by invoking the usual analytical and diagnostic categories of the profession should come later, not at the beginning of a service relationship. That advice is not what most social science, behavioral science, or social work texts suggest, nor is it, I suspect, what many well-intentioned helping professionals actually do. But if we really want to individualize clients, we can only do so from the context of what *we* know best: our experience, and our stake in it.

PHASE IV: ETHNIC COMPETENCE AND POWER

Clearly, individuals who have strong negative feelings about race should not be advising and counseling those who are different from themselves. Even though the Archie Bunker syndrome is now recognizable and generally considered taste-less, it is an unfortunate fact that racism persists as a malevolent and pervasive feature of American life. But what of those who do not consider themselves racists, who want to eliminate racism from their own lives and workplaces, and yet are perplexed by their inability to communicate effectively in cross-cultural encounters? And what of systemic power differentials, the hierarchical arrange-ments of the larger society that create inequalities of race, gender, and language to begin with?

Distressing as it is, it is not uncommon for individuals of genuine goodwill and honest intent to have difficulty communicating across racial and cultural boundaries. I want to suggest several reasons why that is so, reasons that come down to our difficulties with understanding power and the differential access to privilege that power represents. In a discussion of this problem in relations between black clients and white therapists, Jones and Seagull (1977) identify what they see as one important difficulty. As most social workers know, countertrans-ference is projection onto the client of the therapist's feelings and experiences from previous relationships. These feelings may have resulted from prior frustra-tions or from a lifelong pattern of dislike of certain peoples. In the service encoun-ter, they become part of the dynamics of the event and may be difficult to mask or control. Members of minority communities, usually more sensitive to the nuances of cross-racial transactions than many whites appreciate, quickly recog-nize countertransference when it is occurring, and most certainly have their own terms for describing it. Whites who do not understand that often become defen-sive, tentative, even hostile. Neither client nor therapist is anxious to continue the relationship any longer than necessary. This extreme individualizing of ambigu-ous feelings about power and difference is usually difficult to resolve and almost always a barrier to the comparative understanding of those we serve advocated here.

A second problem is guilt. Guilt is the response of social workers who, perhaps too anxious to "do right" for historically "wronged" people, overreact or over-identify with a client's problems. Zealousness, moral crusading, or ingratiation become substitutes for the reality testing that ethnic competence requires, and they limit the worker's potential effectiveness. A rhetoric of "concern" too often repeated, great shows of sympathy, and an "us against them" mentality are symptomatic of the problem. As in the case of countertransference, minority individuals are usually more sensitive to this overreaction than many whites realize. They often perceive it (correctly so, in my view) as patronizing, and they dismiss it. More importantly, it puts an agenda of expiation ahead of the process of learning about cultural differences. It becomes another impediment to the development of a genuinely helpful cross-cultural relationship.

The explicit need for control is a third area of difficulty. As I indicated in the discussion of cross-cultural interviewing (chapter 4), managing the interview is viewed in the profession as one indication of the social worker's skill. Yet in cross-cultural work, the exercise of control is. very complex. The line between control as therapeutic guidance and control as dominance is always problematic, whatever the worker's intentions. The issue is compounded by the client's own perceptions, stereotypes, and misinformation about the social worker, the agency, and service organizations generally.

It is the social worker, not the client, who will have to take the first steps in resolving these difficulties, and that is not easily done. Part of the effort involves self-knowledge and fairly explicit clarification of one's own values and desires. Knowledge of the culture of one's clients, and particularly of the hidden and quiet sources of their community's strengths, is also important. Perhaps part of the effort will require rethinking what "professionalism" means and how the values and practices of a professional subculture either help or confound relations with ethnic communities. If we can approach power that way, at least we can begin thinking about its reality in all cross-cultural encounters.

I have already suggested that service professions are a kind of culture and that service agencies, indeed, every office within a service agency, has its own local culture that more or less replicates that of the sponsoring organization. But these local service cultures have another dimension, which I will argue reproduces in localized form the relationship of the dominant society to specific ethnic groups. For example, the dominant, white, middle-class culture of America (and the many service organizations that function in it) can be thought of as a "host" society that contains within itself a large number of "guest" participants. Some of these "guests" came involuntarily, some were here before the first representatives of the host culture arrived, and some are desperately trying to get in through the host society's borders. But all have been engulfed, followed by varying efforts at absorption, dominance, and control.

This host-guest metaphor can be a provocative one because in some ways service agencies and their personnel are always in host relationships with clients. The cultural formation of hosting tells us something about the implicit cultural features of the dominant group and the people who function as service providers in it. Citing the work of Boekestijn (1984), Furnham and Bochner (1989:230) see the following as some of the important cultural features of host relationships in cross-cultural encounters.

1. Hosts have rules of *territoriality* or "turf." Some of these rules involve competition among agencies for "ownership" of clients or public issues. Turf also involves protective routines and policies that exclude clients and patients from full knowledge of what the agency can or is willing to do for them. These policies and routines, especially those that are in some sense "unspoken," mark the territorial limits of the host agency's culture.

2. Hosts have multiple definitions of their clients. Official definitions are maintained in statutes and administrative directives. Unofficial ones, much richer and more varied, are maintained in shared understandings embedded in agency practice. These are the things that are commonly but privately discussed with coworkers during coffee breaks, between meetings, and in after-work gatherings.

3. Hosts vary in their commitment to their work, their profession, and even the mandate of their agency. Similarly, agency administrators vary in the kinds of reinforcement they give staff. These *identity issues* combine to create agency "morale," an illusive quality that nevertheless translates into service to clients.

4. Hosts vary in their expressions of ethnocentrism or intolerance. Guest outsiders are always sensitive to power differentials, which may be expressed subtly or overtly, by legal mandate or quiet implication. Mechanisms of control are sometimes so routine they are not visible to those who use and rely on them. Suggestions that control may be a response to racial, cultural, linguistic, or class differences often meet with sharp denials.

5. Hosts vary in their willingness to spend the necessary time to work with those who are "hard to reach." Because continuous interaction with others who are not like oneself is physically and psychologically demanding, fatigue is a factor. How well agencies help their workers cope with that fatigue, and how regularly they acknowledge the best efforts of their staff, is an additional measure of an organization's capacity and suitability for working with diverse clients.

None of these five aspects of agency culture is more important than any other, and all must be considered when thinking about how a professional or agency culture responds to the challenge that those who are "different" always represent. But examination of self and agency, as important as that is, cannot be the sole focus when we are considering issues of power. One of the criticisms commonly made of the social service profession, and of cultural awareness approaches to ethnicity, is that they ignore structural inequalities in the larger society. For example, McMahon and Allen-Meares (1992) reviewed 117 articles appearing in a ten-year run of four major journals, *Social Service Review, Social Casework, Child Welfare,* and *Social Work.* They wanted to assess how the literature deals with both individual and institutional racism. Their conclusion, not very flattering, was that "the literature portrays the social work profession as naive and superficial in its antiracist practice. . . . [O]ne of the main remedies proposed for the racism minorities suffer focuses, according to the literature, on *mere change in the awareness of social workers*" (1992:537, my italics).

Similarly, Longres (1991) holds that cultural models of ethnic-sensitive practice may be useful for work among immigrants and refugees, people whose social and historical backgrounds are obviously different from those of most Americans. But for individuals who are members of a long-standing minority group, issues of differential privilege, opportunity, and life chances are more important. He adds that, "If social workers are to be helpful, they need to spend less time thinking about differences in norms and values and more time in thinking about how to operate in encounters between high and low status people. Helping minority clients means changing stratification systems" (1991:55).

I am in basic agreement with these criticisms, but with this qualification. To the extent that cultural differences are seen only as differences in "norms and values," as Longres says, then cultural awareness will never be much more than an adventure into quaint customs and someone else's fun cuisine. The "norms and values" approach is the most superficial one I can imagine, but it is exactly the "safe" and narrow perspective that has driven cross-cultural thinking in social services and its research literature. McMahon and Allen-Meares are right: that kind of cultural awareness is incredibly naive, even damaging, because it distances people from their clients by making the latter objects of exotic otherness. It should be obvious that that is not what I advocate here. Yet there is much more that separates people than their status, be it high or low. Any culture is more than its hierarchical dimensions, and whatever stratification may exist, along lines of race, language, gender, or age, flows from a shared world view of what is acceptable and what is not. We cannot divorce norms and values from power, nor can we limit ourselves to thinking about one at the expense of the other. They always work in tandem.

The host-guest metaphor is a useful device for thinking about what the power differentials really are and, more importantly, how they are manifested. It can help us get beyond thinking about power in raw terms such as high and low, greater or lesser. Power is exercised in practice and routine, especially routine, which is why it is not often visible to those who have it. A cultural approach to agencies and organizations can make what is hidden more evident, and can reveal what the hosts and guests are really doing to and for each other.

PHASE V: THINKING AND WORKING COMPARATIVELY

Genuine cultural awareness must include a comparative, self-critical understanding of how, as a professional, one participates in a system of differential privilege and power (Gutierrez 1990). The host-guest analogy identifies some of the ways hosts (social workers, nurses, doctors, teachers) are in a position to take advantage of those who need their services. The transactional view of ethnicity discussed earlier requires the social worker to see that helping services, "delivered" by a bureaucratic system, are never free of the encumbrances of privilege. Professionals who believe that displays of empathy or cultural "understanding" can overcome inherent inequalities delude themselves. When we see how the professional culture of an agency or an office includes the cultural meanings assigned to power, and their enactment in service relationships, we will be led directly into the heart of inequality, its justifications, and its rationale. Real cultural awareness exposes privilege and may deprive the comfortable of some of their sense of ease.

But there is more to cultural awareness than recognizing problems or discomfiting the complacent. One must seek opportunities for change, options that may not be visible without a special effort to find them. That is why the chapters that follow describe a few of the ethnographic features of prominent minority groups. Every human community is a natural experiment. Each finds a different way of coping with the world and building its own, reasonably coherent system of meaning. People within those communities do the best they can, drawing on what they know, and that is their tradition and their culture. In the case of American ethnic groups, part of their culture involves resistance against, and protections from the predations of the dominant society, as the studies of minority school children and their families by Ogbu (1987) and Kozol (1988, 1991) so eloquently reveal. Cultural awareness must include knowledge of those ethno-graphic choices and practices. Action to resolve inequalities without that kind of information simply reproduces the arrogance of those who know what needs to be fixed but have forgotten to consult the intended beneficiaries.

Real cultural awareness is not a denial of the realities of power. It includes power in the definition of self and others. It acknowledges inequalities in service relationships and their effects on outcomes. But it also foregrounds the strengths that people find in their own traditions, giving them equal weight in problem solving. That cannot but elevate community-based belief and practice to greater parity with the solutions offered by bureaucrats, academics, and professional intervenors. Cultural awareness, in the best sense, cannot be otherwise.

IDENTIFYING ETHNIC COMMUNITIES

A Seattle police officer whose last name is Chan once told a newspaper reporter that when people refer to her as an Oriental, "I just say I'm not a rug." Yet millions of Americans, and not just whites, routinely use ethnic labels such as "Oriental," "black," or "Indian" to describe others as though those terms were accurate descriptive tags. In a training workshop, as we were exploring the complexities of names and naming, an annoyed participant complained that I was making too much of something that was really quite simple and, out of great impatience, she exclaimed, "Why can't we all just be 'Americans'?"

Indeed. Why can't we?

In the discussion on language (chapter 4), I described how the power to name is the power to control. It is important that what people are called, and what they want to be called, be considered carefully. Inappropriate and insensitive labeling is always the banana peel pratfall of cross-cultural communication. Those who are well intended but uninformed are soon on the floor, often without even knowing it. Part of the problem is that labels change, not because people are arbitrary, but because society, politics, and the distribution of power changes. Labels reflect that. There is no final, correct list for what ethnic group members ought to be called or want to be called. But ethnic groups are the final source of authority for the designations that we all use. That is a volatile issue, and in commenting on it here, I do so with full acknowledgment that the terms in use in the 1990s may be "old stuff," even unappreciated old stuff, in later decades. (For an extended discussion of naming and why it is such a complex issue, see Asamoah et al. 1991.)

I will start my consideration of the meaning of names with whites, because they are the politically and socially dominant group at the present time. "White" and "Caucasian" are the two most common (of the polite) terms, "white" being the choice of the U.S. Census Bureau for the 1990 census. What do these two words mean? Physically, no one is really "white" unless they have no pigmenta-tion at all (a condition that occurs in all populations including dark-skinned ones). All people are really brown, for that is the color of the melanin that tints our skin. The word "Caucasian" refers to the Caucasus Mountains, just north of Turkey, and was the name given to a prehistoric skull found there in the late 1700s and believed at that time to be archetypal for all Europeans. "Caucasian" is reflective of the state of the biological and archaeological sciences at the end of the eighteenth century. But now it is a term that has no scientific validity and, more to the point, it designates no one in particular. Spanish speakers sometimes refer to whites as "Anglos," and in certain contexts that is appropriate. "White" is probably the most acceptable term for the present and the one I use in this book. But I do not capitalize it as I do other labels for the reason that whites rarely think of themselves as "ethnic" except when they describe themselves as fractions of European nationalities (Thorne et al. 1983). Given the claims to distinctiveness and ethnic solidarity made by other ethnic communities in recent years, one of the problems posed for whites is just what their "ethnicity" might be anyway. For most, a diffuse idea that they are "generic American" apparently suffices.

The term "black" has its own complex history. For much of the colonial period in North and South America, the Spanish "negro" was the accepted term. During slavery, both in the United States and in the West Indies, there was an extensive and complex vocabulary for presumed degrees of Africanness in the blood. That vocabulary, with words like "octoroon" and "quadroon," was once common in everyday speech but is now so archaic that it can be found only in history books and dictionaries. A capitalized "Negro" and "Colored" were widely used after the Civil War, the word "black" considered at that time a slur. (Hence the continued use of "Colored" in the name of the NAACP, founded early in this century.) Black, first in lower case and then capitalized, became popular during the 1960s, as activists deliberately took on a stigmatized name and turned it into "Black is beautiful." Afro-American, first proposed in the late nineteenth century, and African-American, have been replaced by African American without the hyphen when used as a noun. Many in the black community do not feel they are "hyphenated Americans," and they find the newer usage more descriptive of their origins. African American and black, as of this writing, are used interchangeably by many people of African ancestry although other terms may come into use in the future.

Native Americans were here first, of course, but there was no "America" for most of their 40,000 years of residence. The term "Indian" is a misnomer, from Columbus's mistaken belief that he had discovered India and the East Indies. (The term "West Indian" is equally erroneous, as the native peoples of the Caribbean were quickly exterminated by the Spanish and the region has been overwhelmingly African American since the late seventeenth century.) Generally, the terms Native American and American Indian are acceptable although many Indian people prefer to identify themselves by their tribal affiliation as, for example, members of the Menominee or the Yakama nation. Many tribal names, now compromised by English or French spellings and pronunciation, originally expressed an idea such as "the people" or "the people of the mountain." As names for localities and for historical traditions, they remain important and will not disappear however acculturated some individuals or groups may appear to be.

Spanish speakers often identify themselves with their country of origin as well, as in "Mexican American" or "Puerto Rican." The term "Hispanic" has been widely used, and continues to be, but is losing out to "Latino," "Latina," "Chicano," and "Chicana" in some areas. "Hispanic" was a word originally coined by the Census Bureau, and so it has never had the sense of legitimacy many whites might assume. "Chicana" and "Chicano" came into vogue during the 1960s and 1970s, when some felt that the word "Mexican" conveyed an image of poverty and backwardness. Now even those terms are questioned by those who prefer to think of themselves using a national designation such as Cuban American. As with many of the terms discussed here, more precise designations are better than vague, all encompassing ones, particularly as more and more ethnic groups assert their distinctiveness and their unique cultural identity.

The term "Asian American" is probably the most inclusive and the least descriptive in this list. "Oriental" is definitely out, but Asian American is only a slight improvement. The ethnographic diversity of people of Asian origins in America is staggering: China (with all its regional and ethnic diversity), Japan, Taiwan, Hong Kong, Viet Nam, Malaysia, Indonesia, the Philippines, Micronesia, Polynesia, American Samoa, Guam, Thailand, India, Pakistan, Sri Lanka, and Tibet. People from all these countries, and many more, call themselves Asians and insist, when they become resident here, that they are Asian Americans. Not only is there great national and ethnic diversity represented, but there are significant religious and racial variations too. The Asian American category really explodes the putative melting pot. As in the case of Spanish speakers, many Asian Americans prefer to be identified with a nationality. In all cross-cultural work, what individuals and families are called is *their* choice, and if the choices change with the political or economic climate, that is just what life is in a genuinely pluralistic society. We can't be "just Americans" because we are so much more than that.

What of the more recent expression, "people of color" and others like it, phrases that attempt to be inclusive almost without restriction? There seems to be little consensus about this kind of language. Some individuals like it because of its democratic emphasis on people and its implied claims of a universal opposition between white Europeans, their descendants, and their hegemonic cultures on the one hand and the peoples of Africa, Asia, and the Americas who were colonized and dominated on the other. Others reject the term as too vague, or for perpetuating simplistic ideas about ethnic diversity and the complexity of each ethnic community's historical experience. For this book, I do not use the term "people of color" because for me it belongs to a body of discourse that is essentially political. As a descriptive and analytical phrase, the usefulness of "people of color" must be determined by those interested in ethnic politics and historical patterns of dominance and subordination. In human services, where we work with personal and family needs, and try to individualize clients and patients within their specific cultural tradition, an expression like "people of color" is just too broad to be useful. That does *not* mean we can ignore issues of power and inequity in the way services are provided. I am simply suggesting that sweeping rhetorical forms belong in a forum other than client-worker consultations.

Finally, I want to suggest that in reality all these words of identification are a kind of shorthand, even a fiction. Race, ethnicity, and the language associated with them are constructs that we use for social convenience. They suggest a simple, neat, and orderly world where everyone is slotted into their proper place. But the truth is otherwise, profoundly so, and even well-meaning persons are misled by the vocabulary we all employ. Many of us in America, perhaps *most* of us, are ethnically and *racially* mixed in some sense. But our habits of language and thought do not allow us to perceive that at all. It was as recently as 1967 that the Supreme Court abolished antimiscegenation laws (then existing in fourteen states), some of which had stood for three centuries. The longevity of these laws is evidence that interracial marriage and mating was an old practice and, at least for the lawmakers and their constituencies, a deeply troubling one. But the laws were never enforced in a uniform way, nor could they be, and the evolving physical diversity of the American population is proof of that. Our labels help us deceive ourselves, preserving the fiction that all that mixing, mating, and marrying never went on, when in fact it did.

Consider this. It has been estimated that in terms of family history and genealogical lines, half or more of all African Americans are multiracial (Root 1992). So are almost all Latinos (Fernandez 1992), most American Indians (Wilson 1992), and a significant proportion of whites (Alba and Chamlin 1983). Most whites, unless they have written genealogical records, cannot trace their ancestry further back than three or four generations. Yet the greater the duration of their family "line" in America, the greater the likelihood of interracial ties. (To imagine the possibilities, we have to think of the family "line" not as descent from a common ancestor. That is another fiction. Rather, it starts with oneself and branches out much like a tree, with the tree getting bushier with more connections the further back in time one traces the limbs.) Most of the people in my university classes identify themselves as white, and I believe that many of the students who will use this book are white. I also think that many of them have racially diverse family connections they do not even suspect. In hidden and even secretive ways, most of us are already multiracial because that is a fact of our biological past, although it is usually denied or not known. Whites commonly name multiple European national origins to identify their ethnicity without every considering the possibility of African American racial or ethnic linkages (Alba 1990). Daniel (1992) argues that multiracialism was probably more common in our past than we realize and, further, it will be much more so in our future. He suggests that individuals who "call themselves 'mixed', 'biracial', 'interracial', or 'multi-racial'" are the carriers of a new multiracial consciousness, representing "the next logical step in the progression of civil rights, the expansion of our notion of affirmative action" and especially the affirmation of nonhierarchical ways of constructing personal identity (Daniel 1992:334).

If our future is to include an unapologetic affirmation of multiracial diversity and nonhierarchical ways of thinking about difference, then it should be clear that we can't forget about labels, "just be Americans," and get on with business as usual. First, we have yet to settle what being an "American" means. Second, we have to acknowledge that for many people "being American" is synonymous with being white. Whites control the discourse about what America is. Acknowledging diversity as something more than ethnic holidays and special foods will require that we rethink some very old and pernicious ideas about what our collective experience means to us.

ETHNIC VARIATION WITHIN AND BETWEEN COMMUNITIES

The remainder of this book contains overviews of four major ethnic communities in American life: African Americans, Asian Americans, American Indians, and Spanish-speaking Americans. The rationale for this grouping is not particularly logical but is an artifact of American history and politics: these are the four major groups most commonly recognized as ethnic and minority communities. They are also long-standing communities and have been part of the American experience from virtually the beginnings of nationhood.

Neither is there any assumption about the order of presentation. Suffice it to say that American Indians were here first and may have been living in North America for 40,000 years before the discovery of America by Columbus. Spanish colonizers occupied Florida, the Caribbean, Mexico, and the American Southwest well before the English and other Northern Europeans came along. Particularly in the Southwest and parts of California, Spanish communities were established and the people living there considered themselves long-time residents well before their land was incorporated by war into the current United States. Africans came to North America in bondage, almost with the first whites, and their fortunes have been intertwined with those of the dominant Euro-Americans from the beginning. Asians arrived later but were an "early" group in the sense that they joined whites in the pioneering of the western and Rocky Mountain states. As with African Americans, their lives were part of the white settlement of Indian-occupied lands. Each of these groups now has a lengthy and significant history in this country; they are no longer sojourners or recent arrivals.

Each of the chapters that follow develops a perspective on the meaning of cultural differences as they are expressed and experienced by members of the constituent groups. Each also deals, implicitly if not explicitly, with an issue of considerable importance in social services: individualizing the client. Within specific ethnic groups, there is considerable variation in people's behavior and in their commitment to the prevailing values and practices of their fellows. Intracultural diversity is a fact of social life that the culturally competent social worker must be able to handle. Unfortunately, training in cross-cultural sensitivity has often been built on what might be called "uniformist assumptions" about cultural information. That is, particular cultural traits are identified and treated as though they are typical or uniformly characteristic of a given community. Such approaches, common in both training programs and literature, have been criticized by a number of anthropologists as well as other social scientists (Pelto and Pelto 1975), because they make it easy to apply unthinkingly such labels as "culture of poverty" and "female-centered family" to whole groups of people, including individuals who may or may not exhibit the social and cultural traits that such labels suggest.

For example, descriptors for Spanish-speaking people such as "machismo," "traditionalism," "fatalism," and "present time orientation" have limited explanatory value because they assume that millions of people are basically alike. Although broadscaled, underlying cultural themes are most certainly important in the interpretation of behavior, individual instances of behavior are also the result of situational variables, including the individual's status within the community, the character of social networks, the organization of households, and educational and employment opportunities. The problem for the social worker is to untangle cultural and situational factors in order to comprehend a client's concerns and long-term interests.

Since the approach toward learning I am advocating is an explicitly comparative one, each chapter includes a profile of some (but not all) important cultural themes within each community. But the list is not a grouping of "typical" traits. It is a set of *contrasts* set alongside comparable themes in the dominant, white community. Contrasting white and ethnic communities is a legitimate procedure because most social workers are white and, generally, they set the agenda for the organizing, staffing, and providing of services. It is also important because I am concerned with highlighting a *process* in which the learner acquires ethnographic insight by comparing his or her understanding with that of minority clients. It is the process, not the "typicality" of the statements about whites or minorities in the profiles, that produces the real learning and, ultimately, real empathy and culturally appropriate action.

Exercises in the back of the book give the student a chance to try this learning process and become better informed and more sensitive to cultural meanings and differences. That work can be slow and time-consuming and it requires diligence. But that should not be surprising since that is how we all learned our own culture. How could it be different in learning about the culture of someone else?

6

AFRICAN AMERICANS, DIASPORA, AND SURVIVAL

In 1976, Alex Haley published his monumental work *Roots*, a national best-seller that also became a popular television series. That event was more important than many Americans may have realized, for it was not about literary success or a television special alone. What Haley achieved was permanent installation of an African-centered perspective at the heart of our national discourse on race and ethnicity. He was the historical successor of all those who had argued that there is a distinctively African way of seeing the world, one preserved and elaborated by contemporary African Americans. Earlier voices had made similar claims but were rarely heard outside small academic and literary circles. Haley touched cultural sensibilities on a national scale, perhaps the first African-American writer since Frederick Douglass to do so.

In *Roots* and in subsequent writings, Haley helped establish a national agenda about what we mean by race, oppression, survival, and the African-American experience. It was an agenda that made rich use of history, cultural resources, and language. It was no accident, then, that almost two decades later, when author Toni Morrison accepted her 1993 Nobel Prize in Literature, she too turned to cultural memories, folktales, and language styles to describe her own success and the survival of an entire people (Darnton 1993). The framework for cultural understanding is now well established both in the social sciences and in popular discourse. The task ahead is to apply it in meeting human needs.

INTRODUCTION

As is true of most ethnic groups, the African-American community is diverse, and that diversity has important implications. Most blacks did not come to America by choice, as is well known. Less appreciated is the diversity of ethnic affiliations in Africa and, even under the harsh regime of slavery, the diversity of their communities and activities throughout the Old South. Although most Africans brought to America were involved with the operation of plantations, many "freemen" who had been manumitted by slave owners lived in urban areas where they worked as artisans and small-scale entrepreneurs. These urban-based individuals were the nucleus of a small but growing black middle class. The Civil War ended slavery and the plantation economy but did not change the poverty or racial discrimination that would affect the former slaves and freemen for generations to come.

In the late nineteenth century, blacks began migrating north in significant numbers, usually occupying the poorest sections of large cities such as Chicago, Detroit, Philadelphia, and New York. The work they found—usually in service and domestic occupations—was poorly paid, required few skills, and led to nothing better. Nevertheless, it was for many an improvement over the rural poverty, sharecropping, and Jim Crow racism they left behind. Most migrants who went north improved their circumstances economically and socially but always within the confines of continued discrimination. Not only a revived black middle class but a tiny economic elite appeared. Many members of the latter were of urban Southern origins and had been well established before they migrated north. They were familiar with the operations of the white economic and political world and worked carefully and skillfully in it. After World War I, whole sections of some northern cities evolved complex and socially diversified black communities with their own businesses, newspapers, service organizations, churches, and, in the style of the day, their own political machines. Undoubtedly the most notable of these was Harlem in New York City, which became famous in the 1920s for the cultural florescence known as the "Harlem Renaissance." The success of these northern black enclaves was a terrific magnet to many in the South and migration north became a symbol of upward social mobility.

The Depression of the 1930s undercut the economic vitality of many of these communities as unemployment reached massive proportions. Undercapitalized businesses failed, and underfunded community agencies could not cope with the level of need. The policies of the New Deal, however, established a new relationship between the African-American community and the dominant white society. Legislation friendly to collective bargaining made union participation easier for black workers. Government agencies hired many individuals for white collar positions, establishing government employment as a career option and placing some in positions where they could direct relief programs to their own communities. Jobs in war industries and the desegregation of the military following World War II created new opportunities and also moved workers around the country to areas where they had not had a large historical presence, particularly in the West. Within a hundred years of the termination of slavery, African Americans were so geographically dispersed that they had become a national rather than a regional ethnic minority.

By 1986, African Americans were approximately twelve percent of the U.S. population. Median income was about half that of whites although there were substantial numbers of blacks at all income levels, including a few at the highest. The gap between white and African-American incomes narrowed only slightly during the 1980s. Yet improvements in black educational and occupational achievements were significant in comparison to previous generations and in most cities and towns with a sizable black population there was a well established middle (and sometimes upper) class. African Americans can now be found in the same occupations pursued by whites. Most never come to the attention of social workers nor do they seek out the kinds of professional help social service agencies typically offer.

That is not true of another group of African Americans who, for a variety of reasons, are trapped in circumstances they may never escape and for whom social services of some kind may be needed on a short-term or even long-term basis. In an important book, they have been called by black sociologist William Julius Wilson (1987) "the truly disadvantaged," an "underclass" of extremely impoverished individuals and families concentrated in inner cities where they are effectively isolated. They are, according to Wilson, the victims of two historical trends. First, growing joblessness during the 1970s and 1980s separated people from the workforce and from the acquisition of workforce skills. These individuals now lack the educational and technical preparedness that would serve them when employment conditions improve. Second, this group has been isolated by the withdrawal of other blacks into working and middle-class black neighborhoods and sometimes into predominantly white areas. Those left behind are substantially different from the "inner city" black residents of twenty or thirty years ago; they are more impoverished and they are much more isolated. Wilson refers to this isolation as a "concentration effect," where people "not only infrequently interact with those individuals and families who have had a stable working history and have had little involvement with welfare and public assistance, they also seldom have sustained contact with friends or relatives in more stable areas of the city or the suburbs" (1987:60). Wilson argues that this isolation is a new phenomenon, one of the 1970s and 1980s, and not a legacy of the poverty of the rural South. We can better understand their position, as well as that of other African Americans, by briefly considering the values and institutions that have characterized the black experience generally.

"ROOTS" AND AFRICAN-AMERICAN ETHNICITY

The "roots" phenomenon that Haley created led to searches for an ennobling ancestry by African Americans and by members of other ethnic groups including many whites. Yet a public sense of historical legitimacy is not the same as understanding how that history bears on the problems and conflicts of contemporary life. Billingsley (1968) has provided a useful overview of the African past, one that puts history in a cultural context.

He notes that in West Africa, from which most of the slaves came, family life had great strength and was complex in ways not appreciated by Europeans.

Marriage was not a private arrangement between individuals but a community event, one in which permanent relations between lineages and across villages were established. Those relations had important economic and political significance for the families involved. Consequently, marriage ceremonies were marked by extensive public rituals. These customs had the authority of centuries of tradition and were linked to highly elaborate theological systems and well-defined principles of family organization. In a lineage system traced through the male line, typical of some groups, a man, his sons, their wives, and their children all shared a living area under the senior male's authority. In lineage systems traced through the female line, as was common in other areas, groups of brothers, their wives, and their offspring all lived together, and the brothers acted collectively on behalf of their lineage. In each system, a complex set of rules governed relations between spouses, adults and children, and members of other households. Embedded in larger lineage relationships and ultimately in village and regional linkages, extended family patterns evolved over many generations. It was a way of living that was rewarding to those who grew up in it. Every individual had a place in the world, a place defined by kin connections. Citizenship was equivalent to kinship, and large kinship networks assured that the physical necessities of daily life, as well as moral support in times of crisis, would always be available.

The organization of the slave trade and of the slave-based plantation economy in North and South America and the West Indies made it difficult if not impossible for enslaved Africans to maintain an uninterrupted and secure domestic life. There were various reasons for this. Men were enslaved more often than women because slavery was primarily a labor-supply system; more could be gained by having men rather than women working on plantations. Unlike slavery in Catholic-Iberian areas such as Brazil, colonizers in Protestant and English areas of settlement placed little value on the family life of slaves. Individuals had the status of chattel property and could be sold according to economic need and their owner's sentiments. Family relationships were seen by whites as an impediment to efficient plantation operations. Reproduction and child rearing were expenses most plantation owners wanted to avoid. In addition, a slave's life was short, rarely more than a decade in the early years of slave trading. Older or sick individuals were a liability to an estate, and few were given care of any kind. Almost none lived to old age.

Given these characteristics of the plantation economy, the opportunities for maintaining any kind of family were very limited. The most outstanding characteristic of the slave family was its lack of autonomy. Legal marriage did not exist, and the remembered African marriage rituals that might have been practiced were not tolerated by whites. Whereas some planters encouraged marriage among their slaves, others had little interest in the matter, and none would allow a marriage relationship to interfere with the sale and transfer of a slave. Frequently owners simply assigned specific men and women to share a dwelling, with or without a marriage ceremony. This was done in order to minimize time spent on courting activities and to preserve a measure of domestic peace in the slave cabins. When one partner to the relationship died or was sold to settle an owner's debts, another was supplied as a replacement. Slaves were viewed as units of labor and their personal preferences had little to do with how that labor was exploited.

The economic demands of the plantation regime also interfered with people's ability to establish enduring parental roles. Both men and women were expected to work for the estate, not on behalf of their domestic units. Most of that work was in the fields, although some also worked in the houses of the masters as personal servants, a topic on which there is a rich and often ironic folklore in the African-American community (Abrahams 1964). While their parents labored, small children were tended by old women or by older children. Some estates even had small huts where children were kept during the day. When men and women returned from the fields, their children had been fed and cared for by others, thus limiting the contact of parents with their own offspring. The fact that slaves were required, on their own time, to work small provision grounds to supplement the food supplied by their masters meant that adults were further separated from their children as well as from each other. Their economic roles on the estate came first; domestic responsibilities were secondary. Neither parent could protect the other from abuse or separation by estate owners and neither had much opportunity to supervise children.

Instability in family life was inevitable. Nevertheless, certain patterns did emerge. Men asserted domestic authority when they were able to do so and established close and affectionate ties to their spouses and children within the limits imposed by plantation life. Women were attentive both to their children and to their husbands, and all adults played important roles in instructing children in the etiquette of race relations and physical survival. Often these supportive functions were carried out within a monogamous, nuclear family unit. Where individual planters permitted, older persons and single adults shared quarters with a family, creating an extended family unit. Estate owners generally avoided involvement in domestic relations in the slave quarters unless issues of plantation economics were involved. (The important exception, of course, was the sexual license of white men with female slaves.) Consequently, a small but very limited measure of household control was possible, and men and women could exert their authority within this sphere.

This very limited autonomy was always threatened by the selling of individuals and the dispersal of family members over many estates. Marriages or stabilized mating relationships were often ended this way. Yet the sense of kin ties and obligation, so important in the African homeland, persisted. Vigorous efforts were made by both men and women to be reunited with spouses, children, and other persons regarded as family friends or members. Consequently, kinship linkages and the sentiments of kinship often spanned several plantations. This created a network of communication and even clandestine economic support. It extended people's knowledge of the world beyond individual plantations, including the knowledge that in times of need, help might be available from a distant source. Thus the plantation regime with its stark sense of isolation and helplessness was moderated by an awareness of a larger community, one that could offer limited support in an economic as well as a moral sense.

Recent historical research has suggested that family patterns emerged in pre– and post–Civil War black communities that were distinctive to them and not simply imitations of the norms of Southern whites (Gutman 1976, 1984). These patterns, which initially appeared in the mid-1700s, included an emphasis on extended family networks, strong intergenerational ties, distinctive naming practices, emphasis on sibling loyalties as a model for other relationships, and nurturance of fictive kinship linkages. Fictive kin are unrelated individuals who are treated "as family" and may even have affectionate kinship titles such as "uncle" or "sister." The expansive and inclusive use of kinship terms helped socialize children into the larger community, not just the residential unit, and it enlarged an individual's protective network. It was this emphasis on *kin networks* and *kin-oriented values*, not simply "families" and individual households, that made these black family patterns unique. Gutman (1976) has documented the extensive historical evidence for these patterns—in diaries, plantation account books, letters, newspapers, and legal records—in the South as well as colonial New England. These patterns contributed to a powerful sense of communal awareness and an ethic of generalized obligation and mutuality that often overrode household boundaries. These features—extended family, intergenerational ties, and flexible kinship terminology—continue as important cultural themes among contemporary African Americans.

The common white view that slaves had no family life overlooks these historical facts, yet it remains one of the most persistent stereotypes of African-American culture even today. It has spawned both negative moral judgments and theories of deficiency in the interpretation and understanding of contemporary African-American communities and individuals. Child-rearing practices, household composition, language and communication styles, and religious beliefs have all been viewed not as products of a history of survival but rather as evidence of failure to assimilate to white standards. These misjudgments of the African-American experience continue to have a pernicious impact on the thinking of many Americans about the realities of the black experience. Several examples illustrate the point.

First, academic theories of a "culture of poverty" and the alleged failings of the "female-centered family" have reinforced (and given authoritative justification to) stereotypes that all black people conform to the same set of values and living styles. In fact, there is great diversity in the African-American community, and it is as difficult to summarize the varieties of that experience as it is to typify the family preferences of all whites.

Second, deficit interpretations do not take into account those persons who succeed, either by the standards of their own or the white community. The achievements of individual African Americans, when they are noticed, are taken as proof that the system "works," or that individuals can "rise above" their station in life if they just try hard enough. The social and psychic costs of that mobility, when it occurs, are rarely appreciated or understood.

Third, a view of others that sees them as deviant from so-called mainstream values rather than participants in a parallel cultural tradition ignores the fact that history and tradition are potential sources of strength. Of all the ethnic groups in America, it is the culture of African Americans that has been most thoroughly stigmatized by the larger society; indeed, the debate over the nature of African-American culture continues as artists, writers, politicians, and social critics, black and white, struggle to comprehend the full meaning of our cultural pluralism (Gwaltney 1980, 1986; Steele 1989). Whatever the nature of that parallel tradition, there is no question that it is highly diverse and also something quite distinctive.

VARIATIONS IN THE AFRICAN-AMERICAN COMMUNITY

Many researchers, both black and white, have attempted to describe and summarize the diversity of the African-American community (Green 1970, 1978; Dressler 1985a; Dressler, Hoeppner, and Pitts 1985; McAdoo 1988; Williams 1981). In a recent discussion of the black aged, Stanford argues that "Black older persons should be viewed from the perspective of their own history, without having to suffer the indignity of being compared with those older persons who have, for the most part, had entirely different social, political, and economic experiences" (1990:41). He proposes the concept of "diverse life patterns," the "culmination of the multiple effects of the unique experiences of the black older person" (1990:42), as an important way of identifying the variability that exists among African Americans. Following Stanford's suggestion, I will review several researchers' efforts to describe that internal complexity. In doing so, it is important to recognize that diversity is to some degree a response to the crippling effects of racism and powerlessness over long periods of time, a point well made by Solomon (1976) in her important book on empowerment. But it is also reflective of an inherited tradition of West African origins.

Hill (1971) has identified some of the general social forms and cultural strategies that have been critical to that survival. They are themes that underlie the diversity of the black community and give it coherence. Briefly, they are:

1. Strong kinship bonds linking a variety of households.
2. A strong work orientation in support of family ties.
3. A high level of flexibility in family roles.
4. A marked achievement orientation, particularly in the areas of educational and occupational success.
5. Commitment to religious values and to the African American church as one of the defining and sustaining institutions of the community.
6. Commitment to a language tradition, black English, and appreciation of the skills and subtleties of bilingualism.

It is important if not critical to note that these themes are not associated with deficiency-oriented explanations of cultural difference. They are positive values, contributing to the strength and survival of individuals and families. There is in addition, however, a dimension that is more difficult to define. Solomon (1976:169) has argued that African-American family patterns "for the most part are more humanistic and have greater validity than the hollow values of middle-class American society." She argues that there is a strong sense of hope and integrity that is linked to black religious belief and that this humanistic as well as religious orientation parallels and is different from the values of the dominant white community. If the traditional Puritan work ethic of the white community can be described as task oriented and motivated by economic success, then the African-American community can be described in Solomon's terms as more person oriented, favoring the cultivation of relationships and expressive communication styles. This is a challenging hypothesis, one on which there has been relatively little rigorous comparative research. But it points to an important, perhaps pervasive cultural contrast, one that may distinguish large segments of the African-American community from the politically and economically dominant white world.

In his study of a poor African-American neighborhood in Pittsburgh, Williams (1981, 1992) emphasizes these expressive values as the "genuine" black culture of that community and, by implication, other urban black communities as well. He carefully documents the behavioral and value elements of an explicitly anti-white worldview. They include an emphasis on verbal and body communication that clearly signifies who is and who is not a "true" member of the community; social and economic reciprocity so intense that it significantly reduces the social distance among community members; a preference for public over private locales as sites for intense interaction; and hostility toward other blacks not seen as "genuine" in terms of these values. To enforce their codes, the people Williams studied creatively invented and enacted a variety of "degradation rituals" that mocked not only the values of mainstream American society but also the behavior of blacks who mixed with whites and presumably acquired "white" sensibilities. As sympathetic as Williams was to the problems of these terribly poor neighborhoods, he also saw the culture they generated as self-defeating in some ways, perpetuating an insularity and hostility to even occasional opportunities for economic improvement. Yet they replicated in local terms deeply held black values concerning separateness and self-identity despite the disapproval of the outside world.

In an effort to characterize African-American diversity more explicitly, particularly in urban areas, Hannerz (1969) carried out extensive ethnographic research in Washington, D.C. His work, which popularized the term "lifestyle," moved away from the prevalent culture of poverty and social deficit models. As an anthropologist who relied on in-depth interviews and extensive participant observation for data collection, he saw four major lifestyles in the black neighborhoods he studied:

1. "Mainstreamers" adhere closely to the values they associate with middle-class American life. Usually married, they live in nuclear families and enjoy some

level of economic, educational, and occupational success. This group constitutes the black middle class and is a slowly growing segment of the African-American community in the city.

2. "Swingers" are the children of some of the mainstreamers, young adults who delay settling down and who are intensely involved in a variety of social, political, educational, or athletic activities with their peers. Marriage brings an end to their heavy socializing, mortgages and careers forcing them into the mainstream followed by their parents.

3. "Street families" are found in the poorest parts of the city, are often female headed, and struggle to maintain themselves. Members of street families are highly mobile because of the need to pursue economic opportunities. They are often involved in larger networks of households on whom they rely for some degree of assistance.

4. "Street corner men," while a very small portion of the total black population, are a highly visible part of it. They are often the poorest and least educated individuals in the community, and few have fixed or long-term domestic attachments. They are most likely to come into contact with the larger society's institutions of control.

The degree to which Hannerz's characterizations are accurate can be debated. Other urban centers might reveal lifestyles different from those he found in Washington, D.C. There may be more than the four styles enumerated, as geographical variations and subcommunities within subcommunities are common. This is an important point, although it does not diminish the sensitivity and power of Hannerz's analysis. We need to know how members of a community view diversity among themselves, and Hannerz has succeeded at this where deficit-oriented explanations have failed. The next step is to appreciate how that diversity is experienced on a day-to-day basis.

It is this level of understanding, the emic level, that Martin and Martin (1978) forcefully presented in their study of African-American families in the Chicago area. Studying family issues as community members rather than as outsiders, they attempted to refine previous sociological and anthropological characterizations. They defined the African-American family as:

> *a multigenerational, interdependent kinship system which is welded together by a sense of obligation to relatives; is organized around a "family base" household; is generally guided by a "dominant family figure"; extends across geographical boundaries to connect family units to an extended family network; and has a built in mutual aid system for the welfare of its members and the maintenance of the family as a whole (1978:1).*

In their research, the Martins found that a typical extended family network may include five or more households centered around a base unit, the family "home," where an informally recognized family leader resides. This model of the African-American family is illustrated in Figure 6.1 on page 188. In this example,

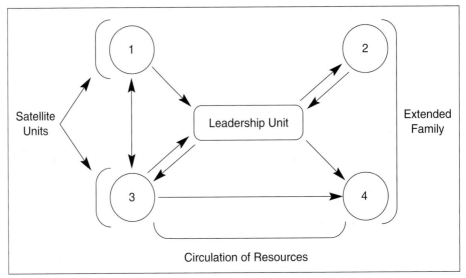

FIGURE 6.1   Model of the African-American family.

Based on Martin, Elmer P., and Joanne M. Martin [1978.] *The Black Extended Family.* Chicago: University of Chicago Press.

the emic view of "family" is a central household connected to satellite units. These units vary in their composition but they all look to the base household for leadership. That leadership is an important source of stability and direction for others in the family network. Satellite households can and do have relationships among themselves, but services and information are often routed through the base household. The base is usually the home of the family's founding couple who, as they age and become grandparents, become increasingly important and powerful in the affairs of the entire family network.

The flexibility of this system is the ease with which individuals are incorporated into households and, consequently, into the total family network. In poorer families, those who attach themselves to a unit may bring added burdens, stretching resources thinner than they already are, but they can also bring new opportunities—a regular paycheck, material goods, connections to other families, and useful knowledge or skills. Pooled resources make it possible for more people to survive, if only marginally better. In her work among very poor African-American families, Stack (1975:6) found one case of fourteen individuals surviving on a yearly income of less than $5000. Family members were discouraged from leaving, and the additional wages even from part-time, low-paying work were critical to the survival of the entire unit.

Martin and Martin found that the senior male in the base household was typically the main provider, not only for his own unit but sometimes for several others. The female head was often responsible for distributing pooled resources among satellite units, caring for young children in them and making decisions affecting everyone in the family. That put her in a very powerful leadership position. When a dominant figure in the base household died, either the surviving spouse assumed the family's leadership position or another adult was informally eased into it. The new leader might be an eldest daughter or another adult child who was close to the family leaders. If no one assumed that position, the family network would be in danger of disintegrating.

This structure of the extended family illustrates Hill's argument that one of the strengths of African-American families is their diversity and flexibility in kinship roles. This flexibility is part of the "social security" that the black family provides. Even when members of satellite units achieve a high level of economic achievement and stability, family traditions of reciprocity in goods, cash, and services often continue (McAdoo 1979). This mutual aid system is based on a moral imperative that the benefits that accrue to a few ought to be made available to others so that the entire family survives. Group interests are expected to predominate over individual ones. This pattern of sharing and the strong value of reciprocity are apparently widespread in African-American communities as well (Zollar 1985).

African traditions are one source of the culture of the African-American community. The values of the larger society, particularly those associated with educational and occupational attainment, are another. Pinderhughes (1979, 1982), however, argues that there is a third force to be considered. She suggests there is a "victim system," a set of self-reinforcing beliefs and practices contributing in some ways to the perpetuation of poverty and hopelessness. Those who possess the least and those whose opportunities are the most diminished, develop a distinctive, protective victim mentality. The victim system emphasizes a present (as against future or past) orientation; trust in religion, magic, or luck; personal impulsiveness and high emotional expressiveness; and manipulativeness in relationships (Pinderhughes 1979:26).

The implications of this argument, if there is in fact a "victim system" in the African-American community, and if it is an indispensable part of being black in America, are enormous. It suggests that a culture is more than its historical backlog of strengths and assets, more than the flexibility and adaptability of its social forms. Each generation is faced with the need to find new responses to new forms of discrimination. What worked in the past may be maladaptive in the present and the celebrated strengths of the past may not assure survival tomorrow. If Pinderhughes is correct, one can be victimized by an obvious and present oppressor, but one can also be victimized by the inappropriateness of old responses to new forms of danger.

The traits listed by Pinderhughes are difficult to interpret, and they may or may not be overstated (Foster and Perry 1982). But either as a set of heroic responses (too often subject to romanticization by outsiders who have not been victims themselves), or as an ideological and emotional trap (thus confirming the biases of those who would blame the victim anyway), they are certainly not characteristic of the whole of the African-American community. Combining the notion of a "victim system," if that is an accurate description, with the diverse heritage of African cultural forms and the horrors of slavery, we get a picture of great cultural complexity. It also becomes apparent that development of ethnic competence in social services for African Americans is more difficult and more fascinating than simplistic integrationist and assimilationist models could ever suggest.

AFRICAN AMERICANS AND SOCIAL SERVICES

With the emergence of the civil rights movement of the l960s, the helping professions were dramatically reminded of the needs of the African-American community and of an unfortunate history of neglect in services to black clients. Indeed, not only was the adequacy of services a point of contention, but racism within social work itself became an issue. A landmark editorial in a 1964 issue of *Social Casework* announced that problems in the relationship of the profession to African Americans could no longer be ignored:

> *The relative dearth of literature on the racial factor in casework treatment, . . . and the conspicuous absence of research on the subject suggest that repressive psychological mechanisms may be at work. Perhaps it is difficult for a profession committed to humanistic tenets to engage in honest appraisal of possible disparities between its ideals and its accomplishments (1964:155).*

That statement was a welcome one in that it recognized the potential for racism within an avowedly helping profession. But it was also a manifestation of the limited understanding of racial issues typical of many professionals at that time, particularly evident in the curious, now almost quaint way the source of the problem was described—"repressive psychological mechanisms may be at work." As a psychological (as against an environmental or sociological) view of the origins of the problem, racism within social services was attributed to ignorance, fear, and guilt. The question of institutional sources of racism, of racism as an endemic feature of the environment of both blacks and whites, was not addressed.

The *Social Casework* editorial did inspire, however, a proliferation of research activities and research reports on how racism might be a potential factor in human services. Typically, the center of this new interest was the client-practitioner relationship. The research literature analyzed, often in psychological terms, the complexities of cross-racial encounters between white workers and black clients (Fibush 1965, Bloch 1968, Simmons 1963); black workers and white clients (Curry 1964); and in racially mixed service settings (Lide 1971, Fibush and Turnquest 1970). The significance of race in interviewing (Kadushin 1972) and in clinical work was also discussed. These studies of the 1960s and 1970s launched a trend that, to some degree, continues. Most of them concluded that racism in some form did indeed exist in social services, that it created problems for communication and worker effectiveness in interracial encounters, and that some of the problems could be overcome when people learned to cope with their feelings about race.

But was that response, with its emphasis on interpersonal encounters and re-examining feelings, an adequate one for the profession? Is race simply a "factor" to be recognized and added to existing intervention formulas for working with clients? Is it sufficient, as one commentator proposed, "to examine and loosen these 'repressive psychological mechanisms' by means of an honest appraisal" (Lide 1971:432)? The reply of some black social workers and of many black critics of social work has been a qualified if not negative one, and they have called for something more ambitious. Their concerns, then and now, focus on three issues.

First, some critics (Devore 1983, and Gwyn and Kilpatrick 1981, for example) have argued that traditional, individualistic approaches to problem solving can do little to improve the lot of many African-American individuals. Intervention based on psychodynamic theories is at best palliative and, at worst, counterproductive to the advancement of blacks as a group. These critics have emphasized that solutions cannot be limited to assisting clients in resolving immediate personal problems; the helping agent must also act to change the system of control itself, a system that creates barriers to productive living for the majority of black people. Thus, an exclusive focus on the mental state of the minority client and the social worker's intellectual and emotional problems in relating to it diverts attention from the ecological sources of that client's problems. Solomon has put it bluntly and forcefully: "Powerlessness is a more virulent stressor than anxiety. Consequently, empowerment becomes a more important treatment goal than reduction of anxiety" (1982:166).

The Black Task Force Report of the Family Service Association of America (Delaney 1979) also illustrates the general critique of individualistic intervention based on psychodynamic models. That report stresses an ecological systems perspective, which "widens the scope of assessment to include the transactions between poor black individuals and the systems within and outside their neighborhoods" (1979:12). This suggestion, while it does not negate a psychodynamic approach, broadens the areas of concern to include structural factors that impinge on the lives of black communities.

A second criticism has been that the strengths of the African-American family have been ignored (Jackson 1993). Years of research and more research dollars than probably can be accounted for have gone into demonstrating the supposed deficiencies of the black family, blaming it for many of the community's problems. These studies culminated in the infamous Moynihan report (1965), a document whose influence persists, despite its weaknesses and the criticisms made against it (Rainwater and Yancey 1967). Moynihan described the African-American family as a "tangle of pathology . . . capable of perpetuating itself without assistance from the white world" (Moynihan 1965:47). This notion of minority families as the source of their own problems has been attractive to conservative interests, to whom it has been convenient to "blame the victim" (Ryan 1969). But the idea also held appeal for a number of liberal, humanistic, mostly white scholars and social workers who were attracted to the "culture of poverty" idea and who, despite a genuine concern for righting the inequalities of racism, were prone to romanticize pathology and find its causes largely in the very people who were being victimized. It is now apparent that these deficiency-oriented explanations and the catchphrases associated with them—"cultural deprivation," "multiple-problem families," "female-centered" family—were seriously misleading.

The ethnographic evidence demonstrates that African-American families and households are often highly flexible and effective in coping with the problems of poverty, although there are conflicting theories as to why this is the case (Fine, Schwebel and James-Myers 1987). Black values centering around children, elders, and the quality of interpersonal relations are more intense and subtle than outsiders have been willing to recognize. These features are all sources of strength and represent, according to Billingsley (1968), a "bundle of complexity" rather than a "tangle of pathology." What that cultural complexity means for the effective delivery of social services is a topic that is finally being addressed in the social work and social science literature (Dedmon and Saur 1983).

A third criticism of the social service system, one often made by African American social workers, is their profession's neglect of indigenous forms of assistance already in place. The black church has served a number of service functions for many years (Solomon 1985). Senior citizen services, day care, credit unions, housing developments, and education in survival skills are just a few services offered by this sometimes overlooked institution. Indeed, the black church in its various forms is probably the oldest helping institution in the African-American community. One religious leader has described it as "the first welfare organization on earth" (Jemison 1982:40). Prior to the American Civil War, there were itinerant black ministers in much of the South, small and scattered congregations, and many mutual aid societies, some of which were the forerunners of contemporary denominations. These societies took care of their members in illness, handled the expenses of burials, and gave small amounts of money to orphans and widows. They were also leaders in literacy and education, using the Bible as a text. All of these groups and their activities constituted an "invisible church," linking black groups both before and after emancipation (Bullock 1967).

One result of this historical experience has been great variety in religious expression among African Americans up to the present time, a variety as great or greater than any other ethnic group. Baer and Singer (1981) have tried to summarize that diversity in what they call a "typology of black sectarianism." They see four major kinds of black religious institutions. Established or mainstream denominations such as the African Methodist Episcopal Church and the National Baptist Convention USA tend to adhere to the values of middle-class America. But they also pursue an agenda of social reform and community improvement. Messianic-nationalist groups repudiate white society and its religious practices while affirming the sovereignty of the black community. Their doctrines foresee a return to former positions of power and integrity, either in Africa or selected parts of America. Black "conversionist" groups often emphasize a strict, even puritanical, ideology, and encourage the spiritual conversion of their members through ecstatic experiences that include energetic singing and dancing. Although unstable in an institutional sense, conversionist groups flourish in most African-American communities, and their combined membership makes up a substantial portion of all black church affiliation. Finally, there are "spiritualist" churches, mostly small and localized, which in addition to their ritual enthusiasm work to help their members solve very practical problems with employment, money, love, family matters, and health (Baer 1981).

Given this social diversity and its historical depth, it is apparent that the African American churches are a major institutional element of the African American world. They meet a variety of human needs and do so in incredibly diverse ways. They are a rich resource not only for those who affiliate with individual congregations but for those who might want to know more about their helping practices and the people who have quietly served for so long.

IDEOLOGY AND CARE

But the African-American church is not the only source of care, aid, and support. The help seeking model directs our attention to other, sometimes less visible, forms of community strength, especially forms that are ideological. One example of this is an ethnomedical system of belief and care that is important not only to a significant portion of the African-American community in the United States but is found in some rural, largely white areas as well. This is a set of beliefs about health, illness, and general well-being derived from older European as well as African sources. The African origins of these beliefs are bodies of knowledge common to the west coast of Africa during the time of slave trading in the seventeenth and eighteenth centuries. The European origins are just as old and were brought to North America by the earliest immigrants. There is no generalized name for this system of knowledge, although terms like "witchcraft" and "spiritualism" have been used and there is a wide range of practitioners, from herbalists and "rootworkers" to faith healers and midwives (Baer 1981). In its contemporary form in the African American community, it is a consistent, self-contained set of principles for accounting for the problems that beset individuals. It is associated with practitioners who, under some circumstances, provide effective assistance to those who seek it. It is not a set of beliefs typical of all African Americans and should not be regarded as such. But it is common in some parts of the United States and is an instructive example of how local belief and practice can coexist with so-called mainstream health institutions.

This ethnomedical system has been studied by a number of anthropologically oriented researchers, not only in this country but also in the West Indies and in Africa (Snow 1973, 1974, 1977, 1978; Whitten 1962; Wintrob 1973). It is thus very widespread and some of its elements appear in a number of communities. The system is based on a fundamental division of illness, mental as well as physical, into two kinds: that which is "natural" and that which is "unnatural." Natural illness results from failure of the individual to properly care for the body. It may also come about as divine punishment for one's misdeeds. In either event, a lack of wellness is due to an improper relationship with natural forces. Cold air, strong drafts, misuse of alcohol, or poor diet can all be responsible for illness and can signify the individual's inattention to basic health and hygiene requirements. Similarly, illness that is a consequence of God's displeasure results from failure to respect principles of decency and morality as they have been established by Biblical and church authorities.

By contrast, unnatural illness is the result of evil influence. Illness may range from obvious physical ailments to psychosomatic symptoms to problems commonly classified as mental health concerns. But they are all similar in that their origin is in the evil intentions and the evil actions of others. Unlike natural illnesses, unnatural ones are initiated by a human agent against a victim and fall outside the orderly domain of the universe established by God and nature. Various terms for this activity are "hexing," "rootwork," "fix," "mojo," and occasionally "witchcraft." It is believed that evil intentions and evil actions are efficacious because all events in the universe are interconnected, and if one knows the interconnections and how to use them, one can have a measure of influence and control over others. It is the wrongful use of this power, not the knowledge of occult things per se, that is evil. Thus, the individual who suffers an inexplicable physical or mental problem has reason to believe that someone else may be the cause of it. It is important, therefore, to find a specialist who can identify the source of the problem and deal with it.

Clearly, neither mental health specialists nor biomedically oriented professionals are in a position to respond to individual complaints based on this kind of conceptualization of illness and misfortune. But there are individuals in the African-American community who are effective as far as they and many of their clients are concerned. These healers are variously known as psychics, rootworkers, counselors, and root doctors. Snow (1973, 1978) has described in detail the skills and procedures of a woman she calls a "voodoo practitioner." What is remarkable are the similarities of her techniques to those of some mental health professionals. The woman's practice was located in her home in the downtown section of a large southwestern American city. Her clients included blacks, whites, Indians, and Mexican Americans. Snow had difficulty locating her because she was known only by word of mouth. Yet her place of business was similar to that of many doctors, counselors, and other professionals. She had an office in which she kept nine-to-five hours, and patients met her in a waiting room. She was trained by her grandmother, who also possessed special healing powers and who was widely known in the local community for her skills. The training consisted of learning ways to utilize her "gift" in helping others, a gift with which she was born and which could not be obtained in any other way. Portions of her therapy involved touching and massage, but much of it involved talking through a problem. Using an idiom with which most black patients were intimately familiar, including the personalities and events of the Bible, she was able to illuminate the sources of personal difficulties and ways of coping with them.

Snow's practitioner made use of the critical distinction between natural and unnatural illnesses, claiming no special medical skills for those problems that were clearly within the domain of medical providers.

"Now an unnatural sickness, well, that's a person that's sick in the mind. Mentally sick. Doctors can't find that. They Xray and they can't find it. . . . And yet they are sick, mentally sick in mind. And then, I'm a counselor, I counsel them. . . . I give 'em medicine you know, through their mind. I call that spiritual medicine" (Snow 1973: 278).

Judged by the enthusiasm of her patients and the size of her clientele, this practitioner was very successful in her community. She did not compete with established medical professionals, as both she and her patients recognized that she dealt with problems that such practitioners were not trained to handle. Furthermore, she had an intimate knowledge of the pressures of life in the African-American community and of how poor people are vulnerable to forces they cannot control. Many of her clients came to her after having seen certified, mainstream counselors and social workers. These clients were disappointed with the kind of treatment they received and had concluded that professionally trained experts could not treat the kinds of problems that afflicted them.

It is especially important to note, as Snow does, that these beliefs in unnatural illness are not simply the legacy of prescientific superstitions. It would be a serious error to interpret them that way. Rather, unnatural illnesses "are those that have to do with the individual's position as a member of society. . . . Some arise from the tensions and anxieties of everyday living. . . . Hostility in interpersonal relationships, on the other hand, may cause the individual to become the target of witchcraft" (Snow 1973:272–273). Where social relationships are strained because of the problems of poverty, discrimination, and exclusion from full participation in the larger society, beliefs in the efficacy of evil influences are a reasonable response to the daily problems of living (Rainwater 1970). A remarkable discussion of this form of healing, rich with case material, can be found in Snow's latest book (1993), documenting the operation of this complex system of traditional belief and community-based care. She effectively makes the argument that it is alive and well in many parts of America.

Foster and Anderson (1978) have identified a number of characteristics of healers and curers, which they believe are the marks of healing individuals in many cultures. These include specialization, selection and training, certification, an aura of capability or professionalism, expectations of payment, and an ambivalent public image. Snow's practitioner fits all these criteria. She has a specialized store of knowledge—the treatment of unnatural mental and physical illness—and she was specially selected and trained for her task. That selection came about through the influence of her grandmother, but it was also a divine choice. "I was born just exactly with the gift," she said. Certification of competence was oral, in the testimony of patients, and did not require framed certificates issued by hallowed institutions. Further, she conducted her practice as a business, and, as she herself admitted, her public image was a mixed one. Some in the community accused her of manipulating dark and forbidden forces. Yet she responded that she was simply implementing the power, the "gift," that God had given her.

To the extent that Snow's respondent had success with her patients, it must be attributed not only to her personal skill in counseling others but also to the sense of legitimacy she enjoyed in her community. It is this legitimacy that strangers and outsiders, stationed in agencies that are themselves outposts of larger, alien bureaucracies, cannot hope to obtain simply through formal training and completion of specialized, degree-granting programs. Outsiders can acknowledge, however, the importance of indigenous help providers such as this practitioner and, to the extent feasible, attempt to learn something of their methods and the reasons for their success. Cultural awareness does not require imitation of the skills of knowledgeable insiders, however desirable that may sometimes be, so much as it presupposes an honest sensibility as to who and what is really helpful and how resources can best be utilized.

CULTURE CONTRASTS AND ETHNIC COMPETENCE

This brief review of the African-American experience and the institutions and ideologies that have emerged within it makes clear that there are major historical differences between blacks and whites. It is important to see those differences as creative and life affirming responses to nearly four centuries of persecution and injustice. The differences have also led to a distinctive cultural configuration within the larger American society. The issue for intervention and for the ethnically competent worker is not simply that these differences exist, but that their meaning and significance be explicitly known in counseling relationships (Gwyn and Kilpatrick 1981).

It is worth repeating that *contrasts,* not just differences, are important in the ethnic competence approach. To identify and describe only difference is to assume an "us versus them" stance: "they" are different from "us"; "we" know what "their" differences mean. Clearly, that is the formula for stereotyping. By emphasizing contrast, however, the worker is put fully into the relationship as an engaged participant. The practitioner, after all, is "different" in the client's eyes, and the client's perceptions of contrast are at least as important to the dynamics of the event as the social worker's. By looking at contrasts rather than differences, everyone is required to evaluate the cultural baggage they bring to the conversation and what that means for quality service.

Table 6.1 presents a series of contrasts in the form of brief statements. They represent a first step toward thinking about differences in legitimately comparative terms. I have brought these statements together from a variety of sources, including my reading, conversations with African-American scholars and social workers, teaching, and years of training workshops. They are not the only items that could have been included in the table, nor are they comprehensive, but they

TABLE 6.1   Selected Cultural Contrasts between the African-American and Anglo-American Communities

African American	Anglo American
Flexibility in family forms is considered normal; the word "family" sometimes refers to a household unit, and sometimes to a network of households containing affiliated kin.	The single-household "nuclear" family is the preferred form, although numerous variations occur and the perceived strengths and/or weaknesses of these variations are topics of discussion and sometimes controversy.
Extended family networks are common, usually centered on a "base" household with specific links to satellite households. Satellites may be newly married couples, single adults with children, or individuals living alone. The term "family" often includes these units.	Extended families in regular contact are believed to be uncommon although they occur in many communities. Individuals linked by kinship have limited obligations to one another and are expected to show loyalty to members of their own household first.
One individual in the base household commonly takes on a leadership role on behalf of all members of the family and their households. This individual is often an older woman, occasionally an older man. She may make day-to-day decisions affecting the welfare of others in the family network, and that leadership provides centrality and stability to the family as an extended unit.	Each household is its own base, a resident adult (often male) its real or nominal head. Adult decisions affect the members of the household, not kin in other units. Interference in the affairs of other units, even when well intended, is viewed as a transgression.
A mutual aid system is typical of extended family networks, and the welfare of others in the network is a primary obligation. Mutual aid is strongly linked to person-centered (in contrast to object-centered) values and to a diffuse sense of humanitarianism, assistance, and sharing.	The primary obligations of adults are to their own children, secondarily to the children of kin or to aged parents. Care of persons outside the nuclear family is a special task, sometimes seen as a hardship, that can intrude on responsibilities to one's immediate family, on one's personal needs, or on career aspirations.
Flexibility of roles is highly valued. Wives may work, older children may supervise younger ones, and children may be informally adopted as the needs of households vary. Relations between men and women are ideally egalitarian. Flexibility is viewed as critical to the survival of households and families.	Although men's and women's roles traditionally have been defined as separate and distinct, role clarity is sometimes difficult to maintain as economic expectations lead to two-career families.

Continued

TABLE 6.1   *Continued*

African American	Anglo American
Older persons are often held in high esteem, their experience in surviving in a hostile world viewed as evidence of skill and wisdom. A strong religious orientation is sometimes associated with aging and authority. Deference to elders sometimes demanded.	Older persons often retain their separateness and independence from the households of their adult children. They sometimes worry about "becoming a burden" on others and are expected to maintain their independence as long as possible.

are important statements and make a good starting point. Some of my sources for this overview include the publications of Barbara Solomon, the author of *Black Empowerment* (1976); Elmer and Joanne Martin, sociologists of the black family; Andrew Billingsley, a well known historian of the African-American experience; and Robert Hill, whose pioneering work with the Urban League identified critical issues confronting the community. But the table's form is not their responsibility. It is my own reading and interpretation of the issues they have said are important.

Among their many concerns, including those political and economic, I have chosen to highlight issues related to the family. My rationale is that myths about African-American families are widespread in American society and in many social services agencies. Further, issues concerning the family and its functioning underlie much of what social services is all about.

My emphasis on contrast rather than difference also suggests that the objective truth of cultural differences may be less important than beliefs about what that truth might be. For example, some blacks and some whites may look at specific items in the table and object: "That isn't me and the people I know!" That may be so and, in fact, in some cases it ought to be. The issue, from the perspective of the ethnic competence model, is: what kind of *generalizable statement* would be *more* true for a specific service population. Statements of cultural contrast are only starting points, *always* provisional and hypothetical. They are to be used for thinking about potential contrasts in values, beliefs, behavior, and social context, exactly the kinds of things social workers refer to when they speak of "individualizing the client." The only legitimate use of the table is in locating areas of potential contrasts, determining their salience for the service to be provided, and revising them as necessary in order to improve service outcomes with individual clients. I want to be as emphatic as I can that the statements are not "insider tips" that tell us what the people in any community are "really" like. They are generalizations, suggested in part by minority scholars and social workers, to help us think comparatively, both about others and about ourselves.

The reader is cautioned, then, that any set of generalizations in this book about a given community may or may not apply to specific individuals. We all vary in our commitment to the norms of our own community and in how we observe them. The contrast statements in the table refer only to general tendencies within groups, not to the attributes of individuals. It is the social worker's responsibility to determine if and how clients approximate those tendencies, and how they might be salient to resolving specific social service issues.

Clearly, the contrasts suggested in Table 6.1 show a strong orientation in the African-American community toward a rich and diverse family life, popular stereotypes notwithstanding. For instance, the concept of "family" is more open and flexible than that commonly used by whites. There is heavy reliance on others within a large network and, because of that, social services are "not necessarily the first and only place poor blacks turn to for help" (Neighbors and Taylor 1985:266). Within the family network there is often a strong sense of obligation and a value orientation that favors group needs over individual preferences. Jones (1983:423) has written that "the sense of 'we-ness', the need for interdependence, and cooperation are major humanistic themes permeating the motivational and behavioral system within black communities." This is not to say that this system of values and behavior always works the way individuals expect it to. Rather, it is a culturally recognizable standard used to judge the correctness of one's own behavior and that of others. It is also a standard for making comparisons, favorable and unfavorable, with the dominant white society. A culturally sensitive assessment, diagnosis, or treatment of African-American clients would have to take these standards, and especially their local and family variations, into account.

In their study of helping traditions within the African-American community, Martin and Martin (1985) identified general areas where inquiry into black family life can usefully begin. Questions they consider important include: How often do family members come to one another's aid? What are the relationships between those family members who are well established financially and those who are struggling? What is the nature of male/female relationships and how do men and women work to advance their joint interests? What are the values adults instill in children and how do they use spiritual resources in family life? How are institutions and networks used to secure aid when it is needed? And finally, "How race conscious are family members, and to what extent is racial consciousness a source of inspiration, pride, therapy, and commitment to black liberation and social change?" (Martin and Martin 1985:86). These are important questions that complement the topics suggested in Table 6.1. Any one of them could be the starting point for a culturally sensitive analysis of a family's needs and for planning appropriate intervention.

DEVELOPING SKILLS FOR SERVICES IN THE AFRICAN-AMERICAN COMMUNITY

Typically, whites (and sometimes members of other ethnic groups) are relatively inexperienced in working with African-American clients. This inexperience can lead to awkwardness and an occasional gaffe. Hunt (1987) has documented some of the most common ones, including pretenses to familiarity with street slang; self-effacement and apologetics for being white or privileged; and promotion of an "us versus the system" stance that the social worker hopes will find favor with minority clients. Name dropping (usually sports or entertainment figures) is only one step removed from the now discredited "some of my best friends are" comment. These errors, as well as others, are quickly recognized by minority persons who are sensitive to how whites respond to their presence (Davis 1984). Sykes (1987) has commented that in cross-racial social work, white counselors often fail to use even the normal interpersonal skills they routinely bring to their work with same-race clients, believing they must make heroic and even theatrical efforts to prove they are trustworthy.

One of the few models of counseling interaction between African Americans and whites is that developed by Gibbs (1981). She notes that there are important ethnic differences in the expectations African Americans and whites bring to a counseling relationship and that these differences have consequences for the encounter's outcome. She argues that "Blacks typically evaluate professional interactions in terms of the *interpersonal* skills demonstrated in initial encounters, while Whites typically evaluate similar interactions in terms of the *instrumental* skills demonstrated" (1981:166–167). Participants who focus on interpersonal skills are most attentive to moods and responses. The emphasis is on the dynamics or flow of the event, especially the flow of language. Those who focus on instrumental skills place more value on the results of the encounter. They are more oriented toward tasks and goal achievement, and language is a secondary device for achieving some desired or remote end.

This does not mean that blacks and whites inhabit entirely different linguistic worlds, or that they are incapable of understanding one another. It means that emphases vary according to cultural traditions and expectations. In her own interactions with schoolteachers during a research project, Gibbs found that blacks and whites each used interpersonal and instrumental ways of responding to others. But she also found that the sequencing varied: "Black teachers tended to respond to us in a very personal, non-task-oriented way in the initial phase of the consultation and became task-oriented much later in the project; while White teachers tended to be very task-oriented initially and developed personal relations with us much later in the project, if at all" (1981:176).

In Gibbs's model, from a black perspective there are five stages and sets of behavior in a consultative relationship. These stages are the "cultural lens" through which African-American clients interpret their meeting with a white counselor. These stages derive from a cultural preference for emphasizing, at least initially, the interpersonal over the instrumental.

In Stage I, which Gibbs calls the "appraisal stage," the client "sizes up" the counselor and minimizes the intensity of the interaction. Whites may interpret this as aloofness, reserve, hostility, or the stereotyped "inability to verbalize." But such distancing gives the client an opportunity to evaluate the counselor for honesty, genuineness, and the potential for trust later on.

Stage II involves the client's more assertive investigation of who and what the counselor is about. The client may ask questions about the counselor's personal life, experiences, and beliefs. He or she is trying to determine how willing the counselor is to go beyond stereotypes, power, or dominance. The search for egalitarianism as a personal (as against professional) quality is being explored.

This stage may be an opportunity to determine if and how race is a factor in a consultation. Jones and Seagull (1981), in their research on black-white interactions, suggest that "the issue of color difference should be brought up early in the relationship, certainly not later than the second session, but preferably in the first. . . . The white therapist should model such openness by examining his or her own feelings if they are relevant to the relationship" (p. 153).

Needless to say, this is a potentially explosive moment in counseling. Workers often dread it, may evade it, and always risk a disruptive faux pas. But to pretend that race is not an issue may be as damaging (and preposterous) as to launch into apologetics for being white, neither being a useful response and both indicating that a social worker is still struggling to get some sense of genuineness and understanding in handling cultural or racial differences. The ethnic competence model calls for veracity, a simple and straightforward statement that race, ethnicity, or general background may be an issue and it should be clarified.

At Stage III, the client "may make overtures to the consultant to establish a personal relationship characterized by the exchange of information, personal favors, [and] mutual obligations" (Gibbs 1981:169–170). Whereas white clients usually prefer to keep the exchange at a strictly professional level, black individuals may place greater emphasis on the willingness of the social worker to identify with the client personally as well as professionally.

Stage IV is the client's commitment to entering into a service plan. The client's language may still be that of personalism (such as expressing personal regard for the counselor), but the client may now be willing to consider the counselor's professional recommendations. Gibbs argues that at this stage white clients may also accept the counselor's program but will express that acceptance more in terms of commitment to the program goals than in terms of their interest in the counselor as a person.

In the last stage, Stage V, the client engages the counselor's program. Again, Gibbs notes the differing cultural agendas that may emerge. "While black persons will make this commitment as a result of their evaluation of the consultant's *interpersonal competence* in the first four stages, white persons will make this commitment in terms of the *instrumental competence* shown by the consultant up to this time" (Gibbs 1981:170).

While the cultural contrasts outlined in Table 6.1 are the beginnings of the social worker's knowledge base, Gibbs's intervention model suggests something of the interpersonal "style" that goes with using and expressing that knowledge. It is important to note that this notion of "style" contrasts dramatically with some of the standard operating procedures of health and social service organizations. While an organization's emphasis is on data gathering for administrative convenience or for short-term, highly focused intervention, the ethnically competent worker will need to find ways of accommodating both agency requirements and the expectations of clients. That in itself may be one of the more difficult tasks in acquiring ethnic competence.

African-American social workers and researchers have often been critical of their profession, especially as it relates to the members of their community. One target of that criticism has been the discipline's emphasis on the intrapsychic state of clients as a way of resolving problems, an approach that too often ignores the need for changes in the social and physical environment. "Talking therapies" are an example. Devore (1983) has called attention instead to the stressful experiences of black families, noting that problem resolution must also take account of the hostile environment in which they live. Similarly, Gwyn and Kilpatrick (1981) question traditional forms of family treatment, urging that it is an "ecological perspective, which treats environmental as well as emotional problems in a cultural framework, that can be most effective" for low-income African-American people (1981:265). They call for greater use of short-term therapy, cooperation with nonprofessional, indigenous counselors, frequent home visits, and careful planning of family tasks. The model proposed by Gibbs, and the knowledge base to be built through comparative understanding, are beginning points for addressing these issues in compassionate and culturally appropriate ways.

OTHER ISSUES OF IMPORTANCE

There are many issues on the agenda of those serving the African-American community. Two—the concerns of black men and needs of the black elderly—are identified here because they have been described as important by black professionals and because they can serve as guides to further discussion and reading about African-American clients.

Social Services and Black Men

Only recently have the special needs of African-American men been addressed by the social service and counseling professions (Gary and Leashore 1982). Historically, black men have had unemployment rates significantly higher than white males, with much lower incomes and very limited access to career ladders in labor, corporate, and professional work. Affirmative action programs have changed these circumstances for some but by no means for all. That African-American men would chose "mainstream" work and family patterns given an opportunity to do so has been demonstrated by sociologist William Julius Wilson (1987) in his studies in inner-city Chicago. Lack of job and career prospects not only reduces a man's ability to contribute to the well-being of a family, but it also isolates the individual from larger economic institutions and especially from the more successful and upwardly mobile men of the black community.

In addition to economic deprivation, Gunnings and Lipscomb (1986) have argued that black men are sometimes unfairly placed in competition with black women for education and employment opportunities, an added stress in families that are economically marginal (Gary 1986). The now infamous Senate confrontation between Clarence Thomas and Anita Hill brought the tension between African-American women and men to public view in a way many black people resented. One aspect of that situation is a phenomenon once rare but now more common, marriages between black men and white women, marriages that have their own special problems of adjustment (Pope 1986).

Finally, African-American men between the ages of 18 and 29 have a suicide rate four times that of black women of similar age (Davis 1982), and violence is a special concern for everyone living in the most depressed parts of urban as well as rural areas (Dressler, Hoeppner, and Pitts 1985; Hampton 1987). The victims of black crime are most often other black people who, because of their economic circumstances, cannot move to safer places to live.

June (1986) summarizes some of the critical issues in counseling African-American men. He argues that they are not usually prepared or willing to disclose personal problems, especially to strangers or to whites. Counseling is stigmatized as something suitable only for those who are "weak." Distrust of service providers is often expressed through distancing, shyness, or a "cool pose" (Vontress 1971; Majors and Nikelly 1983), which insulates the individual from threats. Reluctance is a common response to counselors in social service, educational, and health settings.

Resolving personal, educational, and employment difficulties involves recognizing the sense of oppression, grievance, and rage that many African-American men feel, including men of professional standing (Cose 1993). They are exposed to conflicting messages about what it means to be black in a white-dominated, consumer-oriented, careerist driven society, messages that neither they nor social service counselors can control. June suggests as a starting point—and as a minimal effort—that social workers and their agencies launch an aggressive outreach effort that utilizes a racially diverse service staff, develops ties with places and organizations where African-American men can be found, and explores with black professionals the nuances of communication styles and culturally appropriate counseling skills.

Now that the research and service obsession with the "female-centered, multiple-problem" family may be waning, the special needs of men are finally receiving attention in the professional and even popular literature. Other sources the reader should consult are three special issues of the *Journal of Multicultural Counseling and Development* [April 1985; July 1985; January 1986]; Robert Staples's *Black Masculinity* (1982); McAdoo and McAdoo on *Black Children* (1985); Gibbs's *Young, Black and Male in America* (1988); and the August 1983 issue of *Ebony* magazine.

The Black Elderly

The black elderly are the fastest growing segment of the African-American population and among the oldest of them there is a statistically interesting phenomenon called "cross over" (Markides and Mindel 1987). Generally, American blacks die earlier than whites, but those who survive to old age are on average more robust and live longer than their white counterparts. Thus, a growing number of very old black people will "cross over" to higher age categories as they outlive others in the population. The needs of these elders are considerable, for they are subject to what has been called a "double jeopardy," being both old and members of a minority group (Tally and Kaplan 1956; Jackson 1977; 1980; 1982). That jeopardy is, of course, differentially experienced not only by men and women but by African Americans in different parts of the country, in rural and urban settings, and in different social classes (Harel, McKinney, and Williams 1990). Yet the social science and social services literature of African-American aging often fails to note these differences, partly because it is narrowly focused on issues of "coping" and "survival skills." Although these are important, they are not the totality of the day-to-day experiences of the minority elderly nor are they all that is culturally meaningful and important to older persons (Green 1989).

One of the remarkable features of life among the African-American elderly is the intensity of their social involvement with others. Wylie (1971) asserts that blacks are more likely to demonstrate respect for elders, and more recent statistical studies of national samples appear to support the claim that "Black families do appear to be more involved in exchanges of help across generations" (Mutran 1985:388). There has been extensive discussion of the nature of the social networks that provide this care. Not only are they large but they also show regional variations. In the South, for example, elders are likely to be in regular contact with a sister, a friend, or a neighbor rather than with other kin, especially if the latter lives at an inconvenient distance. "Fictive kin," unrelated persons in kinship-like affectionate relationships, are especially important as sources of companionship and support (Chatters, Taylor, and Jackson 1985, 1986). Fellow church members are also a major source of support, little examined or appreciated in the research literature. Church members often assist with food and clothing, visitations, even church-sponsored housing and financial assistance (Taylor and Chatters 1986; Taylor and Taylor 1982).

An important issue among the elderly in any community is life review, the examining of personal history in a way that helps create a sense of predictability, fulfillment, and completion (Langness and Frank 1981). The need to review a life and establish its points of significance and accomplishment is a particularly critical issue among ethnic minorities (Myerhoff 1978; Myerhoff and Simic 1978; Kaufman 1986). For them, lifelong struggle is a common theme, which may or may not be resolvable. Assisting elders to generate and articulate their sense of integrity based on re-examining of a difficult life well lived is partially dependent on the sensitive worker's knowledge of the traditions of the client's community. The social worker must be able to respond knowledgeably to these culturally specific life reviews with more than a sympathetic ear or polite verbal reinforcement. Active listening, based on cultural knowledge and skill in ethnographic interviewing, goes well beyond more conventional social service concerns with "coping," and it typifies what is best in the ethnic competence approach.

OTHER BLACK COMMUNITIES

Many African Americans born and resident in the United States have family ties to the West Indies. The islands of the Caribbean were settled earlier than the eastern seaboard of this country and it was in the Caribbean that the system of slave-based plantations began. The original Indian inhabitants of the region were virtually exterminated within a century of Columbus's landfall, and African labor and European capital combined to create the system that turned once forested islands into sugar-producing slave societies. The economies of the early North American colonies were closely linked with those of the Caribbean. For several hundred years, ships left European ports with cheap trade goods to exchange for human cargo in West Africa. The infamous "middle passage" was the cross-Atlantic link that carried Africans first to the islands and Brazil and later to the Gulf and southeastern American colonies. Ships carried slaves, raw sugar, molasses, and rum from the Caribbean to southern and New England ports before returning home across the north Atlantic. Slavers from the West Indies and their cargos were a common sight all along the eastern seaboard for more than two hundred years.

It would be a mistake, however, to assume that the island cultures of the Caribbean are identical to their African-American counterparts in North America. Slavery ended throughout the West Indies a full generation earlier than it did in the United States. Whites were a tiny minority in the islands, and in the latter part of the nineteenth century their numbers diminished even further. In the past fifty years, most of the former colonies have become independent countries and, although they may be affiliated with their former colonizers, as is true of many of the British and the French islands, they run their own affairs. The islands are also people-exporting countries, economically dependent on the remittances of massive numbers of labor migrants, men and women, living in the eastern United States, eastern Canada, and the larger cities of England and France. There were well over a million English-speaking West Indians living in this country in 1980; now more than a decade later, their number is probably twice that.

These migrants represent a distinctive group even within their home countries. They tend to be young, many are educated, they are highly motivated to succeed, and they have a view of race and race relations that is their own. They are aware of the bipolar black-white distinction that dominates racial thinking in this country, but their own experience is more complex. Brice (1982) puts it this way:

> A light-skinned British West Indian who comes to the United States is in a dilemma. In the islands, he or she has a certain amount of status, at least more than a Black person. In the United States, however, Whites reject the British West Indian as "another Black," while Blacks may reject or look down on the West Indian because of his or her refusal to identify with other blacks (1982:126–127).

But the issue goes beyond race alone. Most West Indians, including those who become U.S. citizens, continue to assert their ethnic identity as one distinctive from that of North American blacks. They maintain ties with their island of origin, send money home to mothers, often retire to the islands, and continue to use their island patois in addition to the British standard of English they learned in school. They are proud of Caribbean cultural exports, especially calypso and reggae. They may observe island-based forms of Christianity along with African religious creeds, and they often have a "Commonwealth" point of view in matters of politics, soccer pools, and especially cricket.

There is an extensive social science literature on West Indian family patterns (Smith 1988) and the term "matrifocal" comes from an early phase of that research (Clarke 1957). Families of upper-class origins (often of light complexion) tend to adhere to European models of the patriarchal family. Men are expected to be dominant and children quiet and obedient. Great emphasis is placed on formal education, correct English, thrift, ownership of property, fidelity in marriage, and participation in mainstream churches. But most West Indians are not upper class, and it is common for a man and woman of modest origins to live together for many years, have children, and marry only when there is enough money to purchase a house. For them, as for other West Indians, hard work is valued because in the islands the acquisition of property is critical to improving one's status. Also valued is a knowledge of West Indian herbal medicines, use of West Indian folk healers, and beliefs and rituals associated with *obeah*. Pentecostal churches are common in West Indian communities, both in this country and in England and Canada.

There have been very few studies of West Indians in social service settings. Several important ones are those by Thrasher and Anderson (1988), Sewell-Coker, Hamilton-Collins, and Fein (1985), and Watts-Jones (1992). Caribbean migrants tend to come from rural backgrounds, and even those who lived in larger cities such as Port of Spain, Trinidad and Kingston, Jamaica often have important ties to country villages. Consequently, the culture shock of adjusting to life in New York City or Miami is often part of what brings islanders to the attention of social workers. (The study by Watts-Jones, cited above, of a Jamaican women suffering panic disorders is a good example.) West Indian families usually follow a pattern of chain migration in which one member finds a job and a place to live and sends for others as resources permit. Family life, therefore, is very fluid, with new members arriving as they can. Through informal patterns of sharing or "child-minding," children may live with grandmothers, aunts, or other women for years before joining one or both parents in the United States or in England. Given these long separations, family life never picks up where it "left off," and conflicts between children and parents are common.

It is important to note that West Indian migration to this country is often more a matter of women than of men. The "feminization" of Caribbean migration (Ho 1993), as it has been called, means that kinship and family life are really matters of maintaining long-distance, international networks. West Indian family life cannot be thought of in terms of discrete, localized, small household units. It is not that, even for those who remain home in the islands. Men but also women follow economic and educational opportunities where they can and they utilize far-flung friends and relatives to help them care for their children and to channel economic resources. Balancing job and family demands over distances of thousands of miles is costly and exhausting. But those who do it become skilled administrators of their time, money, and energy. Many of the stresses they face, quite apart from racism and adjusting to cultural differences, are the result of heroic efforts to achieve some balance in their obligations to distant people who are dependent on them.

Perhaps as a historical residue of slavery, corporal punishment is common in the Caribbean (Payne 1989). There is also a great emphasis on seniority, with elders as important decision makers on behalf of children. But decision making is not the same for boys and girls. Boys are given much more freedom, whereas there is great concern that girls may "get into trouble" (Sewell-Coker, Hamilton-Collins, and Fein 1985:564), usually meaning teenage pregnancy. There is also a great concern with propriety and its opposite, "rudeness." A rich oral and performative tradition surrounds "rudeness," from inspired calypso lyrics to the verbal stylistics of male-female verbal bantering. But rudeness is not acceptable in children or youth and is often handled by ritualized strapping (Payne 1989:397) or "giving licks." Adults, who place great emphasis on the privacy of family life, are dismayed when what they see as legitimate discipline brings them into contact with protective service workers. In their study of a Brooklyn area population, Thrasher and Anderson (1988) found a high incidence of suspected child abuse and high use (83 percent) of corporal punishment. They noted that "these parents expressed anger and confusion that their belief in physical punishment as an appropriate method of child rearing was in conflict with the dominant society. . . . [and that] it may lead to allegations of child abuse by non-West Indian observers" (1988:175). The same researchers found little in the vast child abuse literature that was applicable or helpful in their attempts to understand West Indian disciplinary practices.

Sewell-Coker, Hamilton-Collins, and Fein (1985) and her associates found that West Indians are neither familiar with nor greatly interested in family therapy counseling models as these have been developed for use with middle-class whites. Their recommendations are for more concrete, short-term forms of intervention such as organizing activities for youth and academic advising. Thrasher and Anderson (1988:176) describe West Indian clients as "formal and distant when interacting with authority figures and professionals," a feature that probably derives from British models of social class hierarchy and elitism that still dominate Caribbean societies. Sewell-Coker, Hamilton-Collins, and Fein (1985:565) go on to argue that "West Indians, a conservative people, do not readily express emotion. . . . [and] say little." Frankly, I find this very surprising. My two years of researching interisland migration in St. Croix taught me that West Indians are exceptionally gregarious, often wonderfully so. Behind their formal, European-style class consciousness is a remarkable sense of individualism and personal animation. Our differing perspectives point to the necessity, I believe, of meeting and knowing West Indians or any ethnic group outside of institutional settings. Clearly, the West Indian community is growing in North America, and there remains a need for "identification of relevant cultural variables and family patterns that influence the[se] immigrants' ability to adapt to their new environment" (Thrasher and Anderson 1988:172).

Fortunately, such information has recently become available. Gopaul-McNicol (1993) has published a major study on West Indian families and she is eminently qualified to do so, having grown up in Trinidad and Tobago. She presents a detailed discussion of West Indian family values and makes an explicit contrast between them and comparable family values in the United States. Her chapter on counseling West Indians and the uses of language in counseling ought to be mandatory reading for professionals working with clients from the islands. Her book also provides assessment, self-concept, and attitude scales that any social worker could use, scales that are sensitive to the cultural distinctiveness of West Indians. The research she reports is an important addition to the social services literature, a literature that for too long has neglected the people of the Caribbean.

Those who want to know more of the social and cultural history of the Caribbean could not do better than Robert Dirks's fascinating *The Black Saturnalia* (1987) or Mervyn Alleyne's *Roots of Jamaican Culture* (1988). Michel Laguerre has written *American Odyssey, Haitians in New York City* (1984), an important reference on issues of Haitian adaptation. Several works address the concerns of women. *Between Two Islands, Dominican International Migration* (1991) by Sherri Grasmuck and Patricia R. Pessar focus on Dominican migration to New York City and Olive Senior's *Working Miracles, Women's Lives in the English-Speaking Caribbean* (1991) covers the day-to-day world of women within the region. Both books address an important issue that has been overlooked, the experiences of women in the local and international workforce. Virginia Kerns's excellent *Women and the Ancestors* (1983) describes kinship from a women's point of view in Belize. Lawrence E. Fisher, in his *Colonial Madness* (1985), has written an intriguing study of a Barbados mental hospital that focuses on cultural sources and styles of mental illness.

Finally, American social workers who have contact with West Indian families should familiarize themselves with the British social work journals. Along with Africans, Indians, and Pakistanis, West Indians have much greater visibility within British social work than they do in North America. Consequently, somewhat more research and journal attention is devoted to their concerns (Atkin and Rollings 1992).

7

AMERICAN INDIANS
IN A NEW WORLD

The Chipewyan are a Canadian-Indian people, widely dispersed from Hudson Bay to the interior of Alaska and linguistically affiliated with the Apache and Navajo much to the south. As recently as seventy-five years ago they hunted caribou for a living, but now they are settled in small villages all across central Canada. One of these, the village of Mission, is home for about 500 Chipewyan. It is an economically depressed place, dominated, as small towns often are, by external institutions, in this case a government school staffed by whites, a Catholic church, and the Hudson Bay Company store.

Some years ago there was a fight in Mission, just outside the school. It followed a hockey game and involved several young men from several different lineages. In addition to accusations that the other side played "dirty" hockey, some of the men had old grievances that for them justified a tiff. But what made this fight locally memorable was that one of the white teachers, fearing damage to school property, rushed to intervene and was briefly struck by a Native American. At first the teacher said he was hit on the coat; later, that he was kicked in the crotch. He filed assault charges with the Royal Canadian Mounted Police, there was a trial, and an Indian man named Charley, one of many people involved in the scuffle, was sentenced to thirty days in the Mission jail.

The people and events of this story are obscure, but for Henry Sharp (1991), an anthropologist who was conducting field research in the town, their significance is not. He was in Mission studying Indian-white relations when the interests of the white schoolteacher, the RCMP, the court, and Charley all collided. Sharp could have interpreted the fight and trial as a local reenactment of Indian powerlessness and Euro-Canadian dominance. An empowerment model would have fit the case. But he felt the situation was more complex than that. Its politics were part of something different and bigger. What interested him was not what "really happened" during the fight—whether the teacher was hit on the coat or in the pants, or whether it was Charley or someone else who landed the offending blow—but what each of the parties *believed* had transpired. How did belief (as against "truth" or "facts") enter into Indian and white versions of the fight, and what does belief have to do with the longer-running story of ethnic identity and ethnic power in the town of Mission and in many American-Indian communities?

Sharp's thesis was that events, such as the fight, do not generate meaning. Rather, meaning precedes and creates events. Whatever "really happened" that day will always be, in some sense, a collusion of fictions—a police fiction, a court fiction, a white teacher fiction, community fictions, and Charley's fiction. Ethnic tensions, in Sharp's view, are really confrontations of fictions, of notions that are already "in the air" that help generate and then "explain" events as they come and go. An objective "truth" about the Mission school fight is not really possible; it is not even the main issue. What is at stake are perspectives, and the only truth about them is that each is different and each is sincerely and energetically be-lieved. The theoretical claim here is that a culture is not a set of objectively describable events and behavior, a categorical trait list of "contents." Rather it is an assemblage of defensible perspectives, of contentious and contending points of view that compete for dominance whenever things need to be explained, or explained away. A culture is a set of transactions of a special kind.

Consider what Sharp learned from ethnographic interviews with those in-volved in the scuffle and from participant observation in the community. The teacher, backed by school officials, insisted he was the victim of an "assault" as defined in Canadian law. But he went further, interpreting the hit as a "rebuke" (not an actionable offense) for his efforts to improve the lot of Indian people. Apparently, the swipe at his coat became a kick in the groin as the meaning of the physical event was transformed from a hit to a rebuke. That is one fiction.

The court had a different interest. Like the schoolteacher, it was not much concerned with what "really happened," for there was little effort by the judge to recreate in court an instant replay of the fight. The court was interested in estab-lishing the identity of the accused, the apparent motivations of the various people involved, and the applicability and appropriateness of Canadian law as a discov-ery procedure for determining who was telling the truth about the alleged slap. The primacy of legal principles, as the court interpreted them, was the second fiction.

Charley and the Chipewyan had their own concerns. The community had long resented white dominance, the high-handedness of the school and church officials, and the exploitive presence of the Company. But they also believed that more education and greater participation in the national economy was the best way for them to improve their circumstances. They wanted to see Indians succeed by what they understood as the standards of the national culture. At the same time they resented the changes that "modernization" brought to their lives, changes that required them to act in non-Indian ways. Competitiveness, asser-tiveness, and structured, hierarchical relations were not to their liking. Their preference was for egalitarian, disinterested, and self-effacing participation in communal activities. The community's ambivalence came together in Charley.

Charley was a physically strong young man with a reputation for being feisty, not a value the Chipewyan traditionally honored. He was also a product of the school and its teachers, but he had not done well as a student. His failings, from a Chipewyan perspective, were that he drifted away from traditional cultural moorings, that he had become belligerent with other Indians, and that he had not taken good advantage of the schooling that was supposed to lead to "improvement" for himself and for all Indians. More fictions.

What "really happened" at Mission was not just a fight but an exercise in reviewing, refining, and reapplying perspectives. The fight was one more occasion among many for asserting meanings about self, others, police, schools, and the noisy and fractious marketplace of competing voices that modernization usually brings. The teachers felt themselves to be unappreciated professionals; the blow that became an assault was a moral affront to their best efforts to help the children and the Indian community. The court looked to Canadian history, legal precedent, and ultimately English common law for its metaphors and created its own legalistic version of what "really happened" after the hockey game. The Chipewyans saw the episode their own way, through tribal eyes, a disrupted history, and great ambivalence about what a school, church, and store had done to one of their own.

Sharp's conclusion is an interesting and challenging one, especially for the field of cross-cultural studies. He claims that the way we know things to be "true" is not from observing "facts" but from defending fictions, our perspectives. We "know" because we assign meanings to events by drawing on our own traditions of knowledge, causality, and expectation. "Facts" and "truth" are squeezed so that our beliefs, and our certainties about them, stay intact. And of all the ethnic communities discussed in this book, none has been more fictionalized, mythologized, and romanticized than that of "the" American Indian (Charles 1987; Albers and James 1986).

WHO IS AN INDIAN?

The 1990 census counted almost two million American Indians in the United States, a dramatic increase of 65 percent in the decade since 1980. Although their total number is less than 1 percent of the overall population, their rate of growth is one of the fastest in the country. That is significant because, at the time of European contact, there was an estimated one million people living in North America. By 1920, their numbers had been reduced by war, disease, and poverty to less than 240,000. There may be more Indians alive now than at any time in their history. But these statistics are deceptive. They hide a complex political and demographic past, one in which it is not always obvious who is an Indian, or what constitutes Indianness. Through intermarriage with whites, African Americans, and other ethnic communities, through government and tribal labeling (usually based on percentages of "blood" in one's ancestry), and through personal choice and opportunity, some people with Indian ancestry do not think of themselves as Indian. Many others do. For some, their Indianness is an identity they can situationally invoke. For others, it is a permanent affirmation. For many, it is a challenge that raises fundamental questions about self and community.

Over half of all those who identify themselves as Indian are married to non-Indians (Greenbaum 1991:107). Degrees of Indian "blood," used as a measure of Indianness, vary widely. Groups in the Southwest, being more isolated, tend to marry out less whereas those in the South, East, and Midwest have long histories of intermarriage with whites and African Americans. Some groups in the Northwest intermarried with Filipinos and other Asian immigrants. Contemporary American Indians tend to be younger than the general population and to have higher fertility rates, although these may have declined somewhat in recent years (John 1988). The composition of Indian households is varied, as would be expected among people affiliated with hundreds of ethnic communities, speaking many languages, and exploiting the ecological diversity of an entire continent. But this cultural variation between tribes is not a "problem" for most Indians; local and regional differences between Indian communities are expected and, for most people, are a point of interest and discussion.

If cultural variation is expected and normal, the question of who and what "an Indian" is remains contentious. As mentioned, "degrees" of blood are a common measure of Indianness. But it is a measure that was imposed by the dominant white society and, although widely used by Indians themselves, it is not indigenous to Native-American cultures. (Nor does it have any scientific basis. There is no naturally occurring entity identifiable as "Indian blood" any more than there is "American blood" or "Chinese blood." Interestingly, many white and black Americans describe themselves as having Indian ancestry or "blood" even though they know little or nothing of the specific genealogical connections. Apparently the popularity of "Indian" values has prestige among non-Indians.) Labeling individuals on the basis of "blood quantum" derives from older racial taxonomies formerly used to classify blacks during slavery. Because there was intermarriage among Indians and Africans, especially in territories bordering on early colonies and slave states, Indians were included in this pernicious form of categorization (Wilson 1992). Porter (1986, cited in Wilson) has argued that far from resulting in ethnic extinction, however, intermarriage with both whites and Africans was a way for Indians to preserve their cultural identity. Indian men and women took mates and lived in "marginal environments," adopting features of the dominant society that made them appear non-Indian while in fact Indian ways of living and thinking persisted (Wilson 1992:113). That may account for the difficulty experienced by some tribes, especially those in the East, of establishing that they are in fact Indians and deserving of recognition by governmental authorities.

Because "degrees of blood" are now significant for claiming entitlements through a tribe, and because tribes set their own standards for what constitutes an appropriate degree of authenticity, the "quantum blood" view of Indianness sets the stage for the divisive struggles between "traditionals" and "moderns" in some Indian communities. It is significant that virtually all contemporary Indian novelists, of which there are many, explore the meaning of this conflict in their writings. "This is not surprising, as most of the writers are mixed bloods and utilize mixed-blood protagonists to deconstruct the tensions of modern Indians gingerly negotiating life strongly influenced by the majority culture" (Wilson 1992:124). It is a struggle that persists among Indians whether they live on reservations or in urban areas. It continues to be discussed, and to be contentious, in virtually all Indian communities and, sometimes, even within families.

Where do contemporary Indian people live? Despite romanticized images suggesting that Indians live more in tune with nature than everyone else, only about one-third of all Indian, Eskimo, and Aleut people currently live on reservations or on Indian designated lands. Most live away from reservations, and a substantial number live in cities and towns. Location is important, for John (1985) has noted that "the deprivation experienced by reservation Indians is substantially greater than urban Indians. In general, the reservation group is poorer, supports more people on its income, has fewer social contacts, lower life satisfaction, and poorer health" (237). Nationally, Indians tend to be concentrated in the West, especially California, Arizona, and New Mexico, some areas of the South (notably North Carolina), Oklahoma, and the states of the upper Midwest, although they are located in virtually all parts of the country and can be found in wealthy suburbs and middle-class neighborhoods as well. Many Indians live in groups that have never been legally recognized as "tribes," yet they keep their sense of ethnic affiliation through their families, community organizations, occupational choices, and residential stability. "It is perhaps remarkable that so many of these groups have retained, in some cases for as many as ten generations, a sense of Indian identity and distinct community organization in spite of the fact that the government has effectively denied their status as Indians" (Greenbaum 1985:362). As with Indian history generally, Indian demography is a picture of geographical dispersion and enormous cultural diversity.

Yet that diversity was neither appreciated by Columbus five hundred years ago or by most of those who came after him. An almost cultivated legacy of ignorance has led to a history of stereotypes that seem truly designed by Hollywood central casting (Bataille and Silet 1980), stereotypes of savages, warriors, cannibals, and humorless stoics. Yet the original peoples of the "new" world were as different among themselves, perhaps even more so, as the peoples, languages, cuisines, and religions of "old" Europe. Many lived a hunting and gathering way of life that was exquisitely attuned to the landscape. Others lived in small, band-like groups in arid regions that supported only a minimal population. Still others were committed to agriculture and permanent urban settlements. Several major civilizations flourished and they, like civilizations elsewhere, occupied themselves with defense, administration, tax collection, and pursuit of higher scientific and religious knowledge. Freebooting his way among a few small, remote islands in the Caribbean, Columbus was grandly ignorant of the complex world he claimed to have discovered. What lay unseen before him were multiple peoples, languages, religions, and economic adaptations. To speak of "the" American

Indian or even "American Indians" generically is one of our most long-standing historical fictions.

The real "discovery," if it can be called that, preceded Columbus by tens of thousands of years. During the last great ice age, a vast amount of seawater was stored on the landmass of North America and Asia in the form of ice sheets and glaciers, significantly lowering ocean levels around the world. That exposed a land bridge nearly 1,000 miles wide, connecting Siberia and Alaska. At the time, no one lived in North America but hunting and gathering populations were common in eastern Asia and its far north. It would be a mistake, however, to assume that people on the Siberian side of the bridge decided one bright morning to set off and "discover" the Western Hemisphere. Small groups simply hunted game and collected available foods as they always had, moving with the seasons and the animals, until over the centuries they followed their food supply all the way to the tip of South America. The habitation of an entire hemisphere occurred relatively fast, by people known to us from archaeology as Paleo-Indians. Their route carried them down through an ice-free corridor in central Canada and onto the high plains, then into central America and points south. Others, at later times, may have come down the northwest coastline at least as far as California. The most recent pre-Columbian migration was that of the present day Eskimo, who moved along the most northerly coastal edges of the continent, exploiting an environment that is harsh but rich in game.

In their thousands of years in the Americas, Paleo-Indians and their descendants pioneered the cultivation of corn, potatoes, pumpkins, squash, beans, sunflowers, peanuts, cotton, tobacco, turkeys, guinea pigs, and llamas. (It is estimated that one-third of all the plant species used to feed people and animals in the world today were first cultivated in the Americas.) They gathered rubber, cocoa, vanilla, and hundreds of pharmaceutical products (including ipecac and quinine) from wild plants. Trade and travel routes were established over which freeways and railroads now run. The confederate government of the Six Nations was a model for the English colonists, and the practice of speaking publicly, but only in turn, was a North American invention, one that we now teach as politeness in children and expect as civility from senators and congressmen. (Contrast our Indian-derived practice of taking turns with the rhetorical styles of the Canadian and British parliaments, with their interruptive shouts and loud table slapping during speeches.) Nor should we omit what may be the ultimate contribution of Indian people to general human knowledge and to the ultimate fate of us all, Vine Deloria's suggestion (tongue in cheek?) that in all likelihood *God is Red* (Deloria 1973).

The earliest Indian people in North America lived by hunting and gathering, a way of life in which large game animals and seasonally available plant foods were important. Of necessity, their bands were highly mobile, their political organization egalitarian, and their numbers small. About 6,000 years ago, however, the archaeological record shows a transition to greater emphasis on foraging and an increased reliance on plants, fish, and smaller animals. There was nothing simple or "primitive" about these early economies, for they required a high level of cooperation between men and women and between children and adults, and an encyclopedic knowledge of animal habits, plant species, ground and water conditions, seasonal variations, weather, geography, and the nearness and movements of other groups of people. Nor was their lithic or stone tool technology in any sense "simple," for it required great skill in manufacture and use. The archaeological evidence also suggests the existence of extensive, almost transcontinental trade routes, for stone tools are commonly found far from where they were quarried and manufactured. The foraging economies of the people of that time were highly varied, as one would expect for a huge continent with a range of ecological niches. They included the sea-oriented fishing of the Northwest, the very difficult small animal and root and seed gathering of the Great Basin, and the game forests and lake and river fishing of the Midwest and the East coast. Buffalo hunting was practiced on the Great Plains, but not until the introduction of horses and guns by the Spanish did it become the wholesale slaughter subsequently indulged by whites and Indians alike.

Agriculture emerged in a number of areas including the central valley of Mexico and in Peru. In North America, the early phases of plant production appeared both in the Southwest and among some groups east of the Mississippi about 5,000 years ago. Sophisticated farming techniques were common in these areas, including field rotation and irrigation. When Europeans arrived in the late 1600s, they found complex farming communities in the Northeast (the Mohawks and Menominees, for example) and in the Southeast (the Creeks, Cherokees, and others).

Like their economies and their various histories, the religious beliefs of the native North Americans were diverse. Olson and Wilson (1984) note that polytheism was common, there being a multitude of deities and many levels of religious hierarchy. One widespread element (which may or may not have been universal) was a belief in a singular, permeating creator spirit. But this spirit is probably not comparable to that of the monotheistic god of the Europeans. Rather, it was explicitly pantheistic; "a fusion of matter, spirit, time, and life, a divine energy unifying all the universe. It was not at all a personal being presiding omnipotently over the salvation or damnation of individual people" (Olson and Wilson 1984:11). Beyond that, however, there was a remarkable profusion of ideas about the spiritual realm, including spirits of animals and natural entities, witches and sorcery, the prophetic power of dreams, individual spirit quests, and a complex organization of the spiritual realm and the afterlife. Similarly, religious rituals varied from place to place, with a wide range of "world renewal" ceremonies, winter ceremonials, cleansing and curing rites, and vision quests. Although most Americans, and some contemporary American Indians, tend to lump all these beliefs and practices together, creating a pan-Indian homogeneity and a singular "great spirit," in fact there was probably far more religious variability among Indian peoples than there was among all the Europeans who arrived after Columbus.

As a part of the homogenizing and romanticizing of native peoples, early Europeans and Americans evolved a popular fiction, more recently abetted by films and the media, suggesting that Indians lived "closer to nature" and were more "natural" and spiritual than whites. This belief, counterpoised to one which held that Indians were only savages and wild animals, led to a mystique, still favored by some, that Indians are more ecologically sensitive. There may be a general truth in this but it has to be seen as an ethnographic and historical one, not as a sentimental or romantic imposition. The Europeans who came to North America viewed the continent as a place for a new beginning, one partly spiritual (as expressed by some of the earliest New England colonists) but mostly economic. In particular, they did not want the "old world's" impediments of class and caste to interfere with their ability to hunt, fish, mine, harvest, produce, and otherwise enrich themselves and provide for their families. As Europeans saw it, the landscape of North America was real estate. It had development potential and unclaimed squatter's rights.

By contrast, many Indians viewed the land as a locale, the place where human and spiritual agencies intermingled. Where Europeans perceived opportunity through modification and use, Indians cultivated rootedness and religiously inspired loyalties to the world as it was. Early generations of Americans acted individualistically, with an "open frontier" and "raw land to be claimed and tamed" mentality. Indian views were more communal, with a strong historical sense of interconnectedness among people, animals, ancestors, and physical places steeped with mythic associations. Their rites and beliefs, in all their diversity, were intended to reinforce that sense of communal purpose and linkage.

The introduction of industrial trade goods (along with literacy, alcohol, diseases, and assimilationist policies) exaggerated and distorted many features of traditional Indian cultures. Guns and horses made hunting, once done entirely on foot, more efficient and ecologically more devastating. Westward expansion by Euroamericans crowded people off of familiar lands, disrupting economic life and contributing to inter-Indian warfare and conflict. While trade goods displaced traditional crafts and skills, Christian missionaries and boarding schools undermined ancient faiths. Despite these impositions, however, the fundamental world view of many Native Americans was always at great variance from that of Euroamericans and, in many quarters, that variance continues with surprising vigor despite superficial appearances of assimilation.

CONTEMPORARY ASPECTS OF INDIAN LIFE

The history of American Indians is much too complex to pursue in detail here, but we must note some of the major events that have influenced the lives of contemporary Indian people. This is important because many Indian people know these events well and discuss them regularly. Unlike whites, Indians generally do not view their history as a boring academic exercise. The allotment acts, the Indian Reorganization Act, the drive for reservation termination, a recently revived Indian militancy, and "self-governing" relations with the Bureau of Indian Affairs are all major concerns for them, worth noting for what they reveal about the fundamental difficulties that have marked relations between Indians and whites. We can usefully think about these events in terms of assimilation and nativism, opposing values that are evident throughout the long and painful history of Indian-white contact.

As noted above, some American-Indian groups were practicing agriculture when Europeans began arriving in North America. But Indians usually thought of their farming as a communal activity, something done to feed everyone as needed. It was never a "job" intended to produce a surplus for sale and profit. Farming as a "business" was a view that motivated Congressional and other reformers who, after the Civil War, believed the solution to the "Indian problem" was the conversion of Indians into small-scale, entrepreneurial farmers. Militarily defeated by the U.S. Army, Indians were moved onto reservations, and the idea was to transform these reservations into family farms, integrated into the prevailing capitalist agricultural economy. These "allotments" were the subject of legislative actions throughout the 1880s, of which the most important was the Dawes Act. It authorized the President, through the Department of the Interior, to create allotments for family farms, usually 160 acres each. Other laws permitted Indians to lease or sell their allotments to non-Indians, who often turned out to be speculators who sold the land to white settlers. The Dawes Act was predictably disastrous. Millions of acres of reservation land were lost by Indians to whites, thousands of Indian families were left without land resources of any kind, and many who did retain titles owned worthless tracts that they could neither farm nor sell.

Following the period of allotments, the U.S. government became more active in regulating Indian affairs. It established a system of boarding schools and the Bureau of Indian Affairs took control of existing tribal schools. The Bureau established a curriculum, some of it modeled after the new schools for freed slaves in the American South, with an emphasis on trades, domestic management or "home economics," and agriculture. In the Indian schools, native languages were prohibited, often brutally so, and Christianity and nineteenth-century notions of industry, thrift and Victorian propriety were imposed with a militaristic ruthlessness and efficiency. The explicit goal of the system was to obliterate traditional Indian cultures within one generation, two or three generations if necessary. While assimilation was the stated goal of this policy, its effect was not assimilation into the mainstream of the American economy but into subservient, marginal positions at its edges. This was especially so for young Indian women, subjected to an extreme regime of boarding school discipline and drudgery that passed as "training." "Habituation to simple labor clearly superseded any truly vocational goals—that is, training for employment—for Indian girls" (Lomawaima 1993: 230). The Bureau of Indian Affairs was not accountable to Indians nor interested in determining their views or their self-determined concerns. "Charged with guarding Indian interests, the BIA also largely determined what those interests were. . . . [Its] supervision was tutelary, intended to break down indigenous social relations and cultural practices and replace them with the socio-cultural patterns of Euro-American society" (Cornell 1984:45).

In the 1920s, however, a reaction set in against the abuses surrounding allotments and Indian education. A new generation of reformers, many of them whites, called for a revived tribalism as a way of reinvigorating Indian communities, and for a new role by the federal government in safeguarding Indian rights. The Indian Reorganization Act of 1934 stopped the selling of Indian lands, in recognition of the failure of the Dawes Act to assimilate Indians and improve the economic life of their communities. Under New Deal legislation, tribes were encouraged to set up tribal governments, and a small amount of land was returned to Indian ownership.

But those who administered the reforms for the federal government underestimated the strength of the opposition to the 1934 Reorganization Act, especially from western congressmen who feared that large tracts of land would be lost to potential development. The reformers also underestimated the uneven response of the various tribes. While some took advantage of the opportunities the act provided, others were severely divided on what they wanted for the future of their communities. The factionalism that was prevalent among so many tribal groups not only forestalled much of what the New Deal planners hoped could be done, but it also contributed to growing Congressional sentiment to "terminate" the tribes and the reservation system altogether.

The desire to terminate all special claims and relationships Indians might have with the federal government had always been favored by some politicians. Termination of reservations was seen as an opportunity to "resolve" the "Indian problem" permanently. During the postwar Communist baiting scares of the 1950s and the national paranoia of McCarthyism, any expression of ethnic independence was seen as a threat to the holy task of containing international Communism. Calls for Indian separateness and tribal revitalization were seen as politically suspect, even treasonous. (This despite the fact that many Indians served honorably in the military during World War II.) In addition, there was no sympathy for allocating funds to Indian interests when so much of the government's financial resources were committed to the emerging military-industrial complex. A demand arose from some politicians to "get the government out of the Indian business," as they described it, an issue that periodically reappears in conservative political circles to this day. Plans for termination called for the dissolution of tribal governments; transfer of tribal civil and criminal jurisdiction to state and county governments; transfer of Indian health and education services to the states; political subordination of reservations to local jurisdictions; and cash inducements to individual Indians who would agree to relinquish all their claims and privileges as Indians.

Predictably, termination proposals were divisive in virtually all Indian communities. Traditionalists and "full bloods," usually resident on reservations, resisted termination of the benefits they had come to expect under the reservation system. (For some tribes, those benefits were and remain the very lucrative sponsorship of bingo and, more recently, multimillion dollar casinos, especially in states where gambling is prohibited. Some less traditional Indians, living off reservations, found the government's offer of a "buy-out" to their personal advantage. Many of these latter individuals were poor and termination promised them, quite literally, a once-in-a-lifetime windfall. But the federal government's efforts at termination were so confounded by economic, jurisdictional, and intraethnic complexities and contradictions that the issue finally died in the early 1960s. However, it did not die before nineteen tribes lost all of their federal support and nearly three million acres of Indian land were sold to outsiders.

During the period of national turmoil marked by the Vietnam war and the rise of ethnic militancy in the 1960s, American-Indian groups were planning and debating a new phase of pan-Indian activism, with an emphasis on tribal self-determination. They confronted the assimilationist policies of allotment and termination directly. The most dramatic examples of this challenge were the much publicized seizure of Alcatraz in San Francisco Bay by a group of Indian militants and armed resistance to the federal government by members of AIM, the American Indian Movement, at the Pine Ridge Reservation in South Dakota. In the Pacific Northwest, Indian "fish-ins" attracted sympathetic celebrities from the entertainment industry and challenged state game departments and white dominance of commercial fisheries. These events, as well as many smaller and less publicized ones, were indicative of a new mood in many Indian communities, a determination to protect local, tribal autonomy and eliminate federal policies restricting the sovereignty of tribes. Assimilation was explicitly rejected. As a troublesome relic from pre–Civil War times (when it was part of the old War Department), the Bureau of Indian Affairs also came under attack. Its usefulness was debated (and continues to be) by Indians and non-Indians alike.

One of the important legacies of the activists of that time was the Indian Self-Determination and Education Assistance Act of 1975. The act declared that:

> *The Congress hereby recognizes the obligation of the United States to respond to the strong expression of the Indian people for self-determination by assuring maximum Indian participation in the direction of educational as well as other Federal services to Indian communities so as to render such services more responsive to the needs and desires of those communities. (Quoted from Olson and Wilson 1984:205).*

Under the act, tribal governments now contract with the Bureau of Indian Affairs and the Department of Health and Human Services for educational, health, and other services. The implementation of social services is generally left to local initiative. Other laws have attempted to maximize Indian control so that the preservation of ethnic identity is both policy and practice. For example, the Indian Child Welfare Act of 1978 restricts the removal of Indian children from Indian families, although there are circumstances under which this regulation has been controversial among both Indians and non-Indians. Differing tribal communities, of course, have their own understandings of the act and sometimes there are conflicts over the interpretation of the laws and regulations that continue to emanate from Washington, D.C. Indians, like anyone else, have differing views of what they want for themselves, their families, or their tribes. Some groups are essentially closed communities, guarding their ethnic distinctiveness with seclusion and social distance, while others work actively with a multitude of local and state agencies. In either case, the preservation of distinctiveness is now the law of the land and that policy is reflected in social services, health, education, and housing.

Paralleling the local implementation of federal policies, Indian people are also working toward preservation of traditional cultural forms. While English is common on most reservations, Indian languages still persist in surprising number. The fact that whites do not often hear them does not mean they are not there. In addition, Indian religions, in their enormous variation, continue to be important. Sweat lodges and winter ceremonials are common, especially among some groups in western states. In recent years public celebrations have become more inclusive, not less so, and there is hardly a weekend where there is not, somewhere, a powwow attracting people from all over the United States. Some ceremonials are open only to Indians or by special invitation. But many are public, and interested outsiders are welcomed and treated graciously. Hospitality, nonintrusiveness, and sharing have been important values in Indian communities literally for millennia. In contemporary America, that is still true.

NATIVE AMERICANS AND SOCIAL SERVICES

As with any underserved community, the range of social service and mental health needs among Native Americans is daunting. But there are special challenges facing social workers who serve American Indian communities. Meketon (1983) has listed some of them. First is the basic issue of language. Most Indians know and use English, but many do not, and many do not use it comfortably. There are over 300 dialects and separate languages in use in contemporary Indian communities and, given the current political mood of ethnic distinctiveness, those languages are valued in a way they were not just a few years ago. One result is that even communication with outsiders who want to be helpful can be awkward and, on occasions, difficult. There is no reason to believe that monolingual social service personnel would be willing or able to learn languages that are complex and phonetically unfamiliar, hence the importance of the word-centered ethnographic interviewing styles described earlier in this book (see chapter 4). But good interviewing skills are no substitute for second language proficiency. Even skilled workers will be at a disadvantage if they do not show at least a minimal interest in local language preferences.

Second, there is enormous cultural diversity among American Indians, far more than among any other ethnic community in America. How can service professionals begin to appreciate how great that diversity is? Anthropologists have often thought of cultural variations in traditional North America in terms of "culture areas." Culture areas are large regions within which more or less similar languages, community organization, religious beliefs, and economic adaptations can be found (Driver 1969). In pre-Columbian times such areas included the Southeast, Midwestern Woodlands, Great Basin, High Plains, Central and Southern California, and the Northwest Coast. While many Indians are highly mobile, and many now live in cities, these large divisions demarcate known and remembered differences that Indian people recognize and respect. However, within these regions, localized diversity is common, a diversity that is made even more complex by urban-rural and reservation–off reservation distinctions (Ross and Moore 1987).

Third, many Indian communities are geographically isolated, which contributes to their cultural uniqueness and has an impact on how services are used. People who live in remote areas find a trip to a clinic or a store a major effort, both in time and money. Old cars, bad roads and weather, nonexistent or unreliable public transportation, and cost are all obstacles to getting help. Home visits by social workers are expensive and costs per client visit may be more than many agencies are willing or able to pay. Those concerns are a reminder that many of our social services are really designed for urban people and for maximizing client contact within an eight-hour day. Some American-Indian communities may require innovative and time-generous ways of delivering services to those who need them, ways that may not always be cost-effective compared with those in urban areas.

Fourth, there are numerous local, state, and federal jurisdictional issues that get in the way of providing effective services to Indian people. They range from overlapping and contradictory laws and policies to turf wars within agencies and between community groups. Resolving some of these obstacles to effective service delivery may be the most important and culturally responsible service some social workers can provide.

In addition to these points, there are complex variations in family life among Native-American people, and most social workers serving Indians probably do not know enough about them. Traditionally, "family" has meant not only household but also extended networks, lineages, and clans. It is rare for individuals, including urbanized ones, to think of family in the narrow sense of the nuclear unit. Particularly in rural areas, where intimate face-to-face relations are common, one's kin are many. Childhood naming ceremonies often establish lifelong linkages between the infant and adults who will share in the responsibilities of child rearing along with biological parents (Shomaker 1989, 1990). In addition, lineage and clan membership may be an important basis for affiliations, cooperation, even marriage choices in later life.

Nor are these variations restricted to rural or reservation life. Red Horse and his associates (1981) documented important differences among Native-American urban families in Minneapolis. They found that some families were "traditional," continuing to use the Ojibway language in the home. While they participated in some of the sports and cultural activities of the larger society, their real loyalties were to powwows and traditional religious observances. "Bicultural" Indian families used English at home, were members of mainstream (usually Catholic) congregations, and saw themselves as highly integrated into the dominant society. In "pantraditional" families, the entertainments and social life of the dominant culture were explicitly rejected; both Ojibway and English were used in the home, and everyone was involved in self-conscious reidentification and re-creation of Indian belief systems drawn from a variety of tribal sources. These diverse family patterns add complexity to the task of understanding Indian communities, both rural and urban. They suggest a world generally hidden from the scrutiny of the larger society, one with which social service personnel need to be more familiar if they are to deliver services in culturally acceptable ways. As Red Horse puts it, "each [family] pattern is legitimate within its own relational field and contributes to a family sense of selfhood" (1981:59). The task of the social worker is to discover why that is so among the Indian clients he or she serves.

THE SPECIAL CASE OF ALCOHOL

Alcohol is perhaps the most serious challenge facing modern Indian people as well as the health and service professionals who work with them. Generally, alcohol use and misuse is more common among minorities than among whites, but for Indians its prevalence is devastating (U.S. Department of Health and Human Services 1985). Compared with the general population, rates of alcoholism among Indians are higher, death rates due to alcohol-related causes are eight times higher, and Indians as a group tend to die younger, often from alcohol and alcohol-aggravated conditions (Christian, Dufour, and Bertolucci 1989).

That said, it is equally important to note that patterns of alcohol consumption are, like Indian cultures, highly variable. Indian drinking, even problem drinking, is a culturally constructed phenomenon, its expression indicative of historical as well as current social circumstances. "Drinking" as a customary practice cannot be treated as a unitary pathology for which a singular treatment modality is recommended. Drinking may also be linked to other conditions, such as depression and suicide, in what some researchers are now calling combinations of "comorbidity" (Maser and Dinges 1992; O'Nell 1992). That is, drinking, depression, and suicide may be linked in ways that are community and culturally specific, their interrelationships undetectable using the decontextualized diagnostic categories of the *DSM-III-R* manual. The possibility of comorbidity enormously complicates any kind of problem assessment. It may be culturally myopic, as an Indian social worker once suggested to me, for anyone to speak of a "treatment of choice" for Indians or their drinking. In this section, I want to suggest some of the reasons for that, and review what the multiplicity of Indian drinking styles suggests for planning and intervention. I also want to affirm, as a necessary and preliminary caution to any generalizations made here, that not all Indians drink, and abstainers as well as moderate users can be found in all Indian communities.

A number of theories of Indian drinking have been proposed, three of which I will discuss briefly following the work of Weisner, Weibel-Orlando, and Long

(1984). First, sociological theories emphasize the history of repression and economic marginalization of Indians over nearly 500 years of European occupation and dominance. Those theories argue that whether Indians are on reservations or in urban areas, they respond to their experiences as do members of poorer or lower-class communities generally. Stress underlies the misuse of alcohol and that, in turn, leads to violence, family disintegration, and all the problems that beset an underclass regardless of its ethnicity. In this perspective, there is nothing culturally unique to excessive Indian drinking; drinking is what oppressed people do, and their unfortunate personal choices in the matter are compounded by society's habit of blaming the victim.

Cultural theories usually begin with the cultural history of a specific community, in addition to experiences of repression and dislocation, looking to the distinctive ways that drinking behavior traditionally have been interpreted. The argument here is that variations in worldview and social organization will correlate with variations in drinking experience. Thus societies with a tradition of the vision quest, or where psychoactive substances were part of religious rituals, will attach less opprobrium to heavy drinking, at least under some circumstances. The "ecstatic" nature of certain patterns of drinking may fit into preexisting explanatory frameworks, making drinking in public and excessive drinking more difficult to control. According to this viewpoint, groups such as the Navajo and Sioux will not have sanctions against destructive drinking. By contrast, Indian societies that are more hierarchical might be expected to place greater sanctions on drinking since outbursts of "deviant" behavior violate strong community norms of order. In these instances, problem drinking could be hypothesized to be a more privatized, secretive activity, one that isolates the individual from the community at large. Eastern Oklahoma Indians (Cherokee, Creek, Choctaw, Chickasaw), for instance, were predominantly horticulturalists rather than nomadic hunters. They used fermented beverages in ceremonies well before white contact and have had longer exposure and experience with European-style alcohol products. Historically, they may have had more institutionalized controls on drinking and, since they reside in what is now the Southern "Bible belt," they have acquired traditional Protestant objections to drinking of any kind. Drinking for them would be a different kind of experience with a differing set of meanings and controls.

As Weisner, Weibel-Orlando, and Long (1984:240) point out, there may be more recent cultural models for Indian drinking as well. California Indians, and perhaps some in other parts of the West, may have adopted a lumberjack or frontiersman model. That model stresses hard, episodic, binge drinking as found in male-centered communities of ranch hands and prospectors. It would be less common among the farmers and merchants who represented the second wave of white encroachment on the frontiers. As "work ethic" types, these second wave Euro-Americans had more privatized drinking styles which would have been less visible to Indians.

Another variant of the cultural approach has been suggested by Morinis (1982) in his work among skid road Indians. He sees alcohol less as a drug than as a symbol of exchange in an urban setting, one that deliberately inverts the standards of the larger society. Thus, urban drinking is bar oriented with intense social interaction. It is episodic rather than ongoing, with heavy consumption tied to brief stints of work and the availability of cash. It is followed by a period of abstention until more money is at hand. Morinis found that police, social workers, and aid car attendants reported Indians to be noncompliant, hostile, poor at communication, and uncooperative when efforts were made to provide them with simple medical care. He argues that the urban Indians he studied in Vancouver, British Columbia, "did not require much alcohol to begin *acting* very drunk" (1982:205), that their offenses were usually alcohol related and not against property or persons, and that display, especially that which was antisocial, was typical of their drunken behavior. If these findings prove to be typical of Indian drinking in urban areas generally, then it is clear that addressing the subcultural meaning of drinking, especially its rejection of the values of the larger society, is as important as understanding clinical symptomotology. Further, intervention techniques that urge compliance with "respectable" standards of work and family life may have little meaning for these clients.

A third set of explanations for Indian drinking are psychological. These theories look to intrapsychic stress, family experiences, life history, role models, peer group attachments, and acculturation difficulties as explanations of alcohol and substance abuse. Studies of "locus of control" are typical of work in this area (Mariano et al. 1989). Researchers often find problem drinkers, including Indian drinkers, to have more "external expectancies" and "perceptions of less personal control" over their drinking (1989:336). That is, their behavior is a response to suggestion and opportunity, and they are unable to control themselves. But from a cultural perspective, interpreting the meaning of "expectancies" and "personal control" among Indians has to be viewed as a conceptual minefield, especially where the analyst has limited understanding of the history and cultural configurations of the specific communities in which Indian drinkers live. Recommendations for relief through social skills training or other standardized modes of clinical intervention are, from an ethnographic perspective, an admission that the analyst does not know how to integrate cultural variables into clinical technique or how to devise a culturally responsive service.

Alcoholism is one of the most vexing problems in American-Indian communities and, as indicated, there are many theories about it. But the fact is that for all the research on Indian drinking, and there has been an enormous amount, very little is known about what "works" to change people's behavior, or under what circumstances a given intervention "works" for the long term. There are, however, some interesting clues.

Based on her analysis of more than fifty Indian alcohol and substance abuse programs in recent years, Weibel-Orlando (1989:153) made the following observations and recommendations. She found that successful efforts to resolve problem drinking involved at least one of several features. They included:

1. Self-generated and self-directed actions by the community that were community rather than individual oriented. Court-directed intervention, and standardized clinical models such as one-on-one and family "ecological" approaches did not usually have a long term impact.

2. A charismatic individual who served as a focus for action. That person could be a shaman, tribal leader, or other high-ranking individual who, as a recovering alcoholic, could make extraordinary demands on the behavior of others.

3. A healing community with historically established values, procedures, apprentice-like relationships, and narrative styles. Explicitly oriented toward healing as a group process, this activity offered a substitute to the values and relationships of local subcommunities of drinking and drinkers.

Weibel-Orlando adds that abstinence and doctrines of the "recovered alcoholic" typical of the Alcoholics Anonymous model did not need to be the operational goals for these healing communities, although they could be. Controlled or moderate drinking could be a legitimate aim, with an emphasis on reducing risks from interpersonal violence, car accidents, and hunting and drowning accidents. Her point, however, is that in successful programs all these activities were locally generated and legitimized. It may be, then, that the most important efforts of social and health care professionals are those that facilitate, in whatever way necessary, the creation of healing communities and the provision of technical assistance only to the extent that its need is recognized by Indian beneficiaries.

NATIVE AMERICAN SUICIDE

Alcohol is only one part of a large set of complex issues affecting Native Americans, another being exceptional rates of suicide in some Indian populations. Rates and patterns of self-destructive behavior vary by tribe, of course, but nationally the figures are alarming. Indians have the highest suicide rate of all U.S. ethnic groups and Indian adolescents have a rate about twice that of their peers in other racial and ethnic communities. (An important document, *The State of Native American Youth Health* [*Division of General Pediatrics and Adolescent Health* 1992] summarizes the current information in this area.) Manson et al. (1989) found that among a cohort of youth who attended an Indian boarding school, fully 23 percent had attempted suicide. By one estimate, for every achieved suicide eight others are attempted (Rosenberg et al. 1987). Among adolescents, significant risk factors included alcohol and suicide attempts by friends or family members. Suicides among Indian youth tend to occur in clusters among people who know one another, several occurring within a short period of time. In some instances alcohol, especially "hard" liquor taken in lethal doses, is the mechanism of death (Grossman, Milligan, and Deyo 1991). The picture that emerges is one of loss of life at near epidemic proportions.

How, from a cross-cultural perspective, can we begin to understand high rates of suicide in any particular Native-American population? Recall that in chapter 2, I suggested that a social problem, and the way a people experience and define it, is in some sense culturally constructed. Each suicide or hunting accident is a distinctive event, but each also invokes a set of implicit cultural themes. The task in culturally sensitive intervention is to find these themes so we can understand better the role they play in how people define and act on their needs. Only then will we be in a position to plan intervention that will make sense to clients. Suicide is an instructive example.

Most whites and many Indians believe that the prevalence of suicide is a consequence of forced and incomplete acculturation. In some instances this is probably true in a general sense, but it is not universally true. It is merely an assumption. The story is more complicated. Levy and Kunitz (1987), an anthropologist and a physician, respectively, looked at the history of suicides in Hopi communities and the prevention programs designed to control them. While many Hopi, especially Hopi elders, attribute increased suicide to the influence of white culture, Levy and Kunitz could not find that suicide rates had changed significantly over many years in these relatively isolated and self-contained communities. They did find, however, that suicide victims were people who occupied a predictable place in the traditional Hopi social order.

Hopi communities are matrilineal. A man marries into the lineage of his wife, and his wife's brothers have considerable influence in their sister's marriage and her household. Although unfamiliar to most white Americans, matrilocal residence is not that rare, and the powerful role of a woman's brothers in her marriage and domestic life is normal in matrilineal societies around the world. Where it occurs, this arrangement is not a problem since everyone expects that the interests of the group, here the matrilineage, take precedence over the wishes of individuals. Further, the Hopi, like many Indian groups, prefer endogamy, marriage within a clan line close to one's own. By marrying within an affiliated line, it is more likely that personal and clan loyalties will coincide and conflict will be reduced. In addition to these expectations, the public ideology of Hopi society is egalitarianism; differences of wealth or rank are said to be slight. However, everyone knows that not all family lines are of equal social status. Some families have control of productive lands while others have access only to marginal areas. Some lineages own important religious ceremonies and songs that only they can use and the ownership of these symbolic goods is very important in most American Indian communities. Clearly, despite professed ideology, not all lineages and clans are equal, and that can generate conflicts.

When considering the effects of demography on marriage patterns—births, sex ratios, residence patterns, and emigration and return—Levy and Kunitz found that some marriages will inevitably be "deviant." They are marriages that link socially unequal clans, lineages, or communities that did not customarily intermarry. "Deviant" marriages challenge the moral differences that distinguish historically distinctive marriage units. They also put at risk the men and women, especially the men, who enter into them since their actions will be heavily scrutinized by the wife's brothers and any disgruntled members of her lineage or clan group. Levy and Kunitz found that individuals in "deviant" marriage relationships, and especially their children, were most exposed to community stigmatizing and were at highest risk for alcoholism and suicide. Not only were these individuals exposed to unusual stresses, but their marriages and subsequent behavior were subject to negative labeling, a highly charged feature of life in small, predominantly face-to-face communities.

The lesson here is that clinical factors alone, and epidemiological factors alone, could not predict who was at risk among the Hopi. A knowledge of community culture and history, especially the history of marriages, was crucial. Levy and Kunitz found the sources of the twin demons of alcoholism and suicide far more elusive than models of "failed" acculturation or clinically defined pathology could predict. In fact, it could be argued on the basis of their evidence that explanations of Indian suicide that rely on acculturation theories or psychological variables alone are essentially ethnocentric. These models originated in the white community, yet they are accepted by whites and Hopi alike. That is because as explanatory models they serve the ideological needs of both groups. For whites, failed acculturation and psychological deficits justify continued efforts to assimilate Indians and treat their deficiencies with individualizing interventions. For Hopi, the models blame the victims and relieve others of having to confront the destructive effects of community-generated labeling and the contradiction of egalitarian beliefs created by historical variations in lineage power.

The Levy and Kunitz analysis is specific to the Hopi situation, but it has a general implication for intervention that is important. Social change, traditional patterns of community organization, local history, and the current activities of service providers and external agencies are complex and intertwined. Models of causation and intervention based on the presumptive importance of specific clinical, diagnostic, or other singular features may not be accurate or adequate. Further, any model of therapeutic intervention carries with it implicit values and preferences, including values about which data are important for an assessment and which are not. So-called treatments of choice are always "someone's choice," and that someone's preferences may or may not be appropriate to small, closed groups where community sentiments have powerful effects on the behavior of others.

Successful suicide prevention may require something exceptional and innovative, perhaps activity that is outside the established institutions of health and benevolence. Levy and Kunitz argue that "an essential task for prevention programs is the identification of community strengths rather than deficits or weaknesses" (1987:938). In the Hopi case, they recommended programs for youth such as wilderness adventures. Those kinds of preventive activities draw upon valued experiences in the community, mix individuals who are and are not "at risk," have explicit goals that do not identify participants as "deviants," and put advisees and counselors in relations that do not carry the stigmata of "client" or "patient." They are also low in cost and have the advantage of reaching individuals before a crisis develops. The disadvantage of their proposal is that it implicitly challenges the assumptions and practices of those whose institutional services are already in place—health and social service agencies, staff, and sometimes funding sources. They also challenge the therapeutic models of many who work in established programs.

CULTURAL CONTRASTS AND ETHNIC COMPETENCE

This brief overview of the Native-American experience and several of the health and service issues that concern Native people identifies some of the complexities professional workers in this area face. American Indians have the oldest cultural traditions on the continent, yet in some ways theirs are the most fragile of any ethnic group. Engulfed by an industrial consumer culture built on unapologetic exploitation of human and natural resources, they have faced everything that is the antithesis of their history and traditions. Exposed to genocidal rates of population loss, Indians have preserved a sense of identity through individual flexibility and high regard for communal traditions. Many Native Americans, especially those who live on reservations and in rural areas, think of themselves as Indians rather than as members of a "minority" group (Neumann et al. 1991). Their sense of cultural distinctiveness may be greater than that of other ethnic peoples, suggesting that social workers who serve Indians will need to make special efforts to understand the rationale of their clients' responses to offers of support and assistance.

In reviewing some of the practices and preferences that distinguish many Native-American peoples from those in the dominant culture, it is worth mentioning again that it is cultural *contrasts*, not just differences, that are important in the ethnic competence approach. An emphasis on difference alone presupposes an "us versus them" relationship; it is essentially adversarial. Clearly, that is not helpful in providing services and it abets the process of stereotyping. In emphasizing contrast, the social worker must put himself or herself into the relationship. The service provider, after all, is "different" too, and the client's perceptions of difference are at least as important. Professionals must examine the cultural baggage they bring from both their institutional and personal backgrounds.

In Table 7.1, a series of very generalized American-Indian–White-American cultural features are contrasted. They represent an initial effort to think about differences in legitimately comparative terms. I have brought them together from a variety of sources, mostly prominent American-Indian scholars and service providers. But I have also had the advantage of drawing on the tradition of anthropological field research in American-Indian communities. Because of the historical presence of anthropologists among Indians and on Indian reservations, a comment on that is useful here, perhaps as a short cautionary tale for social and health service workers.

The love-hate relationship between anthropologists and Indians goes back well over a century to a time when the federal government first began financing research expeditions into Indian territories. The goal was ethnographic information that would lead to enlightened administration, pacification, and speedy assimilation. It was also seen as "pure research" into the disappearing customs of dying cultures, saving for the record whatever could be found before it was gone. Anthropologists and anthropology graduate students inundated Indian settlements until very recent times, their notebooks, tape recorders, and cameras poised and ready. Almost all Indian readers of this book will know that "the

TABLE 7.1   Selected Cultural Contrasts, American-Indian and White-American Communities*

American Indian	White American
Family structure is varied from tribe to tribe and rural to urban areas but extended units in various forms are common.	Nuclear families are assumed to be the norm although there is great variability and experimentation.
Children often have multiple caregivers and live with various relatives as is convenient.	Children are expected to live with biological parents and, in cases of conflict, preference is given to the mother.
Cooperation and sharing are highly valued; individualism, assertiveness, and impulse are discouraged.	Early displays of individualism and lifelong care for the needs of the self are considered normal and even healthy.
Noninterference and respect for the rights and choices of others are highly valued. Confrontation is rarely appropriate.	Assertive (but not aggressive) speech and behavioral styles are favored. Leadership and individual achievement are honored.
Pacing activities according to the needs and expectations of others is more important than observing clock time and abstract schedules.	Punctuality, promptness, and adherence to abstract time schedules are critical to success.
Elders have important ceremonial and sometimes political roles; their views count.	Elders usually live apart and are not expected to exercise political, ceremonial, or financial control over others.
Religious values and ritual practices infuse Indian life and are regarded as critical components in preserving Indian identity and in promoting healing.	Religious and ritual practice is a matter of personal preference with little stigma attached to either participation or avoidance.

*As with all the cultural contrast charts in this book, this list of statements may or may not apply to any specific individual. *These contrasts refer only to general tendencies within groups, not to the attributes of persons.* Individuals vary widely in their commitment to the values of their own culture and to how they choose to observe them in their daily affairs.

anthropologist" is a stock character in their community's history, one more often derided than welcomed. There is good reason for their suspicion and distaste.

Much of American anthropology as an academic discipline was built on Indian studies, yet for the most part anthropology's success has not benefited Indians. But some of it clearly has: many anthropologists have assisted Indian groups with their legal claims for recovery of traditional lands and natural resources and preservation of sacred sites. Some researchers have investigated Indian schools and made recommendations for enlightened teaching and educational policies. Others have studied traditional curing and health beliefs, bringing to the attention of biomedical practitioners the needs of Indian communities and ways these professionals can work with patients more effectively. They have also documented the success of many traditional healing activities. Anthropologists have worked with Indians in developing tribal museums and, through repatriation programs now underway, are helping remove Indian artifacts and skeletons from government and university museums and returning them to their owners. Much of what we now know about the history and diversity of Indians in North America is due to anthropologists who quietly studied and documented changing cultures, religions, and languages. Perhaps the ultimate compliment to those efforts is that some Indians are now anthropologists themselves, reviewing and revising our understanding of their cultures from their own, special perspective. Indians have made the anthropologists learn the meaning of cultural sensitivity; it is appropriate that health and social service professionals be co-partners in the process.

Indian scholars (and scholars of Indians) on whom I have relied include but are not limited to John Red Horse and colleagues (1981), Carolyn Attneave (1982), Spero Manson (1989a, 1989b), Joseph Trimble and associates (1983), Robert John (1985, 1988), and Lou Matheson (1986). They, of course, have nothing to do with the table I have constructed here nor with the interpretations I have made about Indian-white contrasts. As with the other chapters, I have chosen to emphasize family relationships since those are the areas that most concern health and social service personnel. But this table is shorter than other summaries of ethnic group contrasts in this book, and there is a good reason for that. Indians are far too diverse for anyone to summarize their cultures in any meaningful way. The suggestions given here can only be thought of as the most tentative of generalizations, features that each worker in contact with Indian clients will be required to refine and refocus for the community concerned.

As with a listing such as this, its value is not in providing "formulas" for instant understanding of any Indian person or group. That would be absurd, as the discussion of Indian diversity ought to make clear. The proper use of the table is in pointing to areas of contrast and posing questions, such as: If these descriptive contrasts are not true of the community or individuals served, then what contrasts *are* true? What kinds of generalizable characterizations would be *more accurate* for a given situation? Clearly, that approach is a strength for the worker willing to use the table that way. Statements of contrast are not lists of cultural features; they are provisional hypotheses whose accuracy must be explored and examined in every professional encounter. That is especially important since no Indian community is exactly like any other. It is critical for the user to locate potential cultural contrasts in service relationships, assess their salience for the service offered, and revise them in order to improve the cultural meaningfulness and acceptability of the work done. That is the only way clients can be individualized, and it is the only way the cultural context of client experiences can be recognized and respected.

DEVELOPING SKILLS FOR SOCIAL SERVICES WITH INDIAN PEOPLE

As values, contrasts like these frequently emerge in discussions of American Indian cultures. An older body of anthropological literature referred to values such as strength, self-control, obedience, tranquility, cooperation, and protectiveness among the Hopi (Aberle 1951), and conservatism, persistence, generosity, and deference to elders among some groups of Dakotas (Schusky 1970). As reported by Trimble (1981:71), Zintz (1963) adds an interesting value contrast: while whites prefer to win, as much as possible and all the time if they can, Indians prefer to "win once, but let others win also." Trimble (1981) has his own list of traits that appear repeatedly in descriptions of Indian communities, and he wonders if they might not be quite widespread: a strong present-time orientation; time consciousness defined socially rather than by the clock; sharing combined with avoidance of personal acquisitiveness; respect for age and for elders; a preference for cooperation over competition; and an ethical concern for the natural world (Trimble 1981).

While probably valid for large numbers of Indians, these value stances may not be valid for many others. We need to consider that as a possibility rather than taking lists like these as eternal truths. Further, individual adherence to a value such as "noninterference" or "generosity" is certainly not wooden. Values and choices are always situational; individuals act on values, when they choose to, in their own way and with reference to a specific circumstance. Knowing the situation—*in Indian terms*—is absolutely essential to knowing what the values even mean.

Consider, for examples, the meaning of the terms "family" and "family values" in Native-American communities. First of all, there is little consensus. Yet families of some kind have always been at the center of Indian life, and they remain so. Many Indians live in nuclear family units, many others in extended households, and perhaps most in three-generation arrangements of some kind. But knowing the composition of a household is not enough; lineages and clans are also an important part of Indian ideas about family, even among those for whom a lineage may not be operative. A lineage is a group of people related by descent from a common ancestor. The means of tracing those relationships can be through either the male (patrilineal) or female (matrilineal) linkages. Clans are even larger units, containing more than one lineage and often traced far back in time to an ancestor (sometimes an animal) with founder or mythological significance. Lineages and clans create enormous systems of kinship ties and loyalties, and in smaller communities those loyalties will be critical for who does what with whom. So-called family "ecological" perspectives in contemporary social services usually refer to the immediate, nuclear family, sometimes even to extended units. But in many American-Indian communities, the social worker will also have to learn of local clan and lineage affiliations to more fully understand the values that motivate and govern behavior. Clan and lineage ties are background information in the life of any Indian community, things that may not often be commented on but that everyone implicitly understands. The worker who wants to appreciate the local meaning of "traditional family values," therefore, will have to be alert to the significance of these larger kinship ties, in the organization of community life, in ritual activities, and in patterns of sharing and cooperation.

How can that be done? In a useful discussion of family therapy with American Indians, Ho (1987) also begins with a list of presumed, all-Indian values. They include themes we have come to expect: harmony with nature, cooperativeness, a present-time orientation (1987:71), and others. However, Ho does not limit himself to this rather narrow list. He takes it simply as a starting point for moving on to the meaning of cultural relevance in intervention and family therapy with Indian clients. He analyzes cases to help illustrate how values underlie choices and action, offering his own suggestions for service practice as he goes. For example, he remarks on the need to be alert to "American Indian communicative pragmatics" and suggests that "a therapist needs to be attentive, talk less, observe more, and listen actively" (1987:95). He also notes that group interdependence usually takes precedence over personal needs (another value) and that reestablishing harmony within families requires less of psychodynamics and more of group consensus on what needs to be done:

> *As can be expected, group consensus in goal-setting is time consuming, but an American Indian family has a flexible time orientation. The family can wait patiently for a group decision and will experience no urgency in completing certain tasks required of each family member for change. Hence, the time-limited and goal-directed mentality of the therapist may need modification when working with an American Indian family (Ho 1987:97–98).*

Of particular interest is Ho's suggestion for using a "genogram" as an aid to understanding family dynamics. Genograms are graphic devices for mapping family relations but, unlike traditional genealogies that start with a remote ancestor, a genogram begins with oneself. Relations are pictorially mapped out from the point of view of the individual, with other significant data added to the chart as it becomes available: residences and dispersion of kin, household membership, exchange relationships and visiting patterns, types of informal support, and stresses and conflicts. The genogram gives a pictorial representation of an individual's family situation, one that can be added to over time and that gives the reader a quick overview of the resources of individuals and families. Genograms speed up the worker's understanding, not only of the client and his or her family but of relationships and activities (including those based on lineages) that may extend throughout the community. (Chapter 10 contains an exercise based on genograms.)

But knowing about families, lineages, networks, and the values that underlie them is only one area where the social worker needs information and understanding. Another is the relationship of social service and health institutions to indigenous helping patterns and what that means for interpersonal behavior in cross-cultural settings. Several years ago Kahn and associates (1981) helped establish a psychotherapy service for the Papago Indians of the Southwest and they listed what they saw as critical issues in developing a successful Indian-oriented mental health program. Their list included not only the things outside professionals needed to know about the Papago but, just as important, the things service professionals ought to be willing to support in their work. First, service providers needed to respect "the spirit of the clinic" (1981:92), that is, the style and procedures that exemplify an Indian point of view in program management. A suggestion like that may seem obvious enough, except that sometimes that spirit clashed with the canons of administrative practice and efficiency taught in schools of social work and expected by remote state agencies. Yet just because organizations have their own cultures, a genuine cultural awareness would involve learning the style or "spirit" of a local agency and working with it to further the services goals that everyone agrees are important.

Second, the Kahn team noted the importance of appreciating the distinctive work patterns of indigenous service providers. While these individuals often do not have professional degrees, they do have experience that is finely tuned to the needs and expectations of their clients. Professional standards of service, although important, should not be used to challenge local procedures that outsiders do not fully understand.

Third, and following logically from the second point, a good share of any new service provider's time must be spent as a student. A period of sustained learning is critical; later the service specialist will be expected to act as a translator between the standards for service set by outside organizations and the expectations of local staff and clients. Obviously, effective translation of ideas, procedures and expectations, and an ability to find common working agreements, requires commitment to learning not only the culture of the local community but also that of local agencies. That knowledge puts the social worker in a position to recommend locally acceptable ways of carrying out service mandates.

Finally, Kahn concluded that "in working with this particular culture and Indian group [the Papago], a relationship style that is low-key, accepting, and open to input is important. Assertive, pedantic directing styles, especially in any forceful and loud way, would be disastrous in this setting" (1981:94). Obviously, those recommendations cannot be said to apply to all Indian mental-health sites. They are insights that Kahn and his team reached only after careful, patient learning among the Papago. The same, slow procedure would be necessary at any other site before a social worker could come to conclusions appropriate to local clients, indigenous service providers, and a specific Indian community.

OTHER IMPORTANT ISSUES

There are many other concerns related to social and health services for American Indians. Only two will be discussed here, the role of elders and issues in working with teenagers. I have chosen them because they are topics often mentioned by Indians and Indian social workers themselves.

Indian Elders

"Eldercare is an emotionally charged issue that speaks to the essence of tribal life and tradition" (Manson 1989a:40). Good care for older persons is evidence of community concern, yet the resources of caring for Indian elders are not as available as they are for many other Americans, especially those who live in urban areas. The issue is emotional because Indian elders have special roles in their communities, roles that are culturally quite different from those of most white elders. Indians often cite these differences as one way of demonstrating that they are distinctive and, in their view, superior to the country at large.

For most white Americans, the dream of retirement and the so-called golden years is independent living and economic self-sufficiency. The essence of Indian elderhood is grandparenting. Because elders are viewed as the most experienced and knowledgeable members of their community, they are also in the best position to transmit Indian traditions and sensibilities to the next generation. This is not to say that every Indian elder wants to be a grandparent or is good at grandparenting in the traditional sense. But everyone knows how important the task is, and it is generally respected and honored. In collecting life histories from Sioux and Muskogean elders (in South Dakota and Oklahoma, respectively), Weibel-Orlando (1990) identified five distinctive grandparenting styles, of which two were common among her respondents: fictive grandparents and grandparents as cultural conservators. She found that these roles were more common for women than for men and that they were linked to another community expectation, that younger mothers be freed up to participate in the economic life of the community while older women take on child-rearing and culture-transmitting responsibilities.

Fictive grandparents were those who fostered children to whom they were not related. Some of the fictive grandmothers Weibel-Orlando interviewed had well-established reputations for their grandmothering and they were regularly supplied with children to supervise. Some of these children were sent by their parents who, because they lived in urban areas, wanted their children to have an intensive exposure to the basics of the home culture. Other children were orphans or those whose parents could not care for them due to their own struggles with alcohol, the legal system, or unemployment. Fictive grandfathers were rare but some who were knowledgeable in sacred lore and religious traditions took on young boys as apprentices.

Grandparents as cultural conservators were more common than the fictive variety. They were people who actively encouraged their own adult children to relinquish the grandchildren for lengthy periods of time so that they could be instructed in Indian ways of living. One elder woman took her grandchildren with her everywhere: daily visitations in the village, Indian church meetings, senior citizen meetings, memorials, feasts, dances, powwows, giveaways, and rodeos. Her grandchildren attended a school taught both in English and Lakota. They were taken to ceremonials dressed in full regalia, and they helped with the distribution of food and gifts at the giveaways. They were immersed, for months and years at a time, in the minutiae of everyday life. "Through the grandmother's firm, authoritative tutelage, complemented by their gentle and affectionate grandfather, and through the rough and tumble play with rural age-group members . . . they learn, as did nineteenth-century Sioux children (through observation, example, and experimentation), their society's core values and interactional styles" (Weibel-Orlando 1990:122–123).

In many Indian communities, this style of grandmothering is common, and women who are successful grandmothers are powerful personalities in their own right, not easily ignored by their adult children nor by other adults in the community (Shomaker 1990). For grandchildren and grandparents, legacy preservation and transmission, not just companionship, is the "work" of their relationship. For both, the teaching and the learning never stop. Social service professionals would do well to make consultation with grandmothers like these a regular part of their own learning program.

Adolescent Survival

At the other end of the age spectrum, adolescence and especially Indian adolescence can be a turbulent if not deadly time. Alcohol and drug use, in some communities, is well above national averages. What may be most important, however, is that experimentation with alcohol, drugs, and toxic inhalants such as glue and gasoline begins among some at an early age. Beauvais and LaBoueff (1985) found that on the seven reservations they sampled, fully one-third of all children between ages 9 and 12 had used either alcohol or drugs or both. Their sampling was of students in schools; had they reached those not in schools the percentage probably would have been higher. They observe that "Indian alcoholism has usually been seen as an adult problem. The majority of treatment efforts have been slanted toward the adult population, with detox facilities, halfway houses, Alcoholics Anonymous, and one-to-one counseling being the typical responses on the reservation" (1985:149). Where children are involved, prevention and intervention have to be thought of differently.

It is important to note that drug usage has never been typical of Indian peoples historically. Where psychoactive substances such as peyote have been common, they have always been part of religious and ritual activities in which their availability was regulated and their use was related to the acquisition of supernatural power. Drugs for recreation were never sanctioned. Casual use of drugs is an invention of the dominant white society. The fact is that many if not most adult Indians use alcohol very little and drugs not at all.

The reasons for drug use by Native Americans vary, of course, but they may not be entirely due to generalized problems of "acculturation," at least as that is normally understood. Oetting (1980, quoted in Beauvais and LaBoueff 1985) went beyond the usual research formulas by dividing sample subjects into three categories: "traditional," "acculturated," and "bicultural." Survey results showed that the highest rates of drug abuse were among the "acculturated," those who identified least with Indian values of any kind; the next highest group of users were those described as "traditional." The lowest usage was among "bicultural" individuals, those who were effective in both the white and Indian worlds and moved comfortably between them.

How does that relate to younger people? Edwards and Egbert-Edwards argue that "many Indian adolescents have lived with drinking/drug behavior to the extent that they see them as 'Indian' behaviors" (1990:287). Further, they claim that many adults and tribes do not acknowledge that such usage is a problem. "In some situations, substance use and abuse are seen as components of Indian life-styles. A myth is perpetuated that 'everyone' participates in substance abuse" (Edwards and Egbert-Edwards 1990:287–288). Confrontation with drug and alcohol use among teenagers usually occurs when professionals from outside the community demand that "something be done" and bring solutions of their own. The list of programs that have been proposed and tried is impressive and most, according to Edwards and Egbert-Edwards, do not work. They argue that,

> *(1) a simple program aimed at improving self-esteem will fail; (2) a program based on the idea that alcohol is used as a substitute for social acceptance will fail; (3) a program based on the idea that alcohol is taken by depressed, anxious, and otherwise emotionally disturbed youth will fail; (4) a program that uses "socially acceptable" people to reach deviant youth will fail; (5) a program that provides cultural ceremonies and doesn't follow through to ultimately change peer clusters will fail; (6) recreational and social activities that do not actively and completely exclude alcohol will fail (1990:286).*

So what will work? Edwards and Egbert-Edwards (1990) offer overviews of a number of programs that do work, and the interested reader should examine their sources. They include the Soaring Eagles program in Minneapolis, the Indian Youth "Drug Busters" in Colorado, and the Chevak Village Youth Association in Alaska. All of these programs began as community prevention efforts. Their core was a group of local, concerned people, including tribal leaders and elders. As a group, they systematically studied the problem in their own locality through self-identified task groups that included membership from across the community. Outside experts were involved when the task forces felt they needed them, not before, and their assistance was advisory rather than managerial. Schools were the focus of activity—for discussions, planning, implementation— because that is where young people and the drugs are. Because family life and family values are central to Indian communities, whole families, extended and otherwise, were recruited into programs. Family units, not individuals, were the object of "intervention," and counseling, by locals, was on matters of behavior and behavior control, not feelings. Ceremonial and recreational events were frequent, and strong community expectations that everyone participate were made explicit.

A communal approach is not always easy to implement. New research to accurately define the extent of a problem will probably arouse old suspicions because for too long Indians have seen research projects come through their communities with no benefits as a result. Public gatherings and discussions can become difficult if they are not kept on task, especially where there are factions and cliques with their own agendas. But most important, predetermined solutions must be avoided, and local responses must take precedence. Enthusiastic outsiders, however well intentioned, usually lack the knowledge of local history or internal conflicts to comment authoritatively on what Indian people ought to do. Their most important contribution may be encouraging families and groups to invest their time and energy in devising solutions that they can support after all the social workers, applied anthropologists, and health professionals have gone away.

WHO IS AN INDIAN?—AGAIN

Amid all this gloomy discussion of personal pathology and cultural threat, it is important to conclude by noting some of the things that are right about contemporary Native-American communities and the people whose lives are satisfying just because they are Indians. Neumann and associates (1991) surveyed a sample of Southern Cheyenne and Arapaho respondents in Oklahoma. They were interested in those who felt they had been successful and who were proud of their heritage and their achievements.

Individuals who rated high on the numerous scales the researchers used had a number of characteristics in common. All were effectively bicultural, meaning they had significant commitments to activities in both Indian and white communities. They grew up in caring families, were educated at least as far as high school, some had college, and they felt they knew how to navigate the institutional structures of the white world. They participated in Indian community events and some practiced the Indian religion their parents had taught them. Others declared themselves Christians. But all considered Indian ways superior to those of whites. They did not want Indian tribes to change and believed it was important that both they and their children know about their Indian heritage. Rejecting acculturation models, few viewed schooling as a first step toward losing their cultural heritage. Tribal identity, maintenance of the tribal community, and the importance of elders were all rated highly. "Respondents did not agree that the popular public image of an Indian defined them as Indians; that is, they did not define their Indianness by singing and dancing, by using the language, or by dressing in Indian attire. In addition, they did not feel that their degree of Indian identity was defined by their tribe" but was a feature of their observance of Indian ways as they understood and interpreted them (Neumann et al. 1991:109).

So I return to the question raised earlier in this chapter. What is an Indian? Clearly it has much to do with self-identity, commitment to a tradition, and observation of Indian ways in some areas of one's life. It may have something to do with language, ritual, and participation in tribal affairs. It has less to do with how people look, where they live, or what they do for a living. The relationship of Indianness to the larger society, and to the health and social service programs it offers, is always open-ended, always local, and always problematic. But that is a good place for any service professional to start.

8

LATINO CULTURES
AND THEIR CONTINUITY

José Antonio Burciaga is an artist, writer, founder of a comedy group, and Resident Fellow at Stanford. He grew up in El Paso, Texas, in a pious Catholic family, living in the basement of a Jewish synagogue where his father was the caretaker. After a B'nai B'rith meeting or a Bat Mitzvah, the senior Burciaga would gather up unused food and he, young José, and the other children would make deliveries to local Catholic and Baptist orphanages. In the same way, flowers used in Jewish weddings got a ritual recycling at St. Patrick's church and at the convent school. At the elder Burciaga's funeral, a priest said the mass in English, songs were sung in Spanish accompanied by a mandolin, and a representative of the synagogue gave a prayer in Hebrew. Members of Jewish, Catholic, and Baptist congregations sat among one another in the pews and no one thought that particularly unusual since they all knew of Mr. Burciaga's generous way of living. Commenting on that in his recent book of humorous essays, *Drink Cultura: Chicanismo*, son José writes that "I once had the opportunity to describe father's life to the late, great Jewish American writer Bernard Malamud. His only comment was, 'Only in America'!" (1993:118).

The unhappy counterpoint to one man's life of dignified and respectful ecumenicalism is the recent emergence of a new form of cultural chauvinism, the English-Only Movement. Historically, America has never had a national language policy, and restrictive language laws are something new in our political experience. But by 1991, eighteen states had declared English their "official" language: Arizona, Alabama, Arkansas, California, Colorado, Florida, Georgia, Hawaii (with two official languages, English and Hawaiian), Illinois, Indiana, Kentucky, Mississippi, Nebraska, North Carolina, South Carolina, North Dakota, Tennessee, and Virginia. (Crawford [1992] provides a valuable overview of the official English movement.)

Is the driving force behind all this ballot box nativism just a heightened linguistic appreciation of the distinctive sounds of English vowels and consonants, an aural aesthetic newly evolved among native English speakers? Or are there extralinguistic concerns at work here? Hurtado and Rodriguez (1989) think that language, unlike skin color and national heritage, is perceived by some Anglo Americans as the one mutable feature of ethnic groups and therefore the place to begin with encouraging, even demanding, their assimilation to an Anglo norm. The nativist's rationale is that if they can't look like Americans, at least they can learn to talk like them. English-only promoters really have very little interest in language or language learning as such. In a report to the American Psychological Association, Padilla, Lindholm, and Chen (1991) found clear evidence of explicit political agendas in the English-Only Movement. For example, activist individuals and coalitions within it have "close connections to restrictionist, anti-immigration organizations" (1991:120). As propagandists, their appeals are aimed at those Americans who, for whatever reason, have vague, poorly defined grievances and who see in immigrant and ethnic groups the "cause" of various personal and social problems. According to Padilla, several major themes exemplify the appeals of the English-only lobby.

First, the movement's propaganda is marked by unabashed racism and xenophobia. Its publicity, debates in state initiative campaigns, letters to the editor columns, and campaign literature all show a clear pattern of antiforeigner sentiment (Crawford 1989; Huddy and Sears 1990; MacKaye 1990). Second, advocates of English-only habitually advance spurious arguments ranging from assertions that children are "confused" by the burden of learning multiple languages to claims that bilingualism impedes academic and career success. These claims are made despite the fact that educational research invariably suggests just the opposite, that children learn more than one language easily and that those who are comfortable and competent in two or more languages do as well in schools as others, all other factors being equal. In fact, multilingual children may even possess a larger inventory of ideas and expressions than do their monolingual schoolmates. Third, English-only proponents claim that the costs of using translators and multilingual personnel in already stretched education, judicial, health, and social service systems is an unnecessary burden to taxpayers. That, however, is a policy issue, not a linguistic one, and the fact that social service and educational systems are already underfunded can hardly be blamed on the linguistic diversity of the people who use them.

English-only arguments are a smokescreen for groups and individuals whose agendas are essentially antitax, antigovernment, and anti-immigrant. Not surprisingly, exclusivist groups promoting English-only claim to be doing so in the name of a higher good. They assert that enforced use of a single language will promote social unity in an already dangerously divided society. But that argument too is little more than an ethnocentric political agenda parading as a nebulous hope. Multilingualism in itself may or may not promote civil peace—in some countries it does and in some it doesn't, and each is different because of unique political and historical circumstances. What is certain, however, is that the assertions and tactics of the English-only movement have themselves inspired more than a little civil discord and divisiveness (Madrid 1990).

Finally, it must be noted that there is no evidence of any kind that an "official English" policy would reduce the use of other languages in culturally distinctive communities (Piatt 1990). "Home languages" have a tenacity that is remarkable. Denying people the right to use the language in which they can best express their most important concerns would produce little more than frustration and resentment. Certainly the world might be a more manageable place if we all spoke the same language. But it would be more manageable if we all spoke two or three languages as well.

Whatever the political outcome of this sometimes noisy debate, in health and social services the simplistic and denigrating opinions of the pro-English zealots are not an option. Meeting the client "where he or she is at" means taking full account of each individual's speech preferences in useful and positive ways. That does not mean that service professionals are required to achieve fluency in a foreign language as a condition of providing quality services. But it does mean having some sense of the importance of language in people's lives and how they use language to describe and analyze their concerns. As I emphasized in Chapter 4, language is not a neutral tool for communicating information. It is one of the ways people preserve their identity. Social service professionals, therefore, need to be sensitive to the role of language in their work, both as a communicative device and as a signifier of ethnic and communal participation.

After English, Spanish is the most widely spoken language in the United States. According to the 1990 census, over 17,000,000 Americans use Spanish at home. Some cities, counties, and even states are de facto bilingual (even trilingual and more!) and that is likely to become more true rather than less so in the future. In some areas, especially in the Southwest, Spanish has more claim than English to being the historical, traditional language of the region. But not all Spanish speakers use their language the same way or with the same degree of comfort. There are significant dialectic differences between the Spanish of Mexico, Puerto Rico, parts of South America, and the various regions of Spain. More important, not everyone in the United States who identifies with the Spanish language has the same level of proficiency. In studying bilingual communities, linguists commonly distinguish between "communicative" and "symbolic" language (Edwards 1985). Communicative use is that which goes on everyday in routine transactions. It requires a high degree of "performative competence," the ability to speak and understand with fluency. Symbolic attachment to a language is a matter of community affirmation and affiliation, regardless of how well one uses the language of symbolic preference.

While most North American Spanish speakers are fully fluent in their preferred language, some (perhaps many) are not. Eastman (1984) argues that in multilingual nations, including the United States, the link between language and ethnicity is often one of "association" rather than performative competence. She suggests that "a particular 'associated language' is a necessary component of ethnic identity but the language we associate ourselves with need not be the one we use in our day-to-day lives" (1984:259). In fact, an "associated" language may be used only in limited contexts, even imperfectly in the grammatical or lexical sense. That is often true for second and third generation descendants of original immigrants. For them, fluency is less a concern than is loyalty to their community, its traditions, and the associated language. The alert and sympathetic service professional will see that such a stance is not necessarily an anti-assimilation stubbornness (although that is certainly possible) but rather a way for individuals to create an acceptable balance between communal loyalties and participation in a conventionally monolingual society (Keefe and Padilla 1987).

But language habits and choices are more than a matter of communal loyalty, even though that is significant. Espin (1987) has described some of the cognitive and affective issues that surround language use by her Latina clients. Language has a psychodynamic dimension, and in her practice, "even for those Latinas who are fluent in English, Spanish remains the language of emotions because it was in Spanish that affective meanings were originally encoded. . . . To try to decode those affective meanings through the use of another language may be problematic at best" (Espin 1987:496). For most health and social service professionals, the use of English in a consultation is simply a given, but the possibility that clients may want to switch into Spanish (or any other language) must be regarded as therapeutically important, especially where intimate subjects cannot otherwise be well described (Sciarra and Ponterotto 1991). Not only clients but Hispanic practitioners know that Spanish can convey nuances of therapeutic significance (Zuniga 1991). Language choice is not just a political or a communal issue. It is a treatment one as well and requires great flexibility, patience, and a willingness to do what is necessary to further the goals of intervention.

LATINO DIVERSITY

Within the Spanish-speaking population in the United States there is considerable diversity of cultural, racial, ethnic, and national origins. This makes it difficult, if not impossible, to speak of Hispanics as a "consolidated minority." Rather, the situation is one of "a group-in-formation whose boundaries and self definitions are still in a state of flux" (Portes and Truelove 1987:359). That should not be interpreted to mean, however, that Latinos are beginning to "melt" into the larger American pot. Marín (1993) points out that "recently arrived Hispanics, contrary to the experiences of other immigrant groups, seem intent on maintaining their language, cultural values, and other group specific characteristics, requiring that attention be given to the group's characteristics whenever community interventions are designed and implemented" (149). Indeed, in some cases whole communities explicitly defend and actively preserve a distinctive cultural identity, a situation that was typical, for example, of the Chilean political refugees who came to this country after the 1973 coup in their homeland (Eastmond 1993; Gonsalves 1990). The cultural tenacity shown by Latinos in North America is remarkable and it points again to the fact that they, like others, do not abandon their traditions and assimilate but selectively use their cultural background to redefine a sense of identity (Saenz and Aguirre 1991). Each community does that in a way that uniquely suits individual and collective needs. (Keefe and Padilla [1987:211–219] use a 136-item Cultural Awareness and Ethnic Loyalty Scale to measure Chicano ethnicity. Almost half of their questions concern Spanish language use.)

Those who are self-identified as Spanish speakers generally affiliate with one of four major regions of origin: Mexico, Puerto Rico, Latin America, or Cuba. (Many South Americans, however, identify historically with Italy and Germany rather than Spain and those in Brazil, of course, with Portugal. Others stress their Indian heritage rather than that of the colonizing Spanish.) The cultural as well as dialectic differences among these groups are considerable and so too is their geographical distribution within the United States. Yet despite their internal diversity, the terms "Hispanic" and "Latino" have united many Spanish speakers in common political causes. As umbrella terms, they have come into general usage. Latino will be used here, although not without certain qualifications (Giménez, Lopez, and Munoz 1992).

"Hispanic" is not a term invented by the people it identifies. Its general familiarity is the result of a decision made by the U.S. government's Office of Management and Budget in 1978, a decision to help census takers who needed a term for whites (and others) who claimed some degree of Spanish language or cultural affiliation. A definition appeared in the *Federal Register*: a Hispanic is "a person of Mexican, Puerto Rican, Cuban, Central or South American or other Spanish culture or origin, regardless of race" (1978:19269). Like all ethnic definitions and labels, this one is awkward and incomplete. For example, are immigrants from Spain also Hispanics? What of Brazilians who speak Portuguese, or Indians whose Spanish is really just an overlay on a South-American Indian language? What of Spanish speakers from the Philippines or the Dominican Republic? Do those in some parts of the Southwest, whose family lines in the region precede U.S. sovereignty there, think of themselves as Hispanic? And how do any of these people feel about accepting an ethnic label promulgated for them by statisticians and door-to-door head counters?

Some favor the term "Latino" (Hayes-Bautista and Chapa 1987; Pérez-Stable 1987). It has the advantage of both a linguistic association and a geographical referent. But it omits the significant number of South Americans who speak English (Belize, the Guyanas) and those whose family roots extend to Italy, Germany, and some areas of the Mediterranean. The names "Chicano" and "La Raza" have been proposed as well, but they have more limited reference. Chicanos are Mexican Americans north of the border, not Mexicans as such. La Raza, "the race," brings into the labeling a "racial" motif that has not won general acceptance. As identifiers, both Chicano and La Raza were associated with the cultural activism of the 1960s and 1970s, and, whatever the merits of the issues that were addressed then, La Raza is now somewhat dated. So too may be the nominally masculine noun endings of some of the labels proposed, a feature that may be more troublesome for some sensitive whites than for Spanish speakers, but it nevertheless creates an obstacle to universal applicability.

Marín and Marín (1991:24) suggest that when using labels for a population this diverse, primary attention ought to go to people's own affirmations of their ancestry (usually a country of origin) and their preference for whatever cultural features they choose to emphasize. Working in Chicago on the meaning of ethnic labels, Padilla (1985) discovered that what people chose to call themselves was highly situational. While Padilla's research respondents had a generalized "sentimental and ideological identification with a language group," many saw themselves as Latino at one time and Puerto Rican, Mexican American, Cuban, or some other national identity at others (1985:336). Names and labels are always shifting and often controversial, and the discussion that surrounds them is a critical part of the ethnic identity process of both individuals and groups (see especially Giménez, López, and Muñoz [1992] on the politics of ethnic names). The point is that in work with Spanish-speaking clients, as in all cross-cultural activities, labels differ among individuals, families, and communities, even according to who is doing what with whom. If that seems confusing, it is, at least to outsiders. Insiders understand it perfectly well. Therefore the general rule for service providers is: preferences vary, so when you don't know, ask.

There are over 17 million Latinos in the United States, certainly more if the number of residents without official documentation could be known. At current rates of growth, they will be the largest minority in the country within thirty years, about 15 percent of the U.S. population by 2020 (Davis, Haub, and Willette 1988). Before 1950, most Latinos in North America were of Mexican origin and, while Mexican Americans are still the largest group among Spanish speakers, their proportion has declined. The second largest group is that of people from Central and South American countries. Their growth has greatly increased cultural diversity within the Latino population generally. Puerto Ricans are the third largest group, their presence in the United States facilitated by the commonwealth status of their island and freedom of movement to the mainland. Many Puerto Ricans virtually commute, at least on a seasonal basis, between San Juan and the major cities of the East Coast and Midwest. Cubans make up a small and specialized population that is quite distinctive demographically (about 6 percent of all Hispanics) and politically. Concentrated in Florida, many fled the Castro regime and are more properly considered political refugees than labor immigrants. Because of their urban and suburban concentration as well as their business success, they have exerted a powerful influence, relative to their numbers, especially in conservative political circles.

Demographically, Latinos in the United States are relatively young, due to immigration by younger people seeking work and to their high fertility rate. The Hispanic population is on average eight years younger than that of whites and two years younger than blacks, and fully one-third of all North-American Hispanics are under the age of fifteen. The image of Spanish speakers as a predominantly rural, farm-oriented people is prevalent in many western states, but on the East Coast, urban residence for Spanish speakers is the norm. In fact, nearly 85 percent of all Spanish speakers in the United States live in urban areas (Sullivan 1985).

Although Anglo Americans tend to think of all Spanish speakers as "immigrants" and "refugees," the Spanish were well established as colonists in this hemisphere long before the nations of northern Europe. Huge areas of what is now the United States were explored and settled by Spaniards. Mexico once included all of the Southwest, from Texas to California and as far north as Colorado, Utah, and Wyoming. In addition, Spanish attitudes toward commingling socially and sexually with Indians and, later, with slaves taken from Africa, were such that racial mixing (*mestizaje*) was common. (This was in marked contrast to practices in the American colonies established by northern Europeans where mixing, while it certainly happened, was prohibited in law and condemned in practice.) Many of the islands of the Caribbean, the northern coast of South America, and all of Central America were Spanish possessions. Spanish explorers were active in Florida, the Mississippi valley, northern California, and far up the Northwest coast. Indians were "pacified" and missionized and, when they resisted, ruthlessly exterminated so that settlements and trading centers could be established. Many of these once tiny centers still stand, known by their original names: Santa Fe, San Diego, Los Angeles, El Paso.

Mexican sheep and cattle ranchers who called themselves *californios* moved from Mexico northward in the early 1800s, about the same time small-scale cattle entrepreneurs were working their way into what would become Texas, Arizona, and New Mexico (Acosta-Belen and Sjostrom 1988). In addition to founding settlements, the Spanish were active in the American Revolutionary War. Siding with the American colonists, a large *mestizo* army held off the British in the lower Mississippi valley, keeping Gulf ports open for supplies intended for the American colonies (Acosta-Belen and Sjostrom 1988:88). Their contribution is not usually mentioned in American history books although it was critical to the success of the war.

Not until the beginning of the nineteenth century did Anglo Americans begin moving into Texas and the Southwest as colonists, competing politically, economically, and militarily with Latinos who had been resident in the region for nearly two centuries. A short war with Mexico in 1846 and 1847 added a huge landmass to the United States. Spain was forced to give up an empire spreading from Texas and Oklahoma to California, Wyoming and Kansas, establishing the U.S.-Mexican border at about its present location. The *hispanos* who had long family traditions in this massive territory faced then, as now, laws and practices putting them at a disadvantage to the new Anglo occupiers.

Late in the nineteenth century, the U.S. government again became involved with other Spanish colonies. The final decades of that century were the great period of American imperial expansion. Now that the United States was a continental nation and a major trading and military power, politicians and military strategists wanted a canal linking the Pacific and Atlantic oceans. In concert with this was an interest in annexing Puerto Rico and Cuba (and later the Virgin Islands, owned by Denmark) in order to defend the proposed canal. The bombing of a U.S. ship in the Havana harbor in 1898 served as the pretext for the Spanish-American war. The United States seized not only the territories needed to police the Caribbean basin but also the remnants of the Spanish empire in the Pacific: the Philippines, the Hawaiian islands, and Guam. Almost 500 years of Spanish hegemony were replaced by an American political and military presence.

This very brief historical overview suggests something important not only about the diversity of Spanish speakers in North America but also about their durability. Many predominantly Spanish communities and families have a long and distinguished presence in what was once the European's "New World," a presence of greater historical depth than that of the English speakers who currently dominate. That fact raises a familiar but contentious question: what and who is an "American?" It also puts into a larger and more challenging context the claims of the English-only advocates that English is properly the "official" language of the country. The implication that English and the northern European cultural preferences associated with it are somehow "original" and therefore fundamental to American identity is simply not supportable. The Spanish language and Iberian traditions have been here much longer. The idea of a shared cultural ancestry may be difficult for the cultural nativists to accept. But for the rest of us it has to be the starting point in thinking about what it means to be a citizen and what is implied for social and health services in a historically varied population.

SPANISH-SPEAKING COMMUNITIES AND SOCIAL SERVICES

As would be true of any ethnic or minority community, the cultural variability among Spanish speakers challenges us to think about how we might implement an idea like "cultural awareness" in order to better meet their health and social service needs. It is not always obvious what should be done and how. López and Hernandez (1986) surveyed mental health practitioners in California, asking them to describe cases from their clientele where they explicitly used cultural features as an aid to diagnosis and treatment. Most of the cases reported to them involved marital counseling, psychotic symptoms, problems with male adolescents, hospitalization issues, and drinking. While "culture" as a factor was mentioned with some frequency, there was no evidence that the practitioners surveyed had a set of criteria by which to determine that cultural factors were important, or that the cultural features they chose as the basis for interpreting presenting problems were in fact the "right" ones from among the many possibilities. López and Hernandez suggest that in many of these cases, the therapist may have been relying primarily on commonsense understanding of Latino persons generally, and they asked: "Are therapists appropriately taking culture into account, or are they applying stereotypic notions which may not apply to their patients?" (1987:125). The "cultural" half of "cultural sensitivity" was, if not missing, at least not evident.

An important contribution to the cultural awareness issue has been made by Rogler and associates (1987) in a classic paper on defining culturally appropriate interventions. Lloyd Rogler has an especially rich background in research on

Puerto Ricans and mental health in New York City, and he has helped develop innovative approaches to serving second generation Spanish-speaking children there. (Rogler's various publications [1984, 1991] would be useful to anyone who works with Puerto Ricans and his use of *cuento* therapy [Constantino et al. 1986] would interest those who work with children in any community.) Rogler and coworkers suggest that cultural sensitivity be thought of as a pyramidal structure, professional services becoming more creatively and elaborately cross-cultural the higher one rises on the pyramid. There are three levels to the Rogler model, and I will follow his lead in discussing its applicability to health and social services for Spanish-speaking communities. The model is illustrated in Figure 8.1.

Rogler sees the base of the pyramid, level 1, as a historical product of the civil rights movements of the 1960s and 1970s and the rise of community mental health programs on a national scale. The issue at that time, and the one that characterizes level 1, is accessibility. To make services culturally "sensitive," one must first make them available. Consequently there has been, from that time to today, a large and still growing literature on utilization and access barriers. The list of impediments to utilization and their effects on consumers is much too long to summarize here. But for Latino communities, important areas identified for improvement have been (1) a closer match between the client's and professional's understanding of needs and what can be done about them; (2) recognition of alternative forms of help and the skills and procedures of the individuals who offer assistance outside established institutions; (3) surveys and assessments of

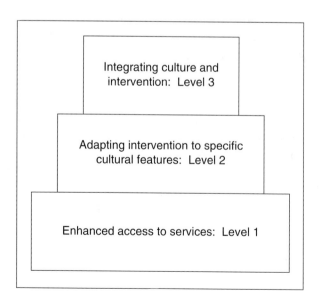

FIGURE 8.1 **Cultural sensitivity increases at each level on the pyramid in Rogler's Model.**

"needs" as they are articulated by the client community; and (4) recognition of the importance of language in providing services to multilingual populations. The latter issue has led to the rise of numerous referral and service agencies targeting specific ethnic communities and making use of native and bilingual speakers and translators. Individuals working in these agencies have become available as consultants to other organizations and are able to activate community-based networks simply because, as cultural compatriots, they are familiar with them.

One rigorous and theoretically well-grounded study of access issues for Hispanics is that of Rodriguez (1987), who looked at how Hispanics in the South Bronx seek help from a variety of social service agencies. That study looked at utilization of mental health, services for the elderly, the disabled, and women heads of households. Not surprisingly, in that area of New York City needs were high and so was utilization. One particularly important finding of the study was that the size of an individual's social network correlates well with service use. Networks are important channels for diffusing information. People with smaller networks, or who relied exclusively on family members for information, were less likely to know of and use services that had potential value for them. It is sometimes thought that large networks are likely to lead clients to alternative help providers. Sometimes that is true, but networks were also important for transmitting information about services from mainstream organizations. Further, Rodriguez's study found that those more familiar with American life, that is, more acculturated, were more likely to use services. Thus, cultural differences, and especially language differences, were significantly related to people's ability to find and use organizations expressly designed to help them.

Rogler identified the level 2 of the pyramid as any effort by service providers to utilize a perceived feature of Latino culture in furtherance of an intervention outcome. It is at this level that we meet again the familiar debate about the appropriateness to minority clients of therapeutic styles originally devised for upper middle class, Victorian-minded, urbanized European and American whites. Is insight therapy really useful for someone needing a job, a house, or vocational training? Does learning to "cope" with one's rage do anything to challenge racism, change divisive public policies, or bring about economic justice?

In general, the answers to these questions, at least as they relate to Latinos, have been negative. Sandoval and De La Roza (1986) examine the clinical implications of Latino cultural features and conclude:

> *Cultural differences in perceptions of health and illness, etiology and treatment, are also reasons why Hispanics do not adequately use mental health services. . . . Cultural differences in personality perceptions might render [insight-oriented] therapeutic modalities as useless. Hispanic perception of personality in general is that of a fixed entity. This leaves little room for therapeutic modalities that solely deal in intrapsychic process and are aimed at promoting personality change, growth and awareness (161).*

To illustrate their point, they look at a number of generalized Hispanic values, including values concerning the family, personalism, individualism, authority, paternalism, machismo, and fatalism, and conclude that in general they are not congruent with the assumptions and treatment styles of most mental health practitioners. Their discussion of individualism is interesting in this regard since that is a value common to many Anglo Americans as well. For them, the Hispanic sense of individualism is distinctive. They cite a popular idiom, "Soy feo pero simpatico"—I am ugly but engaging—to illustrate the subtle difference. For whites, individualism suggests competitiveness, getting ahead, standing out as number one (or "numero uno" to those who know no other Spanish but that). Anglo individualism means being first or the best in a field of like-minded competitors. But the Latino idea of individualism suggests distinctiveness, true difference, including the things that could make someone ugly but charming at the same time. It also implies participation rather than separateness, in the sense that because of differences we all have something unique to offer and for which we can be respected.

In clinical relationships, Sandoval and De La Roza advise the therapist "to overtly accept a client's peculiarities," especially when they are presented as charming features of the individual (1986:170). They cite the example of a young man, Julio, who had repeated encounters with the police because of drinking and who believed that belligerence was one of his unique and valued personality traits. He rejected psychiatric and medical treatment but participated in discussions, apparently informational, about the nature of personality and how behavior could be changed under certain circumstances. The starting point for these talks was his uniqueness, and how belligerence was a distinctive feature of his personality. Once he was able to accept the view that he could modify and even control personality traits, including angry outbursts, and once he had practice in doing so, he was able to bring some stability to his everyday life.

This case is a more sophisticated example of cultural awareness. It requires the identification of a cultural feature—Latino beliefs about personality and this client's commitment to them—and the therapist's willingness to use a feature of Hispanic ethnopsychology as the starting point for intervention. The case illustrates Rogler's point that once we are beyond the first level, that of opening the doors and making access easier, we need to know what kind of background cultural material the client brings to the encounter and how we can use that as part of a helping relationship.

Marín (1993) has discussed this issue at length, especially in relation to community intervention efforts other than those related to mental health. He argues that a culturally appropriate intervention must be based on the cultural values of the group of interest, must adopt strategies that "reflect the subjective cultural characteristics" of the group, and must take account of their behavioral preferences (1993:155). Otherwise outreach and community information programs will have little credibility with those they seek to influence. He cites as an example his own work in anti-smoking campaigns. He found that where whites were more responsive to cessation messages that stressed personal improvement, such as no more coughing, bad breath, or burned clothes (Anglo individualism again), Latinos tended to identify with messages that emphasized family values (smoking as a bad example for one's children, the health risk of "passive" smoke for others in the household). It is widely reported in the literature that familialism is a power-ful cultural value among Hispanics, so the family was a logical and culturally correct focus for health improvement messages. It also made good cultural sense to train nonsmoking family members to support smokers who wanted to quit, a technique that was more effective than the less family-oriented workshops and clinics widely promoted by hospitals and others. Success in this area really began with an understanding of Latino culture and how it might be integrated into the solution of a problem. Shortcuts such as translating into Spanish anti-smoking messages originally written in English, with their cultural assumptions still built in, simply were not as effective and would not qualify as cultural sensitivity.

On level 3 of the Rogler pyramid, the level most fully cognizant of cultural differences and their meaning for therapy, appropriate cultural materials are integrated into whatever intervention is proposed. This raises some interesting and challenging issues: which cultural traits are "appropriate," who is to decide that, and how will they be used? Since communities are not homogeneous, how do we know that a cultural feature is "appropriate" for use with a specific client? Most important, are we to assume that because some value or practice is a feature of the client's culture, it is necessarily a good or useful one that ought to be replicated in therapy? There is, for example, some discussion in the research literature about the power and powerlessness of Mexican-American (Vasquez 1984; Palacios and Franco 1986), Puerto-Rican (Rogler and Cooney 1984), and Cuban women (Ortiz 1985). Some view the position of Latina women vis-à-vis men as submissive and weak. Others claim women's power within the family is much greater than is known or appreciated and that the real disadvantages women face are in the marketplace, not with their husbands. Clearly, this is a complex issue, one that varies among communities, within them, and perhaps within specific families. Before a "trait" can be plucked for use in a treatment regimen, the therapist needs to know a lot not only about the client's community generally but about the needs and interests of individuals and families within it.

One way to prepare for that level of service delivery is to familiarize oneself with the research and ethnographic literature of the community in question. The material below, on health and illness beliefs and what they have to do with help seeking, is only an introduction to a vast literature on Spanish-speaking Ameri-cans. But it does indicate the range of issues one must consider when working with Hispanic clients and patients and where one can begin if a more intensive learning effort is required.

Because Latinos preserve some very old Iberian traditions, as well as others deriving from a lengthy colonial experience quite different from that of Anglo Americans, their views of health, mental health, and healing strategies are distinc-tive. Some of the values and beliefs described below have been dropped, at least by some Latinos in the United States, and others have been preserved or modi-fied. I cannot stress too much, as I have elsewhere in this book, that the persist-ence and strengths of beliefs like those described below are highly variable. They cannot be used as infallible guides to the preferences or practices of specific individuals or families. But many of these beliefs are widely recognized ideas related to well-being, and they are topics that the culturally sensitive social worker will want to know something about. My discussion of them here is just an introduction, and those who will be working with Latino clients and patients will need to do much more study and analysis in this area.

HEALTH, ILLNESS, AND BELIEF SYSTEMS

Given the institutional and ideological predominance of scientific biomedicine and corollary fields such as psychiatry, physical therapy, and even chiropractic medicine, alternative forms of health belief and practice are usually below the horizon of awareness of most Americans. Yet embedded within the Latino community is a large and ancient system of health and mental health practices, derived from Greek, Roman, and Arabic sources and transmitted to this hemisphere in a distinctively Iberian form. In chapter 2, I briefly described several Latino disease categories, *empacho, mal ojo,* and *susto,* to illustrate aspects of the help seeking behavior model. In this section, I will expand on that information, adding other elements of the system to the list. I want it to be clear, however, why this material is here. In presenting it, I am *not* making a case that all Spanish speakers in the United States, or anywhere else, endorse the illness categories, diagnoses, or interventions described. Many do not and, as I have tried to show in the historical overview, there is enormous variation in matters like these as in all areas of life. Aside from the issue of whether people do or do not "believe in" these folk illnesses, most Spanish speakers have heard of them, know something about them, or know of people who accept them as important.

The real concern for social service and health professionals is not *whether* people believe in specific, culturally defined illness syndromes, but rather *how* they believe. The important clinical issue is knowing the circumstances under which a folk illness such as *mal ojo* is regarded as "merely superstition," or as a possible but unlikely diagnosis, or as something clients say "others" believe in but members of their family do not, or as evidence of real forces of maliciousness at loose in the world. People generally do not "believe" in illnesses abstractly. Rather, they know about them in reference to an individual who suffers with one. Similarly, the culturally sensitive practitioner does not have to personally "believe" in a folk illness or diagnosis to appreciate that other people do, and that their beliefs have consequences for their recovery. My claim, simply, is that attention to culturally specific categories of illness is a vital piece of ethnically competent social work and health care. Whether any health or illness belief is "true" in some fundamental, objectifiable sense, as those who rely on *DSM-III-R* might suggest, is only marginally significant.

Why should popular illness categories and variations in local belief be so important to care providers and helpful in intervention? Using participant observation and life history interviews, medical anthropologist Laurie Price (1987) recorded illness narratives from a sample of Ecuadorian patients, most of them women. What is of interest here is not the details of the narratives themselves but rather what she discovered about the importance of naturally occurring discourse about illness as a means for understanding folk beliefs. First, she found that conversations about illness are an occasion for transmitting technical information about symptoms, diagnostic categories, local names, favored remedies, and appropriate helpers. Seemingly casual conversations had an important educational function.

Second, participants in illness narratives often explored and enlarged their theories of illness causation and treatment, building an increasingly global reservoir of information from which to interpret personal experiences. Their theories were not consistent nor scientifically verifiable, but they functioned as all theories do: they generated explanations. Third, narratives often validated treatment actions already taken. They presented the sufferer as someone who had tried to act positively; they helped legitimate the sick role. Finally, narratives intensified social relations and bonds of support. They helped build a small community of sympathizers whose advice and help would be needed before the illness episode was terminated. Recognizing that illness narratives can focus attention this way in any cultural context, we are in a better position to understand the culturally specific illness beliefs that patients and clients present.

In the section that follows, I will examine several categories of popular illness, all of which have varying degrees of explanatory appeal in Spanish-loyal communities. This is not a catalogue of what Latinos "believe" about illnesses, however. Rather, I want to suggest something of the complexity of these cultural themes and note how they supply the material from which patient and client narrative explanations are sometimes built.

The criticism has sometimes been made (Longres 1991, for example) that illness beliefs like those described here are "exotic" and that a cultural approach to social services exaggerates obscure and unusual features of ethnic communities. Yet a 1991 survey conducted at a health clinic for Mexican-American farm workers in central Florida showed that folk illnesses were self-medicated by 53 percent of those in the sample (Baer and Bustillo 1993). Probably many more individuals had knowledge of these health beliefs and may have self-diagnosed as well but still went to a physician. What appears "exotic" to outsiders, or to biomedical and social service professionals, may or may not be unusual to patients and clients and the task of culturally sensitive service providers is to be alert to all the possibilities.

Ataques de Nervios

The cross-cultural psychiatric literature has documented a condition called *ataques de nervios* or an "attack of nerves" for many years, in clinical studies, in epidemiological work, and in studies of people's reactions to natural disasters. The literature on this syndrome is extensive (see especially the various chapters in Davis and Low 1989). Guarnaccia (1993) describes the classic features of an attack as:

> *a culturally sanctioned response to acute stressful experiences, particularly relating to grief, threat, and family conflict. Ataque de nervios is characterized by shouting uncontrollably, trembling, heart palpitations, a sense of heat in the*

chest rising to the head, fainting, and seizure-like episodes. Typical ataques *occur at culturally appropriate times such as funerals, at the scene of an accident, or during a family argument or fight. Ataques mobilize the person's social network. The person usually regains consciousness rapidly and does not remember the* ataque *(158).*

This collection of symptoms, however, is only a culturally naked trait list until we locate it within some larger system of meaning. Guarnaccia notes that an attack occurs only in conjunction with social circumstances that are stressful, that it is not the result of something physiological or of anything "mental." Attacks are responses to distress, to conditions that are social in origin, and for which neither pills nor psychodynamic analysis is necessarily helpful or appropriate. An attack is embedded in a system of culturally specific meanings and resolution requires that those meanings be unraveled and given credence during treatment.

Ataques de nervios were first described in the medical literature in the 1950s, based on studies of Puerto Rican men inducted into the U.S. military. Some of these men were characterized by Army physicians as suicidal, psychopathic, and hysterical and their condition was attributed to personality flaws, child-rearing and weaning practices, and an inability to adapt to the authoritarian structure and competitive values of American military life. Once known (somewhat pejoratively) as the "Puerto Rican syndrome," the condition was later identified by Latino and Anglo mental health researchers as a folk illness also found among Dominicans, Costa Ricans, and some Latin-American immigrants in North America. Guarnaccia, De La Cancela, and Carrillo (1989) describe it as a culturally recognized "expression of anger and grief resulting from the disruption of family systems, the process of migration, and concerns about family members in people's country of origin" (47). They describe four sample cases, all women, who illustrate variant expressions of the syndrome and point to its social origins.

In each case, the patient's attention centers on rage and anger connected to failures in key personal relationships. One elderly woman living in the Northeast had been "abandoned" by her adult children, all of whom had succeeded by American standards of careerism and were not available to her at times of distress. Her narrative description of her *nervios* attacks included references to cutting and self-mutilation. Another woman related an extensive history of physical privation and isolation from important men in her life including her husband and adult son. Her pronounced fears of being alone often initiated an attack. A third client presented a quieter pattern of attacks, describing intense feelings of anger and overwhelming heat and pressure in her chest. She would have trouble breathing and speaking and could not move her hands. Her fear of losing control when she was with friends or neighbors kept her at home, further isolating her from all contact except with the staff of a local clinic who treated her somatic complaints. A fourth case was that of younger woman, only a few months in the United States, who felt threatened by her hard-drinking husband and extremely isolated from family and friends in Central America who could help her. She had seen a priest and a physician, the latter prescribing Valium for her attacks. (Valium is widely used by patients suffering from *ataques* and commonly prescribed by physicians both Anglo and Hispanic.) As with many sufferers, this woman recognized that her seizures were associated with anger, but she did not associate that anger with specific people or events in her life.

In each of these cases, grief and rage (and a subsequent attack) were connected to personal isolation, fear that one might not see friends and relatives in a distant country again, an ongoing crisis in relationships such as marriage or with adult children, and a profound sense that there was nothing that one could do to change anything. Typically, these are conditions symptomatic of immigrants, especially women, who find that in North America they are cut off from traditional supports and that the (ideal) protective functions of male family leadership have collapsed (Espin 1987). In brief, *ataques de nervios* communicate distress, especially powerlessness and anger. "The relationship of these experiences to previous life events in childhood and adulthood shape the individual's current responses in culturally meaningful ways" (Guarnaccia, De La Cancela, and Carrillo 1989:50). *Ataques*, then, cannot be understood as a list of symptoms alone; their significance and amenability to treatment are completely embedded in a culture-specific system of meaning. Outside of that system, the illness is diagnostically incomprehensible, whether it occurs among young Puerto-Rican men or older Central-American immigrant women.

Perhaps as an aside, but not entirely so, I want to note how these clinical understandings were developed by the Guarnaccia team. Their work was interdisciplinary and included a bilingual Anglo anthropologist, a Puerto-Rican psychologist, and a Cuban physician/epidemiologist. All three had extensive communal experience in health and mental health centers. Their subjects had known and documented clinical histories but, importantly, the data in those histories was expanded using open-ended interviews based on Kleinman's health seeking behavior model. Patients were asked individually to name and describe their illness, discuss their beliefs about its causes, produce a narrative of their experiences with it, and describe their history of consultation and treatment. Family histories and migration experiences were prominent in those narratives, and they provided information that went far beyond the usual social histories asked for by clinical staff. All narratives were taken in Spanish, with full attention to the cultural meanings of key terms, and then translated into English. Without that effort, the researchers would not have been able to identify critical features of the *ataque* syndrome or its variations. They would never have been able to "individualize the client." Nor would they have had the material at hand to improve both the accuracy and speed of diagnoses with future clients. Without cultural information, they would have been less perceptive and less efficient as learners and as therapists.

Embrujado

All cultures have folk syndromes, what cross-cultural researchers recognize as locally defined conditions of distress, sets of diagnostic categories, and appropriate intervention techniques. They are "exotic" only to those who do not use or understand them. *Embrujado* is a disorder that, like many in the Spanish-speaking world, employs religious ideology and language in its conceptualization. *Embrujado* hallucinations, paranoid reactions, anxiety, spirit possession, and witchcraft often involve communication with supernatural beings, be they good or evil, and with the dead. Sufferers sometimes invoke the symbolism and ideology of formal religion, which is not surprising given the historical importance of religion and the Catholic church in Iberian cultures. As with *ataques*, the issue is not whether *embrujado* beliefs are "true" in some objective sense but "how" they are true for those who rely on them to frame and narrate their afflictions.

The contrasts between *embrujado* and standard psychiatric categories in understanding mental illness are described by Koss-Chioino and Canive (1993:181). In the former, individuals believe they are powerless to manage daily affairs because an external force, a witch, has overwhelmed their inherent capabilities. The affected individual manifests inappropriate behavior and verbalization including frequent references to the pervasiveness of evil, communication with God and various saints, and fear of future witchcraft attacks. Bodily pains and deviant sexual behavior (if present) are attributed to the hostile attentions of a witch. Failure in a job or in relationships is likewise blamed on evil forces, often many of them converging on the patient in such numbers and strength that they cannot be fought off. Finally, after much struggle and anguish, the individual lapses into apathy and can no longer function in daily activities.

Viewed psychiatrically, the same individual is believed to suffer from a lack of ego strength or a damaged or regressive personality. The problem is generally due to an early life trauma. Anger, hostility, suspiciousness, paranoia, religious ideation, and deviant sexuality all typify the patient's condition, variously diagnosed as paranoid schizophrenia, depression, neurosis, even organic brain dysfunction. Sexual preoccupation is evidence of doubts about one's sexual identity and capability. Obsessions with good and evil, God and the devil, and the pervasiveness of malicious intent in the world at large suggest psychopathological mechanisms at work. Any evident somatizing is an expression of deep psychological conflicts as well as avoidance of the task of resolving them. The individual's energy is consumed by internal conflicts that finally lead to apathy and deep depression. Organic as well as psychological causes may be present.

Koss-Chioino and Canive (1993) studied a sample of Latino patients in a large mental health clinic in New Mexico, patients who believed themselves bewitched. All the patients were men who frequently complained about having been rejected by spouses or spouses-to-be. These women, and sometimes a mother-in-law, were suspected of the bewitching behavior. The men also complained of physical symptoms including tics, temporary paralysis, and back pains. They reported themselves to be filled with evil spirits and often spoke of violence and rage. Religious imagery pervaded much of their talk and they blamed evil forces for leading them away from the kind of life God intended for them. Some of the patients had been taken by their families to a *curendera* but the efforts of these healers had not been helpful. One patient exemplified the condition:

> He said that he wanted help [at the Psychiatric Emergency Unit] because, "my wife advised me to do it if I want to stay married." On further inquiry P.R. revealed that he had lost control and beat his wife. This was the latest in a series of aggressive behaviors that coincided with financial pressures stemming from P.R.'s attempt to run his own business. He felt that a devil had possessed him and "put bad thoughts" into his mind. P.R. appeared somewhat confused to the interviewers, who described his affect as "flat," and showed thought disorder (thought blocking and thought insertion) (Koss-Chioino and Canive 1993:178).

This individual was diagnosed as schizophrenic and treated with antipsychotic medications. His case had a two-year history at the clinic but, following treatment and discharge, his symptoms periodically reappeared. A number of other patients, similarly diagnosed and treated, also had a recurrence of symptoms on an irregular basis.

What is important to note in this study is the differing set of assumptions made in the folk model of *embrujado* and in the medical model of the clinic's staff. For the latter, a patient's talk about evil spirits was likely to be labeled "hallucinatory" or as grandiose religious "ideations." Difficulties in relating intimately with women were prominent in diagnoses and seen as evidence of childhood failures that required reexamination and "resolution." Most important, the clinical diagnoses assumed a flawed intrapsychic state, one that must be identified, labeled, treated (chemically or with counseling or both), and changed, with favorable outcomes expected within a given range of certainty. For their part, the patients were expected to do some kind of healing "work," something that would transform a damaged ego or low sense of self-esteem. That work would be undertaken with a specially trained therapist, not of the patient's culture, and failure of the treatment, if that occurred, would be blamed on insufficient effort on the part of the patient himself or, less likely, an incorrect diagnosis or ineffective therapist. Further, labels such as "schizophrenia" and "depression" suggested to the patient a chronic condition subject to recidivism, and the probability of a lifelong, individual struggle to overcome a very personal failure.

By contrast, a "bewitched" diagnosis would have assumed that the causes of the situation are external to the individual, located in a problematic set of relationships rather than a faulty psychic or organic condition. Issues of intrafamily conflict, power, and control, especially involving wives and mothers-in-law, would have been invoked. Questions of jealousy, spite, and anger over previous slights and hurts would be central to the counseling. Similarly, failures in the job market and expectations of economic success would have been linked to specific work skills and capabilities, with specific plans made for improvement where possible and appropriate. An *embrujado* diagnosis carries with it the implication that, unlike a ruined psyche, a supernatural hex or an external cause can be removed and something of a new start begun.

In addition, a folk diagnosis usually requires that an appropriate healer be found to help treat the condition, one who is willing to work in tandem with clinicians. A dual approach in these matters makes sense because it offers more alternatives for problem resolution (Koss-Chioino 1992). A folk diagnosis also invokes a potentially useful cultural ally, "extended family networks composed of consanguines, affines, and fictive kin acquired through *compadrazgo*" (Koss-Chioino and Canive 1993:184). The individual is absolved of having to bear full responsibility for his or her condition, and those who are emotionally closer than a professional therapist can be part of the treatment. While the *embrujado* strategy has its risks—especially where family networks do not function well and cannot assist the patient—at least as a diagnostic category it affirms that there are stresses in the lives of minority individuals that are not their responsibility alone and that there are acceptable, culturally tested and legitimated ways of dealing with them.

Empacho

While *empacho* is a relatively minor condition, it illustrates several other features of folk illnesses: they may overlap biomedical categories, and they sometimes involve treatments that are not useful, and may be harmful. This is a significant point because I do not want to contribute to the romanticized view that folk healers are necessarily "right" and those who work in established clinics or hospitals are not.

Empacho is a condition in which food or concentrations of saliva are believed to be "stuck" in the stomach, resulting in vomiting, constipation, bloating, diarrhea, lack of appetite, and even chills or fever. An obstruction exists and it must be cleared. *Empacho* can strike infants, children, or adults and can be treated at home, by a physician, or by a specialist called a *santiguador*. The problem has been reported among Mexicans, Mexican Americans, Guatemalans, and, mostly recently, Puerto Ricans in Connecticut. Pachter, Bernstein, and Osorio (1992) did a survey of Puerto Rican families visiting a Hartford hospital in 1990 and found that 90 percent of their sample knew of *empacho* and 67 percent reported that it had afflicted a child in their family. The most popular treatments (in order of their use) were massage, tea, changes in diet, a laxative, and prayer. Over half of the sample said a *santiguador* provided the best treatment, although physicians were consulted as well.

For all Latino communities in which *empacho* has been identified, massage by a folk specialist is the principal method of treatment. Massage usually involves prayer, sometimes rolling an egg over the stomach or pinching up the skin over the small of the back and letting it snap back, presumably to loosen the stomach blockage. Generally, one visit to a *santiguador* is sufficient to effect a cure. But not all treatments can be presumed beneficial. The Pachter team describe a mother who told her physician that she intended to give her infant tea for two days to clear out the "blockage" (she had been feeding the baby whole milk), after which she would shift to the infant formula that had been suggested. The physician opposed the exclusive use of tea for the child but negotiated a two-day regimen in which tea for half a day and formula for the other half would be followed by full-time formula feedings.

Much less benign than tea, however, are other products used for treating *empacho* that are available from herbalists in many parts of the United States. Some are extremely dangerous, especially for children. Trotter (1985) and Bose, Vashistha, and O'Loughlin (1983) describe "azarcon," an orange powder, and "greta," both of which are derived from lead oxide and can result in lead poisoning. Other compounds that have been used for treating *empacho* contain mercury and harmful dyes. Obviously, they are not helpful in treating stomach ailments and their time-honored usage in some communities cannot be assumed to be an advertisement for their desirability.

Complaints of *empacho* may involve little more than indigestion, but an intestinal blockage or bacterial infection is a serious matter. Although not demonstrated scientifically, the condition may be linked to any number of things ranging from the quality of diet to stress associated with eating and family gatherings. It may even have something to do with the frequency or infrequency of eating. Those are hypotheses for the future, but they are important things to know if one's clients are Spanish speakers and *empacho* is part of their vocabulary and their experience. Traditional remedies, while not necessarily suspect, should not be assumed to be efficacious either. Nor should their frequency of use be underestimated. In at least one study, socioeconomic status and acculturation were discovered to have no relationship to use of folk medications (Marsh and Hentges 1988). Over half of the Latino families surveyed treated *empacho* with folk remedies regardless of what they had been given by a physician.

Returning to the issue posed above, it is more important to know how people believe rather than whether their beliefs are true or false. If a condition like *empacho* is common in a client population, understanding it ethnographically and in context is exactly what the culturally alert social service professional must do so that knowledge of it can be incorporated into treatment plans. That kind of professional functioning approaches the highest levels of Rogler's pyramid of cultural awareness.

CULTURAL CONTRASTS AND ETHNIC COMPETENCE

The diversity of the Spanish-speaking population in North America makes it very difficult to offer generalizations. In this section, I have relied on scholars from various Hispanic groups for their views of the commonalities, as well as differences, they feel are important (Table 8.1). As in all the cultural contrast discussions of ethnic communities in this book, the information is most explicitly not intended to provide a trait list for any of the groups in question nor a shortcut to the real effort necessary for learning about an ethnic community. The value of the

TABLE 8.1   Selected Cultural Contrasts in Latino and Anglo-American Communities*

Latino	Anglo American
Commitment to the Spanish language as a marker of ethnic identity is very high, even though not all persons of Latino descent use Spanish regularly.	Language is less important than income, education, occupation, or place of residence as a marker of social class and identity. "Ethnic" identity is sometimes uncertain and national origins may be used as ethnic labels.
Family matters command the individual's loyalty. Other institutions or activities are clearly of secondary importance. Families are thought of in an extended sense and include not only kin but sometimes fictive kin (friends of the family).	Family life is highly valued but sometimes competes with loyalties to career or "outside" interests and activities. Children are encouraged to develop interests and activities outside the home and their involvement in extrafamilial matters interpreted as evidence of maturation and normal development.
Personalism in relations with others is a culturally recognized style and individuals are judged in terms of their behavior with family and friends, less on their roles or position in formal institutions. Strong personal commitment to others and a warm feeling tone in relationships are favored.	Many relationships are expected to be instrumental and utilitarian, especially the important relationships of jobs and community involvement. Competence, knowledge, and skill are highly valued and relations with others are expected to be fair and evenhanded.
Individualism is valued in the sense that the uniqueness and specialness of persons is in what they specifically do and are in their relationships with others, for example, as someone's mother, father, brother, or child. Individualism in this sense is an aspect of one's personality.	Individualism is valued in terms of abstract qualities—skills, knowledge, capability, frugality, for example—that make each person stand out as distinctive in some objective way. Personal desires and "needs" are sometimes contrasted with obligations to others, the latter occasionally seen as impediments to meeting highly valued individual needs.
Respect for hierarchy and authority is important, especially when it is seen as an extension of family relations and values. By contrast, authoritarianism in extrafamilial contexts is subject to challenge and negotiation, especially if it conflicts with family values of hierarchy and clear role structure.	Emphasis is on egalitarianism to the extent that circumstances allow. Children are encouraged to offer their opinions and, ideally, the needs of all are attended to equally.

Continued

TABLE 8.1   *Continued*

Latino	Anglo American
Machismo refers to male leadership (and female complementarity) as an extension of hierarchy and authority. Machismo is most properly associated with concepts of honor, trustworthiness, moral courage, and responsibility, only secondarily with sexual prowess. The honor of women for whom a man is responsible—wife, daughters, sisters, mother—is particularly important.	Male leadership is in providing socially and economically secure circumstances for a family. Changing definitions of male and female roles emphasize egalitarianism in decision making, providing opportunities for personal expression and "growth." Individual needs receive high priority.
Some Latino individuals and families exhibit a philosophy of fatalism, not as a negative or passive view of the world, but as an appreciation of human frailty and limitations. Wisdom is in recognizing limitations but also in the courage to cope with and endure them. Religious belief may support this sense of struggle as a normal part of the human condition.	Change and improvement are desired and problems, properly understood, are less obstacles than they are opportunities. One struggles to achieve and to improve oneself and one's family. Discontent with the status quo and willingness to meet the challenges of everyday life are evidence of a vigorous, positive attitude toward living.

*The contrasted items listed here may or may not apply to individuals. *The contrasts refer only to general tendencies within groups, not to characteristics of specific individuals.* In any culture, people differ in their commitment to approved values and practices.

information is only in highlighting contrasts. Even when the suggested contrasts do not seem to fit exactly, their appearance here is intended to activate more detailed examination of specific clients, families, or a local area, so that a higher level of understanding can be achieved. As usual, when we think in terms of contrasts we are forced to put ourselves into the equation. We come to see that differences as well as similarities are *transactional* features of relationships, not ascribed characteristics of persons different from ourselves.

Marín and Marín (1991) have described what they see as "basic Hispanic cultural values." Their selection is interesting because they are explicitly concerned with culturally sensitive research protocols and their translation into social science practice. They consider seven values which, they note, may not be everyone's choice but for which there is probably general agreement.

Collectivism (or "allocentrism") is a very broad contrast to individualism; it includes the willingness of individuals to seek mutual empathy, to sacrifice self-chosen goals in favor of the interests of the group, to conform to expectations, and to generally trust members of one's own family and community. In these emphases, "Hispanic culture differs in important ways from the individualistic, competitive, achievement-oriented cultures of the non-minority groups in the United States" (Marín and Marín 1991:11). Deference to the group is not always automatic nor painless, but it does confer prestige and respect on those who consistently put the interests of others ahead of their own.

Simpatia is part of a strong group orientation and is both a value and a style. Pleasantness and dignity are important in the presentation of self, and respect is reciprocated. Agreeableness is especially valued, and confrontations and negativism are avoided and discouraged. *Simpatia* requires simple courtesies, time to establish rapport, and small exchanges of gifts or favors. "La platica" or small talk is also important and is a polite way of beginning and ending a conversation. The Anglo value of "getting to the point" and the bureaucratic emphasis on "staying on task" do not inspire *simpatia.*

Not surprising, familialism or familiso rates very high as do loyalty, solidarity, and respectfulness. Loyalty creates obligations that often extend well beyond individual households to include others, both persons more distantly related and compadres or "fictive kin" who are treated "as family." Fictive kin include close friends and especially godparents, the latter a once-common relationship throughout Europe but now more important in southern Europe and South and Central America, areas where the Catholic church has been historically prominent.

Marín and Marín (1991) suggest that these complex ties of affiliation and kinship are not egalitarian but rest on a clear age and gender division of labor and a frank recognition of power differences. In Latino cultures, hierarchy and deference count. So do the native intelligence, education, and wealth that make some individuals more powerful than others. There is nothing inherently wrong in that. Those who enjoy advantages deserve whatever respect and obedience they can command. Teachers, healers, priests, males, and the aged rank high, and those lower in the hierarchy usually see that it is in their own interest to show deference as required. These are values that are hard for some other Americans to accept, however, especially if they are committed to liberal political and social agendas. In an officially egalitarian society, these values are almost too easy to stereotype as regressive, undemocratic, or even archaic. But their functioning in daily personal behavior is more complex than is apparent; moreover, millions of people find satisfaction and meaning in them. Whether they appear autocratic or enabling may be less a matter of objective fact and more one of perspective.

Two other distinctive Latino values mentioned by Marín and Marín (1991) are sensibilities related to space and time. They see Latinos as more "contact" oriented than Anglos, comfortable standing close to one another and with body touch. They also view time, as do many minority communities (and most of the rest of the world, I might add), in a flexible way. Time is always with and for people, it is not an abstraction established by clocks, schedules, and appointment calendars. "Quality time," apparently a recent discovery for some Anglos, is the norm in Latino and other communities all the time.

Finally, gender roles have a particular configuration in Latino cultures, one that we need to address since at least for Anglos stereotypes on the matter abound. Amaro and Rosso (1987) note that the study of Latina women's issues is a relatively new field, one in which there is more stereotyping than reliable information. We know relatively little about migration, immigration, and Latina women's activities in the job market. Most research has been done on the traditional roles of women, not on changes that affect them as they move beyond the sphere of the home. These topics are important to mental health professionals since women who migrate and those who seek education and jobs are at higher risk than are Latino men for depressive symptoms and a variety of health threats (Vega, Kolody, Valle, and Weir 1991; Canino et al. 1987). Women are also exposed to the double jeopardy of gender and ethnicity in jobs and careers.

Gender roles in many Latino communities are carefully defined, even rigidly so by middle-class Anglo standards and by those of some Latina feminists (Comas-Diaz 1987). The code of male honor, well known as *machismo,* defines a man as the provider, protector, and head of his household. He represents the family within the community and, to insure its honor, he enforces communal standards of respectability. While the association of machismo with drinking, fighting, and sexuality is sometimes made, these are not its essential features, although they figure prominently in folklore and stereotypes. It is more appropriate to say that a man with machismo is a man with honor, dignity, and pride, all expressed in the orderly, hierarchical relationships of the household (De La Cancela 1986). The female equivalent, especially in Puerto-Rican culture, is *marianismo,* so named after the Blesed Virgin Mary, of Catholic veneration. Women are often seen as spiritually more sensitive than men, even superior to them on this dimension, and part of that superiority involves a martyr complex, their willingness to take on suffering and self-sacrifice for the good of husband and children. That willingness is the mark of a good mother, a highly prestigious role that is virtually sacred. Women may enjoy certain kinds of power because of that position, but it is a power that is usually exercised quietly and that does not draw attention to itself. Outwardly at least, women are expected to be dependent and docile with men, yet a reliable, capable manager in the home. Comas-Diaz notes that, "on the surface, these traditional sexual codes seem to condone the oppression of one group (female) by another (male); . . . relationships are intricate and complex, and power relationships between the sexes are not straightforward" (1987:463).

For women immigrants, diverse and sometimes contradictory gender-role expectations can combine with early marriage and child rearing to create severe physical and psychological stresses. To cope with these, the newly emerging field of feminist therapy for Latinas emphasizes integrating cultural content into treatment. Comas-Diaz is explicit about including a sociocultural perspective in her work (1987:468). Such an approach can include techniques as diverse as all-female support groups; assertiveness training built around themes and examples taken from Latina daily life; cognitive reframing of female gender and mothering roles; opportunities to discuss the relationship of traumatic experiences to somatization; and couple counseling on shared problems of migration, acculturation, language, and new expectations in a host country.

Work in this and related areas is just beginning, and a useful bibliography on gender values and issues concerning Latino families in North America can be found in Amaro, Russo, and Pares-Avila (1987) as well as in recent issues of the

Hispanic Journal of Behavioral Sciences. Of particular value is the overview article of Fabrega (1990) on the cultural basis of Hispanic mental health research.

OTHER ISSUES OF IMPORTANCE

At the beginning of this chapter, I indicated that one of the demographic features of the Hispanic population in the United States is its youthfulness, relative to other ethnic groups and to whites. That fact has profound implications for both policy and direct social services, matters I want to briefly address here.

In a fascinating, disturbing, and heavily documented study, Hayes-Bautista, Schink, and Chapa (1988) describe what they call a worst-case scenario, based on "grounded speculation," of the short- and long-term implications of an aging Anglo population, mostly baby boomers, and an emerging Latino population that is less well educated and, to varying degrees, alienated by Anglo norms and political dominance. In their scenario, in a hypothetical California between now and the year 2020, the baby boomers reach their old age, consuming huge amounts of state and federal resources, especially for health care. To cover the expenses of treating their chronic illnesses and housing them by the millions in retirement facilities, funds are withdrawn from programs for children, youth, and families. Elementary and secondary schools barely survive by using fewer teachers to teach more children in classrooms that are less and less white. Police and fire protection are more thinly and unevenly distributed, potholes in roads are not fixed. Crowding, pollution, and violence are barely controlled as the baby boomers flee to ever more distant suburbs to escape urban chaos and enjoy their "golden" years.

Meanwhile, the North American Latino population continues to grow as it has over the last fifty years, and along with other ethnic and immigrant groups it is increasingly isolated in cities that are dangerous and dirty. Less well educated than their parents and their grandparents, this generation works (when it can) in low-paying service industries and agricultural production. Business interests outside the state and in distant parts of the Pacific Rim see this as an opportunity. They establish low-wage assembly plants and hire cheap labor to make products for export, few of which are available or affordable to the people who produce them. As the new twenty-first century moves into its teens, California is gradually divided into two social and geographic zones, rural hinterlands overdeveloped with housing, malls, and health care facilities for the graying boomers, and dangerous urban centers (as well as agribusiness processing and packing sites) effectively converted into third world economies, exporting primary foodstuffs and low-tech products to more affluent parts of the world.

In this bifurcated California, the graying baby boomers vote in large numbers, as elders commonly do, and reject candidates and initiatives that would divert health and welfare services from their needs. Alienated urban dwellers and migratory farm workers, then as now, tend not to vote, so the California political system does not respond to their concerns. The government is a gerontocracy, and the populace is too fragmented for effective political action. Civil disorder is a permanent threat, interpersonal violence is common, the physical environment is degraded, and no amount of human services can keep up with needs of the millions who state economists and legislators euphemistically call "marginal."

Perhaps this Orwellian scenario, described by Hayes-Bautista with the help of impressive statistics and charts, will never come about. Maybe it will evolve on a smaller scale instead. It may be confined to California, or it might engulf the industrialized areas of the Northeast as well. Exaggerated or not, the study warns of a potential problem and a devastating possibility. Young people, especially young people in ethnic and minority communities, will be a demographic majority at about the same time that Anglos will be retiring from the workforce in large numbers. At the same time, a huge number of Latino elders will have their own needs when they retire, and this will place additional burdens on their families (Facio 1993). These statistical trends are not guesses; they are already in place. If we believe there is an intergenerational pact now, one that assures that each cohort of elders will be cared for by the taxes of their working juniors, it may not survive past the early twenty-first century. Its fragility will be even greater if the generation gap is a racial and ethnic one as well.

Any effort to improve the education, functional capabilities, and career possibilities of minority children may help forestall the social and economic disaster of which Hayes-Bautista warns. Yet surprisingly little is known about intervention with Latino youth despite all that has been reported about gangs, drugs, and violence by the national media. A cultural approach may be a useful starting point. For example, the value of "familialism" and its greater intensity among Latinos in comparison to Anglos has been well documented in the research literature (Rogler and Cooney 1984). That orientation, argue Rodriguez and Zayas (1990), has important pro-social implications: "Such solidarity implies that Hispanic families may create patterns of conventional behavior even when other factors may dispose adolescents toward deviance" (Rodriguez and Zayas 1990:156).

Juarez (1985) describes some of the clinical issues that are generated by Hispanic values and cultural features and suggests ways of working with them. I have already mentioned the importance of somatization as a means of expressing hostile or dangerous emotions. Juarez notes that this is especially true for women and children: "For example, Hispanic children suffering separation anxiety would present a variety of symptoms expressed through somatization (vomiting, stomachaches, headaches, etc.) and would more likely be taken to a physician" than to a mental health provider (1985:446). This is consistent with a Latino and Iberian view that "good" families do not have "disturbed" children and that if they do it may be related to "bad blood" and other inherited moral conditions.

The linkage of physical and mental states to moral imperatives is not unique to the Latin tradition but it is strongly held there. The importance of "blood" derives in part from medieval humoral theories that depict the body and its moral state as admixtures of four basic elements. These old beliefs are the cultural matrix for some kinds of contemporary behavior and expectation. Thus a child's problems may be attributed to "blood" passed on from parents and grandparents or from others in the family line. Juarez suggests the example of a child separated from its mother because the latter has serious mental health or somatization problems of her own. In such a case, if the child displays depression or mood shifts, they are not likely to be attributed to adjustment problems in a new environment. Rather, "grandparents would feel terrified and helpless that the child is going to 'turn the mother's way.' Thus parents get preoccupied with their child's future behavior which seems to have a destiny of its own beyond the realm of the family's control" (Juarez 1985:447). Destiny and control are linked to beliefs about fatalism, which should be read not as helplessness or acceptance of whatever comes along but rather as vigilance and care in managing what one has in a universe that is not always friendly. Fatalism is not necessarily an arcane viewpoint; it may make sense where the realities of power and especially powerlessness are fully appreciated.

Finally, Juarez mentions adult perceptions of children within the household. One component of Latino familialism is authority, especially that of the father. Anglo stereotypes of "machismo" usually suggest swagger and domination, but Hispanic male authority in the family can more correctly be thought of as economic and moral leadership, protection for women and children, personal and family honor and honorableness, and quiet persistence in overcoming obstacles. Complementary values expressed by women are those of obedience to the husband and nurturance and respect with children. Children, in turn, are expected to defer to siblings who are older. It is clear that within this framework of traditional family values it is hierarchy, not egalitarianism, that is prominent. Hierarchy is associated with unity and especially strength. That has serious implications for family intervention:

> *Children are perceived by many Hispanic parents as extensions of themselves and as objects or property without rights. Typically, they are not allowed to challenge or question their elders, nor do they have the right to voice their opinions. Basically, their behavior revolves around adult feelings (Juarez 1985:447).*

Parents are at liberty to discipline children as they feel is appropriate, since it is they, not the child, who take independent moral action. Similarly, parents are in the best position to plan and make decisions for the child, including long-term ones, and loyalty and self-sacrifice are expected in return. One interesting implication of this value of hierarchy, especially when linked to fatalism, is that children who are disabled in some way may be indulged, for they are seen as less capable, perhaps much less so, than their "normal" siblings. Indulgence does not encourage them to change. The emphasis on "personal growth" and taking control and "ownership" of one's experiences, common among middle-class Anglos, does not appear here. The protection that goes with indulgence is more important. In matters of family intervention, therefore, the culturally sensitive social worker would want to be alert to the presence of these kinds of values and behavior, and especially of their relative strength in differing family units.

Family values carry an aura of sacredness in many Spanish-speaking communities. The Catholic church is an important adjunct to that value, and it remains a force even for those who are not regular church attenders. Yet debilitating family crises do occur, especially in the poorest of neighborhoods. For them, there are options when the protective family life that is so highly prized is not available. Despite unfavorable media treatment, most Latino youth are not involved in gangs precisely because children in strong, hierarchical families do not perceive them as attractive. Yet gang activities are clearly present in most large cities, sometimes lethally so.

Hispanic youth gangs have been studied in detail by Vigil (1983, 1988a, 1988b), who sees in them an alternative to the disrupted family life some barrio teenagers experience. Not surprisingly, generalized Latino values are expressed in gang culture but in exaggerated or destructive ways. (In fact, they are expressed in a very simplified form, a circumstance that has implications for acculturation, to be discussed below.) Likely recruits for gang life are those with few significant family connections and for whom street skills are essential to personal survival. "Gang members are usually reared in poorer homes, mother-centered family situations with more siblings, and marginal, unstable economic conditions" (1988b:425–426). For them, life on the street begins with an extended period of socialization by *veteranos* (veterans) and *carnales* (real and fictive brothers), some of whom are *locos* or "crazies," individuals renowned for outrageous acts of heedless, high-risk behavior. Life on the street is dangerous but also exciting, and it produces intense feelings of camaraderie, much like those that develops among soldiers in war zones. As a full-time gang member, the individual is part of a *klika* (clique), a subunit of the gang, and his primary activity is "protection" of neighborhood territory. Vigil quotes one gang member as saying:

> *If any intruder enters, we get panicked because we feel our community is being threatened. The only way is with violence. We can't talk because of our pride and their pride. No Chicano's going to lay his pride on the line so another can suck it up and make his pride bigger (1988b:428).*

What is interesting about this individual's remark is that it parallels a community value reported by anthropologists who have studied poor, rural villages in Mexico. Known in the research literature as the "image of limited good" (Foster 1965), it asserts that where people have no hope of improvement in their lives, they perceive the availability of the good things they would like as absolutely limited. There is no thought to expanding the size of the pie so that everyone can have a larger slice. Therefore, any improvement in what one has (in goods, luck, or prestige) must come at the expense of someone else. Their slice will be proportionally reduced; others must lose for me to win. So, too, anyone who improves his lot must have done so at my expense. As Vigil's gang member very correctly notes, no one is going to put his pride up for talk and risk its being sucked up and lost. Violence will settle the matter immediately.

For boys and young men active in gangs, masculine identity is closely linked to success in street life and that creates a *cholo* cultural style. In parts of South America the term "cholo" refers to those who are neither metropolitan nor Indian but somewhere in between, that is, marginal to several major cultural communities. Vigil notes that barrio gangs were originally created by second-generation Mexican Americans, beginning in the 1920s in southern California. Later gangs sported the dramatic *pachuco* dress style that came to national attention in the 1940s. Like earlier gangs, modern *cholo* culture adapts some traditional Latin values—*palomilla* (age cohorts) and *camarada* (comradeship)—to the harsh economic conditions of barrio life.

> *The subculture in part is a reforged combination of traditional Mexican palomilla customs of adolescent age cohorts and the complex of cultural values known as machismo. There are many positive machismo traits (strong work ethic, responsibility for family and friends, and patient courage against seemingly insurmountable obstacles) but street life has especially nurtured an emphasis on masculine aggressiveness, dominance, and boastful assertion of individual and group pride (Vigil 1983:59).*

Daily life in gangs is not all fights, however. Since gang members are not usually in school or working at jobs, casual and recreational activities take up much of their time. Pick-up ball games, drinking, gossiping, riding in cars, and watching over one's territory are important areas for learning gang etiquette, developing street skills, and establishing one's own role and style in the *klika*. Nicknames are also important, often denoting some trait of the individual and sanctioning his peculiarities and preferences. *Placas* or graffiti mark gang territory, sending warnings to others. Dress codes distinguish gangs and are matters of personal pride and presentation. The easy availability of guns and the profitability of drugs add to the risks but also the excitement of street living. Gang life creates a semblance of meaningfulness, however thin and temporary. It reproduces hierarchy, offers camaraderie, and creates opportunities to show one's individuality and prowess. In barrios, gangs are *familia*.

Chavez and Roney (1990) suggest that the risks faced by Latino youth, including the risks associated with gang culture, are due to a process of "deculturation." Deculturated individuals and groups are those that are out of contact with both the culture of their heritage and that of the larger, encasing society. *Cholo* describes them accurately: they are people who are set apart, not just in a spatial sense but also in a social and psychological one. They are literally rootless except for the small patch of territory they claim is theirs to defend. With "decultured" individuals, where would the culturally alert social service provider begin?

Individualistic approaches probably would not work, according to Rodriguez and Zayas (1990). They favor instead a program that builds on historical community values and reunites individuals with a tradition. The object of treatment has to be the family, and work with it probably should be undertaken by bilingual therapists. In counseling and planning sessions, the values of family hierarchy, deference of children to adults and younger children to older ones, gender obligations, and the priority of the family over the wishes of individuals ought to be preeminent. Differences in apparent acculturation between children and adults, and between children of different ages, may be important sources of conflict and should be explored comprehensively. Rebuilding intergenerational ties and especially obligations is a high priority, and specific tasks for doing that must be devised and monitored.

Further, community-based interventions should be launched. Schools are one of the most favorable sites for that since social workers can monitor performance both in the home and on school grounds. Recruiting paraprofessionals, "role models" in the parlance of some, ought to be encouraged since they not only add to the available personnel but are another form of community linkage and mentoring. Seniors can be important because they can be asked to share with more acculturated youth traditions that were once important and whose loss is painful. Rogler's *cuento* or folktale therapy, mentioned earlier, has been used with young children, but there is no reason it could not be adapted to work involving elders as living embodiments of valued Hispanic traditions.

Obviously, an effort such as this requires knowledge of a specific neighborhood, a city, and a distant home country. Those are topics as important to effective cross-cultural work as the traditional therapies and interviewing skills more commonly taught to social service professionals. As skills the latter can be useful, but their effectiveness is limited if they are not adapted to the cultural realities of a community's everyday experience.

ACCULTURATION—IS IT FOR EVERYBODY?

In a statistical study of life satisfaction among Cuban Americans in New Jersey, Gómez (1990) found positive correlations of high self-esteem, job satisfaction, and marital adjustment with biculturalism. The latter was measured using a 45-item questionnaire that distinguished individuals who were effectively monocultural (either fully acculturated or not acculturated to any significant degree) from those who were bicultural and saw themselves participating selectively in two valued traditions. He notes that one implication of his study is that "a culturally sensitive mental health service that supports the establishment and development of biculturalism is better equipped to help those with mental problems than a service that neglects the bicultural dimension" (Gómez 1990:387).

Gómez's findings are part of an emerging theme in Latino studies—melting pot enthusiasm was always misplaced and bicultural adjustment is not only possible but desirable. Further, multiculturalism should be the goal of health and social service programs and policies generally.

Several years ago Buriel (1984) emphasized the same theme, arguing in favor of "the seemingly paradoxical hypothesis that integration with traditional Mexican-American culture fosters healthy sociocultural adjustment to mainstream American society" (95). His thesis was that where maladjustment, deviance, or violence occur, it is because individuals have drifted away from sustaining cultural traditions without having replaced them with mainstream American ones. Thus they are vulnerable to the situational effects of poverty, urban decay, and unrelieved personal stress.

Buriel reviewed a large number of studies on Mexican Americans completed by sociologists, psychologists, and educators over a number of years. He gave special attention to differences between generations as it was measured in the various studies. The first generation normally included individuals and families who migrated from Mexico, people who could be expected to retain a strong Mexican cultural orientation. Second-generation individuals were those born in this country but reared in traditional households by their Mexican-born parents. The third generation included all those born in this country and raised by parents also born in North America. According to standard acculturation expectations, later, more acculturated generations should have a mainstream American orientation, having sloughed off their traditional Mexicanness. By contrast, earlier, more traditional generations should show less acculturation and more evidence of difficulty in adapting to American life. It is the "traditionals," in the first and second generations, who would be expected to show the highest incidence of personal and family pathology. Buriel looked carefully at data on use of Spanish, education levels, income, job status, family size, religiosity, and other variables. The outcomes predicted in the acculturation hypothesis were not what the data showed.

Instead, there was a consistent pattern of high levels of achievement and adjustment in the first and especially second generations. The second generation did very well in terms of educational and economic success and general participation in American life. But they also preferred traditional Mexican institutions and practices in their family affairs, their religious participation, and the continued use of Spanish. It was the third generation that displayed the highest levels of personal and family maladjustment. This cohort also showed the least participation in either Mexican or mainstream American cultural values and institutions.

Several examples illustrate what Buriel (1984) found. In numerous studies of educational achievement, second generation Mexican Americans were much more likely to complete high school and college than were their third-generation counterparts. In fact, in some studies first-generation cohorts did better, significantly so, than did third-generation ones. In the workplace, second-generation Mexican Americans consistently had better paying, more professionally oriented jobs than did third-generation samples in the studies reviewed. Although Mexican Catholicism is often compared unfavorably with American Protestantism in terms of its support of a strong work ethic, most of the studies that included religion as a variable showed a high level of church participation in the occupationally successful second generation. Even with gender roles, one of the most stereotyped features of Latino cultures, many studies concluded that women participated in the workforce at almost the same rate as their Anglo sisters.

Further, these women were generally practicing Catholics, had large families, were bilingual who spoke mostly Spanish at home, were very achievement oriented, and were little assimilated to mainstream Anglo values.

Buriel concludes, as have researchers and helping professionals since, that those Hispanic Americans who are most successful are those who are effectively bicultural. And those who have the most difficulties are the least integrated into either traditional Mexican or American cultures.

> [I]ntegration with traditional Mexican-American culture represents a highly adaptive strategy for satisfactorily adjusting to Anglo-American society. . . . Securely embedded in the reinforcing structure of the ancestral culture, these individuals are free to explore new cultural avenues without any threat to their sense of identity, and to adopt the skills, roles, and standards of behavior that are necessary to translate their native ability into conventional forms of success within Anglo-American society. In essence, such individuals are bicultural, which means that they are capable of interacting successfully in both the Mexican-American and the Anglo-American cultural worlds (Buriel 1984:126).

Señor Burciaga, living and working among his Jewish, Catholic, and Baptist neighbors in El Paso, probably would have agreed.

9

ASIANS AND PACIFIC ISLANDERS

Sam Sue is a Chinese American who grew up in a small town in rural Mississippi. Today he is a lawyer in New York City. His story (in Lee 1991) is uniquely his own, but it contains themes that would be recognized by many Asian Americans and recent Asian immigrants and refugees. His father came to the United States in the 1930s at age sixteen and worked in a San Francisco restaurant to earn enough money to bring his wife to America. Eventually, he settled in a rural Mississippi town where he would raise his family and run a small general store for the next thirty years.

Why Mississippi? Much of the rural South at that time was impoverished, land and housing were much cheaper than in California, the town of Clarksdale already had a small number of Chinese families, and a Chinese hardware and grocery man could find an economic niche that no one else filled: selling goods to poor whites and even poorer blacks on credit.

Sue's family lived in the back of the store that was kept open every day of the week, including Christmas, and everyone worked as many hours as was required. Sam's father learned just enough English to get along with his customers; it came out as rural black English with a Chinese accent. Most whites could never understand him. When the family moved out of the store and into a house, it was in the poorer, black part of town because an anonymous caller warned that if they bought in the white area their home would be torched. The elder Sue closed his store in 1978, just two months before his wife died. He still lives in Clarksdale, although he has no affection for the place, because he has no idea where else he might go.

Sam no longer lives in the South, but he is bitter about much that happened to him there. In the rigid, paranoid world of rural Mississippi in the 1950s and 1960s, where separation of blacks and whites was enforced with stunning violence, no Asian found an easy place to alight. Sue recalls that when he went to movies, "I didn't know where I was supposed to sit, so I sat in the white section, and nobody said anything" (Lee 1991:3). He went to a white high school but never dated white girls—they always had a reason not to go to a dance with him. Dating Asian girls was not much of an option since there were few of them and taking one out was, from Sue's point of view, like dating a cousin. His sense of alienation was compounded by his parents' commitment to their store. As he puts it, "One common thread that runs through many Asian lives is that parents spend so much time working for the future needs of their children, that they don't devote enough time to emotional needs. Either the parents are working and can't be there, or if they are at home, they are so tired they can't devote themselves to the children" (Lee 1991:7).

When Sam left the South he went to college in Ohio. But his dilemmas did not end there. He recalls his first visit to a Chinese restaurant, in Cleveland, and his embarrassment at not being able to use chopsticks or read the Chinese portion of the menu. As a monolingual American who cultivated a northern accent by watching television, he resented being treated by both whites and Asians as though he ought to be thoroughly Asian, too. "I don't feel Chinese, and I am not. I identify myself as Asian American. I feel Chinese to some extent, but not necessarily to the extent of knowing much about Chinese culture and tradition" (Lee 1991:8). Just as his father would never return to China, Sam Sue will not return to Mississippi, and just as his father puts up with Clarksdale because he doesn't know where else he might go, Sam tolerates New York City because he feels he doesn't have many other choices.

Sam Sue's life is like that of many Asian Americans—an immigrant family history, the exhausting struggle of his parents' generation to do well financially, their exploitation of a marginal economic niche, a general sense of alienation from their country of origin and America as well, resentment of racism, and the need to survive in a sometimes hostile, sometimes open, but always ambiguous social environment. Those are some of the themes that social and health service workers will see in the lives of many of their clients and patients.

A HISTORICAL OVERVIEW

Asian emigration to the United States is somewhat recent, at least in comparison with other ethnic groups. There are several good histories on the topic but one of the best is that of Chan (1991), whose approach I follow here. She describes how emigration began in the mid and late nineteenth century; five major communities entered the western United States and Canada in three distinctive sequences. The Chinese came first, attracted by the possibility of finding gold and lucrative jobs in the settlement of the American West. Japanese, Korean, and Filipino emigrants came later, usually by way of the sugar plantations in Hawaii. South Asians, primarily Sikhs but Muslims and Hindus as well, represent a smaller but significant migration stream, mostly to limited areas of California and British Columbia. More recently, Vietnamese entered the United States following the Vietnam war, some of them as refugees from settlement camps scattered throughout Southeast

Asia, others as immigrants who could not stay in their home country because of their close affiliation with the Americans during that conflict. While many Asians emigrated because of the economic opportunities available in the American and Canadian West, many, like the Vietnamese, left their homes because they had little choice. Local wars, poverty, colonialism, and the worldwide spread of capitalist institutions all combined to move huge numbers of people throughout the world in the latter half of the nineteenth century and the early decades of this one. The Asian migration to the United States was part of that global event.

Who migrates and why is always important to understanding human relocation. Migration is usually selective, and those who leave their homes are rarely representative of anything but themselves. For example, almost all the Chinese who came to the United States originated in three small regions, each with its own dialect, within one province, Guangdong, in southeastern China. Mostly peasants and landless laborers, they had endured fifteen years of the Taiping Rebellion as well as intense interethnic conflict, and their towns and economies were decimated by it. Similarly, the Meiji Restoration in late nineteenth-century Japan abolished the feudal land system as part of an effort to modernize and industrialize. But it also drove almost half a million peasants off their land because of high taxes and almost uncontrollable inflation. While the government was slow to permit emigration, it finally allowed contract laborers to go to Hawaii to work on sugar plantations. Most came from just seven prefectures in southern Japan.

During the late nineteenth and early twentieth centuries, the United States government and especially private citizens actively promoted migration from Asia. Missionaries, for example, had worked in China for many years, although without much success, and they believed that sending Chinese to live in Christian America would speed up conversions. In Japan, just a handful of American and Japanese businessmen running import/export companies promoted shipments of laborers to Hawaii. An American diplomat in Korea arranged with the government there for Koreans to join the Hawaiian labor flow, which they did for several years. When the United States took possession of the Philippines after the Spanish-American war, Filipino laborers also came to Hawaii, almost all of them from the three most northern provinces of their homeland. Because they had American passports and could travel to the mainland as well, a pattern of chain migration emerged, funneling thousands of Filipinos into the Hawaiian islands and then on to California, Oregon, and Washington State. The experience of Indian Punjabis was selective in its way as well, indicative of the worldwide reach of colonial and capitalist institutions. Punjabis, mostly Sikhs from that North Indian state, had been the police force and soldiers of the British empire and were famed for their willingness to travel in service to the Crown. When opportunities for farming and railroad work appeared in western Canada, small numbers of Punjabi families moved into that region from all over the British empire. But racial hostility toward them quickly grew violent and they moved south to claim and work some of the poorest lands in California and other western states. Through hard labor and quiet persistence, they made their farms productive and highly profitable.

The Vietnamese experience is, of course, the most recent and perhaps the most traumatic. Beginning in April 1975, following the chaotic American exodus from Saigon, over 130,000 Vietnamese were hastily escorted to the United States. The refugees in this initial wave were different from later refugees in that they had had close ties to the American military presence in their country, they were familiar with American customs, they were well educated, they knew English and were lifelong Catholics, and they even had other family members resident in the United States. Later refugees were very different. Many were from that country's minority groups—Cham, Hmong, Khmer, Chinese—and were distrusted and disliked by the Vietnamese who preceded them. Often peasants and laborers, they and their families had fled to huge holding camps late in the war, first in Thailand and Malaysia, and later Indonesia, Hong Kong, and the Philippines. Many waited and wasted for years, until permits for entry into the United States arrived. They were traumatized, poorly educated, and had few job skills when they finally stepped out on American soil. Unlike the first wave, they were not welcome and their resettlement was more difficult. Ultimately, nearly a million Vietnamese came to this country, almost half of them settling on the West Coast and many others in the upper Midwest, Texas, and New York.

ADAPTATIONS TO AMERICAN LIFE

The first large-scale Asian immigration to the United States was that of the Chinese in California, a response to the Gold Rush of the 1850s and the arrival of the railroads. The earliest who came worked as miners, but many others set up businesses to cater to the needs of their countrymen. Chinese importers, merchants, and cooks supplied Chinese laborers with familiar foods, clothing, and medicines. But the opportunities that attracted both Asians and Europeans did not last. Creeks and rivers were soon panned out and the rail tracks laid. Those who had saved money leased small plots of land and began their own fruit and vegetable farms, labor-intensive forms of agriculture that can be profitable with minimal investment. In urban areas such as San Francisco, many Chinese worked in sweatshops where boots, blankets, cigars, and household items were manufactured. The conditions in these factories were as oppressive and brutal as the better-known sweatshops of the East Coast but they offered the new immigrants jobs where none other were available.

The familiar stereotypes of Chinese laundries and restaurants come from this period of early settling in. Chan (1991:33) suggests that these were niche occupations for the Chinese since on the frontier there was a shortage of laundry workers of any kind (at one time laundry was sent from California to Honolulu and back!). In addition, only Chinese cooks could meet the culinary preferences of the immigrant miners and rail and sweatshop workers. Laundry and restaurant work enabled Chinese entrepreneurs to create their own opportunities, not only in California but in the Midwest and the East as well. Chan describes how these businesses were common in blue collar neighborhoods filled with ethnic whites, many of whom lived in boardinghouses and cheap apartments. Restaurants and laundries were low-profile occupations, neither dependent on large numbers of other Asians nor in competition with immigrants from Europe. Very much family businesses, their labor costs were not high and overhead was low. Typically, a few Chinese families could settle into a largely white community and quietly develop their business without arousing nativist fears. Some became prosperous serving the needs of nineteenth-century corporate America's factory workers and clerks. By keeping to themselves and not advertising their success, only their bankers knew how well they were doing.

Unlike the Chinese, many of the Japanese, Koreans, and Filipinos who came at the beginning of this century did so by way of Hawaii and the white-owned sugar plantations there. The history of sugar in the Western hemisphere is a sordid one; the Hawaiian planters needed cheap contract labor as much as their predecessors in the American South needed slaves. Living conditions for the laborers in Hawaii were only marginally better than those in the Old South and many Japanese and Koreans returned home as soon as they could afford passage. Others, however, went on to California, leaving plantation agriculture for migrant harvesting of fruit and vegetable crops instead. Most of the Japanese in California, Oregon, and Washington State through the 1930s were migratory farm laborers who, with their families, did the kinds of work that postwar Americans associate with Mexican labor. But because land was more available in the 1920s and 1930s, in a way it never would be for the Mexicans who came later, many Asians were able to purchase small acreages and establish themselves as truck farmers. Highly dependent on intensive family labor, they supplied fresh produce to nearby urban markets. Some families were very successful and became wealthy, although they risked becoming targets of hate groups because of it. Like the Chinese, many Japanese and Filipinos worked in restaurants and hotels or as domestic servants and gardeners in white households. Some Filipinos in migrant agriculture came in contact with American Indians who were similarly employed and one of the little known stories of American ethnicity is the frequency of Filipino-Indian marriages, especially in parts of the Northwest.

The presence of large numbers of Asians on the West Coast, while filling a labor demand created by the corporatizing of agriculture and the growth of western cities, also generated nativist and racist demands for their containment and even exclusion. Laws were passed to limit Asian wage rates, control buying or leasing of land, impose discriminatory taxes on Asian-owned businesses, and limit naturalization. The Immigration Act of 1924 effectively ended Japanese immigration by, among other things, denying passports to "picture brides," a practice whites disliked intensely. Lacking voting power and due process protections, Asians had almost no ability to influence legislative or judicial actions directed against them. Anti-Chinese race riots were common in the West in the 1880s, both in small towns and virtually all the big coastal cities. Troops were often called up to control mobs because local police neither could nor would. In addition, many states passed laws prohibiting interracial marriage, laws which persisted in some jurisdictions until as late as 1967. While interracial marriage laws had little practical effect, they nevertheless expressed the anti-Asian xeno-phobia common at the time.

In all the resident Asian communities so affected, mutual aid and beneficial societies of many kinds quickly emerged. These were groups organized to represent various Asian interests, to act as power brokers with the institutions of the larger society and even the government of the home country, and to settle disputes among their own membership. Each Asian community followed its own pattern but the historical importance of these organizations is the precedent they set for communal associations still active and important up to the present. Among the Chinese, organizations based on family names or on common dialects were headed by local entrepreneurs and merchants, people who had demonstrated their ability to work with hostile governments and racist business groups. These benefit societies established Chinese language schools, hired white lawyers to fight discriminatory legislation, created rotating credit associations, and arranged for funerals, an especially important function in a community that honors the elderly. Some associations were modeled after trade guilds or unions; others were fraternal bodies complete with secret rites and codes of brotherhood. A few of the latter, known as "tongs," carved up territories and were infamous for the "tong wars" that protected turf and illegal activities in West Coast Chinatowns.

Japanese benefit associations were based on prefects (counties) of origin, and they had special powers and financial support because, through agreement with the Foreign Ministry of Japan, they helped regulate the issuance of visitor certificates for Japanese returning to their home country for personal or commercial visits. Because agriculture was so important in the Japanese immigrant community, some benefit societies were organized as agricultural cooperatives and trade groups. Chan describes how these operations enabled some "to gain vertical control over their own sector of California's agribusiness: Japanese growers out in the countryside or suburbs sold their produce to Japanese commission merchants, who in turn sold it to wholesalers, who then supplied the numerous Japanese retail fruit and produce stores in the city" (1991:70). Like the Chinese, Japanese associations had their criminal counterparts whose activities, in no way typical of the Japanese community, were fodder for sensational journalism aimed at whipping up white fears of the "yellow peril" and other imagined threats to white control in the recently settled West. It is difficult now for whites to imagine the virulence of anti-Japanese racism in the American West for the half century prior to 1941, but it was part of the freebooting individualism and "America first" xenophobia of the time. The oldest Japanese Americans, of course, remember it well, for it had devastating consequences for them after the attack on Pearl Harbor in December, 1941.

In addition to benefit societies and guilds, Christian churches were focal points of Asian community organization. Protestants had long been active as evangelists in China, although the Jesuits got there first in the late 1500s, and they continued their efforts among Asians in the United States. Presbyterians, Methodists, and Baptists aggressively recruited among the Chinese and Japanese, and consequently those denominations are well represented in contemporary Chinatowns and Asian residential areas. For Koreans and Filipinos, Christian churches are a primary form of communal association. Most Christian Filipinos are Catholic due to the colonial presence of Spain in their homeland over several hundred years, and most of their fraternal groups have a religious tone in their statements of purpose and the kinds of activities they encourage. But many Asians are not Christian at all and are firmly committed to other religious traditions. Buddhist temples (sometimes renamed "churches") and their monks are especially important in the Vietnamese community. Among Sikhs, of course, religion defines their ethnicity, as it does for the Hindus and Muslims who also came from South Asia. Sometimes non-Christian immigrants have adapted their religions in superficial ways to meet American expectations. Rutledge (1992:52) describes a group of Vietnamese children in a Port Arthur, Texas, temple singing "Buddha loves me, this I know, for the sutras tell me so"! Despite superficialities such as this, most immigrants are firmly committed to the religious preferences they brought with them and have no intention or desire to give them up. Nor should they be expected to, for their own institutions are usually the best first defense against health and social problems that can afflict immigrant communities.

One of the significant features of the older Asian communities, especially in the years leading up to World War II, was their peculiar demographic shape, a historical circumstance that is very important in the Asian-American experience. Sugar plantations, railroads, and corporate agricultural enterprises were not interested in families. They only wanted younger men willing to work hard, accept minimal pay, and not complain about shoddy and dangerous living conditions. Women were discouraged and at times even prohibited by immigration laws. Chan points out that at the turn of the century the sex ratio among the Chinese in America was 27 men to 1 woman (1991:106). It was only slightly better among the Japanese who, at least at that time, had fewer legal restrictions placed on them.

To resolve this problem, many young Japanese men worked through their parents to arrange for a "picture bride," a woman formally married in Japan to an absentia groom resident in America. The bride then joined her unseen (and often unknown) husband in this country. From the Japanese point of view, this was a simple and logical extension of arranged marriage as they knew it in their own culture. The number of these emigrating brides was controlled and limited largely by the Japanese government, but this pattern of trans-Pacific marriage allowed for the growth of more normal family life in the Japanese community in America until the practice was ended in 1920. White Americans, asserting the 1920s equivalent of the 1990s "traditional family values" argument, opposed picture bride weddings on "moral" grounds and used their objections to fuel anti-Japanese sentiment and racial hysteria.

Beginning in the 1920s and continuing into the 1930s, a first generation of Japanese Americans was born, creating what Chan calls the "second generation dilemma." Because most Asian societies are patriarchal and kinship oriented, generational placement is very important in defining privileges and responsibilities. In some ways, the Japanese are more observant of this than other groups, and their generations in this country are explicitly named. The first immigrants were

Issei; their children, generally born between the war years, are *Nisei*. The first postwar generation are the *Sansei*. The Issei were migrants; their Nisei children were citizens, and that was a significant source of tension. The Nisei were Americanized in a way their parents were not, even though they were often sent to Japanese language schools, and deliberate efforts were made to instruct them in the culture of their parents' homeland. Nisei expected to make more of their own decisions about the use of free time, money they earned, choice of friends, and especially choice of marriage partner. The latter was often a flash point within families since the more traditional Issei expected to make marriage arrangements for their children as had been done for them. Inculcated in the American ideals of personal freedom and choice, Nisei children and young adults were further frustrated by racism and restrictions on job opportunities. Many had a good education and expected to do professional work. Instead, they went into occupations not significantly different from that of their parents: farming, small stores, restaurants, and service occupations. Whatever ambivalence they felt about this, and it was considerable, was overtaken by events following the bombing of Pearl Harbor.

The Camps

Executive Order 9066, signed by President Roosevelt in February 1942, was partly the result of FBI and military scrutiny of the Japanese community that had begun as early as 1918. Under the Order, much of the West Coast, including Alaska, was declared a security zone and arrangements were made to ship all resident Japanese to inland "internment" camps. Arrests of community leaders, teachers, priests, important merchants, benevolent association officers, and others began almost immediately. Within months, thousands of families, many of them including native-born American citizens, were rounded up, searched, tagged, put on trains, and taken to remote desert camps in Nevada, Utah, and as far away as Arkansas. Stores, farms, homes, and personal property were stolen, lost, or sold at such deflated values that even their sale was virtually theft. Liquid assets were frozen, in many cases for the duration of the war, and prosperous households were made destitute almost overnight. Nativist groups demanded the abrogation of American citizenship and deportation of all Japanese back to Japan once the war was over. (Significantly, American citizens of Japanese ancestry who happened to be in Japan when the war began were also treated as potential subversives and were detained and isolated by the Japanese government until hostilities ended.) Japanese living in the Midwest and on the East Coast were not subject to incarceration as were their West Coast compatriots, but they nevertheless suffered the stigma directed against all Japanese at that time.

One effect of the camp experience was to exaggerate the differences already separating Issei and Nisei generations. Nisei insisted on their loyalty to America since it was the only country they knew. Issei insisted on loyalty to family and family traditions, but their argument had little moral force since the senior men had been deprived of property and livelihood. Further, many of these men were separated from their families because of legal charges brought against them, and they spent the war years in separate facilities, often without their wives or children even knowing where they were. Some Nisei chose to demonstrate their loyalty by joining the 442nd Regimental Combat Team, one of the most highly decorated in the Army for its battlefield performance in Italy and France. Others fought lonely personal battles, insisting on their constitutional rights as American citizens, or organizing others and leading protests at the camps. The camp experience remains one of the most vivid among the oldest Japanese still living, and it is a powerful image and memory among their adult children.

The "Model Minority" Stereotype

Following the war, many Japanese returned to their homes, or what was left of them, and began rebuilding. Their hard work and eventual economic success led to a new stereotype, that of the "model minority." The image of a model minority was an appealing one for whites in the 1950s and 1960s, for it suggested that there really were no good reasons for other ethnic groups, blacks and Chicanos is particular, to be protesting in the streets when Asian Americans (called "Orientals" then) had "proved" that through perseverance the system "works." Japanese Americans were notable for having achieved, on average, higher educational levels than whites and, presumably, the higher incomes that go with them. Further, many whites perceived Asians as "deferential" and "polite" and unlikely candidates for noisy street demonstrations. The isolation of Asians in Chinatowns, and in their own businesses and churches, seemed to confirm that they were a minority quietly going about their own business, getting themselves educated, and lifting themselves up by their bootstraps. It was the all-American way.

The fact is that many Asians did surprisingly well, given the economic handicaps and vicious prejudice they faced in 1945. But many did not. Their apparent success, for which whites have been prone to credit "the system" rather than the efforts of the Japanese and Chinese themselves, has to be considered in the context of how it was achieved and how much was actually gained. By some counts, unemployment among Asian Americans seems low. Yet this is due in part to their high representation in low-paying service jobs, one of the growing sectors of the economy in recent years, and their participation in what is essentially cheap family labor in small businesses. For many Asians there is even a preference for underemployment rather than acceptance of government unemployment compensation and the appearance of being "on welfare." Thus, many individuals are not counted in unemployment statistics. While many Asian women are in the workplace, especially Filipinas, their presence there is as much a measure of their need to work as their willingness to do it. Asians tend to have high educational attainments as a group, yet many are underemployed if one compares their job category or income to the amount of education they have acquired.

Finally, regardless of educational and vocational capabilities, Asians tend to cluster in certain occupations. Chan (1991:169) notes that professionals tend to be in engineering, dentistry, and accounting, but not in law, administration, or social services. Asian managers are more likely to be self-employed than working in large corporations. Women tend to be in the garment industry, and few Asians are employed in construction, paper, or chemical operations. The workings of a "model economic system" cannot be seen in the employment patterns of those held to be model citizens.

Recognizing that there are indeed human as well as economic costs associated with membership in a model minority, Asian American activists began working for social change in the 1960s and the 1970s. They did so within the context of a lengthy history of Asian dissent against racism and inequality (Foner and Rosenberg 1993). Espiritu (1992) has documented the politics of this activism in a number of areas, including Asian-oriented social service programs. She notes that as part of the general protest against American cultural institutions and the Vietnam war, Asian activists challenged the traditional power of their own community's historic benevolent associations. They sought to create grassroots, "power to the people" coalitions that would address racism and poverty. Asian students were especially active in these new organizations, launching communal newspapers and setting up local action groups. But when enthusiasm overreached finances, many of these new organizations disappeared. Some of their members gravitated to social work and into governmental positions, hoping to pursue their original interests. Others studied for advanced degrees in public policy, health, and social work. The professionalization of this activist group meant that the influence of the old community elites, as well as that of some of the older organizers, was eclipsed. Those who had the desire to work in large bureaucracies and social service agencies, and who had the skills of grant writing and organizational management, came to prominence.

The institutionalization of Asian activism produced its own set of problems, however. Because of their education, Japanese Americans were often in the best position for leadership roles in Asian-oriented service bureaus and counseling and referral organizations. They were familiar with government funding practices and cultivated the skills of grantsmanship and fund raising. Smaller organizations, and those working with smaller communities such as Samoans or Koreans, found that they needed to ally themselves with government bureaucracies and major funding sources if they wanted to survive. Pan-Asian coalitions emerged, partly because it was less divisive for granting agencies to make awards to multi-ethnic umbrella groups rather than to agencies serving specific, narrowly defined communities. But this also led to friction. Smaller groups resented the power of larger ones; more recently arrived peoples were subject to the procedures and preferences of longer-resident ones. Charges of favoritism arose and some, Filipinos in particular, felt they could do better within their own organizations; they were especially vocal in their criticism of Pan-Asian groups and ideology (Espiritu 1992:103).

Some of these conflicts were ethnic in origin but others clearly related to differences in social class, styles of acculturation, and differences in how people chose to preserve their ethnic identity in a pluralistic society. Consequently, there is no single voice in the Asian community, just as there is no single homeland or historical tradition for Asian Americans. Their diversity is enormous and will become more so as political and especially economic relations among Pacific Rim countries expand.

SOCIAL SERVICE NEEDS AMONG ASIAN AMERICANS

Model minority images notwithstanding, there are serious health and mental health issues among Asian Americans just as there are in other ethnic populations. Uba and Sue (1991) provide a useful overview of needs and services for those they describe as "APIAs," Asian and Pacific-Islander Americans. They note that mental health problems in particular are underestimated and overlooked when they occur in this population. Typically, problems arise from conflicts due to differential acculturation to American practices within families; intergenerational disagreements; trauma due to extreme conditions experienced prior to arrival in this country, especially among Vietnamese and those who spent time in refugee camps; and presumptions of ethnic foreignness by whites, especially toward Asians whose families have lived in America for many generations. These experiences, in addition to exposure to subtle and blatant forms of racism, result in high levels of stress but low levels of service utilization.

Uba and Sue (1991:6–12) list some of the reasons for underutilization. Perhaps most important, many Asian-Americans stigmatize mental health problems to an extreme degree. Concealment is preferable to the shame associated with seeking out a professional service provider or to the humiliation that would result from public knowledge that an individual suffers with a condition that is "psychological." Thus many Asian clients and patients somatize emotional stresses. They report physical rather than mental illnesses, things that can be treated by medicines, acupuncture, or a physician. Sicknesses in a physical sense—generalized aches and pains, stomach upsets, headaches, insomnia—are more acceptable than psychic afflictions. Under certain conditions, mental problems may also be viewed as spiritual ones, requiring the intervention of a spiritual healer of some kind. Differing Asian traditions have different kinds of beliefs and helpers for this kind of service, beliefs usually unfamiliar to Western practitioners who are likely to dismiss them as fantasies and superstitions, or as something to be "overcome" as part of the helping enterprise.

There are also interethnic differences in the value placed on self-control during suffering of any kind. In some communities it is best not to think too much about one's difficulties because to do so may only make them worse. "Indeed, Asians are more likely than whites to believe that one should avoid morbid thinking to maintain mental health. . . . Since treatment often requires self-disclosure of personal and intimate problems (i.e., focusing on morbid thoughts), many APIA clients do not believe that treatment is helpful" (Uba and Sue 1991:10). Formal treatment may even be contraindicated, especially when endurance, quiet patience, and a will to prevail are highly valued as personal characteristics. Pride is at stake, not only for oneself, but for one's family. This is a difficult issue when social services are provided to those unable to pay for them. The stigma of "public welfare" is added to that of mental incapacity. Any suspicions that the sufferer was not able to exert enough self-control to contain and overcome a stressful situation only adds to the burden of admitting to a mental health "problem."

Language differences are also important in underutilization as well. Pain, physical or mental, is never easy to describe even when the patient and professional are users of the same language. Working across linguistic boundaries adds to the frustrations both client and social worker experience. While interpreters can be helpful, reliance on them always slows any interview and, more important, limits the quality as well as the amount of information that can be gathered. The nuances of language carry much of the emotional and informational weight of a counseling exchange, and they do not usually come through in an interpreted interview. When interpreters cannot be found, the common but problematic alternative is dependence on a bilingual youngster, often a member of the client's family. But that stopgap effort usually adds to everyone's frustration, since children may not fully understand what is expected of them, or may want to shield an adult from full disclosure for reasons of family loyalty. In addition, many clients would be understandably reluctant to burden or embarrass children or teenagers with the intimate details of their own problems.

Gender differences are another issue that may influence utilization and the receptiveness of clients to professional suggestions. Song-Kim (1992) suggests that wife battering may be one of the commonest form of family dysfunction among Korean immigrants but that women are unlikely to complain, either to other women or to social service providers. Given the strongly patriarchal organization of Korean households and the belief that beatings are deserved, women are not inclined to "confess" to violence in their own homes. Nor is the problem limited to Koreans. Furuto (1991) describes similar problems among Samoans and Hawaiians and argues strongly for devising culturally appropriate means of helping families adapt to their new circumstances before family violence becomes an issue.

But not all underutilization can be attributed to cultural differences alone. Simple inequities are part of the problem. Murase (1992:102) attributes these to inadequate funding which shunts Asian patients into lower-cost services, wider use of paraprofessionals for Asian patients and clients, and greater use of public rather than private facilities by Asians. These are not problems that can be changed quickly given a national environment of financial constraint, but they are real and need to be corrected.

CULTURAL CONTRASTS AND ETHNIC COMPETENCE

Clearly, the cultural diversity among Asians in the United States is enormous, both between groups and within them. Generalizations are almost impossible to apply, yet there is a need for a starting point for the serious learner. However, I want to state as emphatically as I can that a starting point is only that; anyone who is content to practice social services on the basis of general guidelines has not even begun to move in the direction of ethnic competence. It is also worth repeating, as I have in all the chapters on ethnic communities, that the issue is not one of looking at a list of cultural features and concluding that it represents a summary of what a group of people is "really like." To use tables that are essentially overviews as a kind of laundry list for sizing up clients would be a perversion of their purpose.

What is at issue in the approach taken here is *cultural contrast*—how the social worker sees himself or herself as the "different" one in the helping relationship. The burden of making that mental and emotional readjustment is on the professional, not the client. In engaging cultural differences, the worker is really required to evaluate self-image and self-understanding as part of a caring work style. Cross-cultural empathy, if it is genuine, can proceed only in that way. By thinking in terms of contrasts, rather than differences alone, one can begin to appreciate the role of culture in shaping the dynamics of an interracial or interethnic encounter. That will be true whatever the racial or ethnic affiliations of both worker and client.

Table 9.1 on page 284 lists a series of contrasts in the form of brief statements. I have pulled these statements together from a variety of sources, all made by prominent Asian scholars in several disciplines. I have been particularly dependent on the work of Kitano (1988), Chung (1992), Shon and Ja (1982), and Sue and Sue (1990). They are not responsible in any way for the interpretation I have made of their materials. It is gratifying, nevertheless, that the help seeking behavior model, proposed in the earlier edition of this book, is seen as useful by some of these scholars and practitioners.

As with the tables of cultural features found in other chapters, the reader is cautioned that any generalization offered anywhere in this book may or may not apply to a specific individual or family. "Individualizing the client" means, in part, estimating any individual's commitment and involvement in the norms, values, and practices of his or her cultural tradition. The statements in the tables are only general tendencies, not "facts" in any objective sense. Honing one's skill in ethnic competence means knowing when the statements apply, when they do not, and, always, why that is the case.

The sections that follow give a brief overview of some of the significant health and social service issues for the various groups discussed in this chapter. I emphasize the word "brief" because in communities as varied as these, from so many parts of Asia, an overview is all that can be done. Each of these communities and their human service needs could easily be the subject of an entire book, as most of them are. It is critical, therefore, that students and social workers involved with members of one of these communities actively seek additional information. All the sources I have cited here contain more references and will lead you to additional authors. My intent has been to be suggestive, not exhaustive, and the best use of these sections is as a guide to additional information.

TABLE 9.1   Selected Cultural Contrasts of Asian-American and Anglo-American Communities

Asian American	Anglo American
Strong mutual support, including cooperation, interdependence, and harmony are expected within the family and community.	Individualism, independence, and assertive behavior, which causes individual attributes to stand out and be noticed, are often favored.
A strongly hierarchical, stable pattern of family and community relations is the setting for mutual support, expressed through a strong sense of obligation and duty to others. This duty overrides individual preferences.	Efforts to minimize status and rank differences, to treat individuals equally or on par with one another, expressed through an ideology of growth and development of individual talents.
Relations with those outside the family are an extension of family interests expressed most pointedly in family influence in the choice of friends or a mate.	Relations with those outside the family are a matter of individual preference and limited family control.
Problems are solved within the family and a code of family pride and honor limits the degree to which internal problems should be known outside the family or shared with professional helpers such as counselors.	Problems are solved within the family but a wide range of professional help providers are available and used when needed.
There is great family pressure to succeed, especially through education. Failure is a failure of obligation to one's family.	There is family pressure to succeed, primarily in those areas where one has already shown distinctive talent. Failure is attributed to lack of individual effort and reflects primarily on personal or moral characteristics, secondarily on other members of the family.
Ambiguity in social relations is a source of anxiety.	Lack of structure, informality or "looseness" in social relations is seen as an expression of American egalitarianism. It also creates opportunity for personal and professional growth or advancement.

THE CHINESE

Chinese Americans tend to live on the West and East coasts, mostly in California and New York, but significant numbers reside in Hawaii, Illinois, and Texas as well. Huang (1991:82) notes that a high percentage, almost two-thirds, of all Chinese in the United States are foreign-born. Most of them speak something other than English at home. Their graduation rates from high schools and colleges, for both men and women, are higher than the national average. Yet like other Asians they tend to be underemployed for the amount of education they have, and their incomes lag behind that of similarly educated whites. They tend to cluster in technical and professional fields and in poorly paid service jobs. Poorer Chinese often live in Chinatowns, frequently in substandard housing, while those who can do so live in suburbs.

In the mid-1960s, the United States changed its immigration policies, encouraging whole families to migrate rather than single individuals. Since that time, many Chinese from Hong Kong and other areas have come into the country following the familiar pattern of chain migration (Wong and Hirschman 1983). There are several kinds of families involved in this process, however. "Chinatown Chinese," according to Huang (1988), are working class families who cluster in Chinatowns where language, shopping, and services are familiar. Both husband and wife take low-paying, low-skilled, service sector jobs. Their work schedules may or may not overlap and they may see little of each other or their children except on weekends. Their jobs as cooks, dishwashers, and janitors have no integral relationship to family life, as they might if they were doing the same tasks in a family business. Family values are traditionally hierarchical, which may become a source of conflict where wives earn their own money and children are free to seek their own friendships and entertainments. By contrast, middle class and professional families seek housing in suburbs or gentrified in-town neighborhoods. They see themselves as more American than Chinatown Chinese. Yet they sometimes replicate traditional extended family patterns, with grandparents living in nearby neighborhoods or even in the same apartment building.

In both family types, however, some traditional values remain important. Divorce is rare, and women are expected to accede to the wishes of their husbands, even if that means remaining in an unhappy marriage. Fathers express their authority by maintaining an emotional distance, and mothers expect children to react promptly to commands. Wong suggests that while "Chinese parents may be more indulgent with their young children than parents of the white American culture, discipline is much more strict than that which the typical American child receives" and that punishment, which is immediate, "involves withdrawal from the social life of the family or the deprivation of special privileges or objects rather than physical punishment" (1988:249). Overt expressions of emotion are discouraged; early independence, responsibility, and cooperation are stressed. Older children are expected to help with the younger ones. Sibling rivalry and aggression are not tolerated.

The often-cited central role of the father and the values of hierarchy and respect for age lead one to presume that elders are well taken care of in Chinese families. That is probably the case, especially for families that are financially able to do so, although supporting data for that is rare. Chinese Americans make little use of social services; other family members are the primary sources of support for the aged. Nursing homes in particular do not appeal to most Chinese since placing one's parents in an institution is seen as an admission that one cannot or will not care for them in the expected way.

The circumstances and needs of the Chinese elderly are a useful illustration of a number of issues affecting Asian elders generally. Their adjustment to life in the United States can be particularly traumatic because there is little in American culture that supports their expectations. Their view of the aging process, for example, is considerably different from that of most whites and white elders and even in leisure activities many Chinese American elderly actively maintain their ethnic affiliations (Allison and Geiger 1993). Cheung (1989) lists several beliefs about old age held by these elderly, including their conviction that age is a source of prestige, that their life-knowledge has value and gives them authority, that growing old is pleasant and leads to greater solidarity with one's family, and that they can and should be active as workers and contributors to their family. Clearly, however, the American values of individualism, careerism, and the nuclear family challenge and undermine these traditional expectations. Language differences, problems with literacy, inappropriate work skills, physical immobility, inability to manage public transportation systems, and lack of familiarity with everyday routines such as banking may hinder an elder's ability to act authoritatively or to contribute directly to family welfare. For some of their adult children, especially those with strong career aspirations, a separate residence for an immigrant senior may be preferable to a shared residence as is common in Asia. This may not be an unreasonable choice since suburbs can be as isolating to an elder as an institutional confinement. But it does not relieve the sense of lost power and diluted authority that is typical of the elderly in American society.

Clearly, services directed toward the elderly, as well as to Chinese women and to struggling, low-income families, are important. The special strains experienced by Asian immigrants are well documented in the social work and social science literature (Lee, Patchner, and Balgopal 1991; Dhooper 1991; Le-Doux and Stephens 1992). What is needed is a framework for working with Chinese clients and planning services that will meet their needs in acceptable ways.

Huang (1991:89–93) suggests a number of "principles of practice" for working with Chinese clients and patients. First, most Chinese do not come to the attention of a professional until a problem, be it physical or psychological, is so serious that normal activities cannot be continued. The goal of treatment is symptom relief, and the client expects the social service provider to take charge in naming the malady and suggesting solutions. Both intrusive and indirect questioning may be resisted since the client expects a rapid diagnosis and prompt intervention. (Traditional healers, according to Huang, simply take the patient's pulse and then state what needs to be done.) The ability to quickly assess and name the problem is seen as a sign of the practitioner's competence. Making a reasonable guess about the source of a difficulty and what must be done to correct it is far more acceptable than attempting to access the client's feelings and display empathy by so doing.

Second, competence is displayed when the practitioner reveals a firm but comfortable sense of authority. Since relations in Chinese families tend to be hierarchical, the professional is judged according to how well he or she models hierarchical behavior in the therapeutic relationship. This is a very subtle but critical matter, and it has consequences for the client's willingness to comply with a treatment regimen. Many white social service workers (health services are probably different) prefer an egalitarian style, a friendly openness, and a casualness in the early phases of the relationship. To them "breaking the ice" is a style that shows mutual regard. But to many Chinese it is insulting, even a dereliction of duty, as though the social worker were not taking the problem seriously. A casual manner may make Chinese clients retreat into polite silence, and the therapeutic alliance will never really begin.

Third, many Chinese-American clients see the need to ask for professional advice on personal problems as potentially shameful, and their concern about this should be addressed as soon as is appropriate. They need to be reassured that they are not "crazy" and that the social worker understands that coming in for a counseling session is itself a difficult step. Respect for the client's circumstance can and should be verbalized, but concrete actions are more important. Huang feels that seemingly nonclinical tasks, such as helping a client fill out forms or calling someone in another agency to facilitate an appointment, are much more important as displays of respect than verbal reassurances. The directness of action not only shows the professional's willingness to help but is another sign of authority and competence.

Fourth, personal questions made to the social worker are not out of place, and an honest, straightforward response is a sign that the relationship is a positive one. Some whites view personal inquisitiveness as intrusive, as no one else's business, and not part of the job description. For Chinese clients, however, it is simply another sign that the level of trust is improving.

Fifth, what Huang calls "meta-rules" operate in Chinese communications. These rules govern the appropriate level of disclosure between speakers of different social rank. For example, fathers, physicians, and teachers occupy positions of respect; communicating unpleasant things to them is considered inappropriate, even a faux pas. These meta-rules are exquisitely nuanced in Chinese culture. Outsiders have ignorantly characterized such behavior as "inscrutable" but the culturally sensitive social worker will learn about these matters and recognize them for the finely honed sense of decorum they represent. Such recognition is a skill that takes time and practice; it is probably learnable only through careful mentoring with a sympathetic cultural guide. But it is critical for the professional who sees Chinese clients on a regular basis.

Asian-American mental health professionals generally warn against insight-oriented therapies for Asian clients. Tung (1984, 1991), however, a Chinese American psychotherapist, disagrees. Her observations are especially interesting from a comparative cultural-awareness perspective because she is sensitive to the differences in her work style with white and Asian clients. She finds that Asians are not indifferent to insight and self-revelation therapies, but the focus must be different for them than for whites. Cognitive, didactic discussions of current symptoms and grievances are more important than identification of emotional distortions rooted in the past. It is useful for the therapist to directly teach the client about correct role behavior within the extended family. Asian clients, she feels, are not much concerned with transference issues nor do they need long periods of time to resolve old issues from early family life. Rather, they want to discuss what is culturally proper in Chinese family life and what they can do to return to a state of equilibrium. Typically, fewer treatment sessions are needed with Asian than with white clients because in Tung's practice their task is one of cognitive relearning rather than emotional resolution and redirection. This is consistent with the observation of Shon and Ja (1982) that a good therapeutic alliance with Asian families requires a prompt and firmly directed approach, one in which the therapist proceeds from both a solid ethnographic understanding of Asian family patterns and a genuine empathy for the needs of Asian individuals.

THE JAPANESE

What many Japanese and Japanese Americans think of as their "traditional" family pattern originally came from the *samurai* class of feudal Japan (Tamura and Lau 1992). There the system was one of three-generational families, the eldest son residing with his wife and children in his parents' household. The senior males, a married son and his father, would manage the household and its holdings while younger sons and daughters went elsewhere to start their own families. While relations between fathers and sons were somewhat formal, those between a mother and her children were expected to be emotionally intense. In these stem or multigenerational families, the lowest-ranking adult in the household was the daughter-in-law. She was subservient to all other resident adults and, in daily household chores, answered directly to her mother-in-law. This system, with local variants, was and still is common in much of Asia. It created a distinctive sense of family unity and obligation, one that contrasts markedly with the Western family model. Tamura and Lau define that contrast as one of connectedness versus separateness:

> In British [and American] culture, the importance of the separateness of individuals takes precedence in value over connectedness among the members of a system. . . . [Personal growth] is a process of progressive differentiation of self from an attachment figure. . . . Japanese relate with others on the premise that they are mutually connected. It is like an identity whereby one belongs to a group that can consist of family members, classmates, or company colleagues (1992:332, 334).

This contrast differentiates Japanese and Westerners in a general sense, but there are other important distinguishing features as well. A number of specific, complex, "traditional" values operate within the modern Japanese-American community. They include *amae*, the emphasis on interdependence in preference to individualism; a marked sense of hierarchical order that is important in personal relations; well-defined obligations that attach to one's position in the family and the culture; and *enryo*, respectfulness and modesty. There is also a concern with controlling emotions, doing the best one can in adverse circumstances, and appreciating that there may be limits to what one can do in difficult situations (Fugita et al. 1991:67–70). How this plays out in individual relationships can be complex and subtle.

These values are expressed in an intergenerational structure that emphasizes connectedness and continuity rather than the individualization and separation that is preferred by many whites. In fact, generational marking is so important that each generation is named and its distinctive experiences define the shape of the community. Mass (1981:319) notes that Japanese immigrants were the only ethnic community in America who named their generations and that it is virtually impossible to discuss their history or their personal experiences without knowledge of that. Kitano describes the situation as follows:

> *The Issei generally understood that their own participation in the American mainstream would be limited, but high hopes were placed on their American-born Nisei children. They saw the Nisei as American citizens with the advantage of American education. . . . Issei often thought of themselves as a sacrificial generation; their own lives were to be secondary to the advancement of their children; . . . and it was a familiar sight to see parents in old clothes buying newer clothes for their children and the larger and choicer portions of food going to their sons, with leftovers for the mother (1988:263–264).*

Yanagisako (1985) further argues that not only are there significant differences between Issei and Nisei generations but that to describe them as simply differences in "acculturation" is to miss (and even dismiss) much of their importance. A cultural understanding requires that we know something of the normative rules operating within each generational cohort and that we recognize how those rules have consequences for individuals and for the harmonious functioning of their families.

A major component of the Issei/Nisei intergenerational dynamic is that of family representation (Yanagisako 1985:174). It is generally the case that one individual among the adult Nisei siblings must represent the family and its multiple households, taking leadership on decisions that affect everyone. That is usually the responsibility of the eldest male, who is expected to deal with matters as varied as his Issei parents' health care, maintenance of their home, and general comfort and well-being. He also has important ritual functions connected with the *koden* or mortuary offerings at their funerals.

A second component is the financial responsibility the elder son will assume. Given the strong value of self-sufficiency among Japanese Americans, any form of aid from outside the family (except for social security) is not acceptable. Elders who must accept "welfare" of any kind are pitied and their adult children scorned, especially if the latter are in a position to offer support and do not. The level of support does not have to be high, but it has to be sufficient to keep older parents healthy and comfortable. Younger sons are expected to contribute their financial share as well, leaving it to the eldest to see that funds are properly used. Daughters, by contrast, are not expected to give money toward the financial support of their parents since to do so would mean drawing on the funds their husbands need for support of their own parents.

Third, three-generation households are not considered desirable, even though they may be necessary in some circumstances. It is certainly better to keep an ailing parent in one's own home than to send him or her to an institution. Although in recent years Japanese owned and operated nursing homes have been built, the need for them is far greater than their availability, and many families fear that institutions staffed by non-Japanese may not be truly sensitive to their elder parents' needs. When living with adult children, elder Issei generally prefer to live with daughters rather than sons. Since older Issei women outnumber older men, they are most likely to be the resident elder in a household. Aside from demographics, however, the cultural rationale for this is that mothers and daughters are assumed to have a closer emotional relationship and to be more familiar and comfortable with one another's housekeeping style, thereby reducing the likelihood of friction. These arrangements also add to the solidarity of women within their homes and their ability to exert managerial control even though male elders have titular authority. In addition, daughters, not daughters-in-law or sons, are felt to be better able to provide personal care to an older or disabled parent.

This intergenerational mix of expectations has an additional complicating ingredient. According to Yanagisako, Japanese-American families are marked by very distinctive male and female domains. Especially in the Issei generation, a sharp line is drawn between matters "inside" (*uchi no koto*) and "outside" (*soto no koto*) the family, and these matters are gender marked. Women's actions are defined as "inside," serving the well being of other family members. Even if a women works in an office or a store, her work is "inside" in the sense that it is done in behalf of the family. Men, too, work to support their families but they are also committed to gaining recognition in the extradomestic world, "outside," and that may require giving energy and attention to corporate, professional, or social concerns. Further, given the hierarchical framing of family values and practices, male and female domains are not equal, at least among the Issei, for that which is thought of as "outside" and male encompasses what is "inside" and female. This distinction can have consequences for the harmony that is expected to prevail between men and women:

> *A common theme that runs through the women's accounts of their conjugal relationships is resentment of their husband's interests outside the family. In these complaints, they portray the family and the outside social world as competing for limited resources . . . even respectable interests outside the family were sometimes resented (Yanagisako 1985:103).*

It is worth remembering that many Issei men are and were considerably older than their wives due to the contingencies of earlier immigration laws. Not only their gender but their greater age gave them enormous authority. Yanagisako found that many of the widows she interviewed regarded their husband's death as a personal loss but also as something of a release from their obligations to serve him and from the distractions and expenses of his outside interests.

The Nisei generation has a different sensibility. Nisei downplay but do not deny the importance of *giri* or duty, which motivated their parents and created a powerful sense of obligation. Along with the Sansei, or third generation, they value what they perceive as the more egalitarian nature of "American" marriages. A "Japanese versus American" contrast is common in their descriptions of their own families and how they believe they are different from their parents. Whereas Yanagisako's Issei respondents rarely talked of "love" in reference to their marriages, Nisei and Sansei marriage partners stressed love, intimacy, and communication. Their preference for the conjugal bond over that between parents and children is seen in their strong feeling that older parents should stay in their own homes as long as possible. Yet the clear division of labor based on gender is as characteristic of many Nisei homes as it is of their parents'. Nisei women place high value on working at home or in support of the home if they must work outside it. Like their fathers, men are expected to be good providers through their jobs. But they are not generally expected to share in housework, and at least one Nisei interviewee told Yanagisako that she thought it wasn't "normal" for men to do housework even though she knew that some white women expected that of their husbands. While most Nisei disavowed the rigid gender hierarchy of their parents' generation, they also felt that it was "natural" for men to "lead" the family and act in its behalf (Yanagisako 1985:118).

From this very brief overview of one part of Yanagisako's extensive research, we can identify a number of potential areas in which social service professionals might become involved. First, intergenerational conflicts are possible, not only because of differences in cohort experiences in America, but because conflicts are typical of three-generation families in Japan and other cultures where they occur as well. Fathers and sons may have conflicting expectations of how family resources are to be used, and younger sons may resent the authority of eldest sons in managing what is, after all, common family property. If money is needed to support elderly parents in their own home, wives of junior sons sometimes resent the competition that that creates with the needs of their own households.

Second, female alliances may undercut, or at least modify, the titular authority of men. Older men are increasingly confined to their own homes which are, after all, the "inside" domain. Women can and do make important decisions about money and other resources and those can include decisions about health care. Since mental health conditions are so highly stigmatized in Asian communities, an older man suffering with a disability such as Alzheimer's disease would be especially vulnerable to decisions to keep him away from public awareness or scrutiny, including the awareness of professionals who could help.

Other issues that can be sources of conflict include language, especially when grandchildren cannot communicate well with grandparents; intermarriage between Japanese and white Americans; the necessary mobility of sons who are on career and corporate fast tracks; and divorce, which is particularly shameful and is unfortunately associated with high rates of suicide among women (Ho 1987).

In a valuable review article, Marsella (1993) summarizes the state of knowledge about counseling and psychotherapy with Japanese Americans. Like Yanagisako and Mass, he asserts that ethnic identity among Japanese Americans is not a linear process of movement from traditional-minded immigrants to fully acculturated Americans. The complexity of intergenerational ties and the modification of values derived from Japan make that experience far more complex. Nor can a social service provider be very effective without first knowing how those factors enter into problem identification and resolution.

> *The assumption that a Japanese-American client is acculturated or bicultural simply because of English-language fluency and appearance can result in problems. A thorough assessment must be made of ethnic identity to determine the appropriateness and applicability of different therapeutic styles and approaches (Marsella 1993:201).*

To that end, he suggests that a useful client-therapist relationship must acknowledge and utilize a number of elements that Japanese Americans are likely to bring to the encounter. He lists and discusses the following: a preference to understate or indirectly express a powerful emotion such as grief or anxiety; reference to physical symptoms as metaphors for troubled mental states; conflicts and confusion around ethnic identity and normative expectations; ritualized self-depreciation as a way of emphasizing the primacy of the group over the individual; a willingness to endure and persevere even though suffering may be involved; use of idioms that are unfamiliar to Westerners (ancestors, unusual physical states or appearances) which are not delusional but metaphorical; and careful avoidance of tabooed topics such as alcoholism, family violence, sexual violations, and family finances. These latter are not matters of psychological denial but of loyalty and responsibility to one's family and kin.

Finally, Marsella provides a useful caution on the management of language in therapeutic relationships with Japanese Americans. The practices of verbalization, "venting," and self-disclosure that are sometimes encouraged as an adjunct to therapy, as though universally efficacious with troubled individuals, may be culturally inappropriate with some Japanese Americans. Many of them have high regard for the thoughtful silence, the brief and insightful comment. In their view that is not just a communicative event, it is an emotional one as well. Language establishes the feeling tone of the relationship. A competent counselor will be able to intuit that feeling tone and respond in like manner, without hiding behind a verbal barrage. Instead of talking, he or she will act quickly and authoritatively, quietly and with a clear focus, practically rather than abstractly, in an effort to rebuild family harmony rather than urge personal growth. The worker who can do that will be seen by clients as capable and skilled, and will have given a genuinely professional service.

FILIPINOS

It is unfortunate that there is so little in the social service literature on Filipinos, for they are a sizable community in this country. The Philippines came under American control in 1898 following the Spanish-American war, giving Filipinos access (with limitations) to the United States. Most went initially to Hawaii, where they were recruited by sugar plantation owners and their agents. Generally these were young men from rural areas who had little education and few economic prospects. Their hope was to save enough money to return to their homeland to buy a plot of land and marry.

Many Filipinos also came to California, either by way of Hawaii or directly. Most were not literate, few spoke English, and the only work many could find was "stoop labor" on farms. Others went into domestic service and some into the fishing and canning industries. (Filipinos are still heavily represented in Alaskan fish canneries, some of which provide less than ideal work conditions and have a history of corruption and violence.) Many went into what was to become a "traditional" industry for their community, hotel and restaurant work. As happened to other Asians, Filipinos were the targets of race riots in the 1920s for allegedly competing unfairly with white workers, socializing with white women, and for their presumed "unassimilability." And like other Asians, Filipinos were slow to establish families in this country; labor recruitment favored males and resulted in a severe shortage of Filipino women. After 1965, however, immigration laws were changed, and families and professionals typify the more recent migration stream. These later arrivals provide much of the current leadership in their communities.

Filipinos are concentrated in urban areas, especially Los Angeles, San Francisco, and Honolulu. There are also sizable communities in New York, New Jersey, Illinois, and Washington State. It is noteworthy that Filipinos are heavily involved in the workforce on the mainland. Not only do they experience relatively little unemployment, but an exceptionally high percentage of Filipina women work outside their homes. As a group, they are not poor and both men and women have high rates of graduation from high schools and universities.

Yet in Hawaii, Filipinos are one of that state's poorest groups. They are overrepresented in low-income, low skill jobs and have low levels of educational training and background. They are different from their mainland counterparts in that most are immigrants, not American born, and come from poorer areas of their home country. Like the Vietnamese, those among them who are well educated are often employed well below their skill levels. They suffer "occupational downgrading"; former business owners work as clerks and teachers as teacher's aides. Their resentment is not directed against whites, however, but against Japanese Hawaiians whom they perceive as dominating government and industry to their own advantage.

Filipino families tend to be egalitarian and, in contrast to some other Asian groups, women have a powerful and prominent role in family life. Cordova (1983) makes much of this contrast between "pinay" (or Filipina women) and those from other Asian countries. Pinays, especially in the early years of immigration, were often more highly educated than their husbands, were active in the public life of churches, schools, and businesses, and often controlled family finances. Many were entrepreneurs and many were professionals, working as teachers and nurses. In Cordova's view:

> *The heart and soul of the development of the Filipino American experience were personified in Pinays—particularly first generation women, including those separated from their men, and their second-generation daughters, who tried to emulate their mothers. Pinays have been the yeast that set the men and children rising and the leaven that got their communities producing (1983:153).*

As previously mentioned, there is almost no social service literature on Filipinos, and it would be an error to assume that what applies to Chinese Americans or Japanese Americans will work with Filipinos as well. Like other Asians, however, Filipinos respect the authority of the help provider and expect that person to show leadership in providing solutions. Age confers an advantage since it is presumed that age also leads to greater wisdom. Cross-gender counseling relationships, however, may be difficult to establish since one would not normally confide in someone of the opposite gender. While it is also true that most Filipinos are fluent in English, many use other languages in their homes, and the social worker seeing Filipino clients on a regular basis will need to make at least some effort to become familiar with common phrases and any technical terminology associated with illness or personal distress. At a minimum, such knowledge can open doors and lines of communication in a way that few other activities can.

Being very family oriented, Filipinos may be more comfortable with practical suggestions and prompt guidance than with lengthy, individualized, ongoing sessions emphasizing personal growth and development. Some Filipinos attribute personal or mental distresses to hostile forces in the environment, not to character flaws or personal failings. Thus, the kind of advice they would expect and that they would be likely to act on would be that which focuses on immediate as well as underlying issues: discrimination at work, youth gangs in the neighborhood, disagreements over control of family finances, or a family member's drinking.

There are now over one million Filipinos in the United States, yet relatively little is known about them ethnographically and even less is known about their health and social service needs. One solution to that is greater recruitment and training of Filipino social service professionals. Because many Filipinos are church-oriented, ministers and priests are potential allies in working with social service professionals. Many Filipinos also feel that the larger society's sometimes faddish interest in ethnicity has overlooked them in favor of other Asians and other ethnic groups. Given their substantial numbers in this country, however, they will probably get more attention in the future.

THE VIETNAMESE

The end of the American government's costly and disastrous war in Vietnam in April, 1975 was the beginning of a long period of suffering and transition for many Vietnamese and their families. As noted earlier in this chapter, the two waves of Vietnamese who fled the chaos were different. Those in the first group were well educated and well connected. They had had close ties with the American military, generally spoke English, and had professional and technical skills. The second wave, beginning about 1977, was composed mainly of ethnic groups who fled persecution by the Communist government that took control in the south as well as north. Among these were the "boat people" whose plight was made known to the world by television newscasts over several years. The end of the war generated a complex movement of refugees who fanned out into surrounding countries, disrupting lives, economies, and the precarious political stability of the region for over a decade (Rutledge 1992). Ultimately, almost a quarter million Vietnamese came to this country, although many remained in other parts of Southeast Asia as well.

In the United States, decisions were made at the Federal level that resettlement should involve private and voluntary organizations and that the refugees should be as widely scattered throughout the country as possible. No geographical or cultural "ghettos" were to be encouraged. Once dispersed, they were to be given short-term training in English and occupational self-sufficiency in the expectation that this would help them assimilate, melting pot style, into the larger society. While critics of this policy argued that such a plan would dilute the Vietnamese sense of cultural integrity, proponents replied that no other refugee group was ever given as generous a start-up for their Americanization. They were to be supplied with whatever they needed as they prepared for citizenship and eventual movement into the labor force (Matsuoka 1991). The hope was that quick assimilation would heal memories of Vietnam, both for the Vietnamese themselves and for Americans still troubled by the failed war.

The dispersion of the Vietnamese throughout the country, a policy based on administrative convenience and melting pot simplicities, has been modified both by secondary internal migration and the politics of the Vietnamese community itself. To reestablish old family and friendship ties, many Vietnamese have moved from the point of their original settlement, creating distinctive enclaves in many larger cities. This process began almost immediately after the initial settling in, and for some families it was a major sacrifice since they had to move to communities where they lacked governmental or private sponsors.

Equally important and difficult, some families sought an Asian enclave but were cautious about which Vietnamese they chose as neighbors. There are good historical reasons for this. As indicated, the class and economic differences between original and later wave refugees were considerable. Old hostilities and grievances from the war were not forgotten. In addition, there were significant internal distinctions and stereotypes among the refugees themselves. Rutledge (1992:109) describes the intraethnic competition, even discrimination and stereotyping, that differentiates those from the north of Vietnam, the central areas, and the south. Matters of dialect, religion, previous occupation, and family standing are as important to the Vietnamese as they are to people in other communities and, when combined with the war experience, they can make group solidarity and cooperation difficult. That is a political and ethnographic fact but it is also one with social service implications. No individual Vietnamese can be presumed to speak for others, and outsiders who wish to help promote community institutions need a good sense of the local political landscape before they venture into unfamiliar territory.

Nearly two decades after the war, a number of social service needs remain, and they are typical of those associated with refugee communities. Matsuoka (1991) lists some of them, noting that among the Vietnamese hierarchical views of the family and personal relationships are as important for them as they are for some other Asian groups. I will discuss briefly several of the issues that Matsuoka presents and how they affect delivery of professional services.

Most Vietnamese are Buddhists; others are adherents of Confucianism, Taoism, and, more recently, Catholicism, since the country was once part of the former French colony of Indochina. Confucianism in particular prescribes a mode of social and ethical responsibility that emphasizes the family and the obligations owed to it according to one's age and gender. Filial piety is central to this hierarchical ethos: "son to father, wife to husband, younger brother to elder brother, servant to master, citizen to emperor" (Rutledge 1992:48-49). Elders, especially elder men who are heads of households (called *truong toc*), are senior in moral authority and expect deference from others. Even where they are "incapacitated" by American standards, through sickness, feebleness, or apparent senility, their voice is important in all family decision making. The sensitive social worker will want to be sure that voice is heeded and respected regardless of the seeming inability of an older man to contribute to a discussion. In America, these elders suffer not only the disabilities of normal aging but often increasing isolation as other members of their family adopt American preferences and behavior. Language is often a problem for them since learning any new language is generally a challenge for older persons. They also know that the quality of deference and respect they showed their own parents means little in American culture and that they may be accorded less in the way of family honors than they would like. As Tran (1988:283) points out, in America there is no patrimonial land to dispense nor ancestral graves to maintain. Without other claims to power and authority, older men lose the moral force their age once assured them.

The position of older women is even more precarious in the American context. They have their authority and standing largely through their husbands, not in their own right. Children, who are often under enormous pressure to do well in school and careers, find that their success requires them to leave home, thereby isolating older parents further. Isolation contributes to depression, apathy, and serious illness. Working with senior Vietnamese can be a difficult and challenging task for the health or social service provider. Lappin and Scott (1982) describe their work with a widowed and struggling Vietnamese woman as very slow and based on small, incremental, and very concrete steps. Among other things, she had to be helped with her command of English so as to reduce her dependence on her children as interpreters. She also needed to find others outside the family to whom she could talk confidentially about her concerns. All her needs—English skills, managing grief and depression, and dealing with isolation from friends—had to be dealt with one issue at a time so that she was not overwhelmed with the sheer weight of all that had to be done. In a community of ethnic compatriots that was small and dispersed to begin with, helping her find and use the resources she needed took enormous patience and persistence by the workers. Matsuoka (1993) suggests that Vietnamese women have more negative attitudes toward acculturation than men, partly because they are more closely tied to female kinship networks focused on domestic life. If that is the case, culturally sensitive family therapy techniques may be useful with these clients.

All Vietnamese adults face problems of adjustment. In addition to language skills, employment is a major concern. Many of those in the first wave of refugees took jobs for which they were overeducated. Doctors worked as janitors, and former military officers drove taxis or fried hamburgers. They did this because their tradition emphasizes hard work and self-sufficiency in whatever job one does. This same work ethic prompted many to open their own small businesses, many of which flourished due to the availability of low-cost family labor and the willingness to take entrepreneurial risks. Rutledge (1992:81) notes that "Vietnamese plazas and mini-malls. . . . are becoming somewhat commonplace" in Dallas, Houston, Kansas City, and parts of California. He describes how the Vietnamese prefer to work with other Vietnamese and that in some plants and businesses they are the majority of the workforce.

In their drive to succeed economically, Vietnamese parents place great pressure on children to do well in school. The success of Vietnamese students in business schools and technical programs such as computers and electronics is rapidly becoming a new stereotype on some university campuses. But the fit of student expectations and teacher demands is not always a happy one. In their home country, children (and their parents) learned that teachers were authority figures, their knowledge was not to be questioned, and the preferred style of learning was memorization and repetition. The American practice of classroom discussion and critique, with its democratic emphasis on the worth of everyone's opinion and the disconcerting possibility that no one, including the teacher, has a final, authoritative answer to every question, does not fit with traditional experiences. For many Vietnamese university students, the humanities and social sciences are educational mine fields where disaster lurks in every quiz and test. Reporting disappointing grades to parents is more than some students can handle. When this is added to the American emphasis on peer group association and individualism, both competitors for family loyalty and control, the possibilities for conflict at home are great.

Mention also should be made of a special group of young Vietnamese, many now about college age. They are the *haafus*, children and young adults whose parents were Vietnamese and either black or white American. Many of these children were conceived during the Vietnam war, some later in this country. Those with black parentage would have faced insurmountable discrimination and stigmatizing had they remained in Vietnam. They were held back from education in Vietnam because they were a visible reminder of the former American military presence and they were subject to ostracism and discrimination by other Vietnamese. In an excellent historical overview, Valverde (1992) writes that

"Amerasians have the dual burden of the Vietnamese refugee experience and the marginal multiracial experience. Therefore, their needs are different than those of 'standard' refugees. Uncomfortable in a new land, still without a voice, they continue to carry these burdens" (1992:157). Williams (1992a) describes Amerasians as having "prism lives," their experiences refracted through several cultural lenses. For some, that is a source of pride, but all experience frustrations, within their families, in the Vietnamese community, and in the larger white society.

All of the issues and historical experiences affecting Vietnamese refugees described here create personal stresses, some of which are debilitating. But the vocabulary, even the idea, of "mental health" is not in the inventory of most Vietnamese. Rutledge quotes a Vietnamese physician on the subject:

> *You cannot talk about mental health. I know what you mean, but you will offend people [Vietnamese] if you use those words. In Vietnam, you are crazy if you have mental health [problems]. You can be depressed, or lonely, or afraid. That is okay, but you cannot have a mental health problem. Depression and mental health are not the same to Vietnamese (1992:103).*

Matsuoka believes Vietnamese refugees "experience a significant degree of fatalism and helplessness" (1991:127) and to cope with that they may need skill building, assertiveness training, opportunities to express feelings of survivor's guilt, and activities that promote self-esteem. Unfortunately, how these things are to be done in culturally meaningful ways has yet to be made explicit in the human services literature. A very small number of dedicated Vietnamese have gone into social services. But their knowledge of their own community, and their suggestions for culturally appropriate intervention, have yet to be systematically collected and made available to the larger professional community. Until that happens, social services for the Vietnamese will remain an area of uncertainty, guided more by good intentions than real ethnographic insight and understanding.

SOUTH ASIANS, AMERICA'S MUSLIMS

Sikhs were the first South Asians to come to North America in any considerable number. They came at about the same time as the Chinese, and for about the same reasons. Opportunities for employment and wealth, on railroads, in mines, and as laborers were better in Canada and the United States than in their homeland in the Indian Punjab. Their historical experience in North America, and some of their contemporary concerns as a community and as families, have been well documented by Gibson (1988), Gibson and Ogbu (1991), and Leonard (1992). But Sikhs are not the majority of South Asians in the United States at this time. That distinction belongs to Muslims, and in this section I want to discuss briefly the Muslim community that is increasing in prominence in some areas of the country.

We normally think of Muslims as originating in the Middle East. That is true, but it is also the case that the world's largest Muslim country is in Asia (Indonesia); fully one-third of all Muslims in the United States are from South Asia (India and Pakistan); and Islam is the fastest growing religion in America, partly because of conversion by African Americans but mainly because of immigration. (Muslims, of course, are heavily represented in the ethnic communities of the United Kingdom, although one would not guess that from reading the titles of articles in journals such as the *British Journal of Social Work*.) Thus, my comments about South Asian Muslims will have some validity for Muslims from other parts of the world beyond South Asia, including those from the Middle East.

It is very difficult to know exactly how many Muslims reside in America. Stone (1991) estimates that in 1986 there were around four million, making Islam a small but growing religious presence. (There are many Muslims in Canada, as well, and the proportion of those from South Asia is probably higher since they carry Commonwealth passports, making entry into Canada easier than into the United States.) The number of Muslim immigrants in this country has doubled in the last two decades and that trend continues. Muslims are concentrated in three regions—New York, California, and Illinois—but they live in virtually all parts of the country.

Only in the very largest cities do Muslims tend to cluster in distinctive neighborhoods. Elsewhere they are diffused throughout inner-city neighborhoods and suburbs. Their most distinctive institution is the mosque, and many large cities now have at least one. There are Islamic schools, as well, where children are trained in religious principles and in Arabic so they can read the Quran. Mosques typically contain mixed constituencies, professionals and laborers, Saudis and Indonesians, East Africans and Indians, African Americans and a few white Americans. Whereas prayers are always in Arabic, sermons and meetings are usually in English since that is the only common language for everyone there. The mosque is a critical anchorage for many Muslims, especially those who are less educated and who have difficulty adjusting to life in America. Not only does it offer religious continuity with their home country, it may be the only place where they can find a sympathetic ear and word of comfort as they struggle to make sense of what to them is an incredibly secular and materialistic society.

The head of the mosque is the Imam, the individual who leads Friday prayers. (Friday is the day for religious observances among Muslims worldwide.) There is no formal clergy in Islam and no formal training for an Imam. Only men recognized for their piety are chosen for this position. In America some have taken on the duties of pastoral care typical of a minister, priest, or rabbi although such duties are traditionally not expected of them. Mosques do not offer social services in Islamic countries so the counseling that some Imams do is strictly an American (and probably British and Canadian) adaptation. In their study of Muslims in the United States, one of the very few, Haddad and Lummis (1987) quote a part-time Imam:

> *I do counseling, but my time is limited and I cannot do as much as I would like to do, or what is needed, because of my personal responsibilities. Most of the counseling problems I deal with fall into two categories, one being economic,*

another being marital. . . . Many of the Muslims new to this country do not like to reveal their private life to some stranger. But if the matter is tense, and they have to do something about it, they will come to a place they trust, the mosque. If it is something confidential, it is easier to talk to the Imam than to some social worker (60).

Muslim ways of looking at the world are the product of a religious tradition over 1400 years old, one that defines one's religious commitment as a total way of life. Many features of that tradition conflict with American ways of doing things, leading to confusion and consternation for many Muslims. I want to mention some of these features briefly because they point to areas of cross-cultural understanding, etiquette, and misunderstanding that non-Muslim social service and health professionals might never anticipate.

Gender and inappropriate gender contacts may be the most challenging barriers to communication between Americans and Muslims. The modesty of women—daughters, sisters, wives, and mothers—is central to the integrity and honor of the entire family. Modesty can take many forms, from seclusion of women in the home to the more common practice of covering the head and body to minimize physical exposure. It is quite inappropriate for men, especially strange men including doctors, to see or touch an adult woman. (Shaking hands is reserved for men; men and women who are just meeting one another never shake hands.) It is inappropriate for strange men, including social workers, to be with a woman or to engage her in a lengthy conversation unless some male kinsman is present and has given consent. Even if that is the case, and it would be a rarity, it is most unlikely that a woman would unburden herself to a male counselor. Women social workers and doctors are more likely to be effective in those situations. Similarly, Muslim men are not inclined to reveal themselves, physically or psychologically, to women professionals. They are more likely to talk with other men and, since age confers status, an older male confidante or an Imam is preferable.

Muslims usually have no objections to sending their children to an American public school, and children, unlike many of their mothers, usually dress in Western fashions. Children are expected to observe Islamic holidays along with their parents and may be kept out of school at those times. Prejudice against Muslim children seems rare in this country, although it sometimes flairs up when inspired by political events in the Middle East. Nor do most Muslim families have problems with American holidays such as Thanksgiving and the Fourth of July. Like most Americans, Muslims treat these holidays as opportunities for family gatherings. What is problematic, however, is mixing among girls and boys as they become teenagers. Most parents would prefer that their children marry other Muslims, but their more immediate concern is the appropriateness of dating, American style. The idea of teenage couples out on their own is troublesome. For various reasons, mosques are not able to offer enough activities to keep children and teenagers busy. Consequently, issues of parental control can become explosive, especially in more traditional households. Many of the parents of these teenagers had arranged marriages and may have that expectation for their children. Fidelity to this custom, even in the American context, may be more common than non-Muslims realize.

Islamic practice requires that families respect their aged members and take care of them. Since in most Muslim countries, and certainly in Asian ones, families are both extended and large, there are usually people available to provide that kind of care. The seclusion of women also promotes intense, in-home personal care. But in America, some elderly family members may be too far away to be cared for properly, or career demands may make it difficult for a husband and wife to tend to an aged parent. Unlike Chinese and Japanese cultures, there is no stigma attached to placing an elder in a nursing facility, but most Muslim families do not have the financial means to do so.

American banking practices are troublesome for many Muslims, especially if they decide to buy a home or business, or contract a loan for a car. Orthodox Islam prohibits usury, interest on money, although some Muslims insist the rules only apply to excessive interest. Nonetheless, how to handle money and where to keep it is a dilemma. In addition, most Muslims pay *zakat*, a voluntary tax (usually two percent) put into a common welfare pool. Zakat funds are collected by governments in many Islamic countries and distributed through mosques and established charities, usually to widows and orphans. The extent of zakat contributions among American Muslims is unknown, but where it is practiced the mosque would be the logical place for funds to be collected and distributed to those in need. Accepting zakat is not stigmatizing but is a simple recognition that the community offers some support to those whose have suffered a misfortune.

Dietary restrictions can be a serious problem for Muslims in America, and parents sometimes worry that their children are being served improper foods in school lunch programs or in restaurants. Like observant Jews, Muslims do not eat pork or shellfish. They do not eat foods (soups, hot dogs, cooking oil) where pork or pork products might in any way be involved. Muslim wives quickly become skilled at reading food labels, looking for lard or pork that may be hidden in a product or used in its processing. *Halal* meat, that from which the blood has been drained in a proper fashion, is preferred. For that reason, Muslims sometimes frequent Jewish delicatessens and grocery stores, since for them kosher food is considered halal. Muslim businessmen sometimes request kosher meals on airplanes and in hotels for the same reason. Alcohol is more complex and controversial. Some Muslims say it is forbidden, *haram*; others that it is permitted but only with moderation, and most think it is unhealthy and undesirable. Alcohol is totally inappropriate for children, teenagers, and women of any age.

The issues mentioned here illustrate, but certainly do not encompass, the ethnic distinctiveness of Muslims who have come to America. Once here, they discover that their religion, not their national origin, usually defines their ethnicity. As the Muslim presence in America grows, and it appears that it will, Muslim clients and patients will become more familiar to social service providers. Yet there is almost nothing in the social service literature about them, and they are virtually unknown as a client group. For workers with an immediate need for information, the best sources are Haddad and Lummis (1987), McDermott and Ahsan's (1986) guide for teachers and community workers in Britain, and the recently published *The Muslims of America* edited by Haddad (1991). While Haddad's book does not explicitly address social service issues, it does provide an excellent overview. For health care professionals, Waxler-Morrison, Anderson, and Richardson (1990) and Galanti (1991) have useful information. Combined with the learning principles already outlined in this book, these sources will lead the interested worker into the complexities of America's Islamic community.

CONCLUSION

The diversity of countries and cultures subsumed under the label "Asian and Pacific Islanders" suggests both the unreality of that phrase and the future it portends. It is "unreal" in that it takes in too much; it identifies almost nothing except a huge geographical expanse. The clinician never confronts an Asian or a Pacific Islander. Clients are specific human beings, bearers of a localized and complex tradition in addition to their individual concerns. These clients, as Asians, are also on the leading edge of a century-long trend creating new interconnections among the countries of the Pacific Rim. That trend is more than commerce in cars, cameras, and foodstuffs. It is a new settlement in the United States, but with people from the East instead of the West. The demographics of their resettlement in America are already in place: in just a decade or two the baby boomers will be moving out of the job market and they have not produced enough children to replace themselves, their labor, or their skills. Asians will do that for them. People from Hong Kong, China, Korea, the Philippines, and India, blue collar workers and highly educated professionals, will occupy many of the economic niches the baby boomers leave behind. They will create the commercial and cultural ties that extend American interests across the Pacific, even to the Indian Ocean. And they *will* be American interests, because these Asian and Pacific Islanders will be the new Americans.

They will not, however, be like the old Americans. We delude ourselves if we believe that melting pots, acculturation, or the more recently celebrated pluralism will resolve fundamental differences in outlook, and that given time, "they" will become more like "us." Asian communities in America are not easily accessed by outsiders; they will not be accessed easily when their numbers are larger and their needs greater. Social and health service professionals must be ready to serve populations that will be more diverse in the future, not less so. That diversity, combined with intergenerational conflicts, elders at risk, children lacking nutrition and adequate schools, youth gangs, unemployment and underemployment, can lead to even more dangerous forms of ethnic and racial warfare than we have now. The productive society these future Americans might create will never be possible unless care providers of all kinds begin working now for the ethnic and cultural transformation that is only a few decades away. That work must include nothing less than the ability to help others live their lives according to their own best traditions.

PART **III**

ETHNIC COMPETENCE AND GENERAL PRACTICE

Part III is a series of cross-cultural learning exercises that can be adapted to individual study and classroom use. They are intended to help you develop the skills of ethnic competence as a part of general practice. The exercises are divided into two sections: Section A is a series of cultural awareness activities; Section B outlines ways to build cultural knowledge. A table at the end provides a checklist that relates the exercises to specific areas of general practice.

10

CROSS-CULTURAL LEARNING: HOW IT'S REALLY DONE

Knowledge is one thing; acting on it is another. Putting information to use is critical if we are serious about making a difference in people's lives. Yet how that might be done is not always obvious. Given the complexity of our multicultural society, the long-standing inequities that impede just resolution of old problems, and the limited staffing and resources of service organizations, it is easy to be frustrated. And frustration is the forerunner of cynicism and burnout. So where to begin?

I have two suggestions that I think should guide you as a student as well as a professional social worker, and both are very practical.

1. Go for the small win because the big ones don't usually happen.
2. Get expert advice when you know you need it, but have the expert clearly explain what's in it for you and your clients.

SMALL WINS

I wish I could take credit for this idea but it belongs to psychologist Karl Weick (1984). He analyzed strategies of social and personal change and found that small wins, not hard-fought battles against major foes, are more likely to lead to changes of real consequence. Modesty and quiet persistence often succeed. Heroic stands are gestures, and mostly only that. He cites several interesting examples of the principle, which I paraphrase here.

> Over the last twenty years, the title "Ms." has come into common English usage. That is a direct result of feminist cultural lobbying spearheaded by the editors of the magazine of the same name. It is an impressive achievement because lan-

guages are normally resistant to change. The hope of the proponents was that a new language form, such as a term for address, would lead to new ways of thinking about gender. Yet the same activists failed to secure passage of the Equal Rights Amendment. That we should ignore marital status in forms of address now seems reasonable to most of us. But changing the United States Constitution, for any reason, is something monumental and even alarming for many. The Equal Rights Amendment, aside from its merits, was truly a grand gesture, and seems for now to be dead. But the use of "Ms." is now so common it is hardly noticeable.

Alcoholics Anonymous, and the many spin-off support groups that have adopted its model, does not promise its members a permanent cure. Instead, it asks that they follow a prescribed regimen one day at a time and, sometimes, for just a few hours at a time. In new or difficult cases, they ask for adherence only for as long as it takes to make a phone call for help. The AA time horizon for measuring success can be incredibly short, yet many people have gone for years without alcohol. Changes are incremental, not dramatic, and the ideology of AA says that is the way it must be.

Compared to passage of the ERA, the general use of "Ms." was a small win and, in time, we may hear "Mrs. (followed by husband's first and last name)" only in reruns of 1950s sitcoms. That may or may not change the world fundamentally but it is a change. So is avoiding a drink, one hour and one day at a time, especially in a culture that glamorizes youth, sex appeal, and links them both to alcohol consumption.

Weick defines a small win as "a concrete, complete, implemented outcome of moderate importance"; small wins are "controllable opportunities that produce visible results" (1984:43). More important, "Small wins provide information that facilitates learning and adaptation. Small wins are like miniature experiments that test implicit theories about resistance and opportunity and uncover both resources and barriers that were invisible before the situation was stirred up" (1984:44).

Small wins are always opportunistic, but they are *not* accidental. The people who get small wins have prepared themselves; they have both the mind-set and skills to take advantage of an occasion. They also know that successive small changes are more likely to result in long-term, bigger changes. Goals for change that are too easy or too hard, that do not build on incrementalism, and that do not have a small but noticeable effect, usually have no force.

In addition, small wins are often small pleasures, even when discomfort is present, because they create positive (even comic) relief in chaotic or uncontrollable situations. They define the structure of hope by creating a base for the next win, even if it is only a repetition of the last one, something the AA member would accept as central to recovering sobriety.

The series of exercises that follow are intended to help you accumulate small wins. You only have to be patient and persistent, and mentally ready for the possibilities in every encounter with every client or patient.

ON EXPERTS AND EXPERTISE

Seeking small wins, while a useful strategy in itself, is not enough for developing real cross-cultural interviewing and intervention skills. We think about service to clients in terms of cultural context, and we need to think about that in training as well. What kinds of contexts are most likely to generate high quality professional learning? What contexts trivialize and even defeat real learning?

My second suggestion is that efficient, effective learning generally occurs when two things happen. First, individuals are assigned as apprentices to a person with recognized and validated skills in an area of mutual interest. The "master" in this master-apprentice relationship is qualified not by university degrees or an accumulation of workshop certificates but by "recognized and validated skills." Only that qualifies someone as an "expert." Who experts might be, what it is that they know, and how they can meet the learning needs of apprentices ought to be the only matters of importance.

Second, small groups of learners ought to focus on a limited number of issues and systematically review their success as they go along. (Small wins again.) Review should be done with the expert but also by the learners among themselves, conferring on a regular basis in a systematic way. That helps build learning into the job routine, rather than separating the occasions for learning from daily activities. Experts are important but, in my view, most people can effectively direct their own learning much of the time if it is clear that that is one of their responsibilities and that there are personal and professional benefits in doing so. Calling on experts for help in starting the process and for occasional consultations may be all that is needed from outsiders and specialists. Experts are in a position to validate the progress that has been made and they can legitimize the efforts of individual participants. They usually have useful knowledge to impart, but real change comes because of committed engagement by students and trainees working on issues among themselves.

Learning in a community of apprentices, be that the community of an agency, an office, or a classroom, is quite different from workshop-style training and it produces two effects that the usual kinds of staff training do not. First, apprenticeship learning creates an institutional memory about "how cases like X, Y, and Z are handled in our organization." That is an important administrative concern, especially when turnover of agency personnel is high.

Second, it institutionalizes a work style that generates enthusiasm for skills improvement. That is less likely to happen when workers take released time to go to a distant training site, returning to a job that continues just as it always has. For training "to take," to produce agency and client benefits, it must be part of work routines and everyone has to feel that it enhances their professional performance.

This model has been called "situated learning" by Lave and Wenger (1991). It emphasizes participation in expertly guided performances, not episodic accumulation of facts and skills that have no clear relationship to work tasks. Situated learning has a number of features that distinguish it from traditional classroom education and the cycle of in-service workshops that most of us have experienced (and endured) for most of our student and professional careers.

First, situated learning is democratically "decentered." It is not the property of experts and authorities but is the *experience* of the learning community. Lived learning experiences are what count, not lectures, video tapes, or contrived "role plays." Real learning that has detectable results is "embedded"; it is part of routine job assignments and is done every day. One advantage to thinking of learning as a job activity rather than as something done at a pleasant retreat far from the office is that it encourages a holistic view of what is really going on. One can see more clearly, through the tasks and the learning done with coworkers, the strengths and limits of an agency's goals and capabilities; the real skills of colleagues; the real needs of the community served; and clients' responses to small changes in intervention and practice.

A second and closely related point is that situated learning is always participatory. The "learning curriculum is a field of learning resources in everyday practice *viewed from the perspective of learners*" (Lave and Wenger 1991:97). That means that learning is necessarily opportunistic rather than logically sequential. Writing in the *Journal of Social Work Education*, Nakanishi and Rittner (1992) put it nicely:

> *Intercultural learning is never linear or orderly. It is a process that occurs in complex ways with increasing levels of* cultural self-knowledge *as an integral part of understanding how responses to culturally different persons are manifested (1992:29).*

Only in formally organized classrooms and workshops is education thought of as a linear progression with a beginning, middle, and end. Everywhere else, when each one of us first learned to walk, talk, kiss, or drive a car, learning was opportunistic. Real learning happens when we have need for it. Lectures, training films, and role plays are at best anemic substitutes. They have their uses but by themselves they will never lead anyone to real cultural awareness or ethnic competence.

Third, decentered learning in a community of participation is *transparent*. Informed, critical, self-reflection on our responses to others, especially in challenging situations, is the bedrock of situated learning. That is far, far different from the generic "skills" and heightened "cultural awareness" so often promoted in lectures and training seminars. Through carefully examined cases in which we are a participant, we really begin to see the larger dimensions of our professional activity: the strengths and weakness of the delivery system; the fragility and complexity of human beings; and our personal effectiveness in assisting others. As learning proceeds in an experiential community, hidden personal and institutional agendas are harder to conceal because each learner grows "savvy," not only about how the service system really works but how client communities work as well. That kind of learning inevitably leads to professional maturity and competence.

Fourth, the experiential "discourse of practice," as Lave and Wenger call it, shifts our attention from the abstract to the concrete. We no longer work with "dysfunction families" or "co-dependent spouses." Instead our concern is with how members of the Jones family are managing violence, or how the elderly Smiths are complying with a visiting nurse's suggestions for regular exercise and a better diet. In situated learning, office talk and folklore are less about the presumed characteristics of people in community X and more about stories of how things were done with specific clients having particular needs.

But more than just stories, in this model case accounts are used for explicit, systematic comparisons of those times when an intervention worked, those when it did not, and the reasons why. For case discussions to be more than office gossip, they must be analyzed in comparative terms, understood as Weick's "miniature experiments." Only then can the apparent mysteriousness of good cross-cultural intervention be made explicit and a piece of well-tested practice.

If this idea of "situated learning" sounds wildly idealistic, something hatched by an academic who seems innocent of the "real world" of service agencies, their bureaucracies, budget struggles, office politics, and angry clients, then let me put it in a context that ought to be familiar. What I have described here, following the suggestions of Lave and Wenger, is exactly what makes Alcoholics Anonymous, and many other multiple-step, self-help, and group-support programs successful. They could never have succeeded any other way.

What AA pioneered was apprenticeship learning for people in trouble. In that model, newcomers were given access to full participation through "old timers" (the "experts") who initiated them into a relearning process. The newcomers learned as apprentices always do, one day at a time, opportunistically, with democratic review and consultation on specific, individual cases. An important part of their relearning was adopting a new style of discourse: a new vocabulary, new metaphors of affliction, and new stories illustrating their struggle, all told and retold publicly. No one was allowed secrets, the learning community was transparent, and the warts and strengths of everyone revealed. From that kind of experience, new identities emerged and were maintained because lifelong relearning about alcohol control is what the community is about. Finally, the best recommendation that could be made for the method is that for many people, it works. It is not perfect but it is better than a lot of the alternatives.

Wins in learning most often occur in a community of practice, where committed people work together over a period of time and where cooperation and enthusiasm are institutionalized. This contrasts markedly with the usual methods for teaching skills in social services with their dependence on guest experts invited for one-shot presentations at staffings and workshops. Some states mandate a set number of hours for attendance at this kind of training, apparently in the hope that skilled workers will emerge, fired with eagerness and newly discovered capability. It is sometimes called a "training the trainers" model, the newly converted sent out to win over coworkers. But it is still a top-down approach and I seriously doubt its effectiveness, even though I have taught in many workshops and will probably do more. Its limitations are of two kinds.

First, in traditional methods of training the emphasis is on the guest presentor and the presentor's agenda, as though the trainees had little to offer. The trainer hopes to say something relevant; the trainees hope they will not be bored. Second, there are few opportunities for extended, deliberative engagement with other professionals, a condition that real cross-cultural learning requires. Time is given instead to role plays, responding to videos, and various "sensitizing" and self-disclosure activities. These are not bad in themselves, but they aren't very effective because they have little or no long-term consequence.

I once had the opportunity to help guide a serious training effort for the staff of the Casey Family Program (described in Green and Wilson 1983), one that did not include workshops. Instead, participants were placed for a week in a minority agency and my time as trainer was spent preparing people for their visits, followed by long debriefings with individuals and later the entire group. Real, documentable cultural awareness emerged, mostly through what I would call "comparison stories" made by the staff for and among themselves. Since their experiences were intense, and for some very difficult, they had a lot to say and wanted to say it. As outside specialist, I simply guided conversations, summarized experiences, and commented on cross-cultural issues that were troublesome and would need future attention. I provided handouts and other information as appropriate, but they were only to supplement what the learners themselves agreed they had already learned. To that degree, they set the learning agenda. The agency head participated in the visitation and debriefings along with everyone else, creating what for all of us was a genuinely democratic learning community. Most refreshing, there were no colorful binders full of academic articles, no forced role plays, no bored participants, no badges that said "Hello, My Name Is. . . . "

What is needed are not more workshops but an entirely different division of labor, one in which learning rather than training is the goal, and where a learning curriculum rather than a training curriculum is stressed. The difference between these is really very simple: learning begins with a small community of those who need and want to upgrade their capabilities. They are guided by someone who takes account of their experiences and limitations and helps move them toward a group-selected goal. The "learning effect" is the apprentice's progressive ability to make sense of specific cases and to demonstrate more complex understanding in work with increasingly difficult ones. Learning this way is *efficient*, both in a time management and administrative sense, because knowledge is always additive to what one already knows and new effort goes to acquiring only what one needs, on a case-by-case basis.

Training, by contrast, is hierarchical and authoritative, designed to transmit great principles and keen insights to the less knowledgeable, so that they may hear and go do likewise. It assumes that what the expert offers is identical to what learners need to know. Training is usually decontextualized, offering something for everyone, and it is long on generalities. It is not surprising, then, that training workshop evaluations stress the presentor's performance, not that of the learning community. How well participants "liked" the instructor and his or her teaching style is the measure of success, not whether new skills were acquired, or specifics on how they will be used on the job.

CROSS-CULTURAL LEARNING

Service professions such as social work, health care, and others are rich in training techniques and learning materials. What I have tried to do in the material that follows is to suggest a range of activities that can be expanded, revised, or modified to suit the interests of differing kinds of learners and learning communities. All these activities can be adapted for use by individuals, as part of class or term-paper projects, or in professional settings. I have tried to make them more or less consistent with the ideal of "situated learning" but I am aware that that ideal cannot be easily achieved in all circumstances.

The learning experiences discussed here will give you practice with many of the themes presented in the book. They do so by emphasizing one or more of the basic tenets of an ethnographic or a cross-cultural approach: the emic perspective, contextualization, participant observation, and learning to access real issues affecting real people in a culturally positive way.

Two kinds of activities are listed, and the differences between them are important in terms of learning goals and objectives. I have distinguished *cultural awareness* activities from those emphasizing acquisition of *cultural knowledge*. Cultural awareness refers to a kind of sensibility, a frame of mind about cross-cultural human services. It has to do with qualities of openness, alertness, and in particular, flexibility in relations with others. It focuses on attitudes and values and is, in part, a matter of the inner state of the learner.

But cultural awareness is *not*, and I emphasize this point, the totality of cross-cultural learning. It is only the beginning. Cultural awareness *must* be supplemented with ethnographic information if it is to become more than self-indulgence in training exercises for their own sake. Cultural knowledge activities, therefore, emphasize learning about others within a comparative perspective. As learning experiences, they are outwardly focused and are intended to add to the individual's information base. To the extent possible, learning should be done not about "minorities" or "ethnic groups" in general but about specific communities and with reference to specific needs and services. That way, everyone can begin to see the utility of an ethnographic approach to their professional tasks.

The learning activities listed here should be mixed and matched, modified and expanded according to your needs, those of your co-learners, and most especially those of your patients and clients. Many can be done in classroom settings. Others are more suitable for longer individual and group projects.

Table 10.1 at the end of the chapter can be used as a checklist for working through the exercises. The table also matches exercises to topics of general social work practice so they can be used in conjunction with other texts.

SECTION A. ACTIVITIES IN EXPERIENCING CULTURAL AWARENESS

Exercise 1. First Impressions and the Hidden Assumptions of Culture, Or, The Emics of a Handshake

In American middle-class Anglo culture, there are standardized ways of meeting others, things whites think of as decorum, politeness, or routine civility. But the little rituals of introductory propriety vary from culture to culture, sometimes in striking ways. Knowing that is important, because first impressions are created and individual sensitivities are revealed in such displays. Failure to observe convention may suggest boorishness, usually noticed but rarely commented on until the visitor is out of sight and hearing. Minor gaffs can and do occur and they are an endless source of ethnic humor among almost all people. Humor, in fact, is something very important since jokes, one-liners, lyrics, folktales, and pantomimes often mark and comment on the fault lines that distinguish ethnic communities.

The brief example below is adapted from Keith Basso's wonderful *Portraits of 'The Whiteman'* (1979:45–57) and is used with the kind permission of the author. It is a joking imitation of whites, observed by Basso as it spontaneously occurred in an Apache household when another Apache appeared at the door. It can be thought of as a sociological skit and it was very funny to the Apache who performed it. Knowing why it is funny reveals something of how whites are perceived, at least by one group of Native Americans.

In this sketch, an Apache man in his forties, his wife, and their four children are sitting in their home, about 100 miles east of Phoenix, Arizona, on a pleasant summer evening. The man ("J") is fixing a bridle as his wife ("K") cleans the kitchen following the evening meal. Their four children play quietly on the floor. Another man ("L"), slightly younger and a clan member, walks up to the house and knocks. J goes to the door, sees L, and without prompting begins the joke.

Hello, my friend! How are you doing? How you feeling, L? You feeling good?

(J turns to his family.) *Look who here, everybody! Look who just come in. Sure, it's my Indian friend, L. Pretty good alright!* (J looks L in the eye, grabs his shoulder, and shakes his hand vigorously.)

Come right in, my friend. Don't stay outside in the rain. Better you come in right now. (J drapes an arm around L.)

Sit down! Sit right down! Take your loads off you ass. You hungry? You want some beer? Maybe you want some wine? You want crackers? Bread? You want some sandwich? How 'bout it? You hungry? I don't know. Maybe you get sick. Maybe you don't eat again long time.

(L and K watch J, bemused.)

You sure look good to me, L. You looking pretty fat! Pretty good alright! You got new boots? Where you buy them? Sure pretty good boots! I glad. . . .

(J can't finish the sentence because he, K and L are all laughing together. Finally K says, *"Whitemen are stupid"* and the joke is over.)

Why was this a joke and what, from an emic or Apache point of view, made it funny? The joke has to be analyzed line by line to identify its emic components. Look for the following:

1. The use of the word "friend"
2. Use of names
3. General queries
4. Personal questions
5. Verbal repetitions
6. Attention-getting phrases
7. Body contact
8. References to appearance and to health
9. Offerings of food

Take a sheet of paper and draw a line down the center of it. On the left side, list what you think are the Apache understandings and/or expectations regarding each of the nine items above. On the right side, list the understandings and expectations associated with these categories in your own ethnic community. At the bottom of the page, state something about why this qualifies—from an Apache point of view—as a joke.

On the back of your sheet of paper, write out a list of things that, as a social service provider entering the home of a family in a culture unfamiliar to you, you might want to watch for and be aware of.

To discover the full particulars of this episode, you will want to read Chapter 3 of Basso's interesting and revealing little book, which can be found in most university libraries. Compare your comments on the Apache joke with his detailed analysis. How close did you come to understanding why all of this was so funny? Why did K conclude that "whitemen are stupid"?

If you want to be especially venturesome, list some of the ways you believe you or members of your ethnic community are sometimes perceived by those in differing groups. How does humor draw attention to some of the differences and, as humor, how gentle or pointed can it be?

Exercise 2. Professional Values: Good for Your Mental Health?

The professional values that social workers learn are usually acquired in college and graduate school, when as a student one learns the skills and knowledge of the discipline and begins to develop a sense of professional attachment. The importance of these values in professional socialization has been described by Levy:

> *Social work values constitute a basis for rational choices in professional situations. These are the values to which social workers are expected to be committed. They represent preferences with respect to ways of doing it; preferences with respect to how people are to be regarded who are directly or indirectly affected by what is done or not done; and preferences with respect to safeguards to be accorded such persons, because of the risks and entitlements to which they are subjected or exposed as a result or in the process of its being done (1977:7).*

Now, what might these values which "represent preferences" be? While it is difficult to say that any particular list of values would be typical of the social service profession as a whole, we can nevertheless select two instances which seem to summarize much that has been said on the topic.

Pincus and Minahan (1973:39) believe that social work's two principal values are (1) taking action to ensure that people have access to the resources, services, and opportunities they need to meet various life tasks, alleviate distress, and realize their aspirations; and (2) showing respect for the dignity and individuality of the recipients of those services.

McLeod and Meyer (1967) have been more specific in suggesting principles. Their list includes:

1. Belief in the worth and dignity of the individual human being and the importance of maximizing his or her potential.

2. Belief in the right of every individual to exercise control over his or her own destiny, that is, self-determination.

3. Belief that the group has responsibility for the welfare of its own members.

4. The assertion that individuals should have the security and satisfaction of meeting basic biological and culturally acquired needs in order to achieve self-realization.

5. The notion that scientific and pragmatic problem-solving approaches are optimal.

6. Commitment to social reform, planned change, and progress.

7. Acceptance of diversity and heterogeneity in ideas, values, and lifestyles.

8. Belief that human nature is socially determined and that change often requires environmental alterations.

9. The view that the interdependence of all members of society (group responsibility) supersedes individual autonomy.

10. The notion that all individuals are unique.

This list suggests a good small-group discussion exercise. Try to imagine an instance where you might find one or more of the above statements of value inappropriate for a client, his or her situation, family, or community. For instance, can you visualize an occurrence where the "right of every individual" to manage his or her own affairs might conflict with an obligation to others in a particular community? And what of the "commitment to social reform, planned change and progress"? What assumptions about the "needs" of others are contained in such a "commitment"? How are reforms translated into intervention with clients, and why? Each of these value statements, if explored in reference to specific cases, can help you better understand the difficulties in applying general values uncritically in multicultural relationships.

A second way to handle this list of values is to look at it from the bottom up. In small groups, discuss a specific case that has been supplied by an instructor or that you have seen in a text or journal. After your group has discussed the case and its ramifications, go through both values lists and consider the applicability of each item to the case you have considered. Values, stated in the abstract, often sound unimpeachable. Their utility for specific instances of human need, however, may be something very different.

Exercise 3. Do French Fries Have Identity Crises?

There is nothing French about the hot, greasy, salt-encrusted fast-food specialty that Americans call "French fries." They are generically American. The potato that gives its all for our dining pleasure doesn't much care what it gets called. Americans, however, usually care a lot, especially when they think something of value is at stake. In these times of ethnic consciousness and sensitivity to all kinds of diversity, ethnic names and identities are a public and sometimes private gauge of who and what one is. Among African-American or Latino students, for example, ethnicity as an aspect of personal identity is often easy for them to describe. For whites or Anglos, however, naming ethnicity is sometimes more difficult. Yet simply because most Americans are immigrants or descended from immigrants, everyone is a member of some ethnic group. The issue, then, is not who is ethnic and who is not. It is the relative importance of ethnicity in self-identity and, beyond that, what that has to do with access to social and economic privileges.

The purpose of this exercise is to give you an opportunity to clarify the meaning of your ethnicity in a personal way. We often speak of the importance of "knowing where the client is coming from." But first we need to know where *we* are coming from if we are to feel confident and free of insecurities, whatever label we give ourselves. Kind of like the fry.

In responding to the following statements and questions, it is important to be as precise as possible, keeping in mind that your intuitive sense of family history is as important as what you might be able to verify through old family records or from conversations with senior family members. The goal of this activity is to clarify your perceptions, not establish historical facts. Discussion could be in small groups but this also works well for a group if it is not too large and there is time for everyone to make their contribution.

a. Identify your family origins as far back as you can trace specific ancestors. Specify the earliest dates, names, and places of which you can be sure. If you are unsure, speculate about probable ancestors and how far back you might be able to trace them, as though you were planning to do genealogical research.

b. Why and how did your ancestors come to this country? Speculate on the conditions they left behind and their possible motives for leaving those conditions.

c. When your ancestors arrived here, their ethnic background undoubtedly influenced how they were perceived and treated by others. Describe both a disadvantage and an advantage your ancestors may have experienced because of their ethnicity. Examples might include matters of religion, racial characteristics, economic background, language, family patterns, or political connections.

d. Look at any of the ethnic advantages you have listed. These are often reflected in family strengths, the desirable things people do or experience because they are members of a particular family and a particular ethnic group. Can you name any specific family strengths that you or your family members can link to your family's ethnic background or identity? List these.

e. Look at your list of family strengths. For each one, indicate how that strength has conferred some advantage or privilege on you, or on members of your immediate family. How have you or your family members benefited, or perhaps suffered, because of something you believe to be an important family characteristic?

f. In one or two sentences, name your ethnic background, and describe one specific benefit that you have received or enjoyed as a consequence of your ethnicity.

This exercise should generate data about your family background that illustrates a number of points concerning ethnicity. First, it makes it apparent that we are all "ethnic" in some way.

Second, the data you have on for your family background should have made it clear that ethnicity is something more than old family portraits, heirlooms, or preparation of "ethnic" dishes based on old-country recipes. Ethnicity is a matter of how people define themselves in specific situations, how they are defined by others, and the impact of those definitions on what people aspire to become and what they are able to accomplish. Ethnicity is transactional, not categorical, and how we are perceived ethnically has much to do with how we are treated by others.

Finally, your data should illustrate a fundamental social reality: there are no self-made men or women in this or any other society. What people possess in the way of position, material goods, opportunities, and a sense of importance relates in some measure to their ethnic group membership. Certainly there are "rugged individualists," high achievers, and those who claim to have "pulled themselves up by their own bootstraps." But the fact is that we all started with something fundamental, our communal membership. That gave each of us a position of advantage or disadvantage in relation to all others. Those advantages and disadvantages are often perpetuated over generations. Inherited position and entitlements and how we use them, not grandma's Norwegian Christmas cookies, are what make us ethnic.

Exercise 4. Racism as Rhetorical Form

Racism is an ugly topic and one that is insufficiently discussed by professionals in human service occupations. There are a number of reasons for this. First, the overt expression of racist sentiments is considered poor form in polite circles, although that does not usually prevent it in confidential or "locker room" conversations. Most educated people know the etiquette of racial language and it is the observance of that etiquette that accounts for the controlled expression of racial comments and jokes, especially in a climate of so-called political correctness.

Second, racism is often equated with prejudice and is assumed to represent an ignorant, uninformed, or unworthy attitude. It is something we would expect only of the ill-mannered (and perhaps violent) among us. Identifying these individuals as the carriers of an attitudinal problem pinpoints the blame. It also relieves the rest of us of complicity in their failings.

Third, racism is sometimes viewed as a holdover from our violent and unhappy history. Slavery, detention camps, and Indian hunting are fortunately behind us; the task of the future is creating positive change through education, job training, and service programs. Racism, it is hoped, will disappear along with memories of the circumstances that created it.

These views of racism, as impropriety, as ignorance, and as unfinished national business, are what make racism so difficult to see and to change. I suggest that as well-established public perceptions, they are part of the problem, not its solution. Why should that be so?

According to Barbara E. Shannon, writing some years ago in *Social Casework* (1970), racism really ought to be viewed as a value, like a political or a religious belief, one that serves some useful purpose for those who hold them. The nature of that purpose has been suggested by Wellman (1977), who regards racial speech and ideology as a defense of privileges, be they real or imagined. Racist terminology and jokes, displays of bigotry, or overt acts of discrimination are not simply instances of prejudice. They are rationalizations of advantages and angry responses to fears of their loss.

Wellman describes five kinds of rationales by which inequality is explained, and explained away, by people who normally would not consider themselves bigots. Each rationale is "reasonable," given a particular vantage point; each explanation justifies one's own place in society and the benefits thereby available. These rationales also account for the failure of others to enjoy the same benefits and privileges. I have summarized Wellman's descriptions but the presentation below is my own adaptation of his work. These positions on race, as values statements, are not dissimilar from explanations I have heard many time among students and from some in my workshops.

In this exercise, individuals or small discussion groups are assigned to one of the five statements given below. The groups should analyze their statement carefully, thinking about how or when they have heard comments similar to it before. Add further illustrative examples. Then read the four analytical questions at the end of the list of statements. Use these as the basis of a critique of the values implied in each statement. After discussion, write a brief response to each question that represents the consensus of the group. These can then be shared when the smaller groups are brought together for a general discussion and debriefing.

After you have completed your discussion of the statements and the analytical questions, turn to the short critique at the end of the exercise. Read it only after you have completed your general discussion. Compare and contrast the points presented.

Statements
a. Balance Sheet Justice
Resources are scarce, everyone has to struggle to get what they need, and there is really not enough time, energy, or money to do everything that we would all like to do. Priorities must be established and decisions made. It is too bad that minorities sometimes get shortchanged by government, service agencies, in health care, and other areas of entitlement. But perhaps they should do what others who came to this country have done: get their act together and put pressure on the system to get their fair share. They certainly deserve better than they have been given. But things being as they are, with recessions and public debt, it seems inevitable that the gains of some will be the loss of others. That's how the system works.

b. Changing Others
We live with many contradictions, and it is hard to know what is right. It may be true that in many ways this is a racist society, but there are many caring peope who wish it were otherwise. Discrimination in hiring is wrong but zealotry in affirmative action just alienates people. Better education for minorities would help, but at the same time there is a need to protect academic standards. Admittedly, social service organizations are sometimes inefficient and unfeeling, but if you stop to give special attention to one, then others just pile up at the door making demands of their own. Many of these difficulties will probably be solved when there is better education for everyone and they can find ways to get themselves into the mainstream.

c. Individualized Action
It is clear that there are inequalities. It is also clear that many people from disadvantaged groups make less use of what they do have, limited though it may be. There is a real need for these people to get on with the business of taking control of their lives, owning their own experience, and getting on the same page with everyone else. Ultimately, it all comes down to individual initiative, a little

assertiveness, rolling up your sleeves and really jumping into the job. People need to learn how to clarify what it is they want and then just go after it. Then things will change, at least for them.

d. Improving Communication

Basically, all people are the same and want the same things out of life. Color, class, and ethnic origins really make little difference except when people want them to. When individuals go into agencies, offices, even businesses, they are seeking specific solutions to specific problems. If difficulties and misunderstanding result, that is usually due to a failure of communication, not bad intentions. If people could only communicate better, they would have fewer difficulties. We all need to work on that.

e. Learning to Think Straight

Racism and tension make it impossible for people to really see what is happening to them. People get funny ideas, or they get paranoid and see things that aren't really there. We all have this problem of a limited perspective, of not knowing the impact of a statement or our behavior on others. But race and cultural differences only magnify what is already a complex situation. If people could only straighten out their thoughts and unravel all their feelings about this, it would help a lot. Healing begins with the individual and I devote my time and energy to healing myself. That helps me and it helps make a better world, one person at a time.

Analytical Questions for the Statements

1. Where does each statement assign responsibility for the current state of racial and ethnic tensions?

2. Who is made responsible for change before things can improve in a general sense?

3. In what way does each statement represent an affirmation of values? What are those values and to whom might they be important?

4. What likely agendas for intervention or policy might each statement support?

Complete your discussion, note your observations, then compare your results with those of other groups in a more general discussion.

Now turn to the critique below. Compare the results of all your discussions to the comments presented there.

Critique

As explanations of racial problems and injustice, these statement are, for the most part, liberal and polite accounts. They are not the remarks we would expect to hear from overt bigots. But they all have the function of separating the people who make them from the tragedy and misery they observe in others. They deny the communal nature of social problems and suggest that it is the victim alone who will have to make the changes necessary to improve things. No challenges to the status quo, nor to the privileged position of most whites in it, are contained here. Wellman notes that the essence of racism cannot be simple bigotry or meanness alone. It must include attitudes, acts, and speech patterns that have as their consequence the perpetuation of racially based limitations on other people's opportunities. Intentionally or not, each statement above is an example of that.

Exercise 5. Working through Racial Issues, One Case at a Time

If racism is not just Archie Bunker style bigotry but something more subtle, what are some positive steps that a genuinely concerned person can take? To put it bluntly, how can we move beyond guilt? Shannon (1970) has suggested a number of steps that workers who are members of the dominant group can take.

a. White practitioners can examine more carefully the social context of client beliefs and behavior before concluding that anything in it is destructive or inappropriate. This issue, very simply, is one of ethnocentrism and whether a social worker is imposing on clients behavior or standards that are intended to enhance the worker's own comfort or sense of control.

b. White practitioners need to know about the adaptive patterns common to the client's community and how they can be used to help resolve specific problems. This is partly a matter of having learned the necessary ethnographic background and of having acquired, in practice and participant observation, a well-grounded and informed sense of what is important and why.

c. White practitioners should be aware that their personal values and solutions are not the only ones, even within their own community. Like any ethnic group, the Anglo community is a heterogeneous one. Recommendations to clients must take account of community diversity.

d. White practitioners need to be very critical of research, policy statements, program guidelines, and related information which assumes the desirability of social service procedures when they are based only on white models or on data from white communities and white clients. There is a tendency for whites to unthinkingly assume that what is acceptable to them is equally acceptable to others.

For this activity, you need to recall the details of a case from your experiences in a social service or health care facility, either as a student, intern, or professional. The case must be one that, at the time you observed it, seemed to present special difficulties in cross-cultural communication, agreement on the nature of the problem, or compliance with treatment plans, a case where racial and/or cultural differences also seemed to be a factor.

Present your case to a small group for discussion, reporting what was said and who did what, much as a newspaper reporter would. Once the factual basis of the situation is familiar to everyone in the group, critique and analyze it in terms of the questions below. The questions are based on Shannon's critique. At the end of your discussion, propose specific steps that you or others might have taken to address the difficulties described.

Critique your case using the following questions:

a. What specific things did the staff seem to misunderstand about the client in question?

b. What presumptions did the staff hold about the client as a person, the nature of his or her concerns, and what could or couldn't be done about them?

c. What questions were asked to clarify the nature of the client's presenting problem? How thorough was the questioning? Was the information recorded?

d. What was done with the information the client or patient offered?

e. What questions were asked to ascertain that the client clearly understood the professional advice offered and was prepared to use it in the ways recommended?

The problems posed by Wellman and Shannon are not small ones, and for that reason I have not tried to suggest simplistic exercises to be used in learning about them. There are few simple solutions. These issues of racism, privilege, power and control are always with us and they need to be discussed candidly and frequently in preparing for entry into cross-cultural human services. They are troublesome issues and it is my hope that your discussion left you enlightened but also alerted to some of the hazards involved. As in all cross-cultural work, issues are more effectively analyzed within the context of specific cases rather than general principles. Affirming broad, humane guides to professional behavior is the easy part. It is more important that insight be generated within the context of case analysis and then be applied to other cases as opportunity permits. Only out of continual and explicit comparison will real principles of cross-cultural effectiveness emerge.

Exercise 6. Life in a Glass Box

Some years ago I interviewed an African-American worker about her work in a social service agency. Generally, she liked what she did and was a rising star in the program. We discussed the stresses that affected all the workers in her office—an impossible caseload, not enough time, mountains of paperwork—and also the satisfactions that came from helping people with difficult family and adoption issues.

After the formal interview was over and my note pad was put aside, she began talking about her relations with her peers. She was the only minority person in an office of about 30, and was one of the very few African Americans in the entire organization. Finally she said in an exasperated way that the worst part of her job was not the workload, or even the stresses that are normal in trying to assist frustrated clients. It was all the little presumptions about her made by fellow workers. As she put it, each day she was reminded that she was black and each day she was forced to feel that she was "on" as a minority person. For example, she was expected to have an opinion on prominent sports or pop music figures, especially those who were black. (She cared little about sports.) If someone in the office said they had had lunch at an ethnic restaurant (*any* ethnic restaurant), she would be given an expectant glance as though that was an area of her expertise. Casual questions were put to her about her opinions on the latest in South Africa, or a local news story on a civil rights figure. The questions and comments of her co-workers were always politely and kindly put; they just assumed she must have something to say because she was African American.

She concluded our discussion by stating that going home to her family was the most peaceful time of the day because no one there felt obligated to remind her that she was "an ethnic." At work, as she put it, she was always "on," but at home she could be "off." She could just be herself.

This exercise is one of imagination and creativity. Whatever your racial and/or ethnic affiliation, write down a list of all the things you would be presumed to know about and have opinions on, assuming that you are "on" among people culturally or racially unlike yourself. If you are a member of any ethnic community in America, that should not be too difficult. If you are white, you may have to give it more thought but examples should be forthcoming. Do not stop until you have at least ten items. It matters little how important or trivial the items seem to be. Sometimes, the trivial ones are the most annoying.

In group discussion, share your list. Minority members of the group may want to add personal examples from their experience. Whites who have traveled in other countries certainly should be able to give examples of stereotyping of themselves as Americans. Discuss what it would feel like for you to be "on" all day at work, and how you might feel when you return to home, family, or friends at night.

Done well, this exercise raises consciousness with astounding speed.

Exercise 7. Indulging Your Own Help-Seeking Behavior

We all have our favorite remedies for what ails us. Some are proven cures, some are doubtful but might have good effects, and others just make us feel more comfortable. Beliefs about illnesses, their causes, how they are transmitted, what medicines or foods may do for us when we are afflicted, and what kinds of outcomes we can expect all vary by ethnicity, our region of the country, perhaps by religion or educational level, and probably by generation.

Below is a list of five ailments, ranging from somewhat serious to very serious. You can choose others if you like but you are to use the help seeking behavior model described earlier (see chapter 2) to analyze your response to one of these conditions. Review the model, make a photocopy of the diagram that illustrates it, and on the photocopy write out how you would respond to the illness at each point in the sequence. If everyone in your discussion group chooses the same illness, you can compare the data you collect.

The illnesses are:

1. A "cold"
2. A hangover
3. AIDS
4. Depression
5. Constant headaches

What you are collecting in this exercise is ethnographic data, reflective of your state of knowledge, your beliefs, your best guesses, and perhaps your ignorance. But your information also says something about who and what you are. In your discussion of the data you and others have collected, seek to organize your information under the following headings:

1. The implicit or explicit theories of causation suggested by the data.

2. The historical or contemporary sources of those theories.

3. Evidence for and against the accuracy of the theories.

4. The sequence of help seeking and the kinds of persons one would go to for advice and help.

5. The range of potential remedies and why some were chosen and others not.

6. What you would do if your preferred intervention didn't work.

7. Who else in your community would respond to your help seeking behavior in the same way? Who would not, and why?

Finally, consider why some of the theories, treatments, and beliefs discussed in your group are historically important within specific ethnic communities. What values and behavior reinforce the health seeking behavior you described?

SECTION B. ACTIVITIES FOR BUILDING CULTURAL KNOWLEDGE

Exercise 1. The Pros in the Office: Minority Colleagues

The aim of the following activity is to help you clarify your own expectations about working with minority practitioners and clients—what you anticipate your knowledge and skill needs will be, and how you can expand your capabilities.

Before you can do this exercise, you need to arrange for a minority professional to meet with your group or class. Following the situated learning model,
their role is as a discussant, not a lecturer who will tell you what is right or wrong.
Part of doing this exercise is locating the discussant, explaining to that person
your learning needs, and clarifying how they can assist you and others. Obviously, getting to that point is part of preparing yourself to work cross-culturally
and it is much more than the logistics of simply arranging a meeting. So take your
selection of someone seriously and think through the process and what you
expect to learn from it. You may find some minority professionals who are willing
to give their time to this, and some who are not. That is part of the learning curve,
as well as the reality of race and ethnicity in America. They are busy professionals
too and you will have to make a case for the importance of their commitment of
time to your concerns.

This is a group discussion activity, with a minority professional available as
a mentor, not a presentor. Someone needs to take the role of moderator and lead
the discussion. Each participant is asked to respond to the statements below,
either verbally or in written form. One rule is that everyone must take a stand of
some kind. A polite "pass" on a given question is not acceptable because it defeats
the goal of learning through honest engagement of the issue. Part of the moderator's job is to refuse to accept a "pass" and to encourage a response of some kind
from everyone. There are no right or wrong answers, and each statement and
individual reply is deserving of fair and open discussion.

Statements

a. It is generally best that clients and practitioners be of the same ethnic background if any successful counseling or therapy is to be transacted. Therefore,
minority practitioners ought to assume primary responsibility for caseloads with
ethnic minority clients, because they are better qualified to do so.

b. White practitioners experience fewer discontinuities between personal and
professional values than do minority practitioners.

c. Learning the cultural values and norms of an ethnic minority client and having
some facility in his or her language are absolutely necessary in providing services.

d. There are uniform, established procedures for learning counseling skills and
for providing counseling services. These procedures should be taught and practiced without reference to the ethnicity of the social worker or client.

e. While cultural awareness training can provide important skills in handling
a multi-ethnic client caseload, it is unrealistic to suppose that a white practitioner
can do as well as a bicultural, bilingual practitioner in cross-cultural situations.

f. Minority professionals and dominant-group practitioners have different career paths, goals, and experiences. It is normal, therefore, for them to respond
differently to the expectations of their jobs. Agency and personnel evaluations
should take that into account.

g. While it is important for non-minority practitioners to work cooperatively with their minority colleagues, they should avoid interethnic counseling where they feel a lack of cultural knowledge about prospective clients.

h. Ethnic minority content should be widely dispersed in the social work curriculum, rather than concentrated in a few specialized courses or training programs.

As a follow-up exercise, plan to visit a minority-staffed social service agency in your community. Participants should meet with minority practitioners and discuss the kinds of interventive strategies they use and the value dilemmas or cultural conflicts they encounter on their jobs. These visits should be followed by discussion that compares and contrasts the procedures of the agencies visited with those where learners usually work.

Exercise 2. Social Mapping

This is an ideal exercise for beginning the work of communal learning, although it is really more of a long-term project than an exercise in the usual sense. It can be done in classes, agencies, and individually. It systematically explores the community an agency might serve and it can lead to specific agency benefits, especially where planning and community relations are involved. The various elements of this activity, listed below, could be assigned to "task forces" in a class which could then develop them as term projects.

In describing the concept of social mapping, Cochrane notes that "poverty is not merely a matter of not having things or access to them; it is also a matter of how people behave in particular cultural contexts" (Cochrane 1979:37). Social mapping is a way of learning about those contexts.

The task for the learner is to identify a community for study and become familiar with some of its cultural features in a general sense. The community can be a geographically coherent one or one that is dispersed but within which people experience similar problems and have common concerns. An example of the former would be an ethnically distinct neighborhood and the latter a group of single parents in a large city. The exercise requires collection and study of appropriate documents, including maps and census material; review of whatever sociological and anthropological studies of the community (or ones like it) that can be found; and development of a file of information to be used in training other social workers who may have clients from the community in question.

Following Cochrane's outline, and adapting it to the needs of social service workers, the exercise involves the following steps:

a. Define the community of interest and identify all relevant statistical and demographic information. On a map, draw the boundaries of the group and show any subdivisions that may be appropriate. Special attention should be given to subdivisions that are emically significant within the community. These would include the vernacular names for regions of the community and the significance of those designations. In addition, identify what might be called "local knowledge." For example, what streets do people there consider safe or unsafe? What neighborhoods are desirable for home ownership and which not? Where do those who are employed or upwardly mobile live, and those who are not? Where are older people concentrated, and younger people? What institutions serve the area and what are their reputations?

b. Describe the social organization of the community. Where are resources located, and who controls them? What are the leadership roles, formal and informal, and who occupies them? What types of organizations operate and who is in the important positions in each one? Certain values will probably attach to these organizations, and those values should be made as explicit as possible. Where there are important informal patterns, such as personal networks and cliques or factions, these should be identified and their significance described.

c. Describe the prevailing belief system in the community. What are the predominant values? In what kinds of symbols, ceremonies or community events are they expressed? What variations on prevailing values are permitted, tolerated, or disallowed? Where particular values seem important to the kinds of problems often handled by human service workers, those values should be defined in detail. Their bearing on intervention activities and outcomes should be made explicit. Topics for values analysis are almost endless, but examples include male-female relations, parent-child relations, patterns of sharing and reciprocity, generational differences, the use of wealth, beliefs about the larger society, attitudes toward social services, and the like. The ethnic contrast tables in each of the community chapters are useful for defining areas of interest.

d. Patterns of change, historical and recent, should be described. How has the community in question evolved? What shifts in wealth or political power have occurred? Can these be expected to continue, and what are their implications for social and health services?

e. How members of the community utilize social services should be described. Alternative sources of aid should be noted, and community preferences as well as complaints made explicit. The relationship of wealth, values, and community organization to the use of services is always a complex matter.

To pursue this study agenda in detail is a major task, one that should be broken into discrete pieces and assigned to different individuals for research. But the resulting information can be invaluable as an inventory of the community served and its needs and concerns. All information collected should be stored in a systematic way so that it is always available for training and consulting purposes. It can also serve as a basis for staff meetings and for planning new or revised services and policies.

Exercise 3. The Pleasures of Fieldwork, or, Life Is with People

The purpose of this exercise is to give participants a chance to meet people on their own turf, people that may have previously been known only in institutional settings. Both the chapter on ethnicity and that on language (see Chapters 1 and 4) have stressed the need for a client- and community-based perspective on needs and on how social services fit into local ways of meeting those needs. It is assumed that most participants in this exercise will already have had some kind of field placement or work experience with ethnically distinctive clients. But to know clients in institutional or agency settings is to know them only in the social worker's territory. This exercise reverses that procedure. It requires the participant to leave the safety and emotional supports of the office and enter the client's world.

This activity should *not* be viewed as "slumming." Nor should the learner wear the "social work" or "researcher" label in approaching others. The success of the exercise depends on dropping those role identities and appearing simply as an interested individual who is willing to learn whatever others are willing to share.

In addition to meeting people in naturalistic settings, this exercise introduces an important technique for learning about culturally distinctive communities. A key respondent in participant observation research is an individual who acts as a guide to the community the learner wishes to know more about. A good key respondent is knowledgeable and articulate about the place he or she lives, is willing to share that knowledge, and has the time and interest to accommodate the learner. Finding and establishing a working relationship with a key respondent is a standard feature of all intensive cross-cultural work. Here that technique is applied to the needs of the social service practitioner.

Each participant should identify an agency in which he or she has previously been involved. Make a list of the kinds of clients served: where they came from, what they wanted, how they acted, and how their problems were treated. Then describe in one paragraph how staff members (including the participant) felt about these individuals: Were they likable? Agreeable? Easy to sympathize with? Easy to work with? People one would want to know on a social basis? If staff discussions or remarks can be recalled, write them down as well. This should be a summarizing statement of staff beliefs and attitudes toward a specific group or category of clients. This can be done as an individual assignment or a group activity.

Identify an individual who can serve as a key respondent for several hours or for part of a day. That person may be another social worker, but also could be an acquaintance or former client. The key respondent must be a member of the ethnic community in question; reliance on whites who claim to be knowledgeable (even when they are) is not acceptable. Explain your purposes to the respondent: to learn something of the community as community members see it; to better understand why clients from the community have need of specific services; to appreciate how people use community resources to deal with their problems; to discover how people feel about their relations with the larger society in general and with social service institutions and providers in particular.

You should ask (1) to be taken to the kinds of places where people in the community are likely to gather, or (2) to be taken to an activity that is common in the community. During your visitation, you are to be yourself and simply act natural. If you present yourself as the cool scientific observer or as the enthusiastic, admiring devotee of the quaint and exotic, you will not only offend others and embarrass your respondent, but you will have failed the exercise. Becoming a learner in someone else's culture is a humbling as well as a sensitizing experience. Approach it that way.

After your visit, return to your list about clients. Compare that information with your experience. Are the points made there supported or refuted by what you saw or heard, or by what your key respondent described? Does your initial information need to be modified or amplified in any way? If you were to report back to the staff about your experience, what would you want to tell them that would be useful in improving delivery of services?

Share your list and observations in a group discussion. Discuss your findings in terms of possible discrepancies between the view of clients held by those who see them as "cases" and what you observed. Each participant in the exercise should make one specific suggestion for modifying services or training in terms of what was discovered during the community visit. List these and see if they could be developed into a general statement of service or training recommendations.

Exercise 4. Participant Observation

There are many minority-oriented and operated social service agencies, and their number is growing. They serve every ethnic group and deal with most of the needs handled by professionals in other agencies. But they often have a special tone that sets them apart from more established organizations. Part of that is due to the backgrounds of the clients and social workers, and the distinctive ways in which they interact. Frequently, minority agencies work to emulate in their services some of the cultural characteristics of the communities they serve. They usually do this under serious financial limitations, limitations which are disruptive but which also increase the sense of urgency and importance about the work they do.

A visit to a minority social service agency can be an illuminating experience, not only for social work students but also for established professionals. I used the list of questions and statements below in a study in which white social workers made visits to minority agencies (Green and Wilson 1983). The list was used for training purposes, and it suggests some of the things that social workers can ask about and look for as participant observers.

A word of caution: for an activity like this, the staff of a minority agency must be approached with all the sensitivity that would be involved in any effort to enter an unfamiliar community. Minority professionals are overworked and underpaid, and they get more requests from whites for "resource" assistance than they can reasonably fulfill. White workers who are negotiating informational visits need to make clear what benefits, if any, will accrue to minority agencies for the time and effort they invest.

General Background

a. What is the recent history of minority social service organizations of this type in your area? How and when were they established, and what do they do?

b. What kind of training and experience is common for staff members in agencies of this type?

c. What kinds of relationships do minority agencies have with one another, with large state organizations, and with county and city organizations? What benefits derive from those relationships?

Working with Clients in Minority and Ethnic Group Agencies

a. What are some of the common problems or complaints that are brought by clients to the agency?

b. In making an assessment or diagnosis of some of these issues, what kinds of questions do staff members ask their clients? Are there questions you might not have thought of yourself? Give some examples.

c. Do staff members feel that any of their client's needs are related to class or to the cultural characteristics of their community? If so, describe what these might be.

d. What are some of the treatment plans or intervention strategies most commonly used in the agency? Describe how an intervention plan is developed.

e. Are there any significant ways that these plans differ from those of other minority agencies or from those of agencies serving largely white clients?

f. Do the concerns that clients bring to the agency and the ways staff deal with them suggest norms or values that are typical of the client community? Can these be defined and described?

Adjusting to a New Agency

a. Are there some common errors of assessment, diagnosis, or treatment that a visitor or social worker unfamiliar with the agency or its clients might make? Can you describe an example?

b. Are there any special communication techniques or skills that a visitor or new social worker should know about?

c. Are there any special words or phrases used by clients or staff members that might have a special meaning in the agency or the community? If so, list some and define them.

Exercise 5. Revisiting Minority Professionals

Most minority professionals have special insights into the needs of the communities they serve. In addition, they are usually sensitive to the way social service organizations affect persons of minority background generally. What they know is "insider information," the emic perspective. White social workers can learn much from their minority colleagues if they choose to do so. This activity assumes you have the opportunity to meet with a minority professional to discuss their work. The questions listed below are examples of things that they might be asked. Other questions can and should be added to the list.

Relations with Clients of Minority Groups

a. What are the distinctive problems of the minority clients whom you see?

b. Are there things that minority clients might say to a minority worker that they would probably not tell a white social worker?

c. How do they describe these things to you? Is there any special language or terminology they use?

d. What do clients expect you as a minority professional to understand intuitively about them and their needs?

e. What do you think clients look for in you that they would not expect in a white social worker?

f. Are there any distinctive advantages that you as a minority professional have with your clients?

Relations with White Social Workers

a. In the relations of white social workers with minority clients, as you have seen them, is there anything that troubles you?

b. In your professional relations with white social workers, is there anything that troubles you? How could white social workers be more supportive of you as a minority professional?

c. What do you think white social workers could do or should know if they want to work more effectively with minority clients?

d. If a new social worker were assigned to your agency tomorrow, one who had never worked with minority clients before, and your task was to spend the day getting this worker started, specifically what would you do, and what would you want him or her to know by the end of the day?

Role of Education

a. What in your formal or informal education best prepared you for working with minority clients?

b. What else would have helped?

c. How do you keep up with research and other literature on minority communities and clients? What sources are important to you?

d. What advice would you give to a class of aspiring minority social work students?

Agency and Policy

a. Can you describe instances where you felt the needs of your clients were in conflict with the kind of services offered by your agency, or in conflict with its policies?

b. Can you give an instance where you felt that your agency had failed a minority client? Why do you think that happened?

c. If you could restructure your office, program, or the personnel in it to better serve minority clients, what would you do?

Exercise 6. Describing Cultural Sequences

One technique for acquiring ethnographic information is to record sequences of events that can later be analyzed for their cultural content and significance. Virtually anything can be a sequence in a given culture, provided it is repetitive and is typical of the people there. The possibilities are endless. At the macrolevel, the developmental cycle of the family is a common organizing device. The idea originally came from the work of Fortes (1958), in his studies of African family systems, and it has been widely extended since then. The career of the individual is a potential sequence. Life histories are collected by ethnographers in order to identify cultural themes as they are experienced by individuals (Langness 1965). Goffman (1961) has used the career concept in what he calls the "moral career" of the mental patient. Spradley (1970) has defined and described the career of inner-city tramps, people he called "urban nomads." He was particularly interested in those parts of their careers involving police, jailers, and the courts.

Culturally standardized sequences of interest to social workers are as diverse as the clients their agencies serve. Examples would include: what happens during and after a wife battering episode; the stages of anxiety experienced by foster children when they are shifted into new accommodations; grieving patterns among parents who lose a child; use of folk or over-the-counter medicines by elders; response phases of those who have been informed they have cancer; how the mentally ill in minority communities act out aggression; adjustment to nursing homes, prisons, or other institutions; events leading up to teenage suicides and how they vary from community to community.

There is a common methodology that is usable by social service professionals with an interest in acquiring ethnographic information.

The steps involved in this methodology are as follows:

a. Establish a problem to be investigated. Write it down. Define all the terms as completely as possible. This sets the boundaries of the inquiry.

b. Examine the literature on the problem. Read across disciplines as appropriate. To limit the inquiry to the literature of a single discipline is the formula for parochialism. Read for data, methods, and general conclusions. Summarize these in writing.

c. Define hypotheses, specific problems, or issues to be examined. Be precise and write them down. This is a critical step, for it tells the observer what to look for at the field site. Without it, there can be no disciplined inquiry.

d. Determine appropriate recording techniques. Is the investigator going to take notes, use a tape recorder, or depend on memory? Whatever technique is used, it obviously should be practiced, so that it is not obtrusive.

e. Make repeated, detailed, and accurate observations of all the things relevant to the hypotheses or statements of problems. It will be apparent at this stage whether or not the hypotheses were sufficiently precise to allow identification of only those things that the observer wishes to record. Compile and index the results.

f. Analyze the data. What do they suggest about each of the hypotheses or problem statements? How do they bear on the discussion of the problem as represented in the research literature? How do they advance the learner's knowledge of the culture in question?

g. Draw your conclusions, and state them as new or revised hypotheses. Specify the population to which they apply and to what extent they can be generalized. Relate your findings to what you know about clients of this type generally and to how the information might be used in intervention, in training, and in further research.

These steps do not differ significantly from other forms of social inquiry. But their application to standardized behavior among members of a single community can result in a surprising quantity of data in a short period of time.

Exercise 7. Cover Terms and Attributes

Use of linguistic clues provided by respondents is one of the quickest, most efficient ways of acquiring ethnographic information. The technique, as I have outlined it, is a simple one, although it has been developed by Spradley (1979) as part of a larger and much more complex investigative process, and his publications should be consulted for more details. All that is required by the learner is a linguistic sample from a respondent. For instance, consider the following bit of conversation, taken from my own research notes of an interview with a child protective service worker:

> *I see all kinds of clients. Just recently I worked with a woman who was very disturbed; I'd say she had severe depression. Her child had a number of contusions on the head and arms and the X-rays showed subdural hematoma. I took that as evidence of the battered child syndrome and asked the judge for a preliminary hearing.*

Just this snippet of conversation contains enough cover terms to keep an interview going for an hour or more. Remember that I described a cover term as a word or expression, sometimes in a vernacular, that may be unfamiliar to the interviewer but seems to have particular meaning or importance for the respondent. In this sample, there are at least seven cover terms of interest: clients, disturbed, depression, contusions, subdural hematoma, battered child syndrome, and preliminary hearing. Each term stands for, or "covers," a block of information that is part of the shared subculture of protective service workers, the things they know as members of a specialized and distinctive professional community. (Some of the terms, of course, are shared with other subcultures—other kinds of social workers, doctors, and lawyers, for example—and their meanings may shift somewhat from one professional culture to another.) These words are the emic labels of the professional subculture.

Using the cover terms as guides, we can begin to elicit descriptors which will help us define the cultural world of these social workers. Descriptors are identified by asking questions concerning kinds, qualities, features, characteristics, relationships, and the like. For instance, if this was our first of several interviews with this person, we might ask a global question: "How many kinds of clients are there? Can you list them for me?" For example, the respondent's comments suggest that there is a large category, *disturbed*, of which *depression* is a special case and *severe depression* is an even finer subdivision of the category. We might ask, therefore: "When you say *disturbed*, how many things does that include?" Or we could ask: "Can you tell me some of the characteristics of *depression* that you look for, and what distinguishes *severe* depression from that which is less severe?"

In short, we are asking: How do you know it when you see it? What to you are a category's descriptive characteristics? This same line of questioning can be applied to the other cover terms in the sample. Some terms may be precise, such as the legal or medical ones; others are more generalized. But it is having these terms defined as clearly as possible, and under conceptual control by the worker, that is our goal. Without that, how could we expect to have precision and accuracy in our assessments, diagnoses, and evaluations?

We do not demand full, exhaustive information from one respondent. Where the respondent's knowledge is unclear, that too provides important insight. For example, if the social worker's knowledge of the descriptors for *battered child* syndrome is vague, contradictory, or shifting, that in itself would be important to know since it would tell us that this worker is making decisions about intervention without a clear idea of what is involved. If interviews show that to be true of a number of workers, we would have hard data for making a case for better training. The data would have come to us through ethnographic interviewing.

It is clear that even a tiny fragment of linguistic information is a clue to a great deal of cultural knowledge. The worker need only find the clues, the cover terms, and pursue them in a systematic way. The possibilities for doing this are endless. Spradley and McCurdy (1972) published examples of their students' interviews in a text for college freshmen. Those interviews ranged from subcultures as diverse as airline stewardesses to organized car thieves. Social workers who want to practice the technique can do so with other workers, focusing on the specialized tasks, skills, or client communities associated with their interview partners. Where willing clients are available, they might be interviewed on topics of interest to them.

Exercise 8. Genograms

Most of us have thought about who we are related to and what our family tree looks like. Some people go to great effort and expense to document a family "line," discovering perhaps that they are linked to a famous personage. I put that word line in quotes because a line is not the only way to think about family connections, nor is it the most revealing. Family "trees" (a variant on the line idea) are really fictions since we tend to be selective in how we trace the links. A more accurate way to think of genealogical connections is to start with oneself and then branch out in all directions: back in time; horizontally within one's generation; forward into the future. The graphic representation that results is less like a tree and more like a star, with oneself at the center. Only siblings would have the same star, although the stars of others in the immediate family would overlap considerably.

Ego-centered genealogies roughly shaped like a star have been common in social science research for many years and anthropologists have long used them to graph out relations in traditional societies where kin are one's primary contacts throughout life. They have a proven cross-cultural learning purpose. But could they have clinical utility as well?

Several years ago, Monica McGoldrick and Randy Gerson published an interesting book entitled *Genograms in Family Assessment* (New York: W.W. Norton, 1985). They suggested that genograms can be a valuable clinical tool. They allow one to see in visual form the structural, relational, and evolutionary features of a specific family. They write:

> *Scanning the breadth of the current family context allows the clinician to assess the connectedness of the immediate players in the family drama to each other, as well as to the broader system, and to evaluate the family's strengths and vulnerabilities in relation to the overall situation. . . . Current behavior and the problems of family members can then be traced on the genogram from multiple perspectives (1985:3).*

In addition to mapping a variety of family relationships among current members and how they function, McGoldrick and Gerson suggest specific clinical uses for the data. They show how genograms can be used in family practice to engage a family, clarify the family relationships of each member, "reframe and detoxify" contentious family issues, and aid in family assessment and management of ongoing concerns.

To pursue McGoldrick and Gerson's recommendations in detail, you will need to consult their book, something I strongly recommend. For purposes of this exercise, however, I want to suggest the following activity which is only an introduction to their excellent presentation on genograms.

a. In the first step, create a genogram for yourself. Following McGoldrick and Gerson's conventions, use a small square if you are male and a small circle if you are female. Draw the icon for yourself in the middle of a blank page and start adding on all the family members you can recall. Use vertical lines to represent generational differences. One line straight up from you would connect to a square and circle for your parents. They would be connected by a horizontal line that intersects with your vertical line because they are of the same generation, the one senior to you. Use horizontal lines to link yourself to your siblings and downward vertical lines to connect to any children you may have. Use lowercase letters of your own choosing to mark on each line what it represents: *m* for marriage, *s* for siblings, and the like. Deceased individuals are usually shown with a slant mark over their icon.

Think about some event that was a challenge to you and the members of your family. Perhaps it was a death, a divorce, a serious illness or accident, or a long period of separation. In reference to that event, and how it appeared to you at that time, go through your genogram and write a detailed description of the behavior of the individuals on the chart—what they did; what they didn't do; where misunderstandings were; where the faction line formed. What roles did people play—mediator, fomenter, martyr, spy, tyrant, confessor, bystander, victim, perpetrator, broker? As you can see, if the family is a three-generational one, an extended family, had adoptive relationships, or divorces and remarriages, the potential for rich ethnographic documentation is great. You are beginning to see the emic structure and patterns of a specific family unit—your own.

b. Now turn to information you may have on a client, someone in an agency where you worked or were a volunteer. From memory, attempt to reconstruct their genogram based on your experience with them or agency records you might have seen. Then compare the results to your own genogram. How comprehensive is your data (and understanding) of them when compared to your own family? What does their chart tell you that you might have missed, and what would you have had to do to generate more insight about their family and the circumstances behind the presenting problem they brought to you? How might you use a genogram if you were to work with them again? How would a genogram help you keep track of all the members of a family and their relationships—good, bad, or otherwise?

Exercise 9. NASW Code of Ethics in Cross-Cultural Learning

The National Association of Social Workers publishes a Code of Ethics. Adopted in 1979 and revised in 1990, the Code "is intended to serve as a guide to the everyday conduct of members of the social work profession" and "is based on the fundamental values of the social work profession that include the worth, dignity, and uniqueness of all persons as well as their rights and opportunities" (1990:iii). With the permission of the NASW, I have reproduced here selected portions of the Code, followed by topics for discussion in a class exercise.

Section II-G

Rights and Perogatives of Clients. *The social worker should make every effort to foster maximum self-determination on the part of clients.*

What does "maximum self-determination" mean in reference to minority clients? Review the contrast table in one of the ethnic community chapters and the discussion of family values. Within that cultural context, how might "maximum self-determination" be promoted?

Section V-O

Development of Knowledge. *The social worker should take responsibility for identifying, developing, and fully utilizing knowledge for professional practice.*

How can your experience with clients ethnically or racially different from yourself become part of the knowledge base of your office, agency, or the profession? If you were to make up a list of important things you have learned, however brief or extensive your experience might be, what would be on the list? What additional things would you want to know? How could your private knowledge be made available to others so they could benefit from it? What obstacles in your office or agency keep that from happening? What might you do to improve the situation?

Section VI-P, 3, 4

Promoting the General Welfare. *3. The social worker should act to expand choice and opportunity for all persons, with special regard for disadvantaged or oppressed groups and persons. 4. The social worker should promote conditions that encourage respect for the diversity of cultures which constitute American society.*

What choices and opportunities do clients want in any of the cultural communities you serve? What are some of the limitations on choice that are culturally imposed, limitations on men, women, younger persons, or older persons? Do those constraints seem to contradict norms of the larger society, or of the community you come from? Where they do, what practical limitations do they place on the injunction of the Code "to expand choice and opportunity"?

How are choices constrained by the dynamics of racism and poverty in the larger society? Again, what are some of the limitations the larger society places on men, women, younger persons, or older persons within specific ethnic communities? How do they interfere with expanded choice and opportunity? In specific cases, what can you as a social worker do about it that is also consist with community cultural expectations and practice?

As always, this exercise works best when applied to a case rather than debated in the abstract. Cases are widely available, in the social service journals and in texts. Visiting professionals can also provide examples for discussion. Members of the class who have had direct service experience may also be able to present cases, respecting of course, the privacy of those involved.

TABLE 10.1   Checklist of Cross-Cultural Learning Exercises

Exercise	General Practice
A. Expanding Cultural Awareness	
1. First Impressions	Ethnic Diversity
2. Professional Values	Ecological Issues
3. Identity	Ethnic Diversity
4. Racism and Rhetoric	Race
5. Race and Cases	Engagement
6. Glass Boxes	Engagement
7. Help Seeking Behavior	Data Collection
B. Building Cultural Knowledge	
1. Minority Colleagues	Professional Values
2. Social Mapping	Ecological Issues
3. Fieldwork	Data Collection
4. Participant Observation	Engagement
5. Minority Professionals	Data Collection
6. Cultural Sequences	Assessment
7. Cover Terms	Assessment
8. Genograms	Assessment/Evaluation
9. NASW Code	Practice/Policy

BIBLIOGRAPHY

Aberle, David F.
   1951   "The Psychological Analysis of a Hopi Life-History." *Comparative Psychology Monographs* 21:80–138.

Abrahams, Roger D.
   1964   *Deep Down in the Jungle*. Hatboro, PA: Pennsylvania Folklore Society.
   1970   "A Performance Centered Approach to Gossip." *Man* 5:290–301.
   1972   "Folklore and Literature as Performance." *Journal of the Folklore Institute* 9:75–91.

Abramovitz, Mimi
   1991   "Putting an End to Doublespeak About Race, Gender, and Poverty: An Annotated Glossary for Social Workers." *Social Work* 36:380–384.

Acosta-Belen, Edna and Barbara R. Sjostrom, eds.
   1988   *The Hispanic Experience in the United States*. New York: Praeger.

Aitchison, Jean
   1987   *Words in the Mind*. Oxford: Basil Blackwell.

Alba, Richard D.
   1990   *Ethnic Identity: The Transformation of White America*. New Haven, CT: Yale University Press.

Alba, Richard D., and Mitchell B. Chamlin
   1983   "A Preliminary Examination of Ethnic Identification among Whites." *American Sociological Review* 48:240–247.

Albers, Patricia C., and William R. James
   1986   "On the Dialectics of Ethnicity: To Be or Not To Be a Santee (Sioux)." *Journal of Ethnic Studies* 14:1–27.

Albert, Steven M.
  1990   "Caregiving as a Cultural System." *American Anthropologist* 92:319–331.

Alleyne, Mervyn
  1988   *Roots of Jamaican Culture.* London: Pluto Press.

Allison, Maria T., and Charles W. Geiger
  1993   "The Nature of Leisure Activities among the Chinese-American Elderly." *Leisure Sciences* 15:309–319.

Alasuutari, Pertti
  1992   *Desire and Craving: A Cultural Theory of Alcoholism.* Albany: State University of New York Press.

Amaro, Hortensio, and Nancy Felipe Rosso
  1987   "Hispanic Women and Mental Health, an Overview of Contemporary Issues in Research and Practice." *Psychology of Women Quarterly* 11:393–407.

Amaro, Hortensio, Nancy Felipe Russo, and Jose A. Pares-Avila
  1987   "Contemporary Research on Hispanic Women: A Selected Bibliography of the Social Science Literature." *Psychology of Women Quarterly* 11:523–532.

American Psychiatric Association
  1987   *Diagnostic and Statistical Manual of Mental Disorders, DSM-III-R.* Washington, D.C.: American Psychiatric Association.

Anderson, Benedict
  1983   *Imagined Communities.* London: Verso.

Andre, J.M.
  1979   *The Epidemiology of Alcoholism among American Indians and Natives.* Albuquerque: Indian Health Service.

Arvizu, Steven F., and Warren Snyder
  1977   *Demystifying the Concept of Culture: Conceptual Tools.* Sacramento, CA: Sacramento State University.

Asamoah, Yvonne, Alejandro Garcia, Carmen Ortiz Hendricks, and Joe Walker
  1991   "What We Call Ourselves: Implications for Resources, Policy, and Practice." *Journal of Multicultural Social Work* 1:7–23.

Asian American Community Mental Health Training Center
  1983   *Bridging Cultures: Southeast Asian Refugees in America.* Los Angeles: The Center.

Atkin, Karl, and Janet Rollings
  1992   "Informed Care in Asian and Afro/Caribbean Communities: A Literature Review." *British Journal of Social Work* 22:405–418.

Atkinson, Donald R.
  1983   "Ethnic Similarity in Counseling Psychology: A Review of the Research." *Counseling Psychologist* 11:79–92.

Attneave, Carolyn
  1982   American Indian and Alaska Native Families: Emigrants in Their Own Homeland. In Monica Mc Goldrick, John K. Pearce, and Joseph Giordano, eds. *Ethnicity and Family Therapy*. New York: The Guilford Press.

Baer, Hans A.
  1981   "Black Spiritual Churches: A Neglected Socio-Religious Institution." *Phylon* 42:207–223.

Baer, Hans A., and Merrill Singer
  1981   Toward a Typology of Black Sectarianism as a Response to Racial Stratification. *Anthropological Quarterly* 54:1–14

Baer, Robert D., and Marta Bustillo
  1993   "*Susto* and *Mal de Ojo* among Florida Farmworkers: Emic and Etic Perspectives." *Medical Anthropology Quarterly* 7:90–100.

Bailey, Roy, and Mike Brake, eds.
  1975   *Radical Social Work*. New York: Random House.

Baker, Houston A.
  1972   *Long Black Song: Essays in Black American Literature and Culture*. Charlottesville: University Press of Virginia.
  1984   *Blues, Ideology, and Afro-American Literature: A Vernacular Theory*. Chicago: University of Chicago Press.

Baldwin, James
  1985   *The Evidence of Things Unseen*. New York: Holt, Rinehart, and Winston.

Barker, Philip
  1990   *Clinical Interviews With Children and Adolescents*. New York: W.W. Norton.

Barnow, Victor
  1963   *Culture and Personality*. Homewood IL: Dorsey Press.

Barth, Frederik
  1969   *Ethnic Groups and Boundaries*. Boston: Little, Brown.

Bass, Barbara Ann, Gail Elizabeth Wyatt, and Gloria Johnson Powell, eds.
  1982   *The Afro-American Family: Assessment, Treatment and Research Issues*. New York: Grune and Stratton.

Basso, Keith
  1979   *Portraits of 'The Whiteman': Linguistic Play and Cultural Symbols among the Western Apache*. Cambridge: Cambridge University Press.

Basso, Keith, and Henry A. Shelby, eds.
  1976   *Meaning in Anthropology.* Albuquerque: University of New Mexico Press.

Bataille, Gretchen M., and Charles L. P. Silet
  1980   *The Pretend Indians: Images of Native Americans in the Movies.* Ames, IA: Iowa State
          University Press.

Bauman, Richard, and Joel Sherzer, eds.
  1974   *Explorations in the Ethnography of Speaking.* New York: Cambridge University Press.

Bauwens, Eleanor
  1977   "Medical Beliefs and Practices among Lower Income Anglos." In Edward H.
          Spicer, ed. *Ethnic Medicine in the Southwest.* Tuscon: University of Arizona Press.

Beauvais, Fred, and Steve LaBoueff
  1985   Drug and Alcohol Abuse Intervention in American Indian Communities. *International Journal of Addictions* 2:139–171.

Becker, Howard S., and James W. Carper
  1956   "The Development of Identification with an Occupation," *American Journal of Sociology* 61:289–298.

Bellah, Robert N., Richard Madsen, William M. Sullivan, Ann Swindler, and Steven M.
Tipton
  1985   *Habits of the Heart.* Berkeley: University of California Press.

Benedict, Ruth
  1934   *Patterns of Culture.* New York: New American Library.

Benjamin, Alfred
  1981   *The Helping Interview.* Boston: Houghton Mifflin.

Bennett, Claire J., Julianne Legon, and Felice Zilbertein
  1990   "The Significance of Empathy in Current Hospital Based Practice." *Social Work in Health Care* 14:27–41.

Bennett, John W., ed.
  1975   *The New Ethnicity: Perspectives from Ethnology.* St. Paul: West Publishing Co.

Berger, Charles R., and William Douglas
  1982   "Thought and Talk: 'Excuse Me, But Have I Been Talking to Myself?' " In Frank
          E. X. Dance, ed. *Human Communication Theory.* New York: Harper and Row.

Berger, Peter L.
  1965   "Toward a Sociological Understanding of Psychoanalysis." *Social Research* 32:26–41.

Billingsley, Andrew
  1968   *Black Families in White America.* Englewood Cliffs, NJ: Prentice Hall.

1969   "Family Functioning in the Low Income Black Community." *Social Casework* 50:536–572.

Blanchard, Evelyn
    1983   "The Growth and Development of American Indian and Alaska Native Children." In Gloria Johnson Powell ed. *The Psychosocial Development of Minority Group Children*. New York: Brunner/Mazel.

Blanchard, Evelyn, and Steven Unger
    1977   "Destruction of American Indian Families." *Social Casework* 58:312–314.

Bloch, Julia B.
    1968   "The White Worker and the Negro Client in Psychotherapy." *Social Work* 13:36–42.

Boas, Franz
    1943   "Recent Anthropology." *Science* 98:311–314.

Bochner, Stephen
    1981   *The Mediating Person*. Cambridge, MA: Schenkman.

Boekestijn, C.
    1984   "Intercultural Migration and the Development of Personal Identity." Presented at the *Seventh International Congress of Cross-Cultural Psychology*, Acapulco, Mexico.

Bogdan, Robert
    1972   *Participant Observation in Organizational Settings*. Syracuse, NY: Syracuse University Press.

Bose, Aruna, Krishan Vashistha, and Bernard J. O'Loughlin
    1983   "Azarcon por Empacho—Another Cause of Lead Toxicity." *Pediatrics* 72:106–108.

Boyle, Joyceen S., and Margaret M. Andrews
    1989   *Transcultural Concepts in Nursing Care*. Glenview, IL: Scott, Foresman.

Brice, Janet
    1982   "West Indian Families." In Monica McGoldrick, John K. Pearce, and Joseph Giordano, eds. *Ethnicity and Family Therapy*. New York: The Guilford Press.

Briggs, Charles L.
    1986a   *Learning How to Ask*. Cambridge: Cambridge University Press.

Briggs, Jean
    1986b   "Kapluna Daughter." In Peggy Golde, ed. *Women in the Field: Anthropological Experiences*. Berkeley: University of California Press.

Brislin, Richard W., ed.
    1976   *Topics in Cultural Learning*. Honolulu, HI: East-West Center.

Brislin, Richard W., and Paul Pedersen
    1976   *Cross-Cultural Orientation Programs.* New York: Gardner Press.

Brookhiser, Richard
    1991   *The Way of the Wasp.* New York: The Free Press.

Brown, Linda K., and Kay Mussell, eds.
    1984   *Ethnic and Regional Foodways in the United States.* Knoxville: University of Tennessee Press.

Buijs, Gina, ed.
    1993   *Migrant Women: Crossing Boundaries and Changing Identities.* Oxford: Berg.

Bullock, Henry
    1967   *A History of Negro Education in the South from 1619 to the Present.* Cambridge: Harvard University Press.

Burciaga, José Antonio
    1993   *Drink Cultura: Chicanismo.* Santa Barbara, CA: Capra Press.

Burgest, David R.
    1983   "Principles of Social Casework and the Third World." *International Social Work* 26:7–23.
    1989   *Social Work Practice with Minorities.* Metuchen, NJ: Scarecrow Press.

Buriel, Raymond
    1984   "Integration with Traditional Mexican-American Culture and Sociocultural Adjustment." In Joe L. Martinez, Jr., and Richard H. Mendoza, eds. *Chicano Psychology.* Orlando, FL: Academic Press.

Canino, Glorisa J., Maritza Rubio-Stipec, Patrick Shrout, Milagros Bravo, Robert Stolberg, and Hector R. Bird
    1987   "Sex Differences and Depression in Puerto Rico." *Psychology of Women Quarterly* 11:443–459.

Caplan, Nathan, Marcella H. Choy, and John K. Whitmore
    1992   "Indochinese Refugee Families and Academic Achievement." *Scientific American,* February:36–42.

Caracena, Philip F., and James R. Vicory
    1969   "Correlates of Phenomenological and Judged Empathy." *Journal of Counseling Psychology* 16:510–515.

Carroll, John B., ed.
    1956   *Language, Thought, and Reality: Selected Writings of Benjamin Lee Whorf.* Cambridge: MIT Press.

Chan, Sucheng
    1991   *Asian Americans: An Interpretive History.* Boston: Twayne Publishers.

Charles, James A.
  1987   "The Misrepresentation of American Indians and Their Literature in High School Literature Anthologies." *Journal of Ethnic Studies* 15:131–140.

Chatters, Linda M., Robert Joseph Taylor, and James S. Jackson
  1985   "Size and Comparison of the Informal Helper Networks of Elderly Blacks." *Journal of Gerontology* 40:605–614.
  1986   "Aged Blacks' Choices for an Informal Helper Network." *Journal of Gerontology* 41:94–100.

Chavez, John M., and Collette E. Roney
  1990   "Psychocultural Factors Affecting the Mental Health Status of Mexican American Adolescents." In Arlene Rubin Stiffman, and Larry E. Davis, eds. *Ethnic Issues in Adolescent Mental Health.* Newbury Park, CA: Sage.

Cheng, Li-Rong Lilly
  1987   *Assessing Asian-Language Performance.* Rockville, MD: Aspen.

Cheung, Monit
  1989   "Elderly Chinese Living in the United States: Assimilation or Adjustment?" *Social Work* 34:457–461.

Chin, Jean Lau
  1983   "Diagnostic Considerations in Working With Asian-Americans." *American Journal of Orthopsychiatry* 53:100–109.

Christian, Charles M., Mary Dufour, and Darryl Bertolucci
  1989   "Differential Alcohol-Related Mortality Among American Indian Tribes in Oklahoma, 1968–1978." *Social Science and Medicine* 28:274–285.

Christie, Laird, and Joel M. Halpern
  1990   "Temporal Constructs and Inuit Mental Health." *Social Science and Medicine* 30:739–749.

Christodoulou, Costas
  1991   "Racism—a Challenge to Social Work Education and Practice: The British Experience." *Journal of Multicultural Social Work* 1:99–107.

Chung, Douglas K.
  1992   "Asian Cultural Commonalities: A Comparison with Mainstream American Culture." In Sharlene Maeda Furuto, Renoka Biswas, Douglas K. Chung, Kenji Murase, and Fariyal Ross-Sheriff, eds. *Social Work Practice with Asian Americans.* Newbury Park, CA: Sage.

Chunn, Jay C. III, Patricia J. Dunston, and Fariyal Ross-Sheriff, eds.
  1983   *Mental Health and People of Color.* Washington, DC: Howard University Press.

Clark, Margaret
  1959   *Health in the Mexican-American Culture: A Community Study.* Berkeley: University of California Press.

Clarke, Edith
1957 *My Mother Who Fathered Me.* London: George Allen and Unwin.

Cloward, Richard, and Frances Fox Piven
1975 "Notes Toward a Radical Social Work." In Roy Bailey, and Mike Brake, eds. *Radical Social Work.* New York: Random House.

Cochrane, Glynn
1979 *The Cultural Appraisal of Development Projects.* New York: Praeger.

Cogan, Morris L.
1953 "Toward a Definition of Profession." *Harvard Educational Review* 23: 33–50.

Comas-Diaz, Lillian
1987 "Feminist Therapy with Mainland Puerto Rican Women." *Psychology of Women Quarterly* 11:461–474.

Comas-Diaz, Lillian, and Amado M. Padilla
1992 "The English-Only Movement: Implications for Mental Health Services." *American Journal of Orthopsychiatry* 62:1–6.

Connelly, Naomi
1989 *Race and Change in Social Services Departments.* London: Policy Studies Institute.

Consortium for Research on Black Adolescence
1990 *Black Adolescence: Current Issues and Annotated Bibliography.* Boston: G.K. Hall.

Cordova, Fred
1983 *Filipinos: Forgotten Asian Americans.* Dubuque: Kendall/Hunt.

Cornell, Stephen
1984 "Crisis and Response in Indian-White Relations: 1960–1984." *Social Problems* 32:44–59.

Cose, Ellis
1993 *The Rage of a Privileged Class.* New York: HarperCollins.

Cowger, Charles D.
1977 "Alternative Stances in the Relationship of Social Work to Society." *Journal of Education for Social Work* 13:25–29.

Crawford, James
1989 *Bilingual Education: History, Political Theory, and Practice.* Trenton, NJ: Crane.
1992 *Language Loyalties: A Sourcebook on the Official English Controversy.* Chicago: University of Chicago Press.

Csikszentmihalyi, Mihalyi
1975 *Beyond Boredom and Anxiety.* San Francisco: Jossey-Bass.
1982 "Leisure and Socialization." *Social Forces* 60:332–340.

Csikszentmihalyi, Mihalyi, and Selega Csikszentmihalyi
  1988   *Optimal Experience: Psychological Studies of Flow Consciousness.* Cambridge: Cambridge University Press.

Csordas, Thomas J.
  1990   "The Therapeutic Process." In Thomas M. Johnson, and Carolyn Sargent, eds. *Medical Anthropology: Contemporary Theory and Method.* New York: Praeger.

Csordas, Thomas J., and Arthur Kleinman
  1990   "The Therapeutic Process." In Thomas M. Johnson and Carolyn F. Sargent, eds., *Medical Anthropology, Contemporary Theory and Method.* New York: Praeger.

Curry, Andrew E.
  1964   "The Negro Worker and the White Client: A Commentary on the Treatment Relationship." *Social Casework* 45:131–136.

Dana, Richard H., ed.
  1981   *Human Services for Cultural Minorities.* Baltimore: University Park Press.

Dance, Frank E. X., ed.
  1982   *Human Communication Theory.* New York: Harper and Row.

Daniel, G. Reginald
  1992   *"Beyond Black and White: the New Multiracial Consciousness."* In Maria P. P. Root, ed. *Racially Mixed People in America.* Newbury Park, CA: Sage.

D'Ardenne, Patricia, and Aruna Mahtani
  1989   *Transcultural Counseling in Action.* London: Sage.

Darnton, John
  1993   "Accepting the Nobel, Morrison Proves Power of Words." *The New York Times,* December 8, Section C17.

Dasen, Pierre R., John W. Berry, and Norman Sartorius, eds.
  1988   *Health and Cross-Cultural Psychology: Toward Applications.* Newbury Park, CA: Sage.

Davidson, Ann Locke
  1994   "Student's Situated Selves: Ethnographic Interviewing as Cultural Therapy." In George Spindler, and Louise Spindler. *Pathways to Cultural Awareness: Cultural Awareness with Teachers and Students.* Thousand Oaks, CA: Corwin Press.

Davis, Cary, Carl Haub, and JoAnne L. Willette
  1988   "U.S. Hispanics: Changing the Face of America." In Edna Acosta-Belen, and Barbara R. Sjostrom, eds. *The Spanish Experience in the United States.* New York: Praeger.

Davis, Dona Lee, and Setha M. Low, eds.
  1989   *Gender, Health, and Illness: The Case of Nerves.* New York: Hemisphere Publications.

Davis, Larry E.
   1984a "Essential Components of Group Work with Black Americans." *Social Work with Groups* 7:97–107.
   1984b *Ethnicity in Social Work Practice.* New York: Haworth Press.

Davis, Ossie
   1969   "The Language of Racism: The English Language Is My Enemy." In Neil Postman, Charles Weingartner, and Terence P. Moran, eds. *Language in America.* New York: Pegasus.

Davis, Robert
   1982   "Black Suicide and Support Systems." *Phylon* 43:307–314.

Day, Mary W.
   1987   "Harlem Youth Opportunities Unlimited." In Gladys Walton Holly, Grace C. Clark, Michael A. Creedon, eds. *Advocacy in America: Case Studies in Social Change.* Lanham, MD: University Press of America.

Deal, Terrence E., and Allen A. Kennedy
   1982   *Corporate Cultures: The Rites and Rituals of Corporate Life.* Reading, MA: Addison-Wesley.

Dedmon, Rachel, and William Saur, eds.
   1983   *Rural Mental Health in North Carolina: Social Work Practice and Ethnocultural Issues.* Chapel Hill, NC: University of North Carolina, School of Social Work.

De La Cancela, Victor
   1986   "A Critical Analysis of Puerto Rican Machismo: Implications for Clinical Practice." *Psychotherapy* 23:291–296.

De La Garza, Rodolpho O., Frank D. Bean, Charles M. Bonjean, Ricardo Romo, and Rodolpho Alvarez, eds.
   1985   *The Mexican American Experience: An Interdisciplinary Anthology.* Austin: University of Texas Press.

De La Torre, Adela, and Beatriz M. Pesquera
   1993   *Building with Our Hands: New Directions in Chicana Studies.* Berkeley: University of California Press.

Delaney, Anita J.
   1979   *Black Task Force Report: Project on Ethnicity.* New York: Family Service Association of America.

Deloria, Vine
   1973   *God is Red.* New York: Grosset and Dunlap.

Devore, Wynetta
   1983   "Ethnic Reality: The Life Model and Work with Black Families." *Social Casework* 64:525–531.

Devore, Wynetta, and Elfriede G. Schlesinger
  1987 *Ethnic-Sensitive Social Work Practice.* Columbus, OH: Merrill.

Dhooper, Surjit Singh
  1991 "Toward an Effective Response to the Needs of Asian-Americans." *Journal of Multicultural Social Work* 1:65–81.

Dirks, Robert
  1987 *The Black Saturnalia: Conflict and Its Ritual Expression on British West Indian Slave Plantations.* Gainesville: University of Florida Press.

Division of General Pediatrics and Adolescent Health
  1992 *The State of Native American Youth Health.* Minneapolis: University of Minnesota Health Center.

Douglas, Mary
  1966 *Purity and Danger.* London: Routledge and Kegan Paul.
  1968 "Pollution." *Encyclopedia of the Social Sciences* 12:336–341.
  1971 "Deciphering a Meal." In Clifford Geertz. *Myth, Symbol, and Culture.* New York: Norton.
  1975 *Implicit Meanings.* London: Routledge and Kegan Paul.

Dow, James
  1986 "Universal Aspects of Symbolic Healing: A Theoretical Synthesis." *American Anthropologist* 88:56–69.

Dressler, William W.
  1985 "Extended Family Relationships, Social Support, and Mental Health in a Southern Black Community." *Journal of Health and Social Behavior* 26:39–48.

Dressler, William W., Susan Hoeppner, and Barbara Pitts.
  1985 "Household Structure in a Southern Black Community." *American Anthropologist* 87:853–862.

Driver, Harold E.
  1969 *Indians of North America.* Chicago: University of Chicago Press.

Dufort, Molly E.
  1992 "Disability Management in Cross-Cultural Contexts." *Practicing Anthropology* 14:14–16.

Dunlop, Burton D.
  1979 *The Growth of Nursing Home Care.* Lexington, MA: Lexington Books.

Eastman, Carol M.
  1984 "Language, Ethnic Identity and Change." In John Edwards, ed. *Linguistic Minorities, Policies and Pluralism.* London: Academic Press.

Eastmond, Marita
    1993   "Reconstructing Life: Chilean Refugee Women and the Dilemmas of Exile." In Gina Buijs, ed. *Migrant Women: Crossing Boundaries and Changing Identities.* Oxford: Berg.

Edwards, E. Daniel, and Margie Egbert-Edwards
    1984   "Group Work Practice with American Indians." *Social Work with Groups* 7:7–22.
    1990   "American Indian Adolescents: Combating Problems of Substance Use and Abuse Through a Community Model." In Arlene Rubin Stiffman and Larry E. Davis, eds., *Ethic Issues in Adolescent Mental Health.* Newbury Park, CA: Sage

Edwards, John, ed.
    1985   *Language, Society and Identity.* Oxford: Basil Blackwell.
    1988   *Linguistic Minorities, Policies and Pluralism.* London: Academic Press.

Efired, Cathy M.
    1988   "Enhancing the Use of Mental Health Services." In Susan E. Keefe, ed. *Appalachian Mental Health.* Lexington: University Press of Kentucky.

Egan, Gerard
    1986   *The Skilled Helper: A Systematic Approach to Effective Helping.* Pacific Grove, CA: Brooks/Cole.

Eisenberg, Leon, and Arthur Kleinman, eds.
    1981   *The Relevance of Social Science for Medicine.* Boston: Reidel.

Ejaz, Farida Kassin
    1989   "The Nature of Social Casework in India: A Study of Social Worker's Perceptions in Bombay." *International Social Work* 32:25–38.
    1991   "Self-Determination: Lessons to Be Learned from Social Work Practice in India." *The British Journal of Social Work* 22:187–191.

Epstein, Laura
    1985   *Talking and Listening: A Guide to the Helping Interview.* St. Louis: Times Mirror/Mosby.

Espin, Oliva M.
    1987   "Psychological Impact of Migration on Latinas." *Psychology of Women Quarterly* 11:489–503.

Espiritu, Yen Le
    1992   *Asian American Panethnicity: Bridging Institutions and Identities.* Philadelphia: Temple University Press.

Estroff, Sue E.
    1981   *Making It Crazy.* Berkeley: University of California Press.

Evans, A. Donald
  1988   "Strange Bedfellows: Language, Deafness, and Knowledge." *Symbolic Interaction* 11:235–255.
  1991   "Maintaining Relationships in a School for the Deaf." In William B. Shaffir, and Robert A. Stebbins. *Experiencing Fieldwork.* Newbury Park, CA: Sage.

Fabrega, Horacio, Jr.
  1990   "Hispanic Mental Health Research: A Case for Cultural Psychiatry." *Hispanic Journal of Behavioral Sciences* 12:339–365.

Facio, Elisa
  1993   "Gender and the Life Course: A Case Study of Chicana Elderly." In Adela De La Torre, and Beatriz M. Pesquera. *Building with Our Hands: New Directions in Chicana Studies.* Berkeley: University of California Press.

Ferguson, Frances N.
  1976   "Stake Theory as an Explanatory Device in Navajo Alcoholism Treatment Response." *Human Organization* 35:65–78.

Fernandez, Carlos A.
  1992   "La Raza and the Melting Pot: A Comparative Look at Multiethnicity." In Maria P. P. Root, ed. *Racially Mixed People in America.* Newbury Park, CA: Sage.

Fibush, Esther
  1965   "The White Worker and the Negro Client." *Social Casework* 46:271–277.

Fibush, Esther, and Bealva Turnquest
  1970   "A Black and White Approach to the Problem of Racism." *Social Casework* 51:459–466.

Fine, Mark, Andrew I. Schwebel, and Linda James-Myers
  1987   "Family Stability in Black Families: Values Underlying Three Perspectives." *Journal of Comparative Family Studies* 18:1–23.

Finkler, Kaja
  1985   *Spiritualist Healers in Mexico.* South Hadley, MA: Bergin and Garvey.

Fisher, Lawrence E.
  1985   *Colonial Madness: Mental Health in the Barbadian Social Order.* New Brunswick, NJ: Rutgers University Press.

Foner, Philip S., and Daniel Rosenberg
  1993   *Racism, Dissent and Asian Americans from 1850 to the Present.* Westport, CT: Greenwood Press.

Fortes, M.
  1958   "Introduction." In J. R. Goody, ed. *The Developmental Cycle in Domestic Groups.* Cambridge: Cambridge University Press: 1–14.

Foster, George M.
  1965   "Peasant Society and the Image of Limited Good." *American Anthropologist* 67:293–315.

Foster, George M., and Barbara Gallatin Anderson
  1978   *Medical Anthropology.* New York: John Wiley and Sons.

Foster, Madison, and Lorraine R. Perry
  1982   "Self-Valuation among Blacks." *Social Work* 27:60–66.

Fugita, Stephen, Karen L. Ito, Jennifer Abe, and David T. Takeuchi
  1991   "Japanese Americans." In Noreen Mokuau, ed. *Handbook of Social Services for Asian and Pacific Islanders.* New York: Greenwood Press.

Furnham, Adrian, and Stephen Bochner
  1989   *Culture Shock: Psychological Reactions to Unfamiliar Environments.* London: Routledge.

Furuto, Sharlene Maeda
  1991   "Family Violence among Pacific Islanders." In Noreen Mokuau, ed. *Handbook of Social Services for Asian and Pacific Islanders.* New York: Greenwood Press.

Furuto, Sharlene Maeda, Renoka Biswas, Douglas K. Chung, Kenji Murase, and Fariyal Ross-Sheriff, eds.
  1992   *Social Work Practice with Asian Americans.* Newbury Park, CA: Sage.

Galanti, Geri-Ann
  1991   *Caring for Patients from Different Cultures.* Philadelphia: University of Pennsylvania Press.

Gallegos, Joseph S.
  1984   "The Ethnic Competence Model for Social Work Education." in Barbara W. White, ed. *Color in a White Society.* Silver Spring, MD: National Association of Social Workers.

García-Castañon, Juan
  1994   "Training among Refugee Students: Chicano Anthropologist as Cultural Therapist." In George Spindler, and Louise Spindler. *Pathways to Cultural Awareness: Cultural Awareness with Teachers and Students.* Thousand Oaks, CA: Corwin Press.

Gary, Lawrence E.
  1986   "Predicting Interpersonal Conflict between Men and Women: The Case of Black Men." *American Behavioral Scientist* 29:635–646.

Gary, Lawrence E., and Bogart E. Leashore
  1982   "High-Risk Status of Black Men." *Social Work* 27:54–58.

Geertz, Clifford
  1971   *Myth, Symbol, and Culture.* New York: Norton.
  1975   "On the Nature of Anthropological Understanding." *American Scientist* 63:47–53.

1976   "'From the Native's Point of View': On the Nature of Anthropological Under-
         standing." In Keith Basso, and Henry A. Shelby, eds. *Meaning in Anthropology.*
         Albuquerque: University of New Mexico Press.
1983   *Local Knowledge.* New York: Basic Books.

Gelman, Sheldon R.
1980   "Esoterica: A Zero Sum Game in the Helping Professions." *Social Casework* 61:48–53.

Ghali, Sonia Badillo
1977   "Cultural Sensitivity and the Puerto Rican Client." *Social Casework* 58:459–468.

Gibbs, Jewelle Taylor
1981   "The Interpersonal Orientation in Mental Health Consultation: Toward a Model
         of Ethnic Variations in Consultation." In Richard H. Dana, ed. *Human Services for
         Cultural Minorities.* Baltimore: University Park Press.
1988   *Young, Black and Male in America: An Endangered Species.* Dover, MA: Auburn House.

Gibbs, Jewelle Taylor, and Larke Nahme Huang, eds.
1989   *Children of Color: Psychological Interventions with Minority Youth.* San Francisco:
         Jossey-Bass.

Gibson, Margaret, and Steven F. Arvizu
1977   *Demystifying the Concept of Culture: Methodological Tools.* Sacramento: Sacramento
         State University.

Gibson, Margaret A.
1988   *Accommodation without Assimilation: Sikh Immigrants in an American High School.*
         Ithaca: Cornell University Press.

Gibson, Margaret A., and John Ogbu, eds.
1991   *Minority Status and Schooling: A Comparative Study of Immigrant and Involuntary
         Minorities.* New York: Garland.

Gilligan, Carol
1982   *In a Different Voice.* Cambridge: Harvard University Press.

Gilligan, Carol, and John Murphy
1979   "Development from Adolescence to Adulthood: The Philosopher and the 'Di-
         lemma of the Fact.'" In Deanna Kuhn, ed. *Intellectual Development beyond Child-
         hood.* San Francisco: Jossey-Bass.

Gilligan, Carol, and Mary F. Belenky
1980   "A Naturalistic Study of Abortion Decisions." In Robert L. Selman, and Regina
         Yande, eds. *Clinical-Developmental Psychology.* San Francisco: Jossey-Bass.

Giménez, Marta E., Fred A. Lopez, and Carlos Munoz, Jr.
1992   "The Politics of Ethnic Construction: Hispanic, Chicano, Latino?" *Latin American
         Perspectives* 19:1–106.

Ginsburg, Faye D.
  1989   *Contested Lives, the Abortion Debate in an American Community.* Berkeley: University of California Press.

Glasgow, Eilene K.
  1991   *Second Language Learner's Development of Literacy Behaviors in the First Grade Classroom.* Seattle: University of Washington, Unpublished Doctoral Dissertation.

Glasser, Irene
  1983   "Guidelines for Using an Interpreter in Social Work." *Child Welfare* 57:468–470.
  1988   *More Than Bread: Ethnography of a Soup Kitchen.* Tuscaloosa: University of Alabama Press.

Glazer, Nathan, and Daniel Patrick Moynihan
  1963   *Beyond the Melting Pot.* Cambridge: MIT Press.

Gleave, Danica, and Arturo S. Manes
  1990   "The Central Americans." In Nancy Waxler-Morrison, Joan Anderson, and Elizabeth Richardson, eds., *Cross-Cultural Caring, a Handbook.* Vancouver: University of British Columbia Press.

Goffman, Erving
  1959   *The Presentation of Self in Everyday Life.* New York: Doubleday.
  1961   *Asylums.* Garden City, New York: Doubleday.

Golde, Peggy, ed.
  1986   *Women in the Field: Anthropological Experiences.* Berkeley: University of California Press.

Gómez, Manuel R.
  1990   "Biculturalism and Subjective Mental Health among Cuban Americans." *Social Service Review* 64:375–389.

Gonsalves, Carlos J.
  1990   "The Psychological Effects of Political Repression on Chilean Exiles in the U.S." *American Journal of Orthopsychiatry* 60:143–153.

Good, Mary-Jo DelVecchio, Paul E. Brodwin, Byron Good, and Arthur Kleinman, eds.
  1992   *Pain as a Human Experience: An Anthropological Perspective.* Berkeley: University of California Press.

Good Tracks, Jimm G.
  1973   "Native-American Non-Interference." *Social Work* 18:30–34.

Goode, William J.
  1957   "Community Within a Community: The Professions." *American Sociological Review* 22:194–200.

Goodenough, Ward H.
  1957   "Cultural Anthropology and Linguistics." In P. L. Garvin, ed. *Report of the Seventh Annual Round Table Meeting on Linguistics and Language Study.* Washington, D.C.: Georgetown University: 1–4.

Gopaul-McNicol, Sharon-Ann
  1993   *Working with West Indian Families.* New York: Guilford Press.

Gordon, Raymond L.
  1969   *Interviewing.* Homewood, IL: The Dorsey Press.

Grafton, Jr., Hull H.
  1982   "Child Welfare Services to Native Americans." *Social Casework* 63:340–347.

Grasmuck, Sherri, and Patricia R. Pessar
  1991   *Between Two Islands: Dominican International Migration.* Berkeley: University of California Press.

Graves, Theodore D.
  1967   "Acculturation, Access and Alcohol in a Tri-Ethnic Community." *American Anthropologist* 69:306–321.

Green, James W.
  1973   "The British West Indian Alien Labor Problem in the Virgin Islands." *Caribbean Studies* 12:56–75.
  1989   "Aging and Ethnicity: An Emergent Issue in Social Gerontology." *Journal of Cross-Cultural Gerontology* 4:377–383.

Green, James W., and James Leigh
  1989   "Teaching Ethnographic Methods to Social Service Workers." *Practicing Anthropology* 11:8–10.

Green, James W., and Linda Wilson
  1983   "An Experiential Approach to Cultural Awareness Training." *Child Welfare* 63:303–311.

Green, Vera
  1970   "The Confrontation of Diversity in the Black Community." *Human Organization* 29:267–272.
  1978   "The Black Extended Family in the United States: Some Research Suggestions." In Demitri B. Shimkin, Edith M Shimkin, and Dennis A. Frate, eds. *The Extended Family in Black Societies.* The Hague: Mouton.

Greenbaum, Susan
  1985   "In Search of Lost Tribes: Anthropology and the Federal Acknowledgement Process." *Human Organization* 44:361–367.
  1991   "What's in a Label? Identity Problems of Southern Tribes." *Journal of Ethnic Studies* 19:107–126.

Gregory, Steven
    1992   "The Changing Significance of Race and Class in an African American Community." *American Anthropologist* 94:255–271.

Grossman, Daniel C., Carol Milligan, and Richard A. Deyo
    1991   "Risk Factors for Suicide Attempts among Navaho Adolescents." *American Journal of Public Health* 81: 870–874.

Guarnaccia, Peter J.
    1993   *"Ataques de Nervios* in Puerto Rico: Culture-Bound Syndrome or Popular Illness?" *Medical Anthropology* 15:157–170.

Guarnaccia, Peter J., Victor De La Cancela, and Emilio Carrillo
    1989   "The Multiple Meanings of Ataques de Nervios in the Latino Community." *Medical Anthropology* 11:47–62.

Gubrium, Jaber F.
    1991   "Recognizing and Analyzing Local Cultures." In William B. Shaffir, and Robert A. Stebbins. *Experiencing Fieldwork.* Newbury Park, CA: Sage.

Gutiérrez, Lorraine M.
    1990   "Working with Women of Color: An Empowerment Perspective." *Social Work* 35:149–153.

Gudykunst, William B., and Young Yun Kim
    1984   *Communicating with Strangers: An Approach to Intercultural Communication.* New York: Random House.

Gumperz, John J., and Dell Hymes, eds.
    1972   *Directions in Sociolinguistics.* New York: Holt, Rinehart and Winston.

Gunnings, Thomas S., and Wanda D. Lipscomb
    1986   "Psychotherapy for Black Men: A Systemic Approach." *Journal of Multicultural Counseling and Development* 14:17–24.

Gutman, Herbert G.
    1976   *The Black Family in Slavery and Freedom.* New York: Random House.
    1984   "Afro-American Kinship Before and After Emancipation in North America." In Hans Medick and David Warren Sabeam, eds. *Interest and Emotion.* Cambridge: Cambridge University Press.
    1986   *The Dissenters: Voices From Contemporary America.* New York: Random House.

Gwaltney, John L.
    1980   *Drylongso: a Self-Portrait of Black America.* New York: Random House.
    1986   *The Dissenters: Voices from Contemporary America.* New York: Random House.

Gwyn, Felisha S., and Allie C. Kilpatrick
    1981   "Family Therapy with Low-Income Blacks: A Tool or Turn-Off?" *Social Casework* 62:259–266.

Haddad, Yvonne Yazbeck, ed.
    1991   *The Muslims of America.* New York: Oxford University Press.

Haddad, Yvonne Yazbeck, and Adair T. Lummis
    1987   *Islamic Values in the United States.* New York: Oxford University Press.

Haley, Alex
    1976   *Roots.* Garden City, New York: Doubleday.

Hampton, Robert L., ed.
    1987   *Violence in the Black Family.* Lexington, MA: D.C. Heath.

Handelman, Don
    1976   "Bureaucratic Transactions: The Development of Offical-Client Relationships in Israel." In Bruce Kapferer, ed. *Transaction and Meaning.* Philadelphia: Institute for the Study of Human Issues: 223–275.

Hannerz, Ulf
    1969   *Soulside: Inquiries in Ghetto Culture and Community.* New York: Columbia University Press.
    1986   "Theory in Anthropology: Small is Beautiful? The Problem of Complex Cultures." *Comparative Studies in Society and History* 28:362–367.

Harel, Zev, Edward A. McKinney, and Michael Williams, eds.
    1990   *Black Aged: Understanding Diversity and Service Needs.* Newbury Park, CA: Sage.

Harris, Marvin
    1968   *The Rise of Anthropological Theory.* New York: Crowell.

Harvey, Aminifur R., ed.
    1985   *The Black Family: An Afro-Centric Perspective.* New York: United Church of Christ.

Harwood, Alan
    1987   *Rx: Spiritist as Needed, a Study of Puerto Rican Community Mental Health.* Ithaca, NY: Cornell University Press.

Hayes-Bautista, David E.
    1978   "Chicano Patients and Medical Practitioners: A Sociology of Knowledge Paradigm of Lay-Professional Interaction." *Social Science and Medicine* 12:83–90.

Hayes-Bautista, David E., and Jorge Chapa
    1987   "Latino Terminology: Conceptual Bases for Standardized Terminology." *American Journal of Public Health* 77:61–68.

Hayes-Bautista, David E., Werner O. Schink, and Jorge Chapa
    1988   *The Burden of Support: Young Latinos in an Aging Society.* Stanford: Stanford University Press.

Hess, David J.
   1993   *Science in the New Age: The Paranormal, Its Defenders and Debunkers, and American Culture."* Madison: University of Wisconsin Press.

Hill, Robert B.
   1971   *The Strengths of Black Families.* New York: National Urban League.

Hill, Thomas W.
   1978   "Drunken Comportment of Urban Indians: "Time-Out" Behavior?" *Journal of Anthropological Research* 34:442–467.

Ho, Christine G. T.
   1993   "The Internationalization of Kinship and the Feminization of Caribbean Migration: The Case of Afro-Trinidadian Immigrants in Los Angeles." *Human Organization* 52:32–40.

Ho, Man Keung
   1987   *Family Therapy with Ethnic Minorities.* Newbury Park, CA: Sage.

Hogan, Robert
   1969   "Development of an Empathy Scale." *Journal of Counseling and Clinical Psychology* 33:307–316.

Holland, Dorothy, and Naomi Quinn, eds.
   1987   *Cultural Models in Language and Thought.* Cambridge: Cambridge University Press.

Holly, Gladys Walton
   1987   *Advocacy in America: Case Studies in Social Change.* Lanham, MD: University Press of America.

Hoopes, David S., Paul B. Pedersen, and George Renwick, eds.
   1978   *Overview of Intercultural Education, Training and Research.* Washington, D.C.: SIETAR.

Hopps, June G.
   1982   "Oppression Based on Color." *Social Work* 27:3–6.

Huang, Karen
   1991   "Chinese Americans." In Noreen Mokuau, ed. *Handbook of Social Services for Asian and Pacific Islanders.* New York: Greenwood Press.

Huang, Lucy Jen
   1988   "The Chinese Family in America." In Charles H. Mindel, Robert W. Habenstein, and Roosevelt Wright, Jr. *Ethnic Families in America: Patterns and Variations.* New York: Elesevier.

Huddy, Leonie, and David O. Sears
   1990   "Qualified Public Support for Bilingual Education: Some Policy Implications." *The Annals of the American Academy of Political Science* 508:119–134.

Hunt, Portia
  1987   "Black Clients: Implications for Supervision of Trainees." *Psychotherapy* 24:114–119.

Hurtado, Aída, and Raul Rodriguez
  1989   "Language as a Social Problem: The Repression of Spanish in South Texas." *Journal of Multilingual and Multicultural Development* 10:401–419.

Ivey, Allen E.
  1971   *Microcounseling.* Springfield, IL: Charles C. Thomas.
  1983   *Intentional Interviewing and Counseling.* Monterey, CA: Brooks/Cole.

Jackson, Eileen M.
  1993   "Whiting Out Difference: Why U.S. Nursing Research Fails Black Families." *Medical Anthropology Quarterly* 7:363–385.

Jackson, Jacquelyne J.
  1977   "The Black Aging: A Demographic Overview." In Richard A.. Kalish, ed. *The Later Years: Social Applications of Gerontology.* Monterey, CA: Brooks/Cole.
  1980   *Minorities and Aging.* Belmont, CA: Wadsworth.
  1982   "Death Rates of Aged Blacks and Whites, 1964–1978." *The Black Scholar* 13:36–48.

Jacobs, Carolyn, and Dorcas D. Bowles, eds.
  1988   *Ethnicity and Race: Critical Concepts in Social Work.* Silver Spring, MD: National Association of Social Workers.

Jacobs, Sue-Ellen
  1974a "Action and Advocacy Anthropology." *Human Organization* 33:209–214.
  1974b "Doing It Our Way and Mostly for Our Own." *Human Organization* 33:380–382.
  1979   "Our Babies Shall Not Die: A Community's Response to Medical Neglect." *Human Organization* 38:120–133.

Jemison, T. J.
  1982   "As Christians We Must Do More to Help Other People." *The Crisis* 89:9.

Jenkins, Shirley
  1981   *The Ethnic Dilemma in Social Services.* New York: The Free Press.

Joans, Barbara
  1992   "Problems in Pocatello: A Study in Linguistic Understanding." In Aaron Podolefsky, and Peter J. Brown, eds. *Applying Anthropology.* Mountain View, CA: Mayfield.

John, Robert
  1985   "Service Needs and Support Networks of Elderly Native Americans: Family, Friends, and Social Service Agencies." In Warren A. Peterson, and Jill Quadagno, eds. *Social Bonds in Later Life: Aging and Independence.* Beverly Hills, CA: Sage.
  1988   "The Native American Family." In Charles H. Mindel, Robert W. Habenstein, and Roosevelt Wright, Jr. *Ethnic Families in America: Patterns and Variations.* New York: Elsevier.

Johnson, Colleen L.
  1987   "The Institutional Segregation of the Aged." In Philip Silverman, ed. *The Elderly as Modern Pioneers.* Bloomington: Indiana University Press.
  1989   "In-law Relationships in the American Kinship System: The Impact of Divorce and Remarriage." *American Ethnologist* 16:87–99.

Johnson, Colleen L., and Leslie A. Grant
  1985   *The Nursing Home in America.* Baltimore: Johns Hopkins University Press.

Johnson, John M.
  1975   *Doing Field Research.* New York: The Free Press.

Johnson, Thomas M., and Carolyn Sargent, eds.
  1990   *Medical Anthropology: Contemporary Theory and Method.* New York: Praeger.

Jones, Alison, and Arthur A. Seagull
  1977   "Dimensions of the Relationship between the Black Client and the White Therapist: A Theoretical Overview." *American Psychologist* 32:850–855.

Jones, Dorothy M.
  1974   *The Urban Native Encounters the Social Service System.* Fairbanks: University of Alaska.
  1976   "The Mystique of Expertise in the Social Services." *Journal of Sociology and Social Welfare* 3:332–346.

Jones, Michael O., Michael D. Moore, and Richard C. Snyder
  1988   *Inside Organizations: Understanding the Human Dimension.* Newbury Park, CA: Sage.

Jones, Reginald L., ed.
  1989   *Black Adult Development and Aging.* Berkeley, CA: Cobbs and Henry.

Jones, Richard L.
  1983   "Increasing Staff Sensitivity to the Black Client." *Social Casework* 64:419–425.

Juarez, Reina
  1985   "Core Issues in Psychotherapy with Hispanic Children." *Psychotherapy* 22:441–448.

June, Lee N.
  1986   "Enhancing the Delivery of Mental Health and Counseling Services to Black Males: Critical Agency and Provider Responsibilities." *Journal of Multicultural Counseling and Development* 14:39–44.

Kadushin, Alfred
  1972   *The Social Work Interview.* New York: Columbia University Press.
  1990   *The Social Work Interview: a Guide for Human Service Professionals.* New York: Columbia University Press.

Kahn, Marvin W., Cecil Williams, Eugene Galvez, Linda Lejero, Rex Conrad, and George Goldstein
  1981   "The Papago Psychology Service, a Community Mental Health Program on an American Indian Reservation." In Richard H. Dana, ed. *Human Services for Cultural Minorities*. Baltimore: University Park Press.

Kalcik, Susan
  1984   "Ethnic Foodways in America: Symbol and the Performance of Identity." In Linda K. Brown, and Kay Mussell, eds. *Ethnic and Regional Foodways in the United States*. Knoxville: University of Tennessee Press.

Kalish, Richard A., ed.
  1977   *The Later Years: Social Applications of Gerontology*. Monterey CA: Brooks/Cole.

Kaneshige, Edward
  1973   "Cultural Factors in Group Counseling and Interaction." *Personnel and Guidance Journal* 51:407–412.

Kaufman, Sharon R.
  1986   *The Ageless Self: Sources of Meaning in Late Life*. Madison: University of Wisconsin Press.

Kearney, Michael
  1975   "World View Theory and Study." In Bernard J. Siegel, Alan R. Beals, and Stephen A. Tyler, eds. *Annual Review of Anthropology*. Palo Alto: Annual Reviews 4:247–270.

Keefe, Susan E., ed.
  1988   *Appalachian Mental Health*. Lexington: University Press of Kentucky.

Keefe, Susan E., and Amado M. Padilla
  1987   *Chicano Ethnicity*. Albuquerque: University of New Mexico Press.

Keith, Jennie
  1982   *Old People, New Lives: Community Creation in a Retirement Residence*. Chicago: University of Chicago Press.

Kelly, G. P.
  1977   *From Vietnam to America: A Chronicle of Vietnamese Immigration to the United States*. Boulder, CO: Westview Press.

Kerns, Virginia
  1983   *Women and the Ancestors, Black Carib Kinship and Ritual*. Urbana: University of Illinois Press.

Keyes, Charles F.
  1977   *The Golden Peninsula*. New York: Macmillan.

Kitano, Harry H. L.
    1988   "The Japanese American Family." In Charles H. Mindel, Robert W. Habenstein, and Roosevelt Wright, Jr. *Ethnic Families in America: Patterns and Variations.* New York: Elsevier.

Klein, Richard E.
    1989   *The Human Career.* Chicago: University of Chicago Press.

Kleinman, Arthur
    1973   "Medicine's Symbolic Reality, on a Central Problem in the Philosophy of Medicine." *Inquiry* 16:206–213.
    1974   "Social, Cultural and Historical Themes in the Study of Medicine in Chinese Societies: Problems and Prospects for the Comparative Study of Medicine and Psychiatry." In Arthur Kleinman, Peter Kunstadter, E. Russell Alexander, and James L. Gale, eds. *Medicine in Chinese Cultures.* Washington, D.C.: Department of Health, Education and Welfare.
    1977   "Lessons from a Clinical Approach to Medical Anthropology Research." *Medical Anthropology Newsletter* 8:11–16.
    1978a   "Concepts and a Model for the Comparison of Medical Systems as Cultural Systems." *Social Science and Medicine* 12:85–93.
    1978b   International Healthcare Planning from an Ethnomedical Perspective: Critique and Recommendations for Change." *Medical Anthropology* 2:71–94.
    1978c   "Rethinking the Social and Cultural Context of Psychopathology and Psychiatric Care." In Theo C. Manschreck, and Arthur Kleinman, eds. *Renewal in Psychiatry.* New York: John Wiley and Sons.
    1980   *Patients and Healers in the Context of Culture.* Berkeley: University of California Press.
    1982   "Neurasthenia and Depression: A Study of Socialization and Culture in China." *Culture, Medicine, and Psychiatry* 6:117–190.
    1986   *Social Origins of Distress and Disease: Depression, Neurasthenia and Pain in Modern China.* New Haven, CT: Yale University Press.
    1988a   *The Illness Narratives: Suffering, Healing and the Human Condition.* New York: Basic Books.
    1988b   *Rethinking Psychiatry: From Cultural Category to Personal Experience.* New York: The Free Press.
    1992   "Pain as a Human Experience: An Introduction." In Mary-Jo DelVecchio, Paul E. Brodwin, Byron Good, and Arthur Kleinman, eds. *Pain as a Human Experience: An Anthropological Perspective.* Berkeley: University of California Press.

Kleinman, Arthur, and Byron Good, eds.
    1985   *Culture and Depression.* Berkeley: University of California Press.

Kleinman, Arthur, and Joan Kleinman
    1991   "Suffering and its Professional Transformation: Toward an Ethnography of Interpersonal Experience." *Culture, Medicine, and Psychiatry* 15:275–301.

Kleinman, Arthur, Peter Kunstadter, E. Russell Alexander, and James L. Gale, eds.
    1974   *Medicine in Chinese Cultures.* Washington, D.C.: Department of Health, Education and Welfare.

Kluckhohn, Florence R., and Fred L. Strodtbeck
    1961   *Variations in Value Orientations.* Evanston, IL: Row, Peterson.

Kochman, Thomas L.
    1970   "Toward an Ethnography of Black American Speech Behavior." In Norman E. Whitten, and John F. Szwed, eds. *Afro-American Anthropology: Contemporary Perspectives.* New York: Free Press.
    1981   *Black and White Styles in Conflict.* Chicago: University of Chicago Press.

Kohut, Heinz
    1959   "Introspection, Empathy, and Psychoanalysis: An Examination of the Relationship Between Mode of Observation and Theory." *Journal of the American Psychoanalysis Association* 7:459–483.
    1971   *Analysis of Self: A Systematic Approach to the Psychoanalytic Treatment of Narcissistic Personality Disorders.* New York: International Universities Press.

Kopp, Judy
    1989   "Self-Observation: An Empowerment Strategy in Assessment." *Social Casework* 70:276–284.

Korbin, Jill
    1976   "Anthropological Contributions to the Study of Child Abuse." Manuscript.
    1981   *Child Abuse and Neglect: Cross-Cultural Perspectives.* Berkeley: University of California Press.

Koss-Chioino, Joan
    1992   *Women as Healers, Women as Patients: Mental Health Care and Traditional Healing in Puerto Rico.* Boulder, CO: Westview.

Koss-Chioino, Joan, and Jose M. Canive
    1993   "The Interaction of Popular and Clinical Diagnostic Labeling: The Case of Embrujado." *Medical Anthropology* 15:171–188.

Kozol, Jonathan
    1988   *Savage Inequalities: Children in America's Schools.* New York: Crown.
    1991   *Rachel and Her Children: Homeless Families in America.* New York: Crown.

Kracke, Waud H.
    1994   "Reflections on the Savage Self: Introspection, Empathy, and Anthropology." In Marcelo Suarez-Orozco, George Spindler, and Louise Spindler, eds. *The Making of Psychological Anthropology II.* Fort Worth: Harcourt Brace.

Kroeber, A. L., and C. Kluckhohn
    1952   *Culture: A Critical Review of Concepts and Definitions.* Cambridge, MA: Papers of the Peabody Museum, No. 47.

Kuhn, Deanna, ed.
    1979   *Intellectual Development Beyond Childhood.* San Francisco: Jossey-Bass.

Kupferer, Harriet J.
   1979   "A Case of Sanctioned Drinking: The Rupert's House Cree." *Anthropological Quarterly* 52:198–203.

Labov, William, and David Fanshel
   1977   *Therapeutic Discourse: Psychotherapy as Conversation.* New York: Academic Press.

Laguerre, Michel S.
   1984   *American Odyssey: Haitians in New York City.* Ithaca: Cornell University Press.

Lakoff, George
   1972   "Hedges: a Study of Meaning Criteria and the Logic of Fuzzy Concepts." *Papers of the Eighth Regional Meeting.* Chicago: Chicago Linguistics Society.

Lakoff, George, and Mark Johnson
   1980   *Metaphors We Live By.* Chicago: University of Chicago Press.

Landrine, Hope
   1992   "Clinical Implications of Cultural Differences: The Referential vs. Indexical Self." *Clinical Psychology Review* 12:401–415.

Lang, Gretchen C.
   1990   Talking About a New Illness with the Dakota: Reflections on Diabetes, Food and Culture. In Robert H. Winthrop, ed. *Culture and the Anthropological Tradition.* Lanham, MD: University Press of America.

Langness, L. L.
   1965   *The Life History in Anthropological Science.* New York: Holt.

Langness, L. L., and Gelya Frank
   1981   *Lives: An Anthropological Approach to Biography.* Novato, CA: Chandler and Sharp.

Lappin, Jay, and Sam Scott
   1982   "Intervention in a Vietnamese Refugee Family." In Monica McGoldrick, John K. Pearce, and Joseph Giordano, eds. *Ethnicity and Family Therapy.* New York: The Guilford Press.

Lave, Jean, and Etienne Wenger
   1991   *Situated Learning, Legitimate Peripheral Participation.* Cambridge: Cambridge University Press.

Leach, Edmund
   1968   *A Runaway World?* New York: Oxford University Press.

Le-Doux, Cora, and King S. Stephens
   1992   "Refugee and Immigrant Social Service Delivery: Critical Management Issues." *Journal of Multicultural Social Work* 2:31–45.

Lee, Jik-Joen, Michael R. Patchner, and Pallassana R. Balgopal
   1991   "Essential Dimensions for Developing and Delivering Service for the Asian American Elderly." *Journal of Multicultural Social Work* 1:3–11.

Lee, Joanne Faung Jean
   1991   *Asian American Experiences in the United States.* Jefferson, NC: McFarland.

Lee, Judith A. B.
   1980   "The Helping Professional's Use of Language in Describing the Poor." *American Journal of Orthopsychiatry* 50:580–584.

Lee, Raymond
   1993   *Doing Research on Sensitive Topics.* Newbury Park, CA: Sage.

Lefley, Harriet P., and Paul B. Pedersen, eds.
   1986   *Cross-Cultural Training for Mental Health Professionals.* Springfield, IL: Charles C. Thomas.

Leininger, Madeleine
   1970   *Nursing and Anthropology: Two Worlds to Blend.* New York: John Wiley.
   1978   *Transcultural Nursing: Concepts, Theories, and Practice.* New York: Wiley.

Lemert, E. M.
   1954   *Alcohol and the Northwest Coast Indians.* Berkeley: University of California Press.

Leonard, Karen Isaksen
   1992   *Making Ethnic Choices: California's Punjabi Mexican Americans.* Philadelphia: Temple University Press.

Leong, Frederick T. L.
   1986   "Counseling and Psychotherapy with Asian Americans: Review of the Literature." *Review of Counseling Psychology* 33:196–206.

Levin, Jeffrey, and H. Vanderpool
   1987   "Is Frequent Religious Attendance Really Conducive to Better Health? Toward an Epidemiology of Religion." *Social Science and Religion* 24:589–600.

Levine, Robert
   1982   *Culture, Behavior, and Personality.* New York: Aldine.

Levy, Charles C.
   1976   *Social Work Ethics.* New York: Human Sciences Press.
   1977   "Values in Social Work Education." In Boyd E. Oviatt, ed. *Values in Social Work Education: Cliché or Reality?* University of Utah: Graduate School of Social Work: 1–9.

Levy, Jerrold E., and Stephen J. Kunitz
   1974   *Indian Drinking: Navajo Practices and Anglo-American Theories.* New York: John Wiley and Sons.

1987   "A Suicide Prevention Program for Hopi Youth." *Social Science and Medicine* 25:931–940.

Lide, Pauline D.
1971   "Dialogue on Racism: A Prologue to Action?" *Social Casework* 52:432–437.

Lieberman, Alicia F.
1990   "Culturally Sensitive Intervention with Children and Families." *Child and Adolescent Social Work* 7:101–120.

Lieberson, S.
1985   "Stereotypes: Their Consequences for Race and Ethnic Interaction." In Cora Bagley Merrett, and Cheryl Leggon, eds. *Research in Race and Ethnic Relations.* Greenwich, CT: JAI Press.

Liebow, Elliot
1967   *Tally's Corner.* Boston: Little, Brown.

Locklear, Herbert H.
1977   "American Indian Alcoholism: Program for Treatment." *Social Work* 22:202–207.

Lofland, John
1971   *Analyzing Social Settings.* Belmont CA: Wadsworth.

Lomawaima, K. Tsianina
1993   "Domesticity in the Federal Indian Schools: The Power of Authority over Mind and Body." *American Ethnologist* 20:227–240.

Longres, John F.
1991   "Toward a Status Model of Ethnic Sensitive Practice." *Journal of Multicultural Social Work* 1:41–57.

López, Steven, and Priscilla Hernandez
1986   "How Culture is Considered in Evaluations of Psychopathology." *Journal of Nervous and Mental Disease* 176:598–606.

Loring, Marti, and Brian Powell
1988   "Gender, Race, and DSM III: A Study of the Objectivity of Psychiatric Diagnostic Behavior." *Journal of Health and Social Behavior* 29:1–22.

Lum, Doman
1986   *Social Work Practice and People of Color: A Process-Stage Approach.* Monterey, CA: Brooks/Cole.
1992   *Social Work Practice and People of Color: A Process-Stage Approach,* 2nd ed. Pacific Grove, CA: Brooks/Cole.

Lutz, Catherine A.
1988   *Unnatural Emotions.* Chicago: University of Chicago Press.

MacAndrew, Craig, and Robert B. Edgerton
  1969   *Drunken Comportment.* Chicago: Aldine.

MacKaye, Susannah D. A.
  1990   "California Proposition 63: Language Attitudes Reflected in the Public Debate."
          Annals of the American Academy of Political and Social Science 508:135–146.

Madrid, Arturo
  1990   "Official English: A False Policy Issue." *Annals of the American Academy of Political
          and Social Science* 508:62–65.

Madsen, William
  1964   *Mexican-Americans of South Texas.* New York: Holt, Rinehart and Winston.

Maduro, Renaldo
  1983   "Curanderismo and Latin Views on Disease and Curing." *Western Journal of
          Medicine* 139:64–70.

Mandelbaum, David G., ed.
  1949   *Language, Culture and Personality: Selected Writings of Edward Sapir.* Berkeley:
          University of California Press.

Manschreck, Theo C., and Arthur Kleinman, eds.
  1978   *Renewal in Psychiatry.* New York: John Wiley and Sons.

Manson, Spero M., J. Beals, R. W. Dick, and C. Duclos
  1989   "Risk Factors for Suicide Among Indian Adolescents at a Boarding School."
          Public Health Report 104:609–614.
  1989a "Long-Term Care in American Indian Communities: Issues for Planning and
          Research." *The Gerontologist* 29:38–44.

Manson, Spero M.
  1989b Provider Assumptions about Long-Term Care in American Indian Communi-
          ties." *The Gerontologist* 29:355–358.

Mariano, Anthony J., Dennis M. Donovan, Patricia Silk Walker, Mary Jean Mariano, and
  R. Dale Walker
  1989   "Drinking-Related Locus of Control and the Drinking Status of Urban Native
          Americans." *Journal of Studies of Alcohol* 50:331–338.

Marín, Gerardo
  1993   "Defining Culturally Appropriate Community Interventions: Hispanics as a
          Case Study." *Journal of Community Psychology* 21:149–161.

Marín, Gerardo, and Barbara VanOss Marín
  1991   *Research with Hispanic Populations.* Newbury Park, CA: Sage.

Markides, Kyriakos S., and Charles H. Mindel
  1987   *Aging and Ethnicity.* Beverly Hills, CA: Sage.

Marsella, Anthony J.
   1993   "Counseling and Psychotherapy with Japanese Americans: Cross-Cultural Considerations." *American Journal of Orthopsychiatry* 63:200–208.

Marsh, Wallace W., and Kae Hentges
   1988   "Mexican Folk Remedies and Conventional Medical Care." *American Family Physician* 37:257–262.

Martin, Elmer P., and Joanne M. Martin
   1978   *The Black Extended Family.* Chicago: University of Chicago Press.

Martin, Joanne M., and Elmer P. Martin
   1985   *The Helping Tradition in the Black Family and Community.* Silver Spring, MD: National Association of Social Workers.

Martinez, Cervando, and Harry W. Martin
   1966   "Folk Diseases among Urban Mexican-Americans: Etiology, Symptoms and Treatment." *Journal of the American Medical Association* 196:147–150.

Martinez, Joe L., Jr., and Richard H. Mendoza, eds.
   1984   *Chicano Psychology.* Orlando: Academic Press.

Maser, Jack D., and Norman Dinges
   1992   "Comorbidity: Meaning and Uses in Cross-Cultural Clinical Research." *Culture, Medicine, and Psychiatry* 16:409–425.

Maslow, Abraham
   1965   "Humanistic Science and Transcendent Experience." *Journal of Humanistic Psychology* 5:219–227.
   1971   *The Farther Reaches of Human Nature.* New York: Viking.

Mass, Amy Iwasaki
   1976   "Asians as Individuals: The Japanese Community." *Social Casework* 57:160–164.
   1981   "Asians as Individuals—the Japanese Community." In Richard H. Dana, ed. Human Services for Cultural Minorities. Baltimore: University Park Press.

Matheson, Lou
   1986   "If You Are Not An Indian, How Do You Treat An Indian?" In Harriet P. Lefley, and Paul P. Pedersen eds. *Cross-Cultural Training for Mental Health Professionals.* Springfield, IL: Charles C. Thomas.

Matsuoka, Jon K.
   1991   "Vietnamese Americans." In Noreen Mokuau, ed. *Handbook of Social Services for Asian and Pacific Islanders.* New York: Greenwood Press.
   1993   "Demographic Characteristics as Determinants of Qualitative Differences in the Adjustment of Vietnamese Refugees." Journal of Social Services Research 17:1–21.

Mayes, Nathaniel H.
  1978 "Teacher Training for Cultural Awareness. In David S. Hoopes, Paul B. Pedersen, and George Renwick, eds. *Overview of Intercultural Education, Training and Research.* Washington, DC: SIETAR

McAdoo, Harriette P.
  1977 "Family Therapy in the Black Community." *American Journal of Orthopsychiatry* 47:75–79.
  1979 "Black Kinship." *Psychology Today* 12:64ff.
  1988 *Black Families.* Beverly Hills, CA: Sage.

McAdoo, Harriette P., and John P. McAdoo
  1985 *Black Children.* Beverly Hills, CA: Sage.

McCready, William, ed.
  1983 *Culture, Ethnicity, and Identity.* New York: Academic Press.

McDermott, Mustafa Yusuf, and Mahammad Manazir Ahsan
  1986 *The Muslim Guide.* London: The Islamic Foundation.

McFee, Malcolm
  1968 "The 150% Man, a Product of Blackfeet Acculturation." *American Anthropologist* 70:1096–1103.

McGoldrick, Monica, John K. Pearce, and Joseph Giordano, eds.
  1982 *Ethnicity and Family Therapy.* New York: The Guilford Press.

McGoldrick, Monica, and Randy Gerson
  1985 *Genograms in Family Assessment.* New York: W. W. Norton.

McLeod, Beverly
  1981 "The Mediating Person and Cultural Identity." In Stephen Bochner. *The Mediating Person.* Cambridge, MA: Schenkman.

McLeod, Donna L., and Henry J. Meyer
  1967 "A Study of the Values of Social Workers." In E. J. Thomas, ed. *Behavioral Science for Social Workers.* New York: Collier-Macmillan: 401–416.

McMahon, Anthony, and Paula Allen-Meares
  1992 "Is Social Work Racist? A Content Analysis of Recent Literature." *Social Work* 37:533–539.

Mechling, Jay
  1990 "Theory and the Other; or, Is This Session the Text?" *American Behavioral Scientist* 34:153–164.

Medick, Hans, and David Warren Sabeam, eds.
  1984 *Interest and Emotion.* Cambridge: Cambridge University Press.

Mehrabian, Albert, and Norman Epstein
    1972   "A Measure of Emotional Empathy." *Journal of Personality* 40:525–543.

Meketon, Melvin Jerry
    1983   "Indian Mental Health: An Orientation." *American Journal of Orthopsychiatry* 53:110–115.

Menicucci, Linda C., and Laurie Wermuth
    1989   "Expanding the Family Systems Approach: Culture, Class, Developmental and Gender Influences in Drug Abuse." *American Journal of Family Therapy* 17:129–142.

Merrett, Cora Bagley, and Cheryl Leggon, eds.
    1985   *Research in Race and Ethnic Relations.* Greenwich CT: JAI Press.

Mindel, Charles H., Robert W. Habenstein, and Roosevelt Wright, Jr.
    1988   *Ethnic Families in America: Patterns and Variations.* New York: Elsevier.

Moffatt, Michael
    1986   "The Discourse of the Dorm: Race, Friendship and 'Culture' among College Youth." In Herve Varenne. *Symbolizing America.* Lincoln: University of Nebraska Press.
    1989   *Coming of Age in New Jersey: College and American Culture.* New Brunswick, NJ: Rutgers University Press.

Mokuau, Noreen, ed.
    1991   *Handbook of Social Services for Asian and Pacific Islanders.* New York: Greenwood Press.

Montero, Darrell
    1979   "Vietnamese Refugees in America: Toward a Theory of Spontaneous International Migration." *International Migration Review* 13:624–648.

Moore, Pat
    1989   "The Incredible Aging Woman." *The Guardian.* August 1, page 17.

Morales, Armando
    1986   *Social Work: A Profession of Many Faces.* Boston: Allyn and Bacon.

Morinis, E. Alan
    1982   "'Getting Straight': Behavioral Patterns in a Skid Row Indian Community." *Urban Anthropology* 11:193–214.

Moynihan, Daniel P.
    1965   *The Negro Family: The Case for National Action.* Washington DC.: Department of Labor.

Murase, Kenji
  1992   "Models of Service Delivery in Asian American Communities." In Sharlene
          Maeda Furuto, Renuka Biswas, Douglas K. Chung, Kenji Murase, Fariyal Ross-
          Sheriff, eds. *Social Work Practice with Asian Americans*. Newbury Park, CA: Sage.

Mutran, Elizabeth
  1985   "Intergenerational Family Support among Blacks and Whites: Response to Cul-
          tural and Socioeconomic Differences." *Journal of Gerontology* 3:382–389.

Myerhoff, Barbara
  1978   *Number Our Days*. New York: Simon and Schuster.
  1982   "Rites of Passage: Process and Paradox." In Victor Turner. *Studies in Festivity and
          Ritual*. Washington, DC: Smithsonian Institution Press.

Myerhoff, Barbara, and Andrei Simic, eds.
  1978   *Life's Career*. Beverly Hills, CA: Sage.

Nakanishi, Manuel, and Barbara Rittner
  1992   "The Inclusionary Cultural Model." *Journal of Social Work Education* 28:27–35.

Nash, Manning
  1989   *The Cauldron of Ethnicity in the Modern World*. Chicago: University of Chicago
          Press.

National Association of Social Workers
  1990   *Code of Ethics of the National Association of Social Workers*. Silver Spring, MD:
          NASW Press.

Neighbors, Harold W., and Robert J. Taylor
  1985   "The Use of Social Service Agencies by Black Americans." *Social Service Review*
          59:258–268.

Neumann, Alfred K., Velma Mason, Emmett Chase, and Bernard Albaugh
  1991   "Factors Associated with Success among Southern Cheyenne and Arapaho."
          Journal of Commmunity Mental Health 16:103–115.

Neutra, R., J. Levy, and D. Parker
  1977   "Cultural Expectations versus Reality in Navaho Seizure Patterns and Sick
          Roles." *Culture, Medicine and Psychiatry* 1:225–275.

Norton, Dolores G., et al.
  1978   *The Dual Perspective*. New York: Council on Social Work Education.

Nurge, Ethel C.
  1970   *The Modern Sioux: Social Systems and Reservation Culture*. Lincoln: University of
          Nebraska Press.

Oetting, E. R., R. Edwards, G. S. Goldstein, V. Garcia-Mason
    1980   "Drug Use among Adolescents in Five Southwestern Native American Tribes." *International Journal of Addictions* 15:439–445.

Ogbu, John V.
    1974   *The Next Generation.* London: Academic Press.
    1978   *Minority Education and Caste: The American System in Cross Cultural Perspective."* New York: Academic Press.
    1987   "Variability in Minority School Performance: A Problem in Search of an Explanation." *Anthropology and Education* 18:312–334.

Olson, James S., and Raymond Wilson
    1984   *Native Americans in the Twentieth Century.* Urbana: University of Illinois Press.

Omni, Michael, and Howard Winant
    1986   *Racial Formation in the United States from the 1960s to the 1980s.* New York: Routledge and Kegan Paul.

O'Nell, Carl W.
    1976   "An Investigation of Reported 'Fright' as a Factor in the Etiology of Susto, 'Magical Fright'." *Ethos* 3:41–63.

O'Nell, Theresa D.
    1992   " 'Feeling Worthless': An Ethnographic Investigation of Depression and Problem Drinking at the Flathead Reservation." *Culture, Medicine and Psychiatry* 16:447–469.

Ortiz, Karol R.
    1985   "Mental Health Consequences of the Life History Method." *Ethos* 9:99–120.

Pachter, Lee M., Bruce Bernstein, and Adalberto Osorio
    1992   "Clinical Implications of a Folk Illness: *Empacho* in Mainland Puerto Ricans." *Medical Anthropology* 13:285–299.

Padilla, Amado M., Kathryn Lindholm, and Andrew Chen
    1991   "The English-Only Movement: Myths, Reality, and Implications for Psychology." *American Psychologist* 46:120–130.

Padilla, Felix M.
    1985   "On the Nature of Latino Ethnicity." In Rodolpho O. De La Garza, Frank D. Bean, Charles M. Bonjean, Ricardo Romo, and Rodolpho Alvarez, eds. *The Mexican American Experience: An Interdisciplinary Anthology.* Austin: University of Texas Press.

Page, J. Bryan, Dale D. Chitwood, Prince C. Smith, Narmie Kane, and Duane C. McBride
    1990   "Intravenous Drug Use and HIV Infection in Miami." Medical Anthropology Quarterly 4:56–71.

Palacios, Maria, and Juan N. Franco
1986 "Counseling Mexican-American Women." *Journal of Multicultural Counseling and Development* 14:124–131.

Parke, Ross D., and Candace Whitmer Collmer
1975 *Child Abuse: An Interdisciplinary Analysis.* Chicago: University of Chicago Press.

Parry, Joan K.
1990 *Social Work Practice with the Terminally Ill: A Transcultural Perspective.* Springfield, IL: Charles C. Thomas.

Payne, Monica A.
1989 "Use and Abuse of Corporal Punishment: A Caribbean View." *Child Abuse and Neglect* 13:389–401.

Pedersen, Paul, ed.
1976 "The Field of Intercultural Counseling." In Paul Pedersen, Walter J. Lonner, and Juris G. Draguns, eds. Counseling across Cultures. Honolulu: University of Hawaii Press: 17–41.
1985 *Handbook of Cross-Cultural Counseling and Therapy.* Westport, CT: Greenwood Press.

Pedersen, Paul B., Juris G. Draguns, Walter J. Lonner, and Joseph Trimble
1981 *Counseling across Cultures.* Honolulu: University of Hawaii Press.

Pedersen, Paul B., Mary Fukuyama, and Anne Heath
1989a "Client, Counselor, and Contextual Varieties in Multicultural Counseling." In Paul B. Pedersen, Mary Fukuyama, and Anne Heath. *Counseling across Cultures.* Honolulu: University of Hawaii Press.
1989b *Counseling across Cultures.* Honolulu: University of Hawaii Press.

Pelto, Pertti J., and Gretel H. Pelto
1975 "Intra-Cultural Diversity: Some Theoretical Issues." *American Ethnologist* 2:1–18.
1978 *Anthropological Research: The Structure of Inquiry.* Cambridge: Cambridge University Press.

Pérez-Stable, E. J.
1987 "Issues in Latino Health Care." *Western Journal of Medicine* 146:213–218.

Peterson, Warren A., and Jill Quadagno, eds.
1985 *Social Bonds in Later Life: Aging and Independence.* Beverly Hills, CA: Sage.

Pfeifferling, J. H.
1981 "A Cultural Prescription for Medicocentrism." In Leon Eisenberg, and Arthur Kleinman, eds. *The Relevance of Social Science for Medicine.* Boston: Reidel.

Philips, Susan V.
1974 "Warm Springs 'Indian Time.'" In Richard Bauman, and Joel Sherzer, eds. *Explorations in the Ethnography of Speaking.* New York: Cambridge University Press.

Piatt, Bill
    1990   *Only English? Law and Language Policy in the United States.* Albuquerque: University of New Mexico Press.

Pincus, Allen, and Anne Minahan
    1973   *Social Work Practice: Model and Method.* Itasca, IL: F. E. Peacock Publishers.

Pinderhughes, Elaine
    1979   "Afro-America and Economic Dependency." *Urban and Social Change Review* 12:24–27.
    1982a   "Family Functioning of Afro-America." *Social Work* 27: 91–96.
    1982b   "Afro-American Families and the Victim System." In Monica McGoldrick, John K. Pearce, and Joseph Giordano, eds. *Ethnicity and Family Therapy.* New York: The Guilford Press.

Podolefsky, Aaron, and Peter J. Brown, eds.
    1992   *Applying Anthropology.* Mountain View, CA: Mayfield.

Ponterotto, Joseph G., and J. Manuel Casas, eds.
    1991   *Handbook of Racial/Ethnic Minority Counseling Research.* Springfield, IL: Charles C. Thomas.

Ponterotto, Joseph G., and Haresh B. Sabnani
    1989   "'Classics' in Multicultural Counseling: A Systematic Five-Year Content Analysis." *Journal of Multicultural Counseling and Development* 17:23–37.

Pope, Bonita R.
    1986   "Black Men in Interracial Relationships: Psychological and Therapeutic Issues." *Journal of Multicultural Counseling and Development.* 14:10–19.

Porter, Frank W., ed.
    1986   *Strategies for Survival: American Indians in the Eastern United States.* Westport, CT: Greenwood Press.

Portes, Alejandro, and Cynthia Truelove
    1987   "Making Sense of Diversity: Recent Research on Hispanic Minorities in the United States." *Annual Review of Sociology* 13:359–385.

Postman, Neil, Charles Weingartner, and Terence P. Moran, eds.
    1969   *Language in America.* New York: Pegasus.

Powell, Gloria Johnson, ed.
    1983   *The Psychosocial Development of Minority Group Children.* New York: Brunner/ Mazel.

Price, John A.
    1975   "An Applied Analysis of North American Indian Drinking Patterns." *Human Organization* 34:17–26.

Price, Laurie
  1987   "Ecuadoran Illness Stories: Cultural Knowledge in Natural Discourse." In Dorothy Holland, and Naomi Quinn, eds. *Cultural Models in Language and Thought.* Cambridge: Cambridge University Press.

Putsch, Robert W. III
  1985   "Cross-Cultural Communication: The Special Case of Interpreters in Health Care." *Journal of the American Medical Association* 254:3344–3348.

Rahe, R. H., et al.
  1976   "Psychiatric Consultation in a Vietnamese Refugee Camp." *American Journal of Psychiatry* 135:185–190.

Rainwater, Lee
  1970   *Behind Ghetto Walls.* Chicago: Aldine.

Rainwater, Lee, and William Yancey, eds.
  1967   *The Moynihan Report and the Politics of Controversy.* Cambridge: MIT Press.

Ratliff, Nancy
  1988   "Stress and Burnout in the Helping Professions." *Social Casework* 69:147–154.

Red Horse, John G., Ronald Lewis, Marvin Feit, and James Decker
  1981   "Family Behavior of Urban American Indians." In Richard H. Dana, ed. *Human Services for Cultural Minorities.* Baltimore: University Park Press.

Rhodes, Lorna
  1991   *Emptying Beds: The Work of an Emergency Psychiatric Unit.* Berkeley: University of California Press.

Robbins, Susan P.
  1984   "Anglo Concepts and Indian Reality: A Study of Juvenile Delinquency." *Social Casework* 65:235–241.

Rodriguez, Orlando
  1987   *Hispanics and Human Services: Help-Seeking in the Inner City."* Bronx, NY: Fordham University Hispanic Research Center.

Rodriguez, Orlando, and Luis H. Zayas
  1990   "Hispanic Adolescents and Antisocial Behavior: Sociocultural Factors and Treatment Implications." In Arlene Rubin Stiffman, and Larry E. Davis, eds. *Ethnic Issues in Adolescent Mental Health.* Newbury Park, CA: Sage.

Rodwell, Mary K., and Adell Blankebaker
  1992   "Strategies for Developing Cross-Cultural Sensitivity: Wounding as a Metaphor." *Journal of Social Work Education* 28:153–165.

Rogler, Lloyd H., and Rosemary Santana-Cooney
    1983   *A Conceptual Framework for Mental Health Research on Hispanic Populations.* New York: Fordham University.
    1984   *Puerto Rican Families in New York City: Intergenerational Processes.* Maplewood, NJ: Waterfront Press.

Rogler, Lloyd H., and August B. Hollingshead
    1985   *Trapped: Puerto Rican Families and Schizophrenia.* Maplewood, NJ: Waterfront Press.

Rogler, Lloyd, Robert G. Malgady, Giuseppe Costantino, and Rena Blumenthal
    1987   "What Do Culturally Sensitive Mental Health Services Mean? The Case of Hispanics." *American Psychologist* 42:565–570.

Root, Maria P. P., ed.
    1992   *Racially Mixed People in America.* Newbury Park, CA: Sage.

Rose, Stephen M., and Bruce L. Black
    1985   *Advocacy and Empowerment: Mental Health Care in the Community.* Boston: Routledge and Kegan Paul.

Rosenberg, M. L., J. C. Smith, L. E. Davidson, and J. M. Conn
    1987   "The Emergence of Youth Suicide: An Epidemiologic Analysis and Public Health Perspective." *American Review of Public Health* 8:417–440.

Ross, E. Lamar, ed.
    1978   *Interethnic Communication.* Athens: University of Georgia Press.

Ross, Thomas E., and Tyrel G. Moore
    1987   *A Cultural Geography of North American Indians.* Boulder, CO: Westview Press.

Rubel, Arthur J.
    1960   "Concepts of Disease in Mexican-American Culture." *American Anthropologist* 62:795–814.
    1964   "The Epidemiology of a Folk Illness: Susto in Hispanic America." *Ethnology* 3:268–283.
    1966   *Across the Tracks: Mexican-Americans in a Texas City.* Austin: University of Texas Press.
    1984   *Susto, a Folk Illness.* Berkeley: University of California Press.

Rubin, David C.
    1986   *Autobiographical Memory.* Cambridge: Cambridge University Press.

Rumelhart, Marilyn Austin
    1984   "When Understanding the Situation is the Real Problem." *Social Casework* 65:27–33.

Rutledge, Paul James
    1992   *The Vietnamese Experience.* Bloomington: Indiana University Press.

Ryan, William
  1969   *Blaming the Victim.* New York: Pantheon Press.

Saenz, Rogelio, and Benigno E. Aguirre
  1991   "The Dynamics of Mexican Ethnic Identity." *Ethnic Groups* 9:17–32.

Sanday, Peggy Reeves, ed.
  1976   *Anthropology and the Public Interest.* New York: Academic Press.

Sandoval, Mercedes C., and Maria C. De La Roza
  1986   "A Cultural Perspective for Serving the Hispanic Client." In Harriet P. Lefley, and
         Paul B. Pedersen, eds. *Cross-Cultural Training for Mental Health Professionals.*
         Springfield, IL: Charles C. Thomas.

Sands, Roberta G.
  1988   "Sociolinguistic Analysis of a Mental Health Interview." *Social Work* 33:149–154.

Saunders, Lyle
  1954   *Cultural Difference and Medical Care: The Case of the Spanish Speaking People of the
         Southwest.* New York: Russell Sage Foundation.

Schaik, Eileen Van
  1989   "Paradigms Underlying the Study of Nerves as a Popular Illness Term in Eastern
         Kentucky." *Medical Anthropology* 11:15–28.

Schensul, Stephen L., and Jean J. Schensul
  1978   "Advocacy and Applied Anthropology." In George H. Weber, and George J.
         McCall, eds. *Social Scientists as Advocates.* Beverly Hills, CA: Sage: 121–166.

Schon, Donald
  1990   *Educating the Reflective Practitioner.* San Francisco: Jossey-Bass.

Schubert, Margaret
  1982   *Interviewing in Social Work Practice: An Introduction.* New York: Council on Social
         Work Education.

Schusky, Ernest L.
  1970   "Cultural Change and Continuity in the Lower Brule Community." In Ethel C.
         Nurge. *The Modern Sioux: Social Systems and Reservation Culture.* Lincoln: Univer-
         sity of Nebraska Press.

Sciarra, Daniel T., and Joseph G. Ponterotto
  1991   "Counseling the Hispanic Bilingual Family: Challenge to the Therapeutic Pro-
         cess." *Psychotherapy* 28:473–479.

Selman, Robert L., and Regina Yande, eds.
  1980   *Clinical-Developmental Psychology.* San Francisco: Jossey-Bass.

Senior, Olive
   1991   *Working Miracles: Women's Lives in the English-Speaking Caribbean.* Bloomington: Indiana University Press.

Sewell-Coker, Beverly, Joyce Hamilton-Collins, and Edith Fein
   1985   "Social Work Practice with West Indian Immigrants." *Social Casework* 66:563–568.

Shaffir, William B., and Robert A. Stebbins
   1991   *Experiencing Fieldwork.* Newbury Park, CA: Sage.

Shannon, Barbara E.
   1970   "Implications of White Racism for Social Work Practice." Social Casework 51:270–276.

Sharp, Henry S.
   1991   "Memory, Meaning, and Imaginary Time." *Ethnohistory* 38:149–175.

Shield, Renee Rose
   1988   *Uneasy Endings: Daily Life in an American Nursing Home.* Ithaca: Cornell University Press.

Shimkin, Demitri B., Edith M. Shimkin, and Dennis A. Frate, eds.
   1978   *The Extended Family in Black Societies.* The Hague: Mouton.

Shon, Steven P., and Davis Y. Ja
   1982   "Asian Families." In Monica McGoldrick, John K. Pearce, and Joseph Giordano, eds. *Ethnicity and Family Therapy.* New York: The Guilford Press.

Shomaker, Dianna J.
   1989   "Transfer of Children and the Importance of Grandmothers among Navaho Indians." *Journal of Cross-Cultural Gerontology* 4:1–18.
   1990   "Health Care, Cultural Expectations and Frail Elderly Navajo Grandmothers." *Journal of Cross-Cultural Gerontology* 5:21–34.

Shore, James H., and Spero Manson
   1983   "American Indian Psychiatric and Social Problems." *Transcultural Psychiatric Research Review* 20:159–179.

Shweder, Richard A.
   1985   "Menstrual Pollution, Soul Loss, and the Comparative Study of Emotions." In Arthur Kleinman, and Byron Good, eds. *Culture and Depression.* Berkeley: University of California Press.
   1991   *Thinking Through Cultures: Expeditions in Cultural Psychology."* Cambridge: Harvard University Press.

Siegel, Bernard J., Alan R. Beals, and Stephen A. Tyler, eds.
   1989   *Annual Review of Anthropology, 18.* Palo Alto CA: Annual Reviews, Inc.

Silverman, Philip, ed.
1987   *The Elderly as Modern Pioneers.* Bloomington: Indiana University Press.

Simmons, Leonard C.
1963   "'Jim Crow': Implications for Social Work." *Social Work* 8:24–30.

Smith, Raymond T.
1988   *Kinship and Class in the West Indies.* Cambridge: Cambridge University Press.

Snow, Loudell F.
1973   "'I was Born Just Exactly with the Gift.' An Interview with a Voodoo Practitioner." *Journal of American Folklore* 86:272–281.
1974   "Folk Medical Beliefs and Their Implications for Care of Patients." *Annals of Internal Medicine* 81:82–96.
1977   "Popular Medicine in a Black Neighborhood." In Edward H. Spicer, ed. *Ethnic Medicine in the Southwest.* Tucson: University of Arizona Press.
1978   "Sorcerers, Saints, and Charlatans: Black Folk Healers in Urban America." *Culture, Medicine and Psychiatry* 2:69–106.
1993   *Walkin' over Medicine.* Boulder, CO: Westview Press.

Social Casework
1964   "Editorial Notes: Race Relations in Social Work." *Social Casework* 45:155.

Sokolovsky, Jay
1990a   "Bringing Culture Back Home: Aging, Ethnicity, and Family Support." In Jay Sokolovsky. *The Cultural Context of Aging.* New York: Bergin and Garvey.
1990b   *The Cultural Context of Aging.* New York: Bergin and Garvey.

Solomon, Barbara B.
1976   *Black Empowerment: Social Work in Oppressed Communities.* New York: Columbia University Press.
1982   "The Delivery of Mental Health Services to Afro-American Individuals and Families: Translating Theory into Practice." In Barbara Ann Bass, Gail Elizabeth Wyatt, and Gloria Johnson Powell, eds. *The Afro-American Family: Assessment, Treatment, and Research Issues.* New York: Grune and Stratton.
1985   "The Inner-City Church: A Non-traditional Setting for Mental Health Services." In Aminifur R. Harvey, ed. *The Black Family: An Afro-Centric Perspective.* New York: United Church of Christ.

Song-Kim, Young I.
1992   "Battered Korean Women in [the] Urban United States." In Sharlene Maeda Furuto, Renoka Biswas, Douglas K. Chung, Kenji Murase, and Fariyal Ross-Sheriff, eds. *Social Work Practice with Asian Americans.* Newbury Park, CA: Sage.

Sotomayor, Marta
1977   "Language, Culture and Ethnicity in Developing Self-Concept." *Social Casework* 58:195–203.

Spicer, Edward H., ed.
    1977   *Ethnic Medicine in the Southwest.* Tucson: University of Arizona Press.

Spindler, George
    1982   *Doing the Ethnography of Schooling: Educational Anthropology in Action.* New York: Holt, Rinehart and Winston.
    1987   *Interpretive Ethnography of Education at Home and Abroad.* Hillsdale, NJ: Erlbaum.

Spindler, George, and Louise Spindler
    1994   *Pathways to Cultural Awareness: Cultural Awareness with Teachers and Students.* Thousand Oaks, CA: Corwin Press.

Spradley, James P.
    1970   *You Owe Yourself a Drunk: An Ethnography of Urban Nomads.* Boston: Little, Brown.
    1972   *Culture and Cognition.* San Francisco: Chandler Publishing Co.
    1979   *The Ethnographic Interview.* New York: Holt, Rinehart and Winston.
    1980   *Participant Observation.* New York: Holt, Rinehart and Winston.

Spradley, James P., and David W. McCurdy
    1972   *The Cultural Experience.* Chicago: Science Research Associates.
    1975   *Anthropology: The Cultural Perspective.* New York: John Wiley and Sons.

Squier, Roger W.
    1990   "A Model of Empathic Understanding and Adherence to Treatment Regimes in Practitioner-Patient Relationships. *Social Science and Medicine* 30:325–339.

Stack, Carol B.
    1970   "The Kindred of Viola Jackson: Residence and Family Organization of an Urban Black Family." In Norman E. Whitten, and John F. Szwed, eds. *Afro-American Anthropology: Contemporary Perspectives.* New York: Free Press.
    1975   *All Our Kin: Strategies for Survival in the Black Community.* New York: Harper and Row.

Stanford, E. Percil
    1990   "Diverse Black Aged." In Zev Harel, Edward A. McKinney, and Michael Williams, eds. *Black Aged: Understanding Diversity and Service Needs.* Newbury Park, CA: Sage.

Staples, Robert
    1982   *Black Masculinity: The Black Man's Role in American Society."* San Francisco: Black Scholar Press.

Statham, Daphne
    1978   *Radicals in Social Work.* London: Routledge and Kegan Paul.

Steele, Shelby
    1988   "I'm Black, You're White, Who's Innocent?" *Harpers,* June.

1989   "Being Black and Feeling Blue." *The American Scholar* 3:497–513.

Stewart, E. C., J. Danielian, and R. J. Festes
  1969   *Simulating Intercultural Communication through Role Playing.* Alexandria, VA: Human Resources Research Organization.

Stiffman, Arlene Rubin, and Larry E. Davis, eds.
  1990   *Ethnic Issues in Adolescent Mental Health.* Newbury Park, CA: Sage.

Stone, Carol L.
  1991   "Estimate of Muslims Living in America." In Yvonne Yazbeck Haddad, ed. *The Muslims of America.* New York: Oxford University Press.

Suarez-Orozco, Marcelo, George Spindler, and Louise Spindler, eds.
  1994   *The Making of Psychological Anthropology: II.* Fort Worth: Harcourt Brace.

Sue, Derald Wing, and David Sue
  1990   *Counseling the Culturally Different.* New York: John Wiley and Sons.

Sue, Stanley
  1988   "Psychotherapeutic Services to Ethnic Minorities: Two Decades of Research Findings."*American Psychologist* 43:301–308.

Sue, Stanley, and Herman McKinney
  1975   "Asian Americans in the Community Mental Health Care System." *American Journal of Orthopsychiatry* 45:111–118.

Sue, Stanley, and Nolan Zane
  1987   "The Role of Culture and Cultural Techniques in Psychotherapy." *American Psychologist* 42:37–45.

Sullivan, Teresa A.
  1985   "A Demographic Portrait." In Pastora San Juan Cafferty, and William C. McCready, eds. *Hispanics in the United States, a New Social Agenda.* New Brunswick, NJ: Transaction Books.

Sundberg, Norman D.
  1976   "Toward Research Evaluating Intercultural Counseling." In Paul Pedersen, Walter J. Lonner, and Juris G. Draguns, eds. *Counseling across Cultures.* Honolulu: University of Hawaii Press: 139–169.

Sykes, Donald K., Jr.
  1987   "An Approach to Working with Black Youth in Cross Cultural Therapy." *Clinical Social Work Journal* 15:260–271.

Taft, Ronald
  1977   "Coping with Unfamiliar Cultures." In Neil Warren, ed. *Studies in Cross-Cultural Psychology.* New York: Academic Press.

1981   "The Role and Personality of the Mediator." In Stephen Bochner. *The Mediating Person*. Cambridge, MA: Schenkman.

Tally, T., and J. Kaplan
  1956   "The Negro Aged." *Gerontological Society Newsletter* 3:4.

Tamura, Takeshi, and Annie Lau
  1992   "Connectedness versus Separateness: Applicability of Family Therapy to Japanese Families." *Family Process* 31:319–340.

Taylor, Eleanor D.
  1987   *From Issue to Action: An Advocacy Program Model*. Lancaster, CA: Family and Children's Services.

Taylor, Robert Joseph, and Linda M. Chatters
  1986   "Patterns of Informal Support to Elderly Black Adults: Family, Friends and Church Members." *Social Work* 31:432–438.

Taylor, Robert Joseph, and Willie H. Taylor
  1982   "The Social and Economic Status of the Black Elderly." *Phylon* 43:295–306.

Taylor, Ronald L.
  1994   *Minority Families in the United States*. Englewood Cliffs, NJ: Prentice Hall.

Thompson, Richard W.
  1989   *Theories of Ethnicity: A Critical Appraisal*. Westport, CT: Greenwood Press.

Thorne, Barrie, Cheris Kramarae, and Nancy Henly, eds.
  1983   *Language, Gender and Society*. Rowley, MA: Newbury House.

Thrasher, Shirley, and Gary Anderson
  1988   "The West Indian Family: Treatment Challenges." *Social Casework* 69:171–176.

Tran, Thanh Van
  1988   "The Vietnamese American Family." In Charles H. Mindel, Robert W. Habenstien, and Roosevelt Wright, Jr. *Ethnic Families in America: Patterns and Variations*. New York: Elsevier.

Trimble, Joseph E.
  1981   "Value Differences among American Indians: Concerns for the Concerned Counselor." In Paul Pedersen, Juris G. Draguns, Walter J. Lonner, And Joseph E. Trimble, eds. *Counseling across Cultures*. Honolulu: University of Hawaii Press.

Trimble, Joseph E., Teresa D. LaFromboise, Duane H. Mackey, and Gary A. France
  1983   "American Indians, Psychology and Curriculum Development: A Proposed Reform with Reservations." In Jay C. Chunn III, Patricia J. Dunston, and Fariyal Ross-Sheriff, eds. *Mental Health and People of Color*. Washington, DC: Howard University Press.

Trotter, Robert T.
 1985   "Folk Medicine in the Southwest." *Folk Medicine* 78:167–179.

Truax, Charles B., and Kevin M. Mitchell
 1971   "Research on Certain Therapist Interpersonal Skills in Relation to Process and Outcome." In Allen Bergin and Sol Garfield, eds. *Handbook of Psychotherapy and Behavior Change.* New York: John Wiley and Sons: 299–344.

Tsui, Philip, and Gail L. Schultz
 1985   "Failure of Rapport: Why Psychotherapeutic Engagement Fails in the Treatment of Asian Clients." *American Journal of Psychotherapy* 55:561–569.
 1988   "Ethnic Factors in Group Process: Cultural Dynamics in Multi-Ethnic Therapy Groups." *American Journal of Psychotherapy* 58:136–142.

Tung, May
 1984   "Insight-Oriented Psychotherapy and the Chinese Patient." *American Journal of Orthopsychiatry* 61:186–194.
 1991   "Life Values, Psychotherapy, and East-West Integration." *Psychiatry* 47:285–292.

Turner, Victor
 1968   *The Drums of Affliction.* Oxford: Clarendon Press.
 1969   *The Ritual Process.* Ithaca: Cornell University Press.
 1982   *Studies in Festivity and Ritual.* Washington, DC: Smithsonian Institution Press.

Tyler, Forrest B., Deborah Ridley Sussewell, and Janice Williams-McCoy
 1985   "Ethnic Validity in Psychotherapy." *Psychotherapy* 22:311–320.

Uba, Laura, and Stanley Sue
 1991   "Nature and Scope of Services for Asian and Pacific Islander Americans." In Noreen Mokuau, ed. *Handbook of Social Services for Asian and Pacific Islanders.* New York: Greenwood Press.

Ucko, Lenora Greenbaum
 1983   "The Use of Folktales in Social Work Practice." *Social Casework* 64:414–418.

U.S. Department of Health and Human Services
 1984   *Fifth Special Report to the U.S. Congress on Alcohol and Health.* Washington, DC: U.S. Government Printing Office.
 1985   *Health Status of Minorities and Low Income Groups.* Washington, DC: Government Printing Office.

Valverde, Kieu-Linh Caroline
 1992   "From Dust to Gold: The Vietnamese Amerasian Experience." In Maria P. P. Root, ed. *Racially Mixed People in America.* Newbury Park, CA: Sage.

Varenne, Herve
 1977   *Americans Together.* New York: Teachers College Press.
 1986   *Symbolizing America.* Lincoln: University of Nebraska Press.

Vasquez, Melba J. T.
    1984   "Power and Status of the Chicana: A Social-Psychological Perspective." In Joe L.
            Martinez, Jr., and Richard H. Mendoza, eds. *Chicano Psychology*. Orlando, FL:
            Academic Press.

Vega, William A., Bohdan Kolody, Ramon Valle, and Judy Weir
    1991   "Social Networks, Social Support, and Their Relation to Depression among Im-
            migrant Mexican Women." *Human Organization* 50:154–162.

Vigil, James Diego
    1983   "Chicano Gangs: One Response to Mexican Urban Adaptation in the Los Ange-
            les Area." *Urban Anthropology* 12:45–75.
    1988a   *Barrio Gangs: Street Life and Identity in Southern California.* Austin: University of
            Texas Press.
    1988b   "Group Processes and Street Identity: Adolescent Chicano Gang Members."
            Ethos 16:421–445.

Vontress, Clemmont E.
    1971   *Counseling Negroes.* New York: Houghton Mifflin.
    1976   "Racial and Ethnic Barriers in Counseling." In Paul Pedersen, Walter J. Lonner,
            and Juris G. Draguns, eds. *Counseling across Cultures*. Honolulu: University of
            Hawaii Press: 42–64.
    1981   "Racial and Ethnic Barriers in Counseling." In Paul Pedersen, Juris G. Draguns,
            Walter J. Lonner, and Joseph E. Trimble. *Counseling across Cultures*. Honolulu:
            University of Hawaii Press.

Vuong, Thuy G.
    1976   *Getting to Know the Vietnamese and Their Culture.* New York: Frederick Ungar.

Waddell, Jack O., and Michael W. Everett
    1980   *Drinking Behavior among Southwest Indians: An Anthropological Perspective.* Tuscon:
            University of Arizona Press.

Wallace, Anthony F. C.
    1956   "Mazeway Resynthesis: A Bio-Cultural Theory of Religious Inspiration." *Trans-
            actions of the New York Academy of Science* 18:626–638.
    1970   *Culture and Personality.* New York: Random House.

Wallman, Sandra
    1979   *Ethnicity at Work.* London: Macmillan.

Warren, Neil, ed.
    1977   *Studies in Cross-Cultural Psychology.* New York: Academic Press.

Watts-Jones, Darielle
    1992   "Cultural and Integrative Therapy Issues in the Treatment of a Jamaican Woman
            with Panic Disorder." *Family Process* 31:105–113.

Wax, Rosalie, and Robert K. Thomas
    1961   "American Indians and White People." *Phylon* 22:305–317.

Waxler-Morrison, Nancy, Joan Anderson, and Elizabeth Richardson, eds.
    1990   *Cross-Cultural Caring: A Handbook for Health Professionals in Western Canada.* Vancouver: University of British Columbia Press.

Weaver, Jerry L.
    1977   *National Health Policy and the Underserved.* St. Louis: C.V. Mosby.

Weibel-Orlando, Joan
    1989   "Hooked on Healing: Anthropologists, Alcohol and Intervention." *Human Organization* 48:148–155.
    1990   "Grandparenting Style: Native American Perspectives." In Jay Sokolovsky. *The Cultural Context of Aging.* New York: Bergin and Garvey.

Weick, Karl E.
    1984   "Small Wins: Redefining the Scale of Social Problems." *American Psychologist* 39:40–49.

Weisner, Thomas S., Joan Crofut Weibel-Orlando, and John Long
    1984   " 'Serious Drinking,' 'White Man's Drinking' and 'Teetotling': Drinking Levels and Styles in an Urban American Indian Population." *Journal of Studies on Alcohol* 45:237–250.

Wellman, David T.
    1977   *Portraits of White Racism.* London: Cambridge University Press.
    1993   *Portraits of White Racism.* London: Cambridge University Press.

Wharton, Carol S.
    1989   "Splintered Visions: Staff/Client Disjunctions and Their Consequences for Human Service Organizations." *Journal of Contemporary Ethnography* 18:50–71.

White, Barbara W., ed.
    1984   *Color in a White Society.* Silver Spring, MD: National Association of Social Workers.

Whitten, Norman E.
    1962   "Contemporary Patterns of Malign Occultism among Negroes in North Carolina." *Journal of American Folklore* 75:311–325.

Whitten, Norman E., and John F. Szwed, eds.
    1970   *Afro-American Anthropology: Contemporary Perspectives.* New York: Free Press.

Wiener, Carolyn L., and Jeanie Kayser-Jones
    1989   "Defensive Work in Nursing Homes: Accountability Gone Amok." *Social Science and Medicine* 28:37–44.

Williams, Brackette F.
   1989   "A Class Act: Anthropology and the Race to Nation across Ethnic Terrain." In
           Bernard J. Siegel, Alan R. Beals, and Stephen A. Tyler, eds. *Annual Review of
           Anthropology, 18.* Palo Alto, CA: Annual Reviews, Inc.

Williams, Constance Willard
   1991   *Black Teenage Mothers: Pregnancy and Childrearing from Their Perspective."* Lex-
           ington, MA: D.C. Heath.

Williams, Melvin D.
   1981   *On the Street Where I Lived.* New York: Holt, Rinehart and Winston.
   1992   *The Human Dilemma: A Decade Later in Belmar.* Forth Worth, TX: Harcourt Brace
           Jovanovich.

Williams, Teresa Kay
   1992   "Prism Lives: Identity of Binational Amerasians." In Maria P. P. Root, ed. *Racially
           Mixed People in America.* Newbury Park, CA: Sage.

Wilson, Terry P.
   1992   Blood Quantum: Native American Mixed Bloods. In Maria P. P. Root, ed. *Racially
           Mixed People in America.* Newbury Park, CA: Sage.

Wilson, William Julius
   1980   *The Declining Significance of Race: Blacks and Changing American Institutions.* Chi-
           cago: University of Chicago Press.
   1987   *The Truly Disadvantaged: The Inner City, the Underclass, and Public Policy.* Chicago:
           University of Chicago Press.

Winthrop, Robert H., ed.
   1990   *Culture and the Anthropological Tradition.* Lanham, MD: University Press of Amer-
           ica.

Wintrob, R. M.
   1973   "The Influence of Others: Witchcraft and Rootwork as Explanations of Behavior
           Disturbances." *Journal of Nervous and Mental Disorders* 156:318–326.

Wise, Fred, and Nancy B. Miller
   1983   "The Mental Health of American Indian Children." In Gloria Johnson Powell, ed.
           The Psychosocial Development of Minority Group Children. New York: Brunner/
           Mazel.

Wolf, Eric R.
   1982   *Europe and the People without History.* Berkeley: University of California Press.

Wong, Morrison G.
   1988   "The Chinese American Family." In Charles H. Mindel, Robert W. Habenstein,
           and Roosevelt Wright, Jr. *Ethnic Families in America: Patterns and Variations.* New
           York: Elsevier.

Wong, Morrison G., and Charles Hirschman
    1983   "The New Asian Immigrants." In William McCready, ed. *Culture, Ethnicity, and Identity.* New York: Academic Press.

Wylie, F. M.
    1971   "Attitudes toward Aging and the Aged among Black Americans: Some Historical Perspectives." *Aging and Human Development* 2:66–70.

Yanagisako, Sylvia Junko
    1975   "Two Processes of Change in Japanese-American Kinship." *Journal of Anthropological Research* 31:196–224.
    1985   *Transforming the Past: Tradition and Kinship among Japanese Americans.* Stanford: Stanford University Press.

Yancey, William L., Eugene P. Ericksen, and Richard N. Juliani
    1976   "Emergent Ethnicity: A Review and Reformulation." *American Sociological Review* 41:391–403.

Youngman, Geraldine, and Margaret Sadongei
    1974   "Counseling the American Indian Child." *Elementary School Guidance and Counseling* 8:272–277.

Zintz, M. V.
    1963   *Education across Cultures.* Dubuque, IA: William Brown.

Zola, I. K.
    1972   "The Concept of Trouble and Sources of Medical Assistance." *Social Science and Medicine* 6:673–680.

Zollar, Ann Creighton
    1985   *A Member of the Family: Strategies for Black Family Continuity.* Chicago: Nelson-Hall.

Zuniga, Maria E.
    1991   "'Dichos' as Metaphorical Tools for Resistant Latino Clients." *Psychotherapy* 28:480–483.

INDEX

McLeod, Donna L., 314

McMahon, Anthony, 171–172

Mead, Margaret, 11, 95, 138

Mechling, Jay, 52, 57

Media, influence of, 54–55, 64, 67, 96, 213, 216

Mediation, techniques in, 37–38

Mehrabian, Albert, 110

Meiji Restoration, 273

Meketon, Melvin Jerry, 220

Melting pot model, 25–26

Men, 128, 202–203, 262, 265

Menicucci, Linda C., 8

Menominees, and agriculture, 215

Menomini, and alcohol use, 60

Mental health issues, 22, 222–227, 253–256

Mental health services. *See also* Healers
 alternatives to, 51–53, 67
 history of, 247
 and language, 118
 and power, 77

Mental illness
 and participant observation, 101–102
 stigmatization of, 75, 281, 287, 291, 298

Mental lexicon metaphor, 124, 141

Metaphors
 for blood, 12, 212–213
 family as, 63
 mental lexicon, 124, 141
 150 percent man, 96

Meta-rules, for communication, 287

Mexicans/Mexican Americans. *See also* Latinos
 and age, 269–270
 definition of, 175, 243
 demography of, 244
 and gangs, 267
 and gender, 250
 health survey of, 252
 social services for, 35

Mexican War, 245

Mexico, 3, 21

Meyer, Henry J., 314

Miami (FL), drug use in, 108–109

Middle class, lifestyle of, 162–163, 170, 180, 186

Migration, 48, 206–207. *See also* Immigration; Refugees

Military-industrial complex, 218

Minahan, Anne, 314

Mindel, Charles H., 45

Minneapolis (MN), American Indians in, 221

Minorities. *See also* Ethnic groups
 and alcohol use, 222
 definition of, 15–16, 242
 as social workers, 5, 38–39, 98–99, 154, 202, 287, 321–325, 329–331
 writings by, 99–100

Missionary, in client relationships, 37–38, 42–43

Mission (village in Canada), 209

Mitchell, Kevin M., 86

Models. *See also* Help seeking behavior model
 basis of, 320–321
 of cultural awareness, 46
 of empathy, 111–114, *112*
 of ethnic competence, 44–49, *47*
 for participant observation, 107–108
 of social behavior, 103
 for social work, 8–10

Modernization, and Chipewyan, 210

Moffatt, Michael, 24

Mohawks, and agriculture, 215

Monolingualism, 147

Moore, Pat, 83–84

Moral career, of mental patients, 331

Morinis, E. Alan, 223–224

Mormons, and religious issues, 45

Morrison, Toni, 179

Mortality rates, 33, 222

Movies, stereotypes in, 213, 216

Moynihan, Daniel Patrick, 25, 191

Ms., use of, 307

Multiculturalism, 268–270

Multilingualism
 and legal aid services, 6
 maintenance of, 26

versus monolingualism, 147
 and translators, 146–148, *147*, 240, 254, 282

Multiracialism, 176–177

Murase, Kenji, 282

Museums, of American Indians, 230

Muskogean, and role of elders, 234

Muslims, lifestyles of, 277, 298–302

Mutual aid societies, 192

Myerhoff, Barbara, 79, 104–105

NAACP (National Association for the Advancement of Colored People), 174

Nakanishi, Manuel, 308

Name dropping, 200

Names/naming, 29, 173, 221. *See also* Labels

Nash, Manning, 19–20, 22, 39

National Association of Social Workers, 8, 32, 34, 335–337

National Baptist Convention USA, 192

Nationality, concept of, 12–13, 18, 21, 174, 315–317

Native Americans. *See* American Indians

Nativism, 217–219, 240

Navajo, lifestyles of, 60, 209, 223

Negro (label), 174

Nerves, attacks of, 252–254

Networks, 204, 248, 257

Neumann, Alfred K., 237

New Deal, 180, 218

New Mexico, health survey in, 255–256

Nisei (second generation), 278–279, 289–291

Nobel Prize in Literature, 179

North America, discovery of, 214

Northwest Coast Indians, lifestyles of, 89, 126, 219

Nursing, skills for, 44–45, 91, 141

Nursing homes, 43, 77–79

Obeah, 206

Objectivity, and ethnicity, 18–19